# IMAGINE WANTING ONLY THIS

IMAGINE
ONLY

# WANTING THIS

# KRISTEN RADTKE

Pantheon Books
New York

All rights reserved. Published in the United States by Pantheon
Books, a division of Penguin Random House LLC, New York, and
distributed in Canada by Random House of Canada, a division
of Penguin Random House Canada Limited, Toronto.

Pantheon Books and colophon are registered trademarks of
Penguin Random House LLC.

Library of Congress Cataloging-in-Publication Data
Name: Radtke, Kristen, author.
Title: Imagine wanting only this / Kristen Radtke.
Description: First edition. New York : Pantheon, 2017.
Identifiers: LCCN 2016034575 (print). LCCN 2016035188 (ebook).
ISBN 9781101870839 (hardcover). ISBN 9781101870846 (ebook).
Subjects: LCSH: Radtke, Kristen—Psychology—Comic books, strips,
etc. Radtke, Kristen—Travel—Comic books, strips, etc. Cartoonists—
United States—Biography. Loss (Psychology)—Comic books, strips,
etc. Graphic novels. BISAC: COMICS & GRAPHIC NOVELS / Literary.
COMICS & GRAPHIC NOVELS / Contemporary Women.
Classification: LCC PN6727.R334 Z46 2017 (print). LCC PN6727.
R334 (ebook). DDC 741.5 973—dc23.
LC record available at lccn.loc.gov/2016034575

www.pantheonbooks.com

Printed in China
First Edition
2 4 6 8 9 7 5 3 1

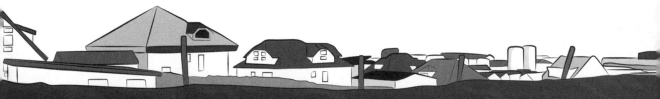

For Danno

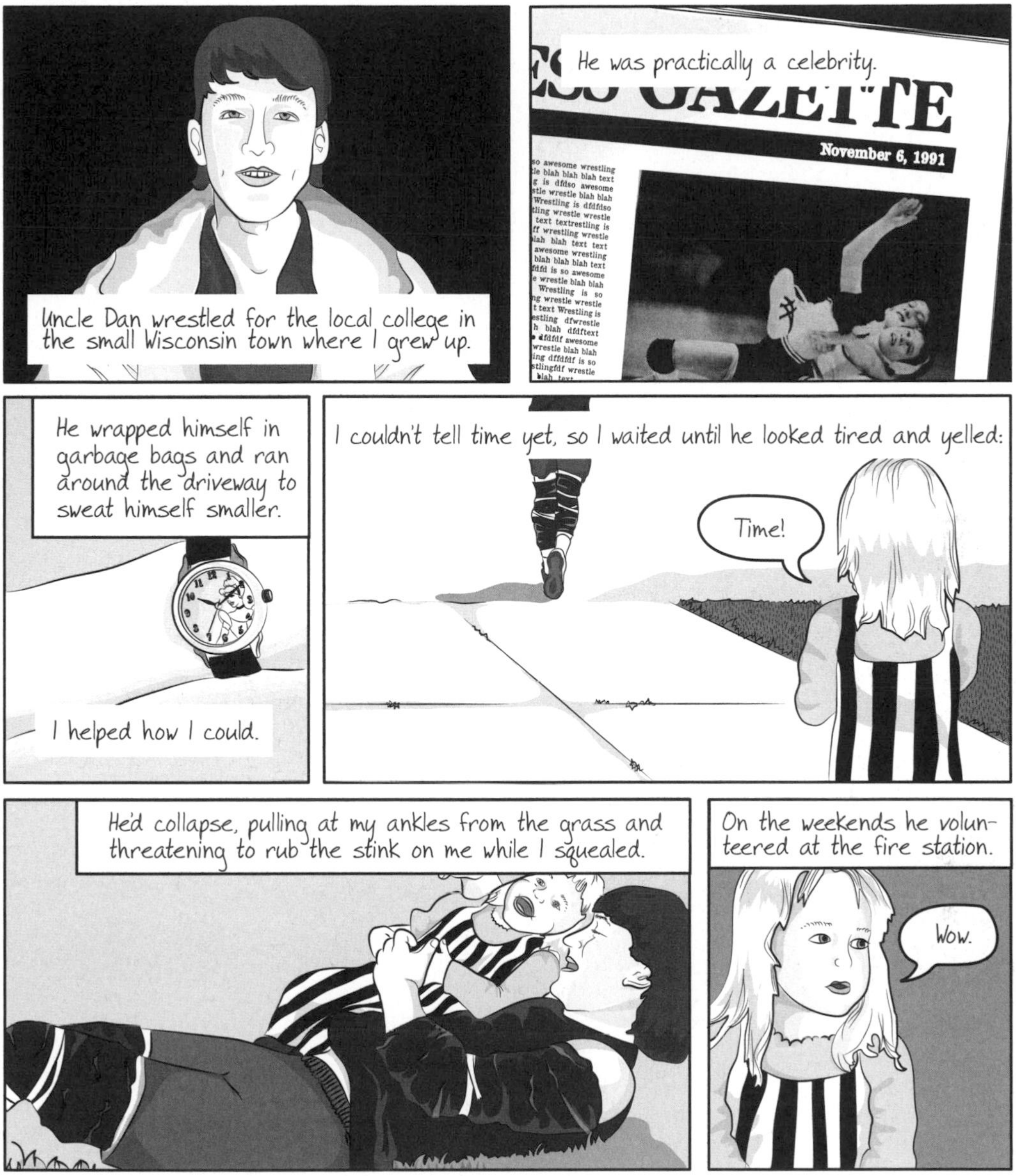
Uncle Dan wrestled for the local college in the small Wisconsin town where I grew up.
He was practically a celebrity.
GAZETTE
November 6, 1991
He wrapped himself in garbage bags and ran around the driveway to sweat himself smaller.
I helped how I could.
I couldn't tell time yet, so I waited until he looked tired and yelled:
Time!
He'd collapse, pulling at my ankles from the grass and threatening to rub the stink on me while I squealed.
On the weekends he volunteered at the fire station.
Wow.

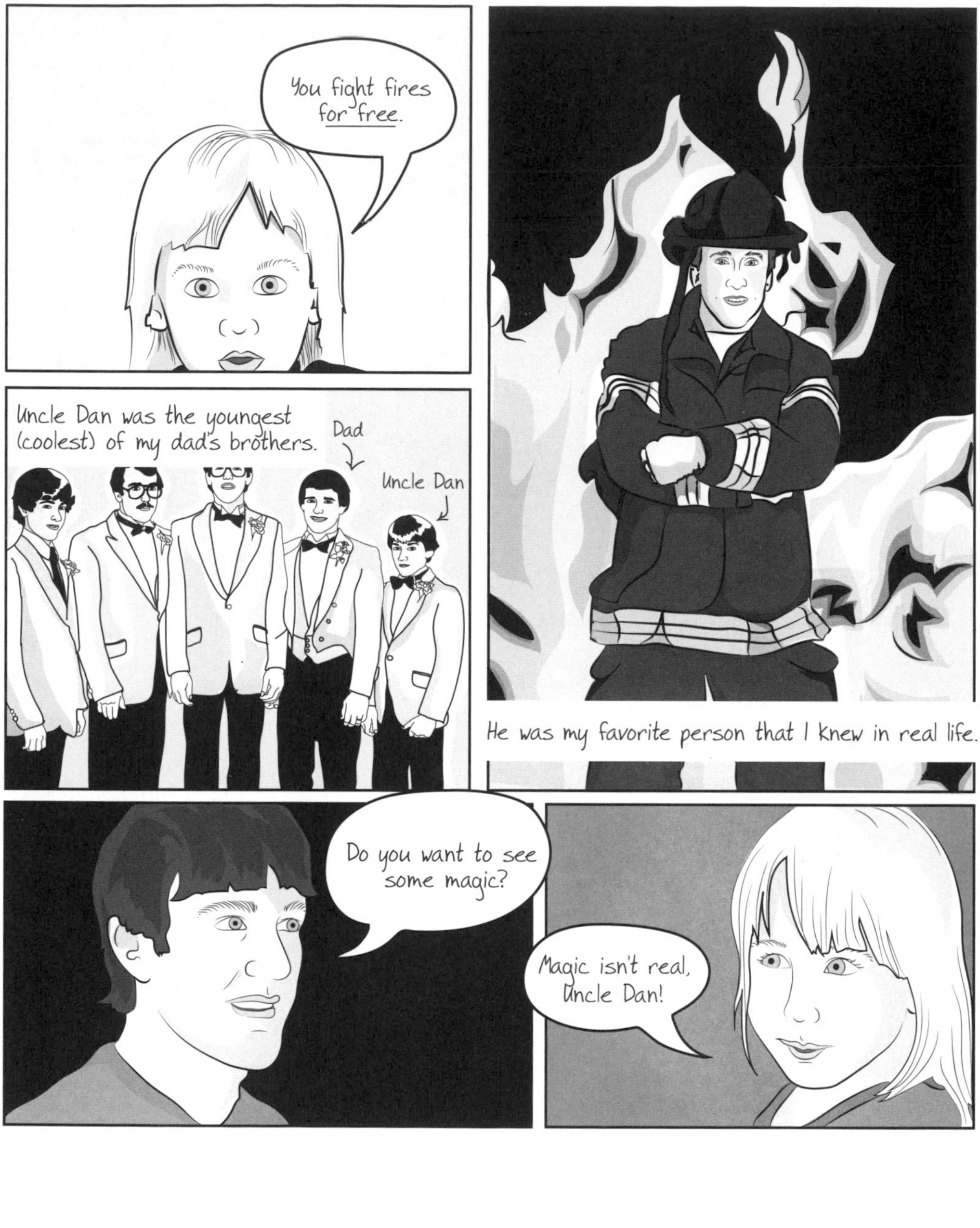
You fight fires for free.
Uncle Dan was the youngest (coolest) of my dad's brothers.
Dad
Uncle Dan
He was my favorite person that I knew in real life.
Do you want to see some magic?
Magic isn't real, Uncle Dan!

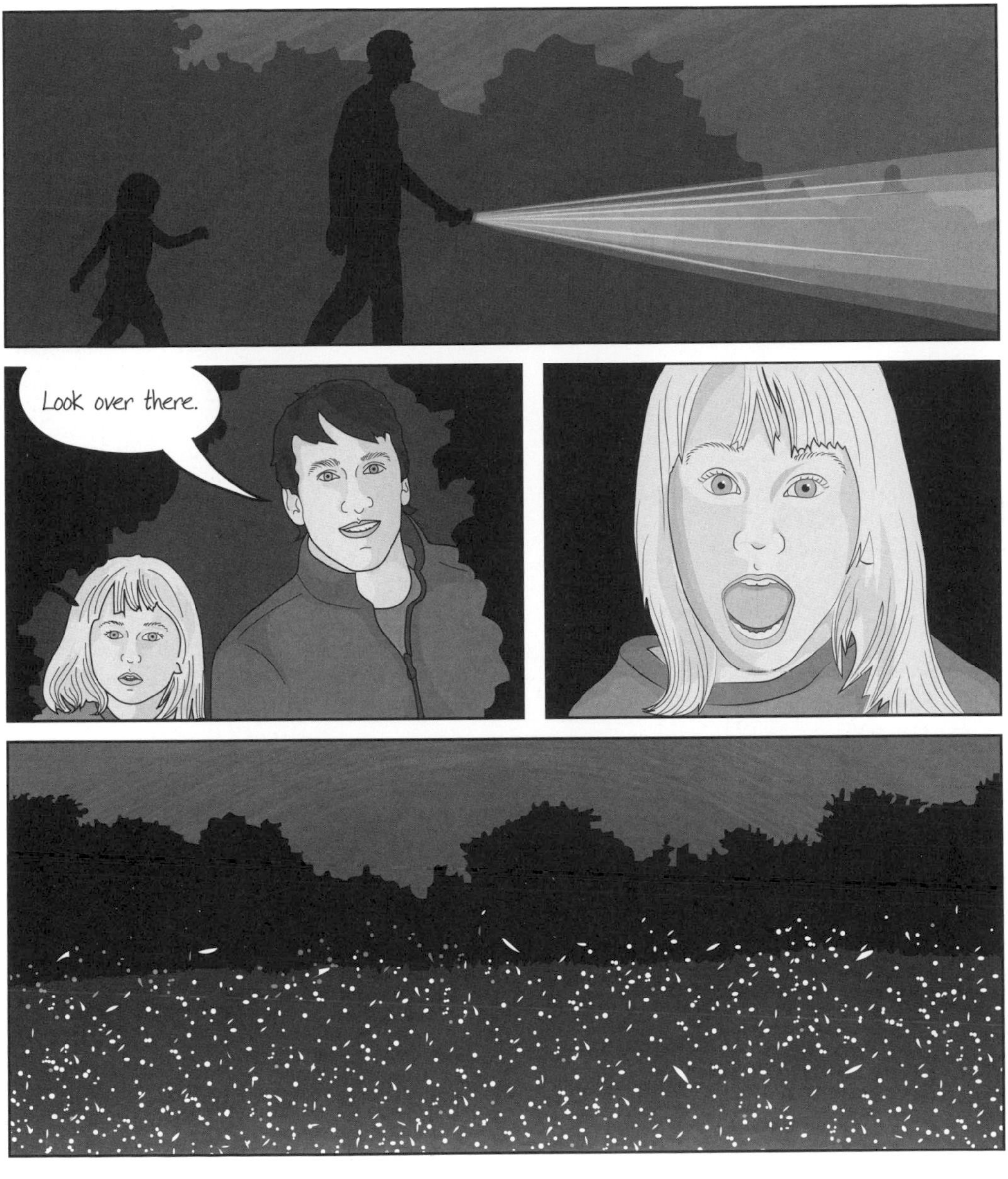
Look over there.

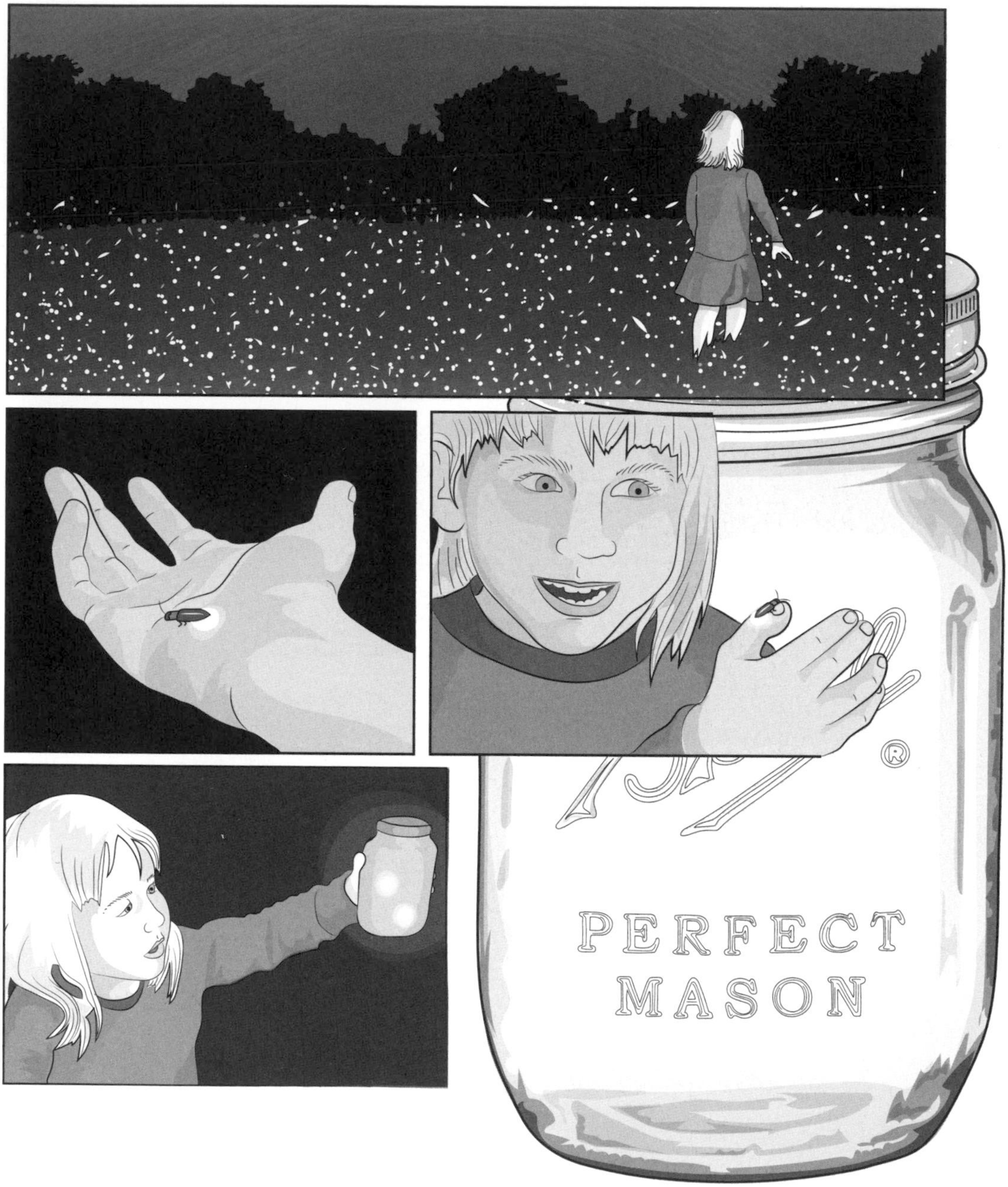
PERFECT
MASON

I have one fuzzy memory of my dad's and uncles' mother, who died when I was three.

Grandma

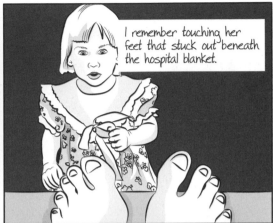

I remember touching her feet that stuck out beneath the hospital blanket.

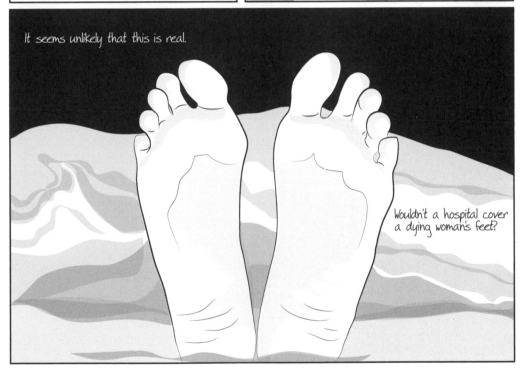

It seems unlikely that this is real.

Wouldn't a hospital cover a dying woman's feet?

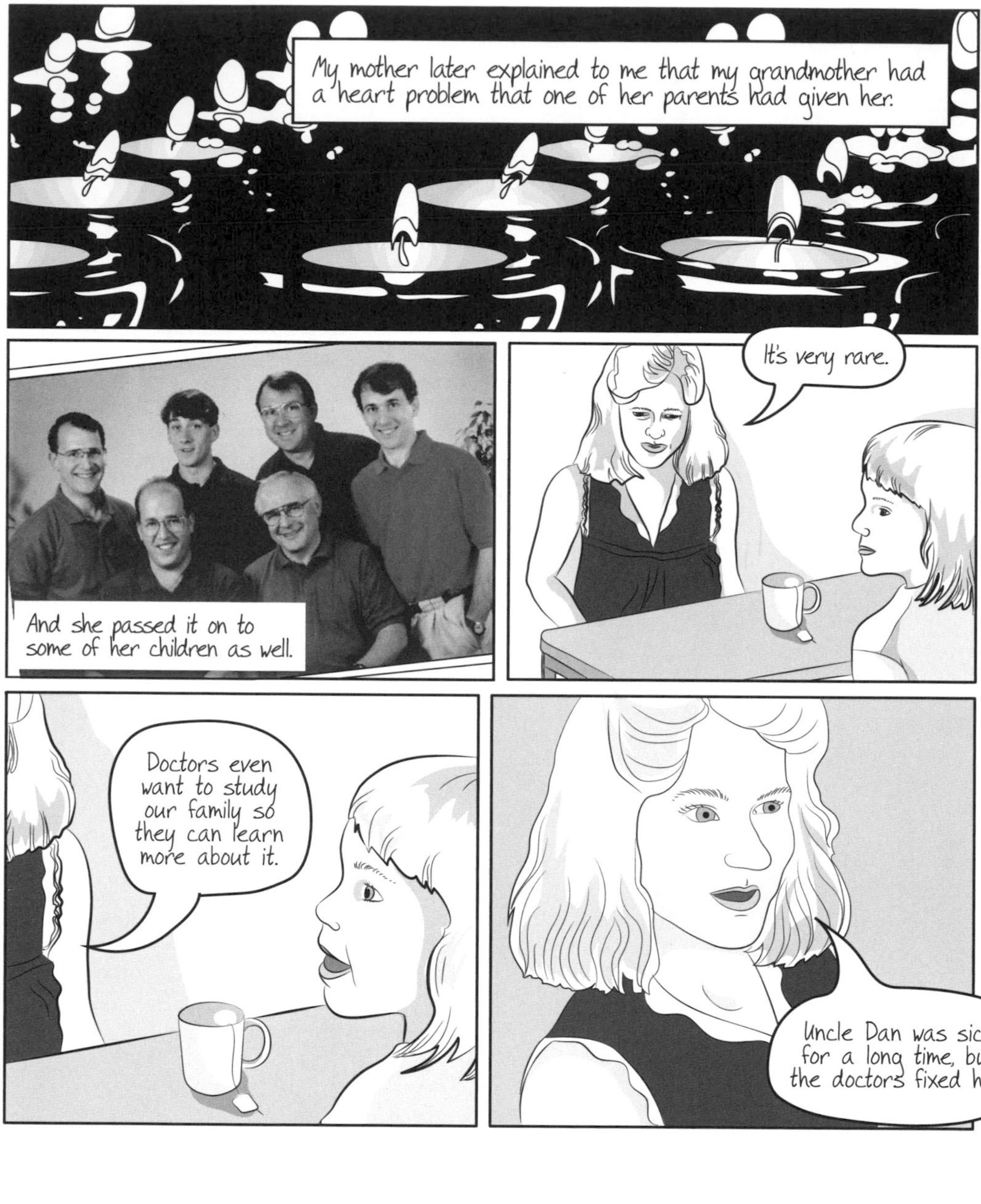
My mother later explained to me that my grandmother had a heart problem that one of her parents had given her.
And she passed it on to some of her children as well.
It's very rare.
Doctors even want to study our family so they can learn more about it.
Uncle Dan was sick for a long time, but the doctors fixed him.

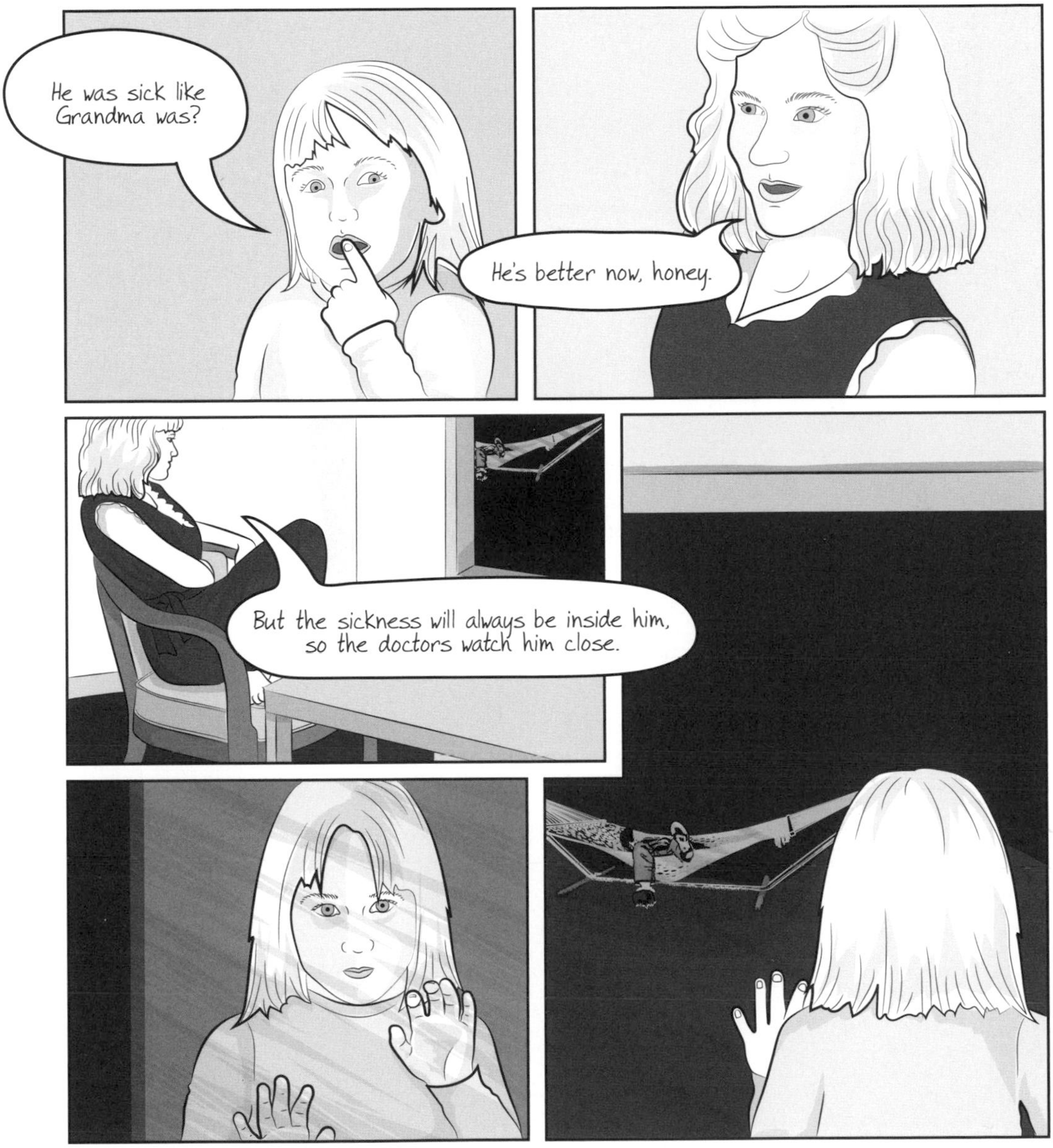
He was sick like Grandma was?
He's better now, honey.
But the sickness will always be inside him, so the doctors watch him close.

I counted on Uncle Dan to offer a clearer explanation.

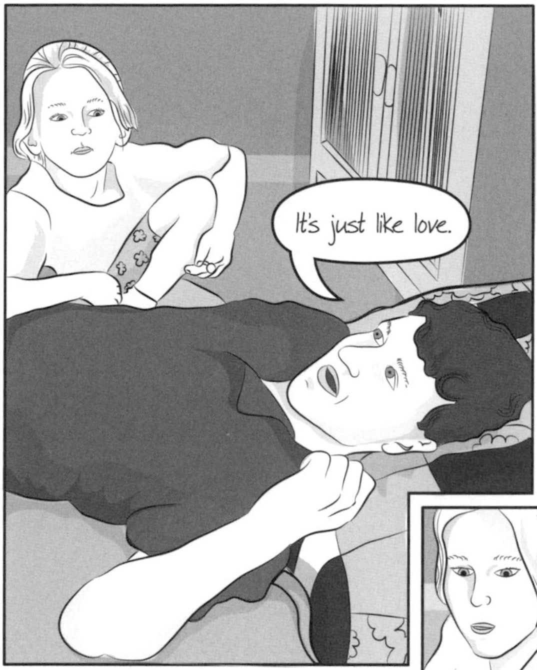
It's just like love.

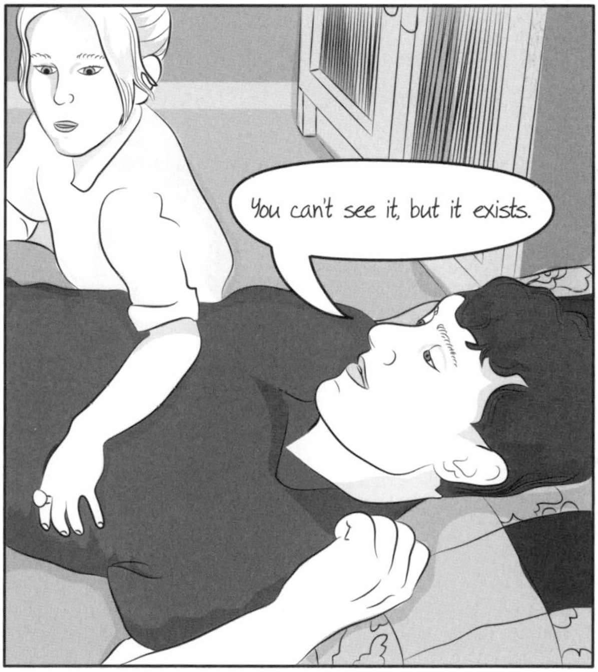
You can't see it, but it exists.

# Chapter 1

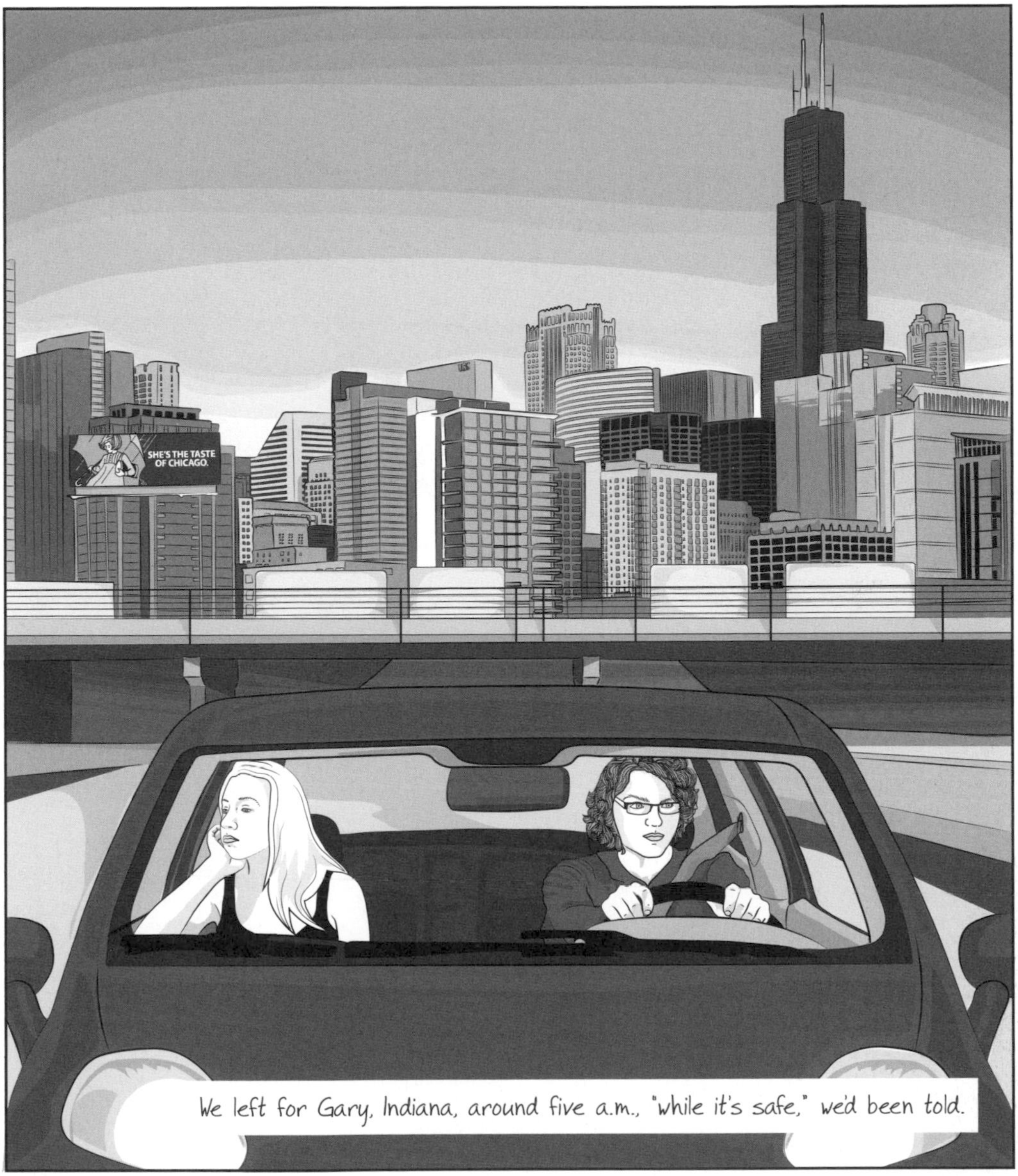
SHE'S THE TASTE OF CHICAGO.
We left for Gary, Indiana, around five a.m., "while it's safe," we'd been told.

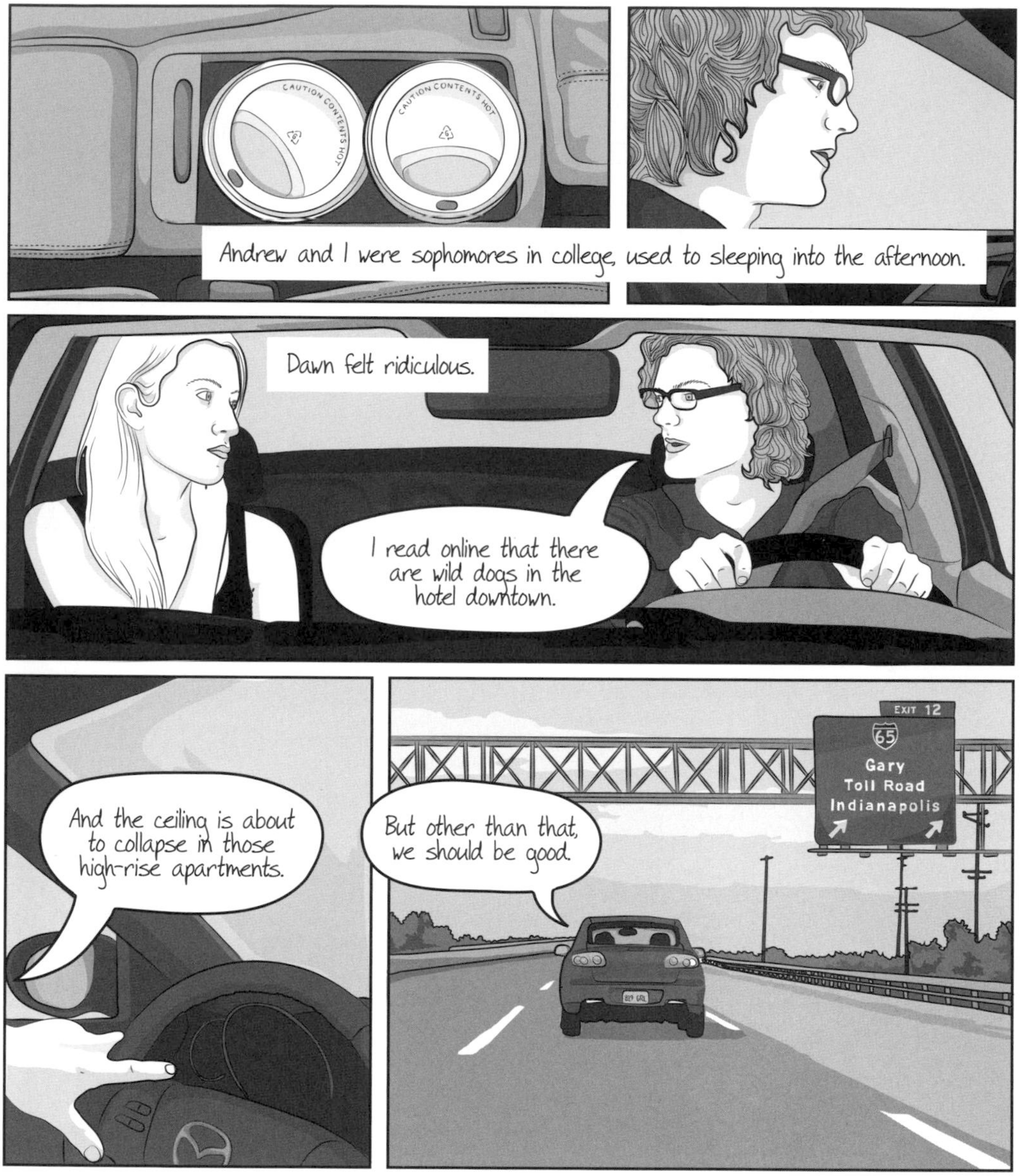
CAUTION CONTENTS HOT
CAUTION CONTENTS HOT
Andrew and I were sophomores in college, used to sleeping into the afternoon.
Dawn felt ridiculous.
I read online that there are wild dogs in the hotel downtown.
And the ceiling is about to collapse in those high-rise apartments.
But other than that, we should be good.
EXIT 12
65
Gary
Toll Road
Indianapolis

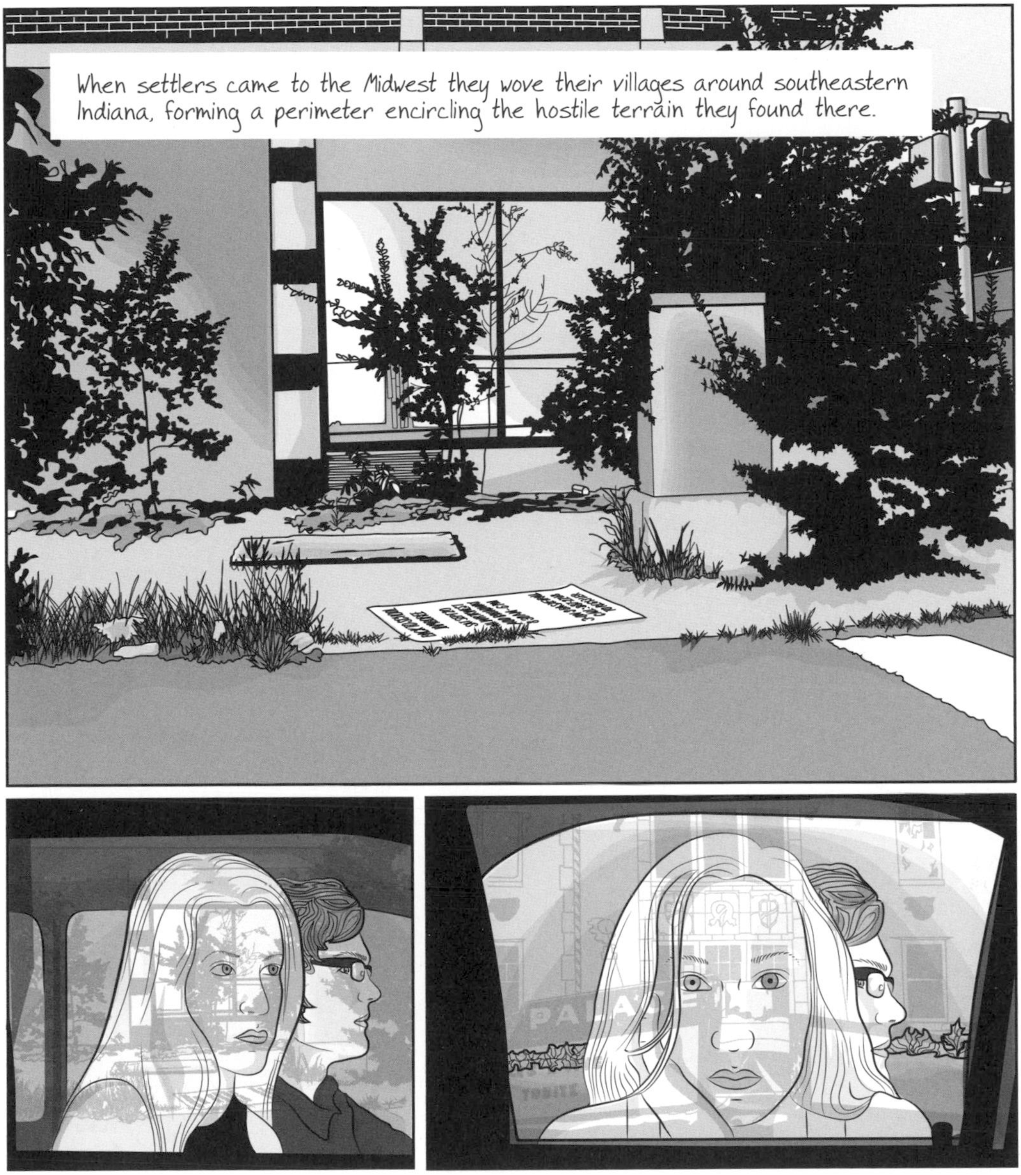
When settlers came to the Midwest they wove their villages around southeastern Indiana, forming a perimeter encircling the hostile terrain they found there.

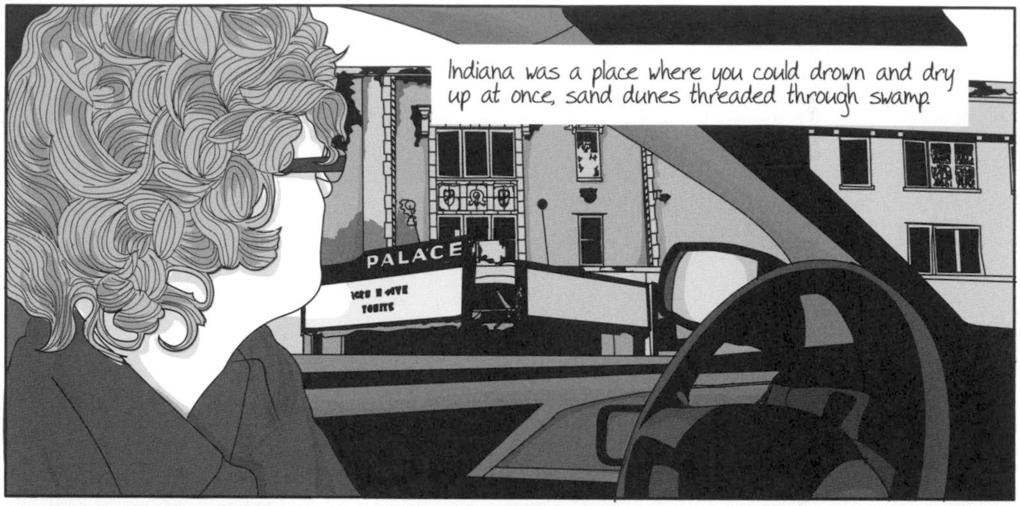
Indiana was a place where you could drown and dry up at once, sand dunes threaded through swamp.
PALACE

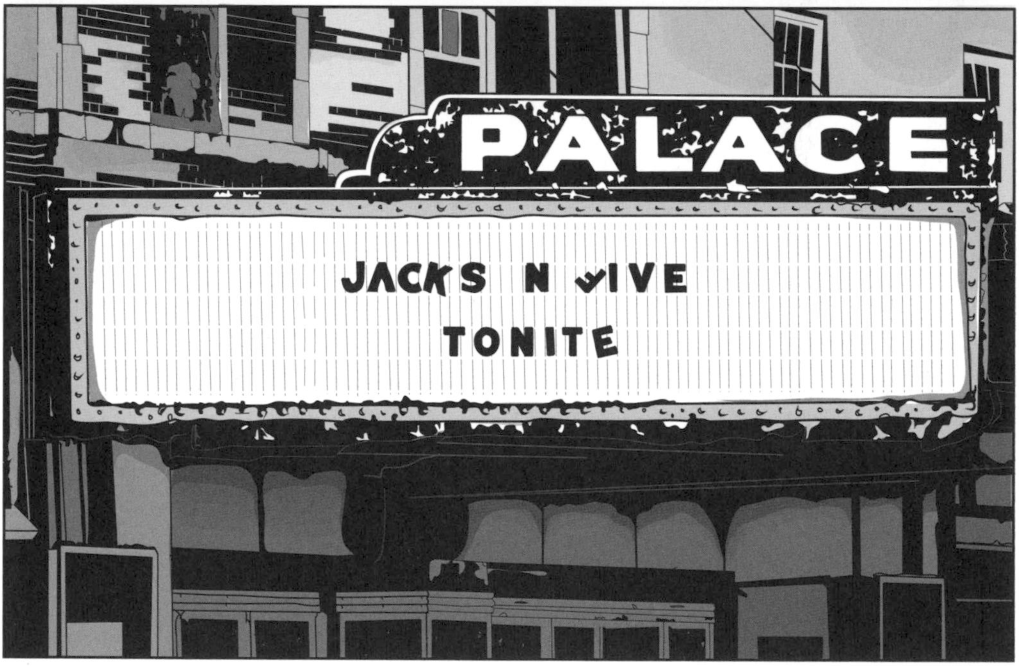
PALACE
JACKS N JIVE
TONITE

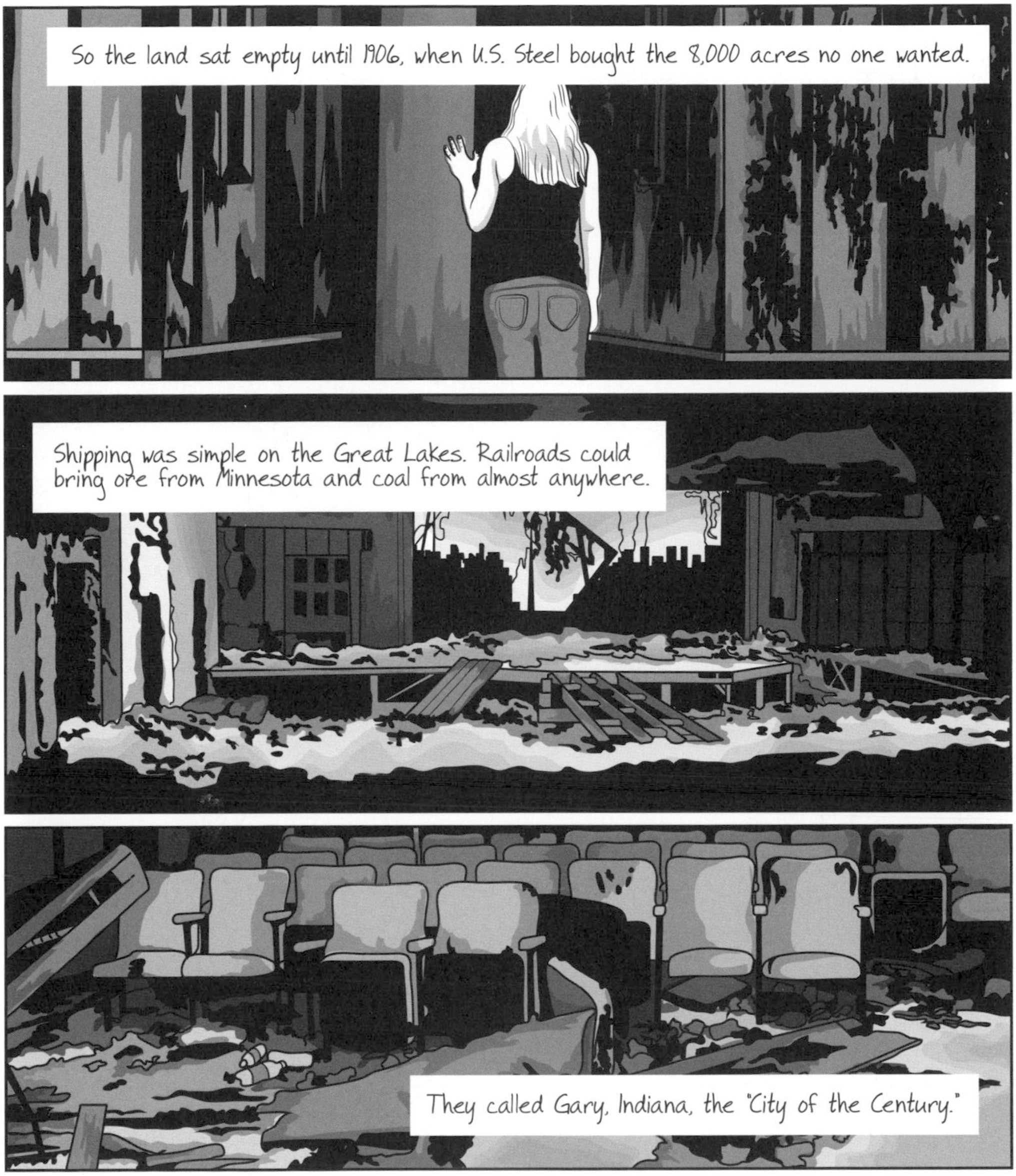
So the land sat empty until 1906, when U.S. Steel bought the 8,000 acres no one wanted.
Shipping was simple on the Great Lakes. Railroads could bring ore from Minnesota and coal from almost anywhere.
They called Gary, Indiana, the "City of the Century."

The state border was only a forty-minute drive from Chicago, where I attended an art school that held classes almost exclusively at night.

I liked the simple fact of filling a space, the comfort of sitting with spotlights and worn easels in a quiet room before being released into dark, empty streets.

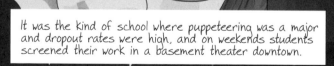

It was the kind of school where puppeteering was a major and dropout rates were high, and on weekends students screened their work in a basement theater downtown.

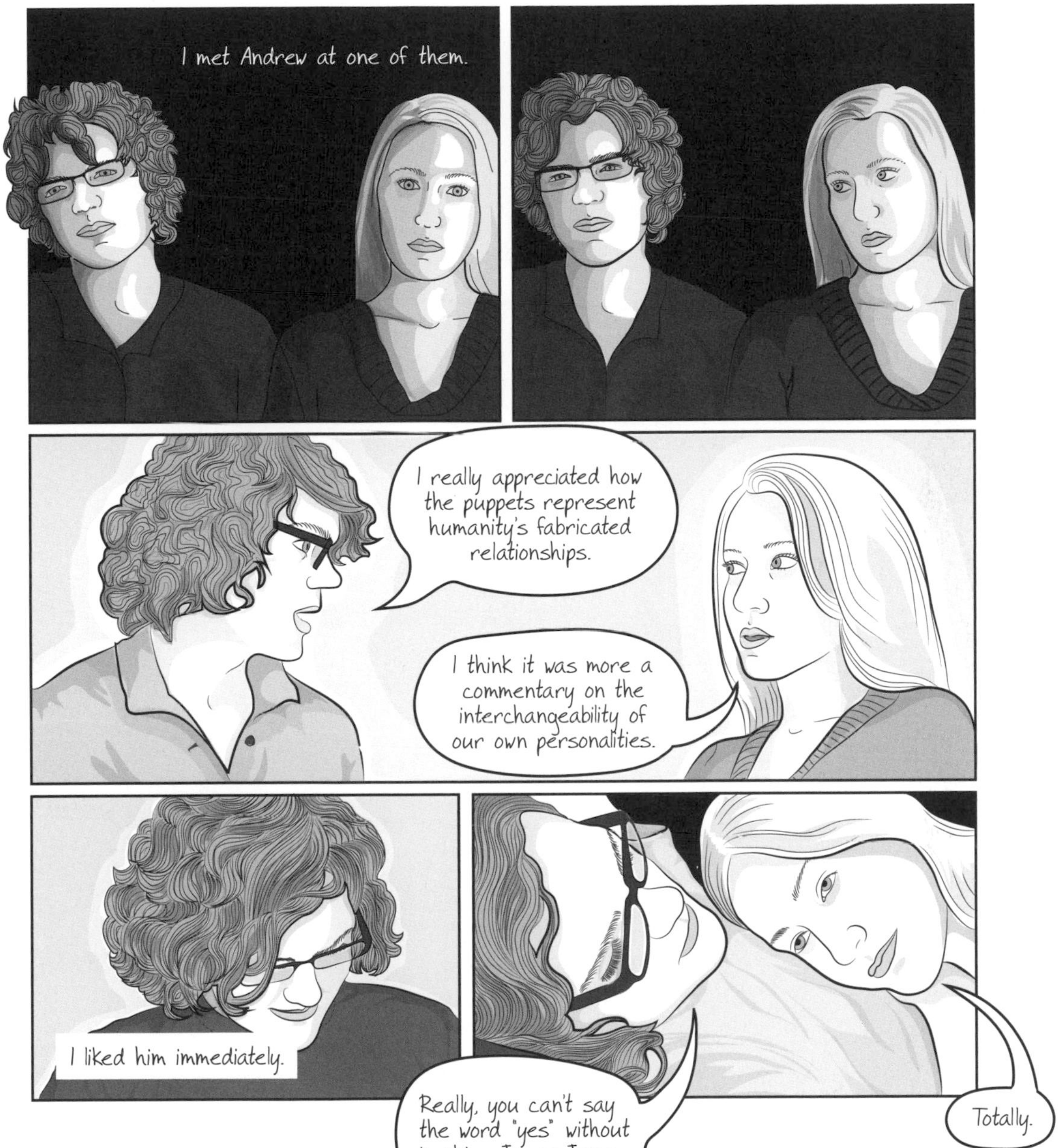
I met Andrew at one of them.
I really appreciated how the puppets represent humanity's fabricated relationships.
I think it was more a commentary on the interchangeability of our own personalities.
I liked him immediately.
Really, you can't say the word "yes" without invoking James Joyce.
Totally.

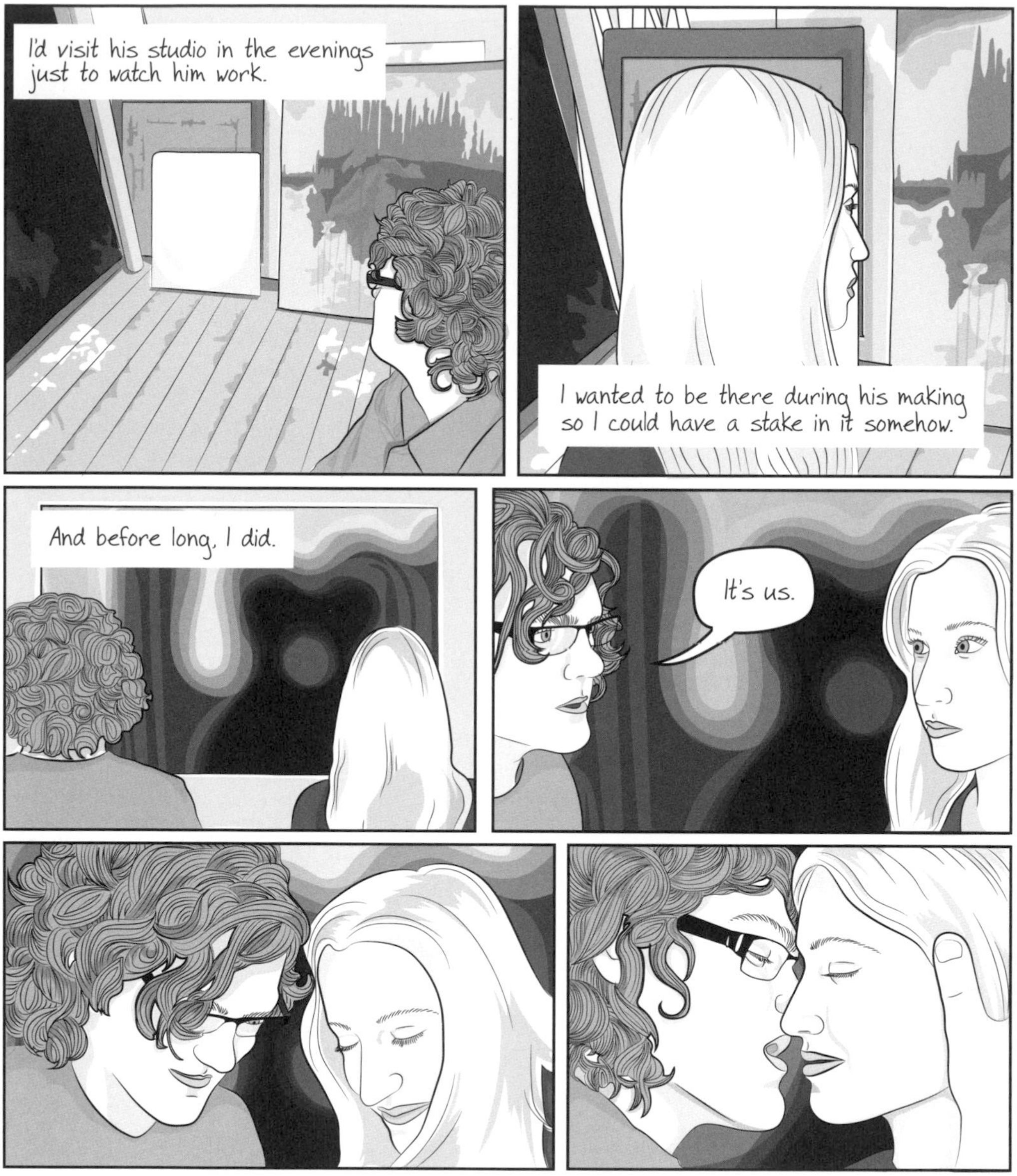
I'd visit his studio in the evenings just to watch him work.
I wanted to be there during his making so I could have a stake in it somehow.
And before long, I did.
It's us.

The photography department was down the hall from Andrew's painting studio.

I loved the way everything looked in the darkroom, smoothed and forgiven, and the sound of it, enclosed and somehow secret atop the trickle of cold water and chemicals I touched so compulsively that the skin began peeling from my palms.

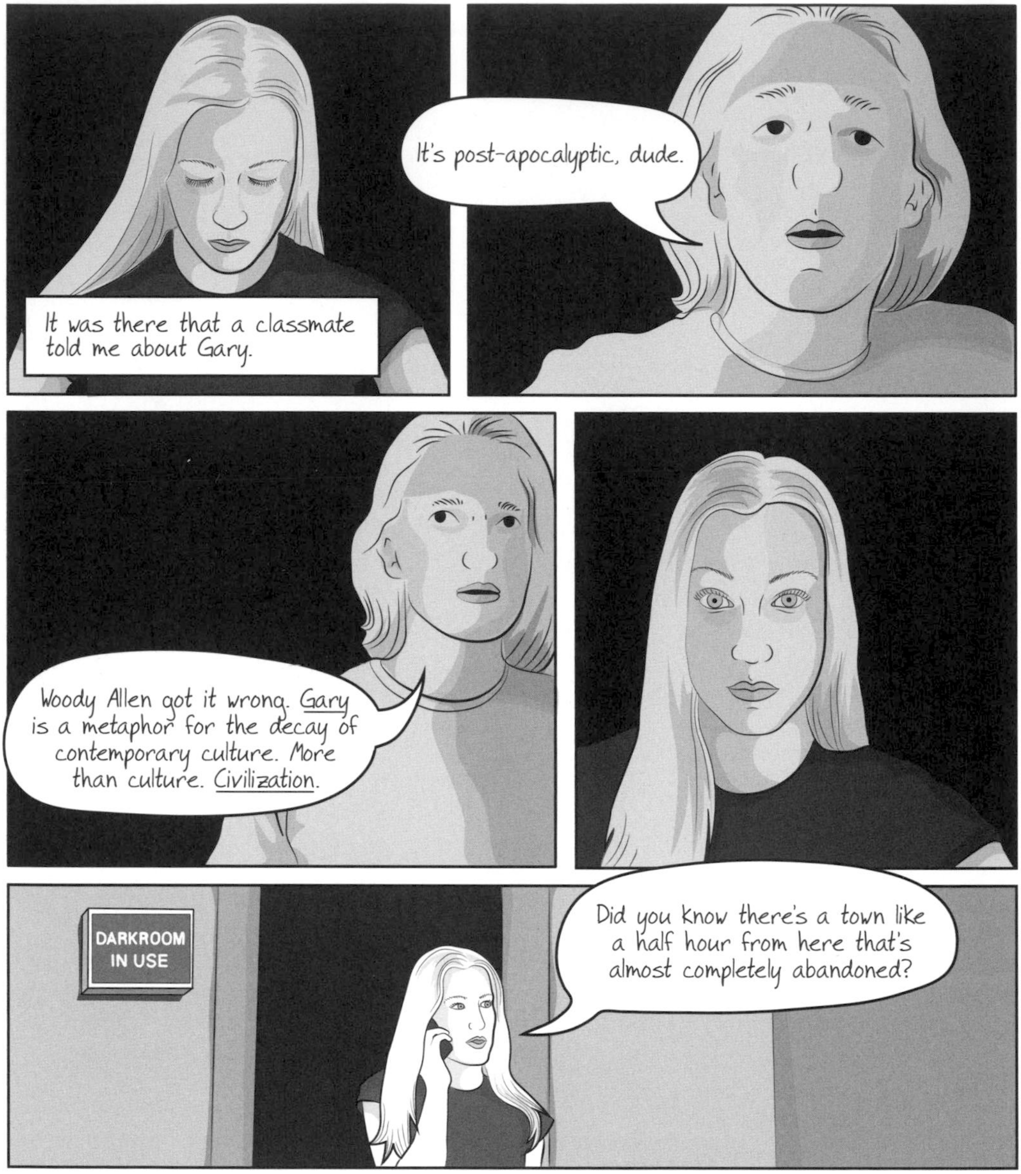
It was there that a classmate told me about Gary.
It's post-apocalyptic, dude.
Woody Allen got it wrong. Gary is a metaphor for the decay of contemporary culture. More than culture. Civilization.
DARKROOM IN USE
Did you know there's a town like a half hour from here that's almost completely abandoned?

GREETINGS FROM GARY
FOR SALE
JACKSON ARMS
It's like someone pulled a fire alarm and no one ever came back.

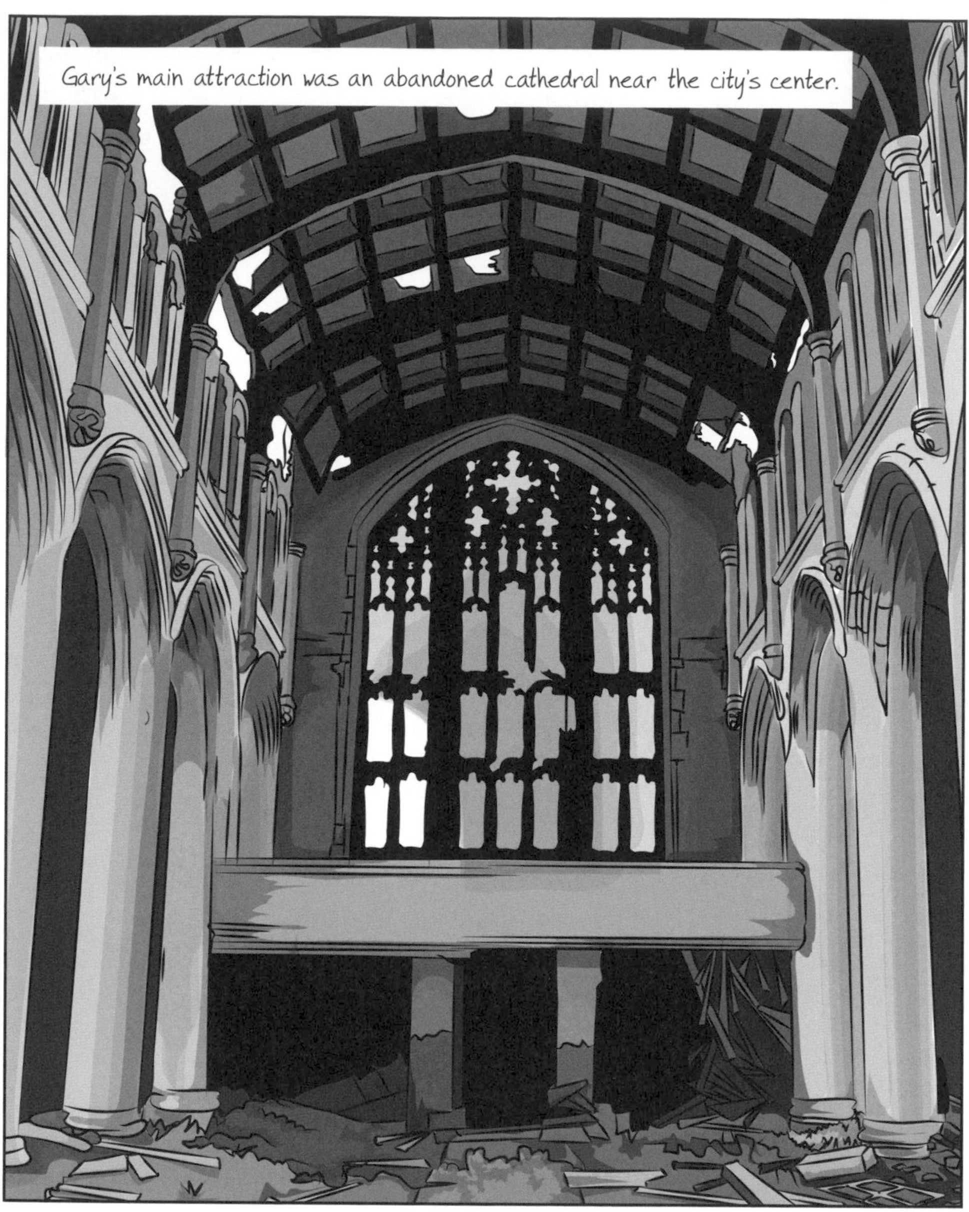
Gary's main attraction was an abandoned cathedral near the city's center.

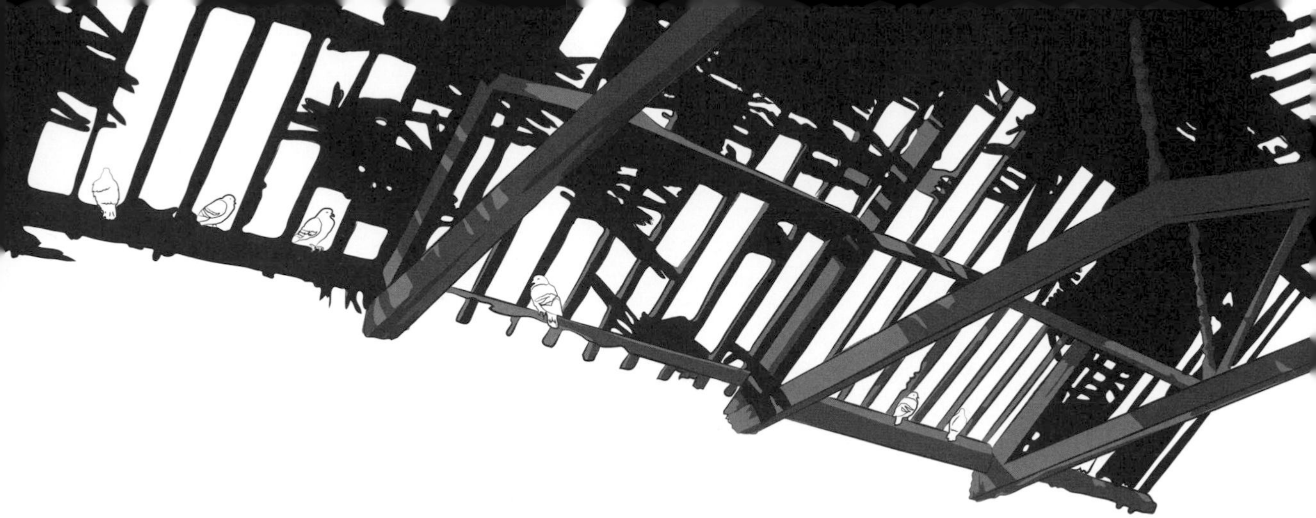

We pulled ourselves up from the snarled foliage of the courtyard and through stone arches where the walls had fallen, stepping around thick chunks of plaster mazed beneath the collapsing ceiling of the sacristy. The stained glass was still intact below the rafters, too high for rocks or looters.

Ivy overtook the corroding walls as it does in storybooks, covering the slated stone with spindles of earthy web.

The tarnished pedals of a shattered organ lay in the corner, its broken keys like piles of pulled teeth.

When we were quiet, the pigeons came down from their towers as we perched on the splintered floorboards, gently easing our feet along the rotting wood.

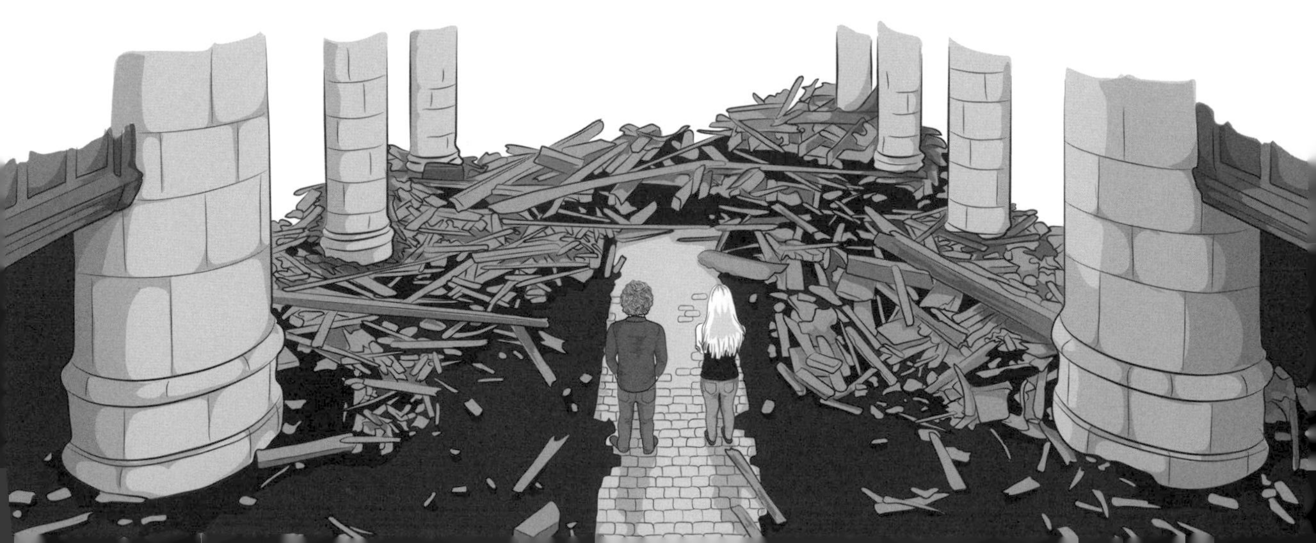

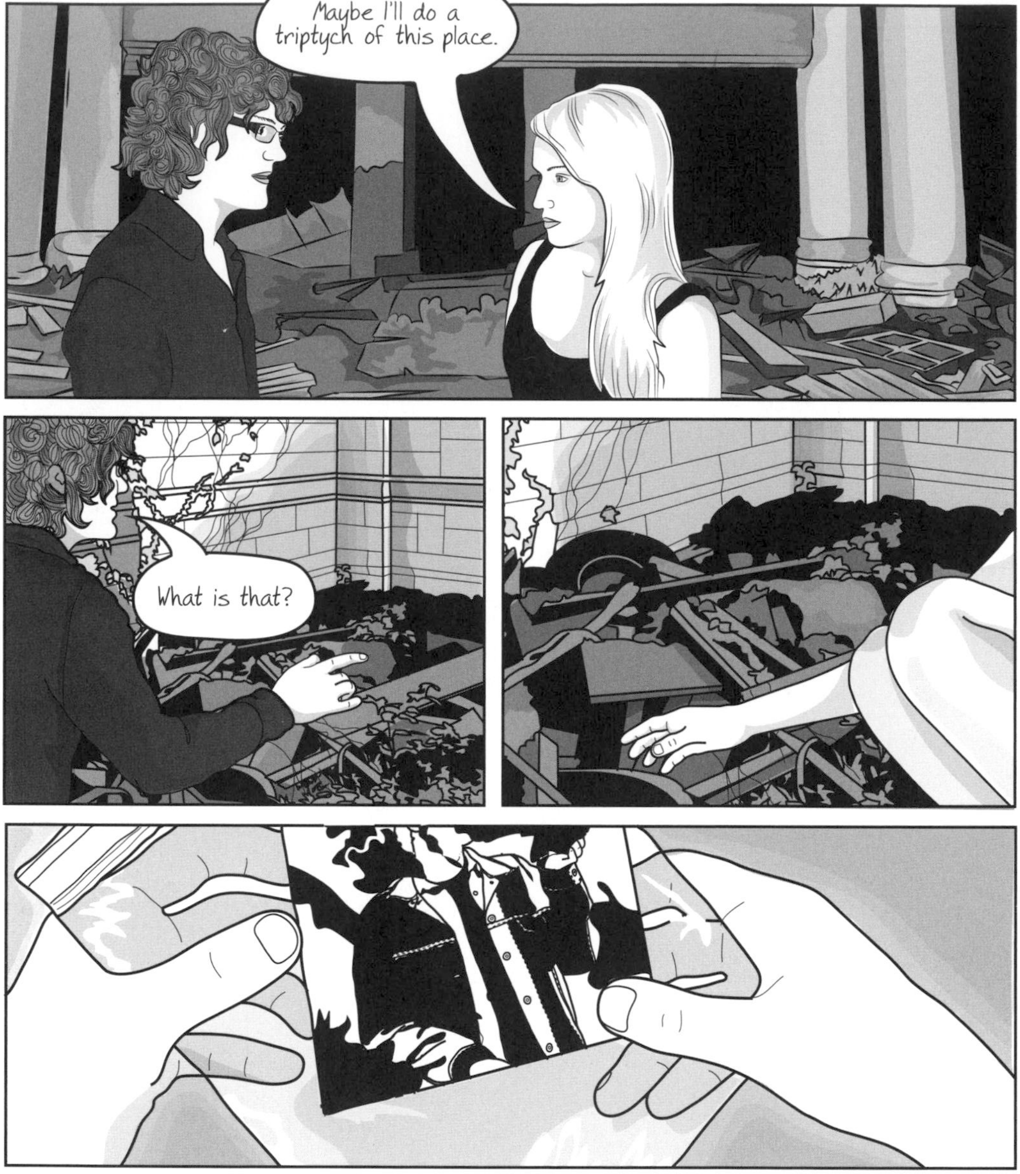
Maybe I'll do a triptych of this place.
What is that?

There are tons of them.

Let's take them. For an installation.

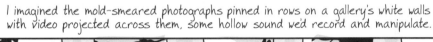

I imagined the mold-smeared photographs pinned in rows on a gallery's white walls with video projected across them, some hollow sound we'd record and manipulate.

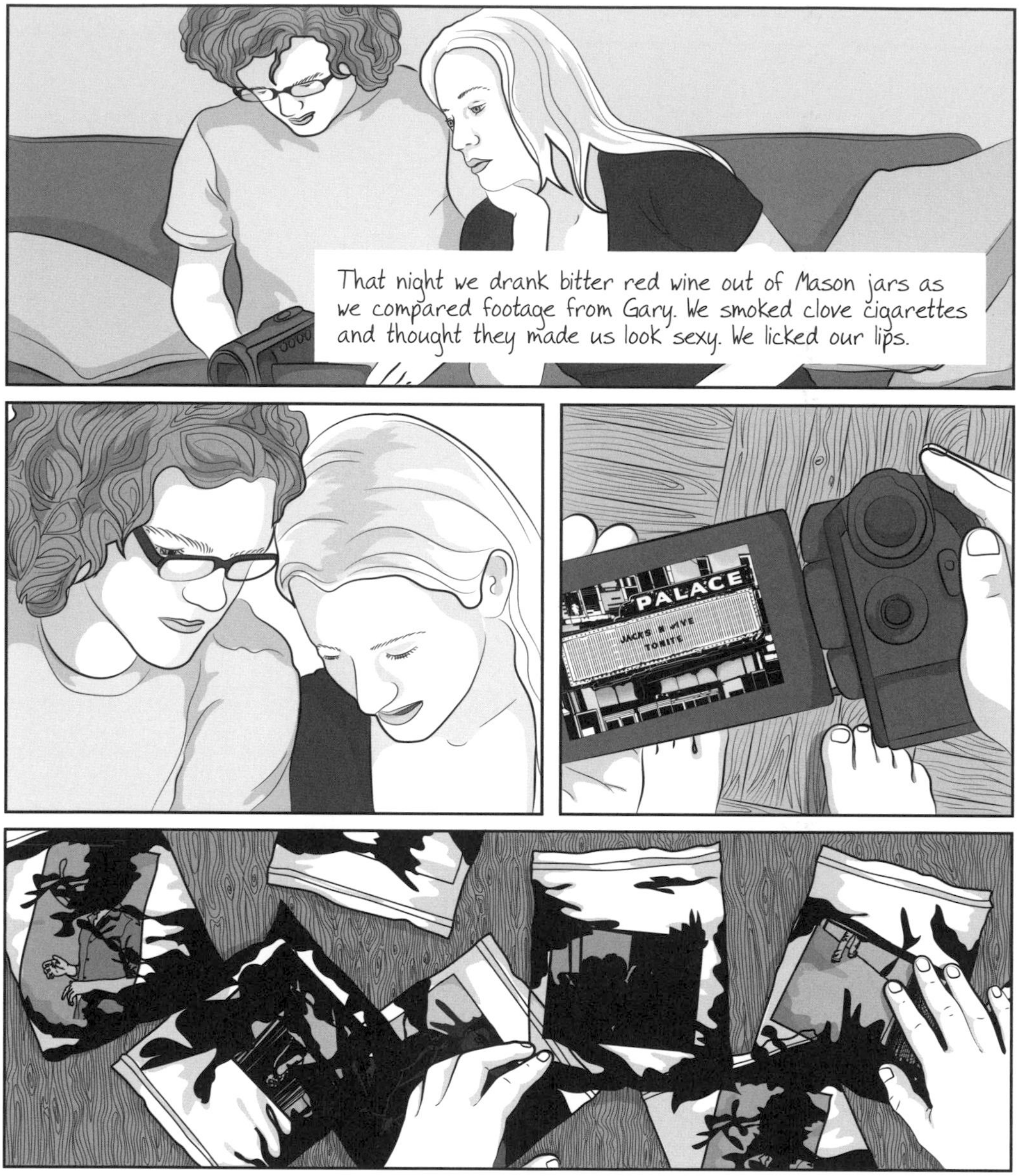
That night we drank bitter red wine out of Mason jars as we compared footage from Gary. We smoked clove cigarettes and thought they made us look sexy. We licked our lips.
PALACE
JACKS N JIVE
TONITE

NORTH
HOTEL
TIP TOP
FOOD & LIQUOR
T&C MEA
MOVED
2701 W NORTH
T&C MEATS
INSTANT CASH
BEST CASH PAID FOR GOLD
We'd just moved to a crumbling neighborhood on Chicago's west side.
A rapidly changing cast of roommates rotated around us, but the place felt like ours.
Obama'08
NUKE FREE
The fact of the house's missing façade and its boarded front windows seemed of little concern.

The ceilings were vaulted high and white, a crooked and cold kind of rehabbed interior that looked expensive until you touched it.

Paris

turtle

free furniture

Buddha

We spent most weeks talking about art we did not understand, creating earnest impersonations that are the hallmarks of young art students, and the house was the backdrop for all of it.

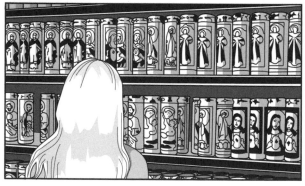

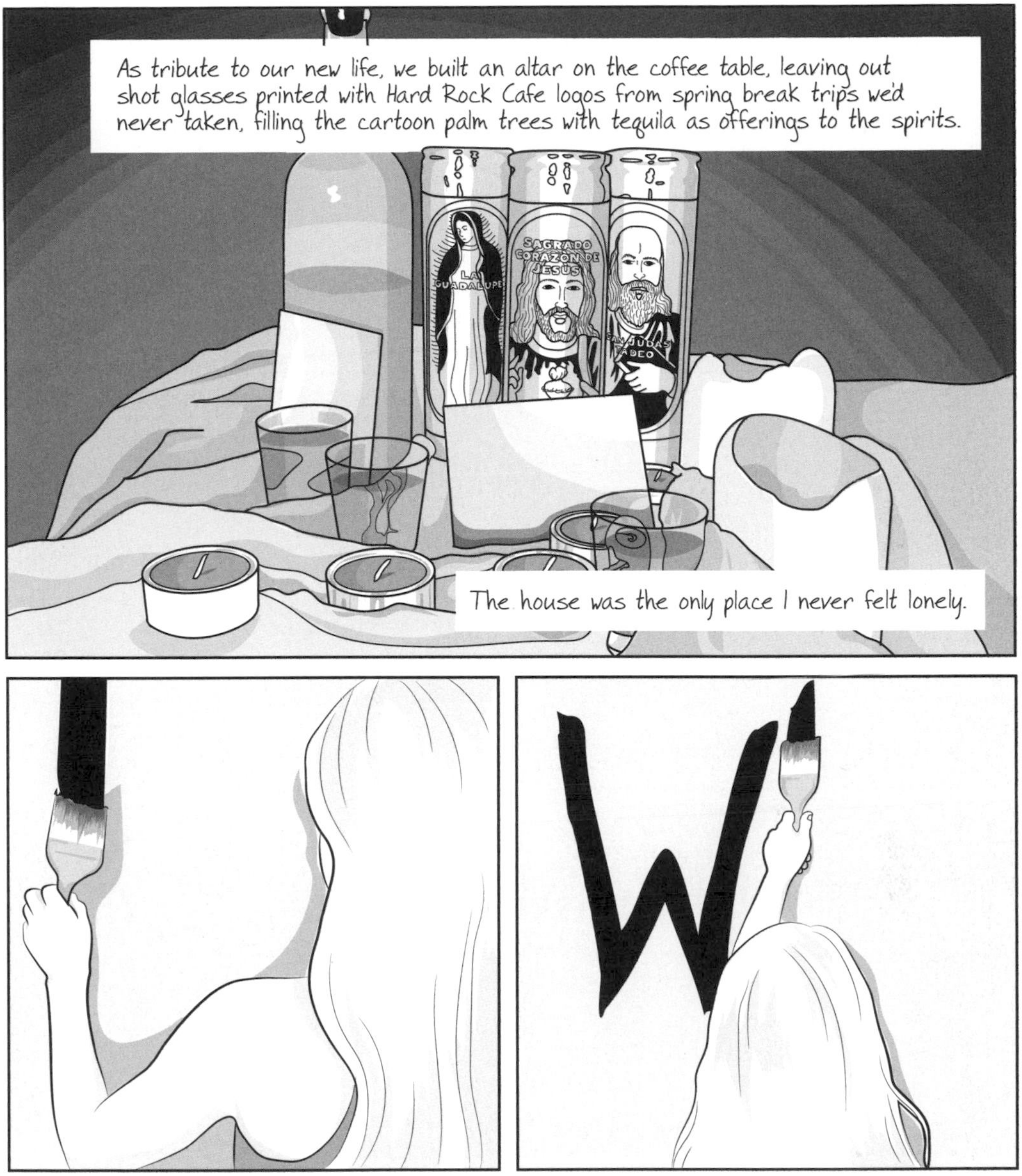

As tribute to our new life, we built an altar on the coffee table, leaving out shot glasses printed with Hard Rock Cafe logos from spring break trips we'd never taken, filling the cartoon palm trees with tequila as offerings to the spirits.
LA GUADALUPE
SAGRADO CORAZON DE JESUS
The house was the only place I never felt lonely.
W

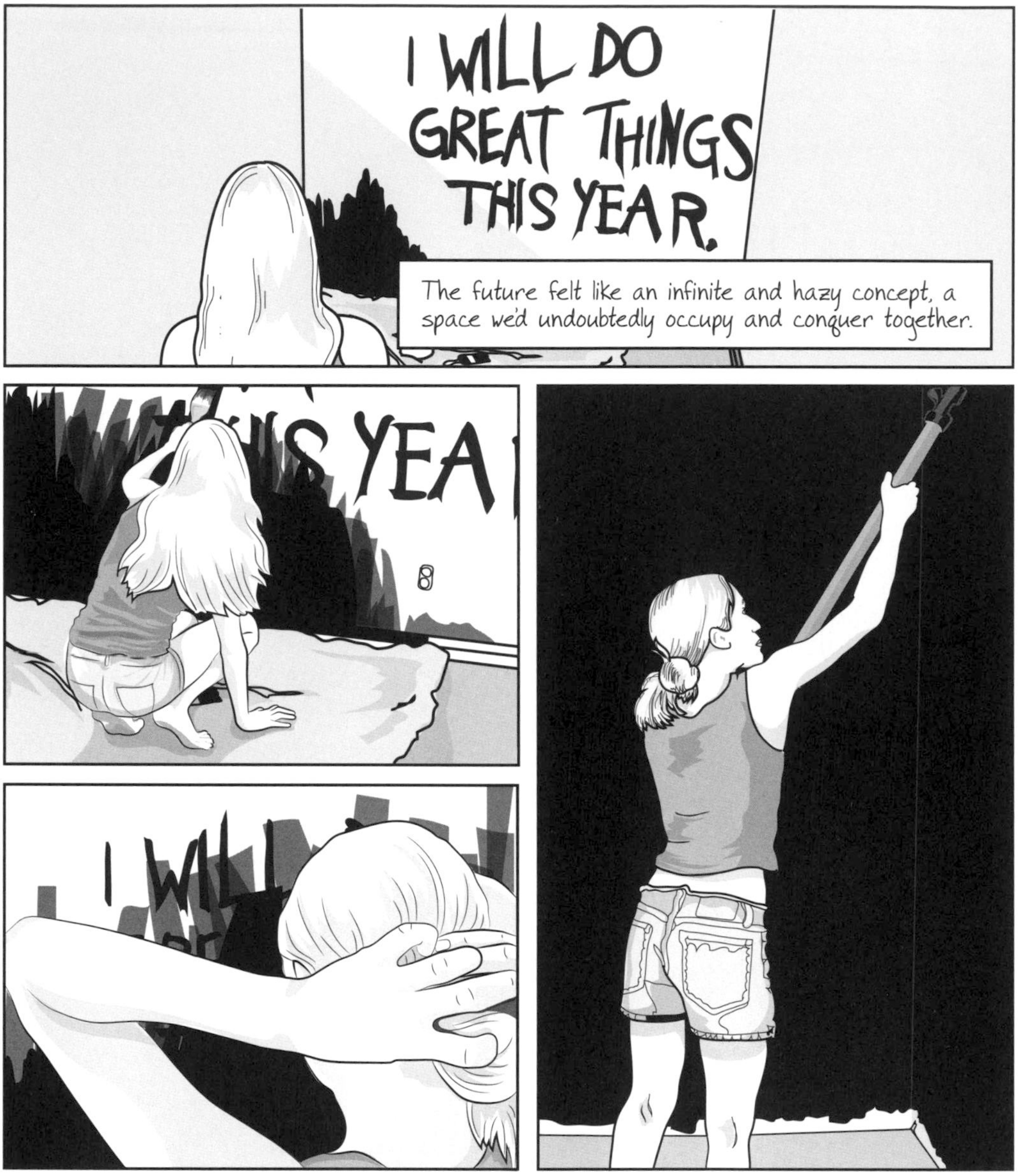
I WILL DO GREAT THINGS THIS YEAR.
The future felt like an infinite and hazy concept, a space we'd undoubtedly occupy and conquer together.
YEA
I WILL

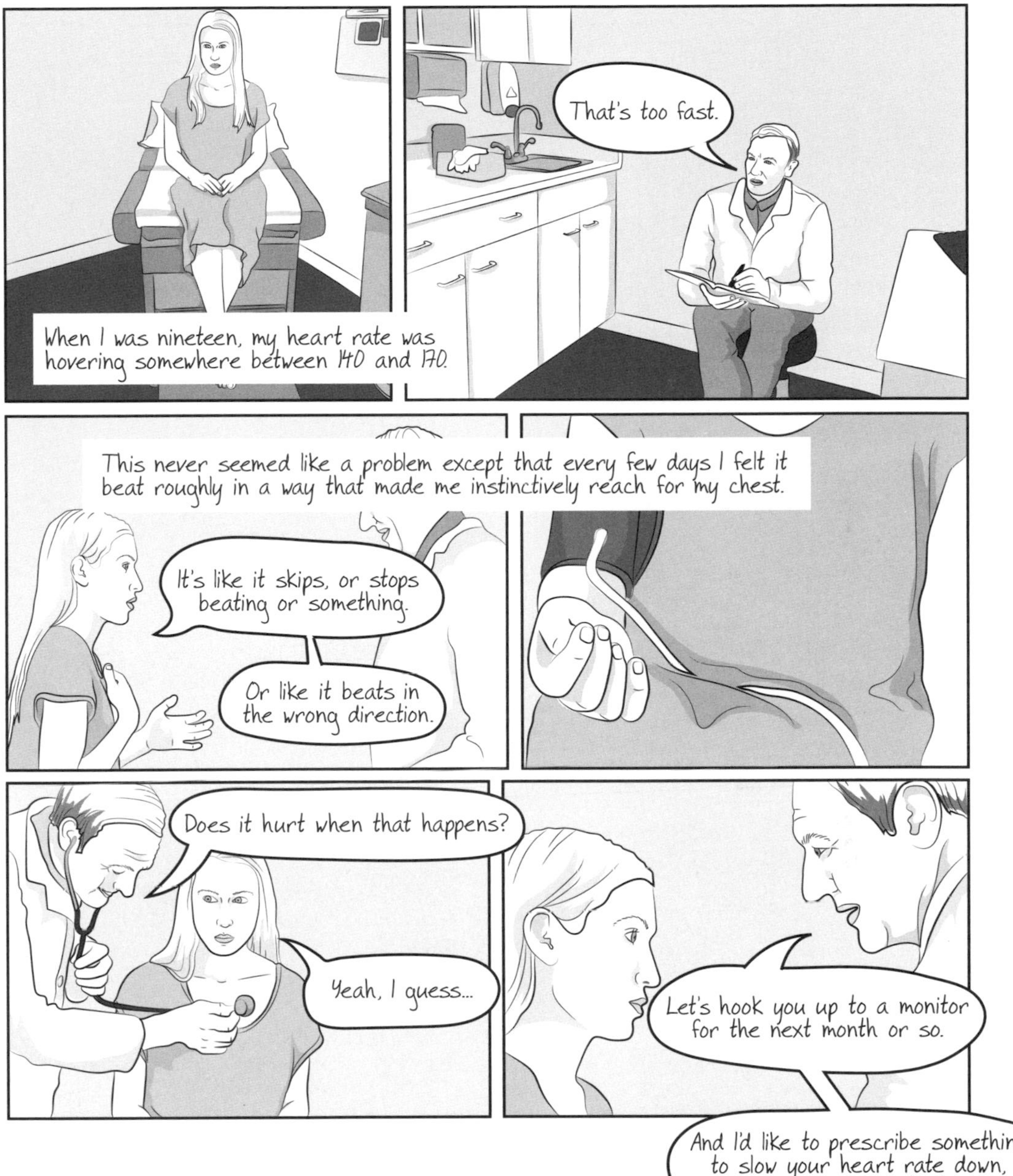
When I was nineteen, my heart rate was hovering somewhere between 140 and 170.
That's too fast.
This never seemed like a problem except that every few days I felt it beat roughly in a way that made me instinctively reach for my chest.
It's like it skips, or stops beating or something.
Or like it beats in the wrong direction.
Does it hurt when that happens?
Yeah, I guess...
Let's hook you up to a monitor for the next month or so.
And I'd like to prescribe something to slow your heart rate down, given your family history.

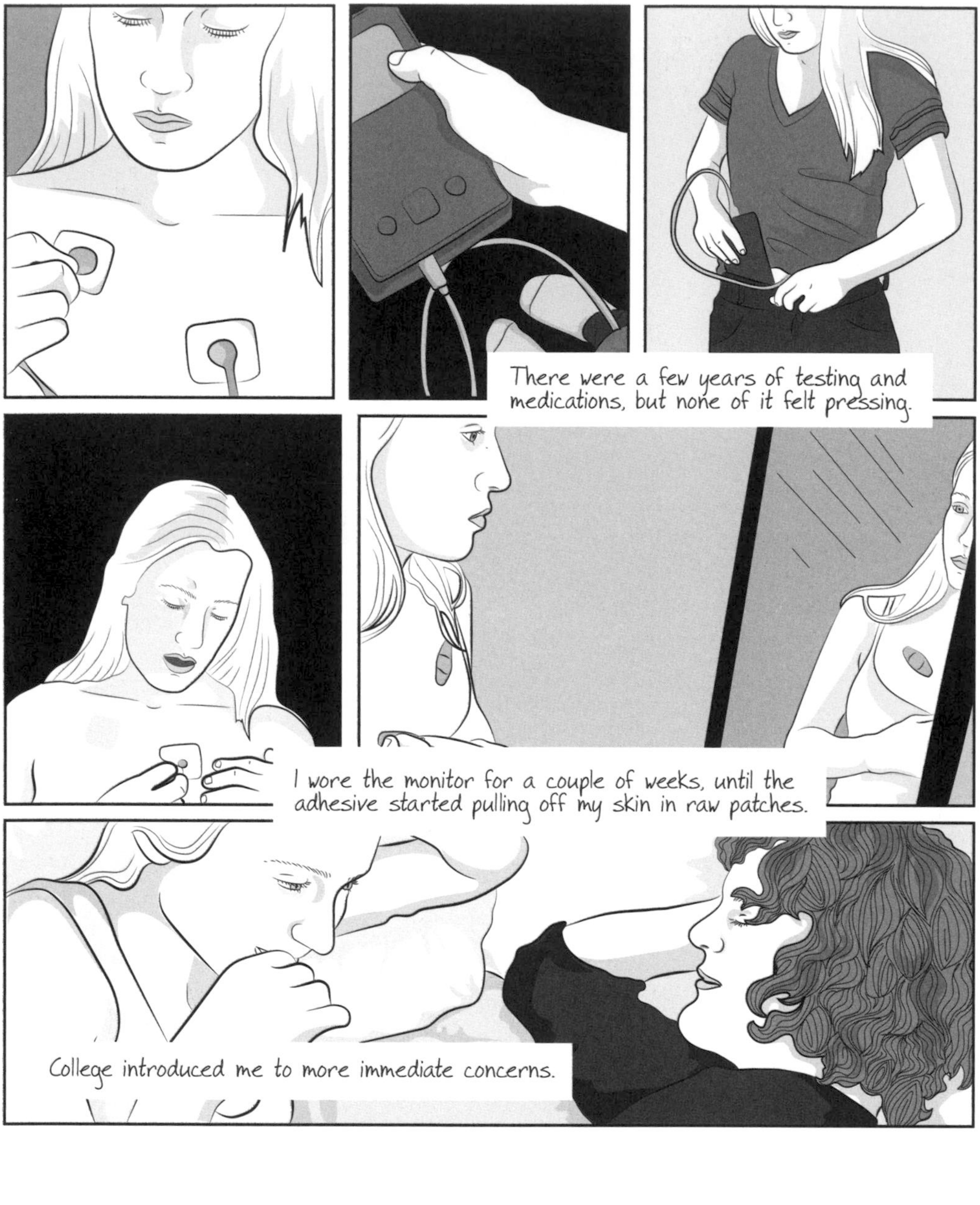
There were a few years of testing and medications, but none of it felt pressing.
I wore the monitor for a couple of weeks, until the adhesive started pulling off my skin in raw patches.
College introduced me to more immediate concerns.

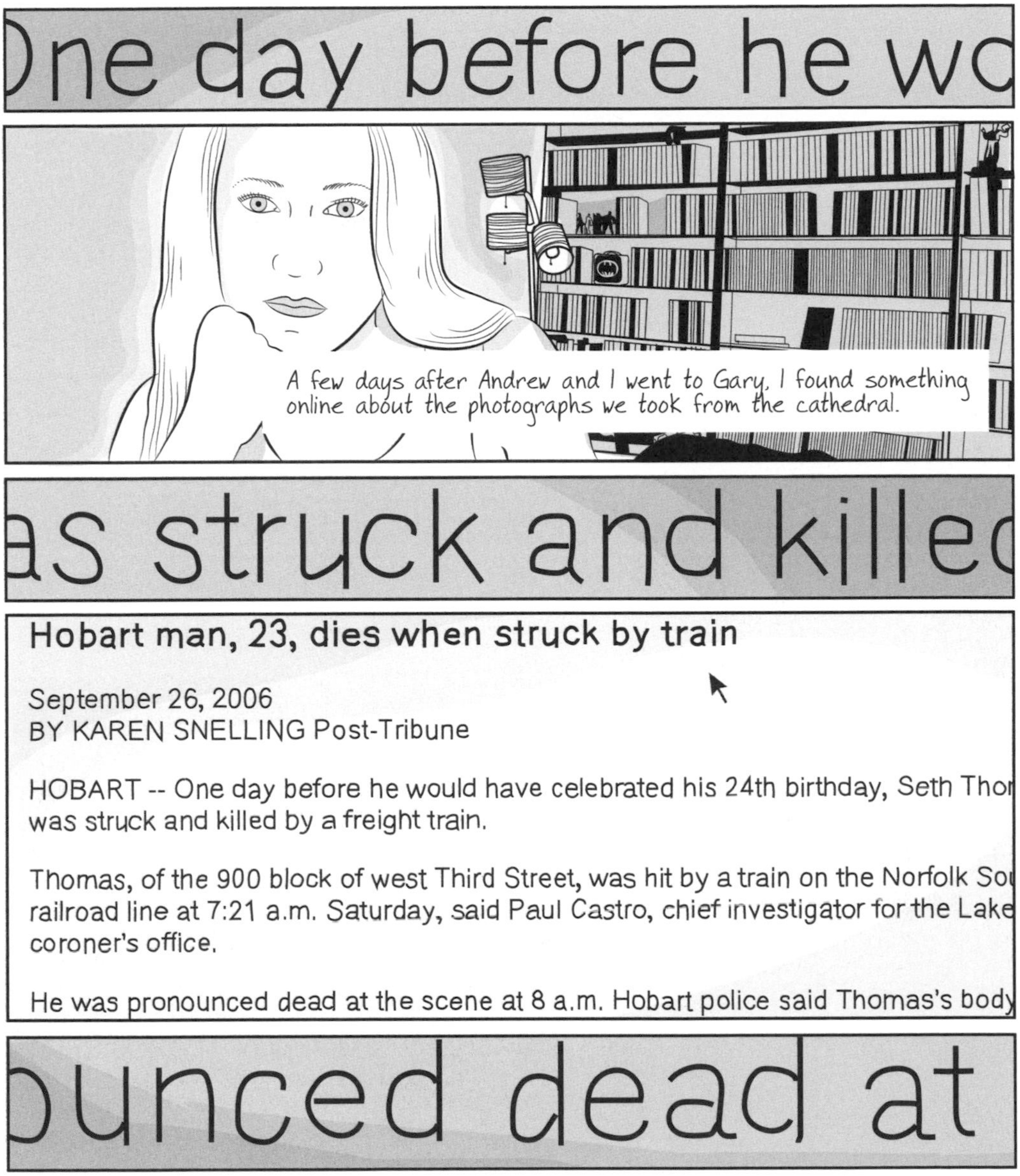
One day before he wo
A few days after Andrew and I went to Gary, I found something online about the photographs we took from the cathedral.
as struck and killed
Hobart man, 23, dies when struck by train
September 26, 2006
BY KAREN SNELLING Post-Tribune
HOBART -- One day before he would have celebrated his 24th birthday, Seth Thor
was struck and killed by a freight train.
Thomas, of the 900 block of west Third Street, was hit by a train on the Norfolk So
railroad line at 7:21 a.m. Saturday, said Paul Castro, chief investigator for the Lake
coroner's office.
He was pronounced dead at the scene at 8 a.m. Hobart police said Thomas's body
ounced dead at

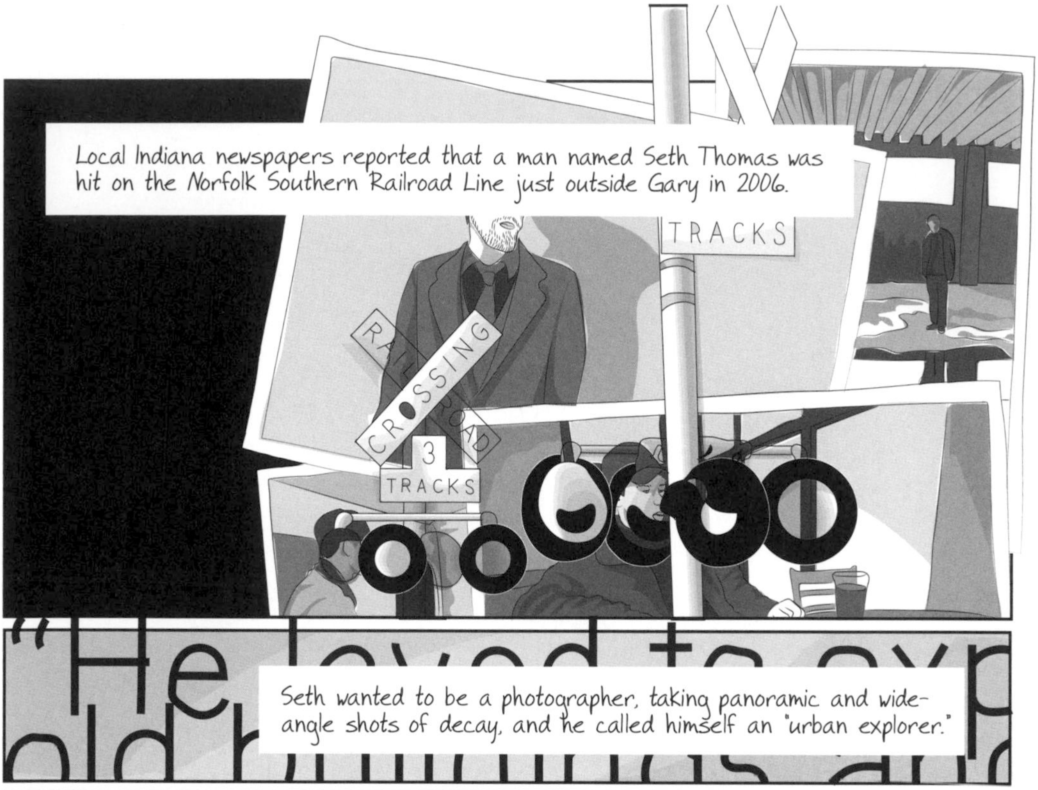
Local Indiana newspapers reported that a man named Seth Thomas was hit on the Norfolk Southern Railroad Line just outside Gary in 2006.
TRACKS
RAILROAD CROSSING
3
TRACKS
Seth wanted to be a photographer, taking panoramic and wide-angle shots of decay, and he called himself an "urban explorer."

**eth Thomas saw beauty in abandoned buildings**

onday, October 9, 2006 12:29 AM CDT

Y ADELE L. MACKANOS

hrough the lenses of his camera, Seth Thomas saw beauty, even in the interior and e
ructures of old, abandoned buildings.

lext to working to get his degree in engineering, photography was my son's greatest
teve Thomas said. "He loved to explore old buildings and even went as far as Detroit
em. He took photos there of the Packard plant and the Motown building."

www.futurespeak.net/myspic/fisher21/slides/fisher05.html

His camera was found, shattered, near his body.

Exposure: 2.0s : F/2.8 @ ISO 100

previous | index | next

So he was taking a picture of the train, the people who knew Seth Thomas insisted, not jumping in front of it.

Eight days after he stood on the tracks, held the camera to his face, and felt or did not feel the train pull his body apart, his friends hosted a memorial service in the abandoned City Methodist Church, his favorite place to photograph.

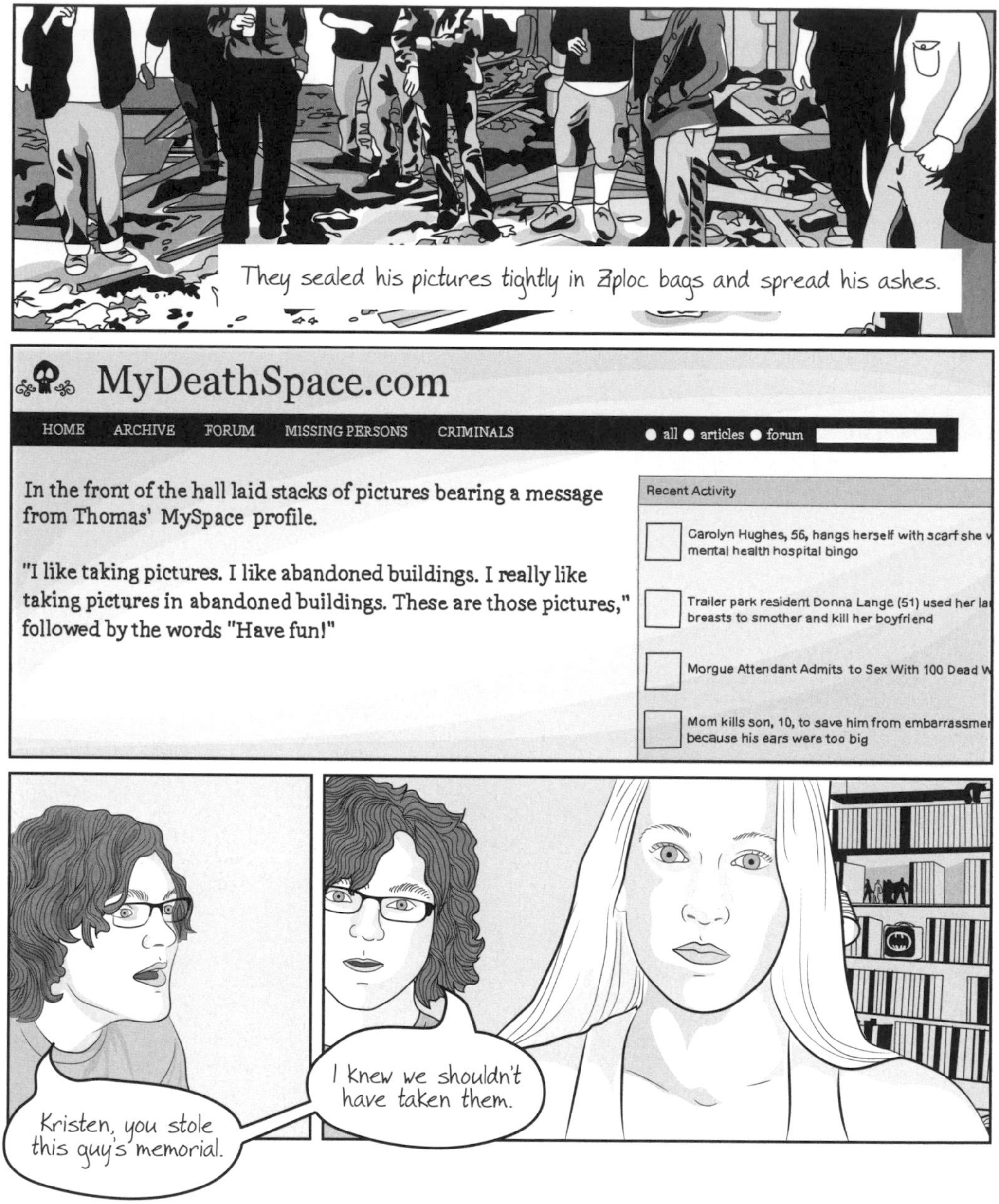
They sealed his pictures tightly in Ziploc bags and spread his ashes.
MyDeathSpace.com
HOME ARCHIVE FORUM MISSING PERSONS CRIMINALS
all articles forum
In the front of the hall laid stacks of pictures bearing a message from Thomas' MySpace profile.
"I like taking pictures. I like abandoned buildings. I really like taking pictures in abandoned buildings. These are those pictures," followed by the words "Have fun!"
Recent Activity
Carolyn Hughes, 56, hangs herself with scarf she
mental health hospital bingo
Trailer park resident Donna Lange (51) used her
breasts to smother and kill her boyfriend
Morgue Attendant Admits to Sex With 100 Dead
Mom kills son, 10, to save him from
because his ears were too big
Kristen, you stole this guy's memorial.
I knew we shouldn't have taken them.

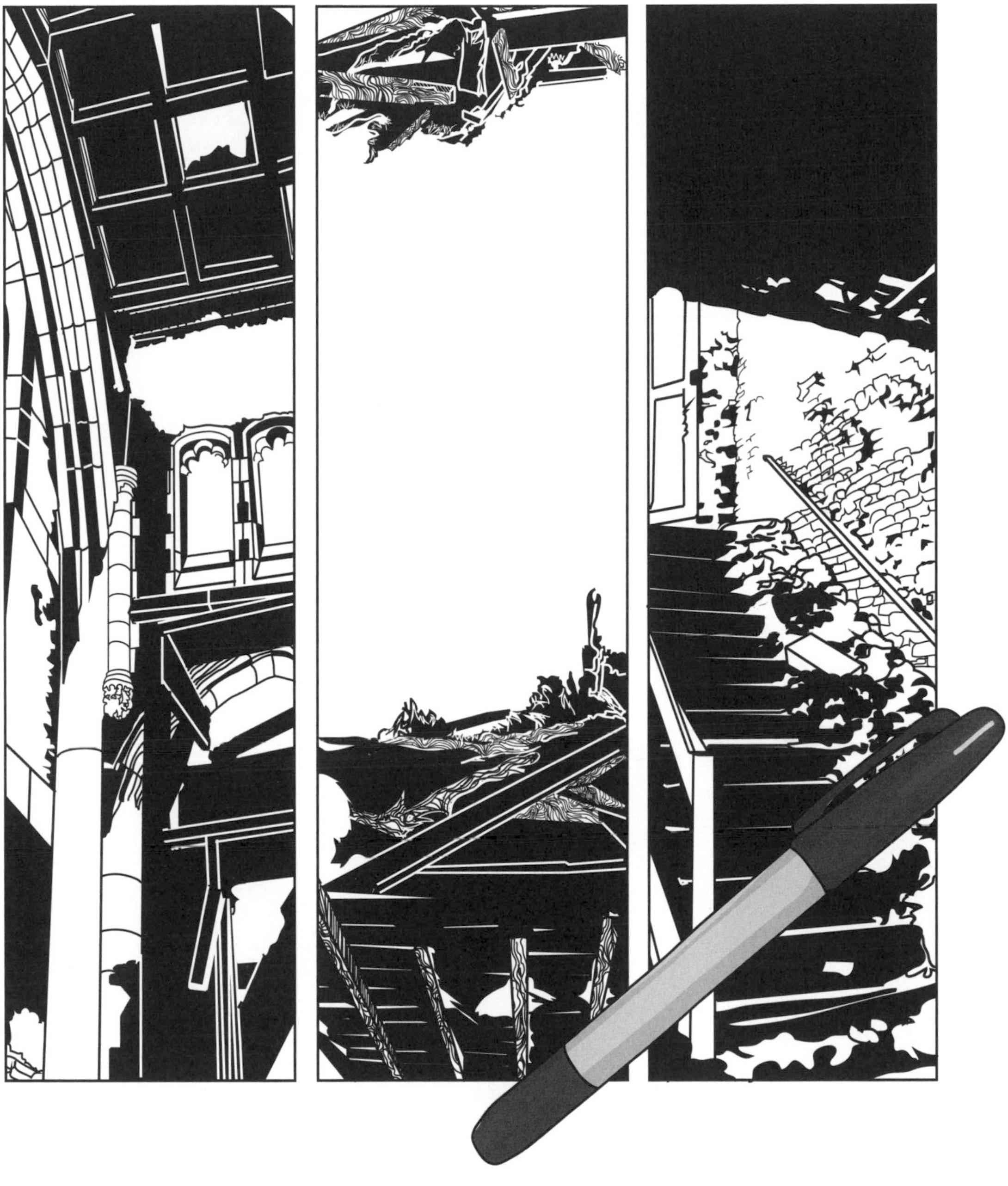

# Chapter 2

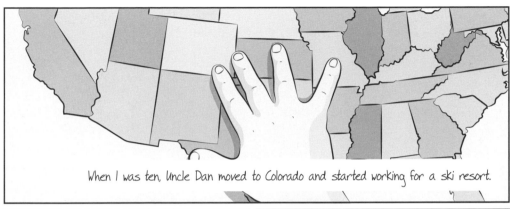

When I was ten, Uncle Dan moved to Colorado and started working for a ski resort.

It sounded very glamorous.

Who is _she_?

He met Sonia there, a woman who'd just moved to town.

The story never lost its romance.

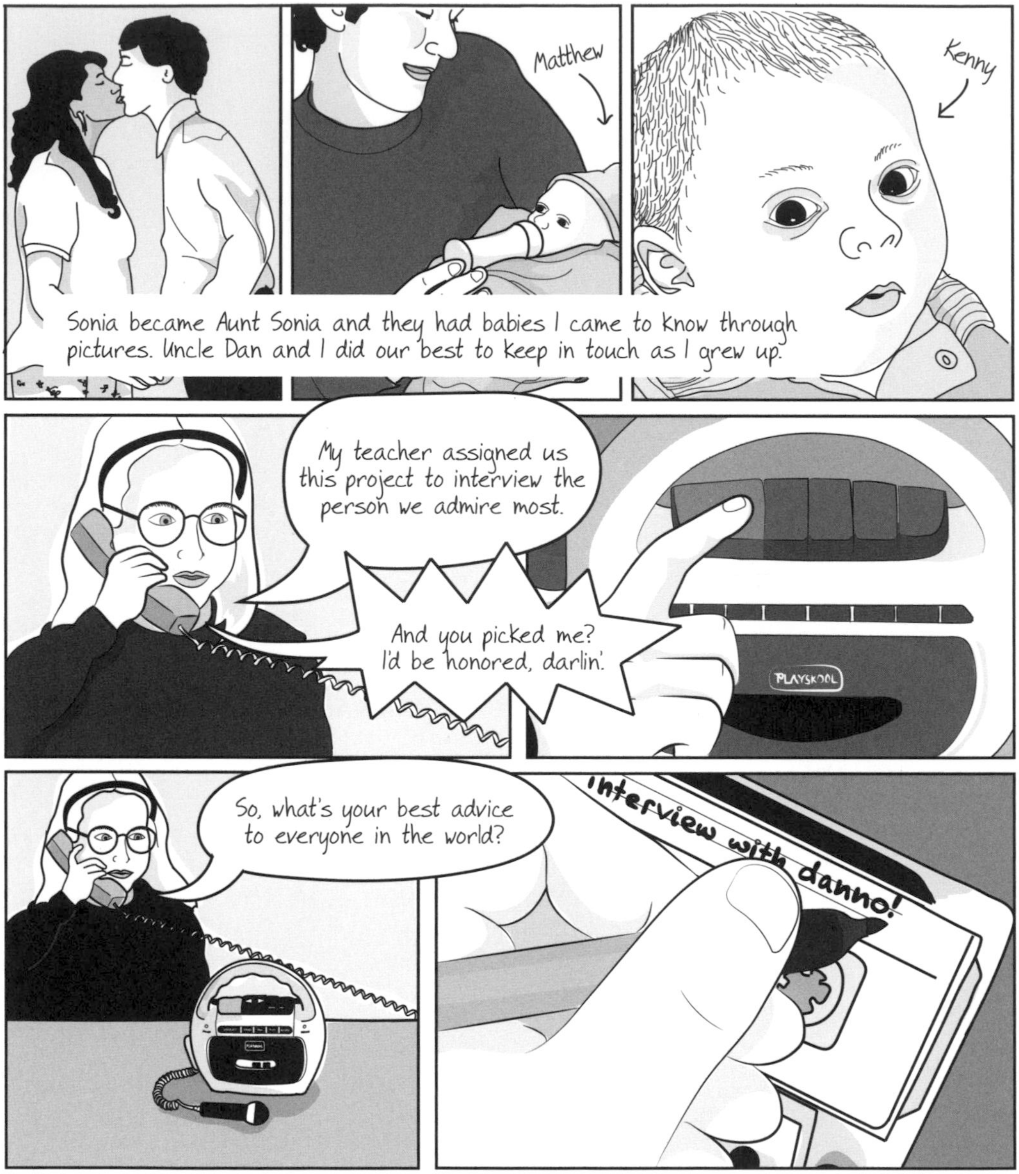
Matthew
Kenny
Sonia became Aunt Sonia and they had babies I came to know through pictures. Uncle Dan and I did our best to keep in touch as I grew up.
My teacher assigned us this project to interview the person we admire most.
And you picked me? I'd be honored, darlin'.
PLAYSKOOL
So, what's your best advice to everyone in the world?
interview with danno!

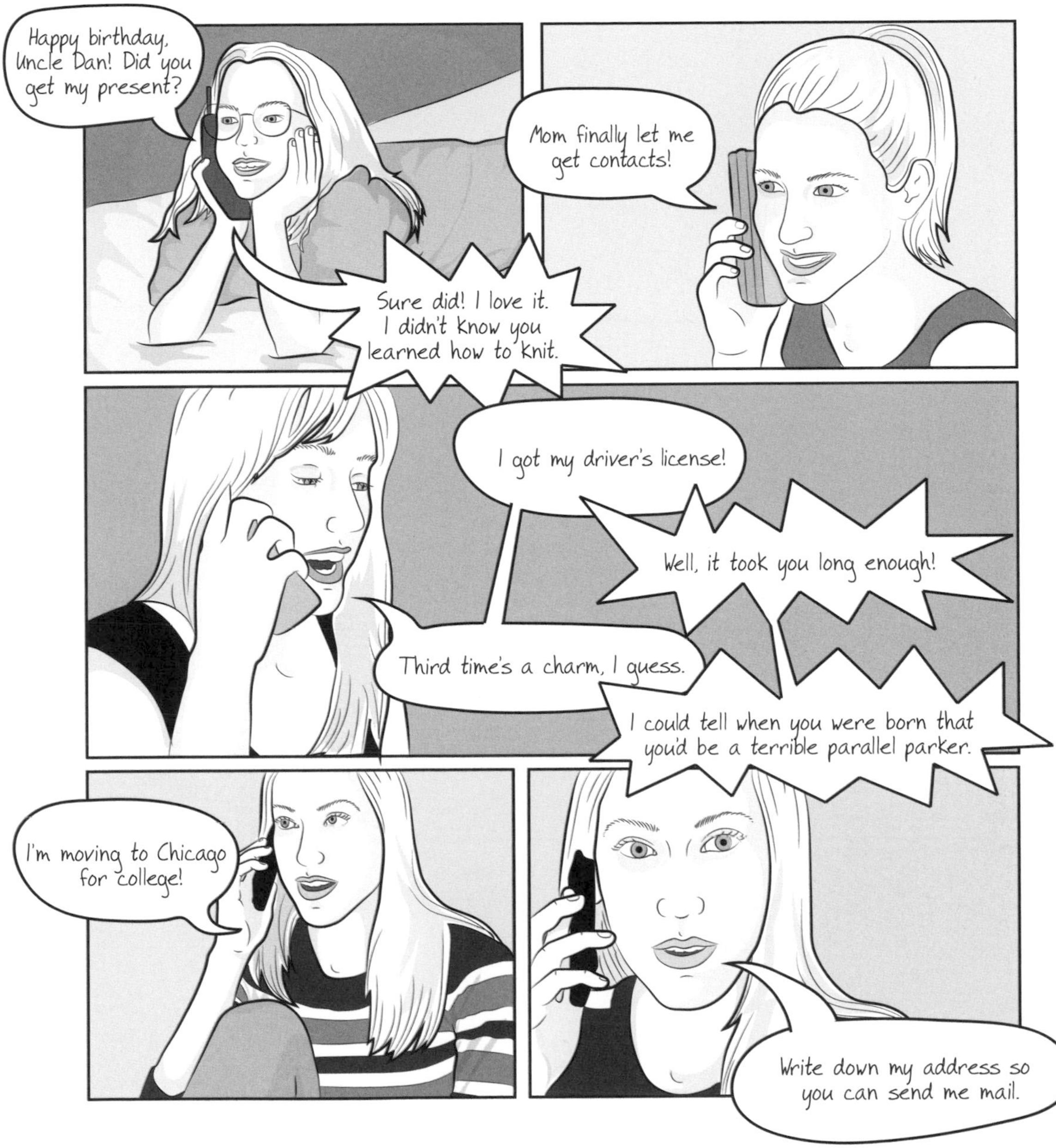
Happy birthday, Uncle Dan! Did you get my present?
Mom finally let me get contacts!
Sure did! I love it. I didn't know you learned how to knit.
I got my driver's license!
Well, it took you long enough!
Third time's a charm, I guess.
I could tell when you were born that you'd be a terrible parallel parker.
I'm moving to Chicago for college!
Write down my address so you can send me mail.

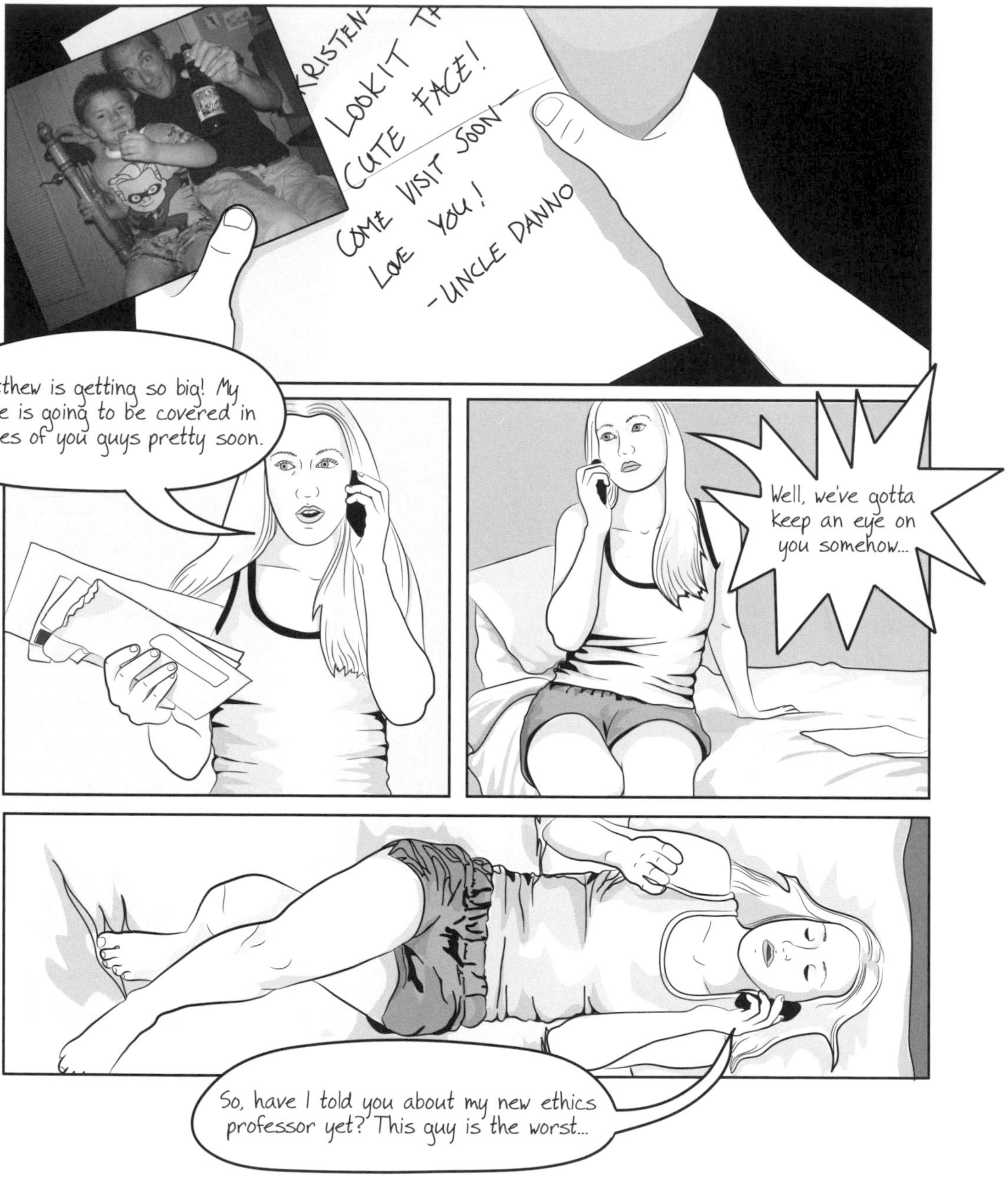
KRISTEN—
LOOKIT TH
CUTE FACE!
COME VISIT SOON—
LOVE YOU!
-UNCLE DANNO
Matthew is getting so big! My fridge is going to be covered in pictures of you guys pretty soon.
Well, we've gotta keep an eye on you somehow...
So, have I told you about my new ethics professor yet? This guy is the worst...

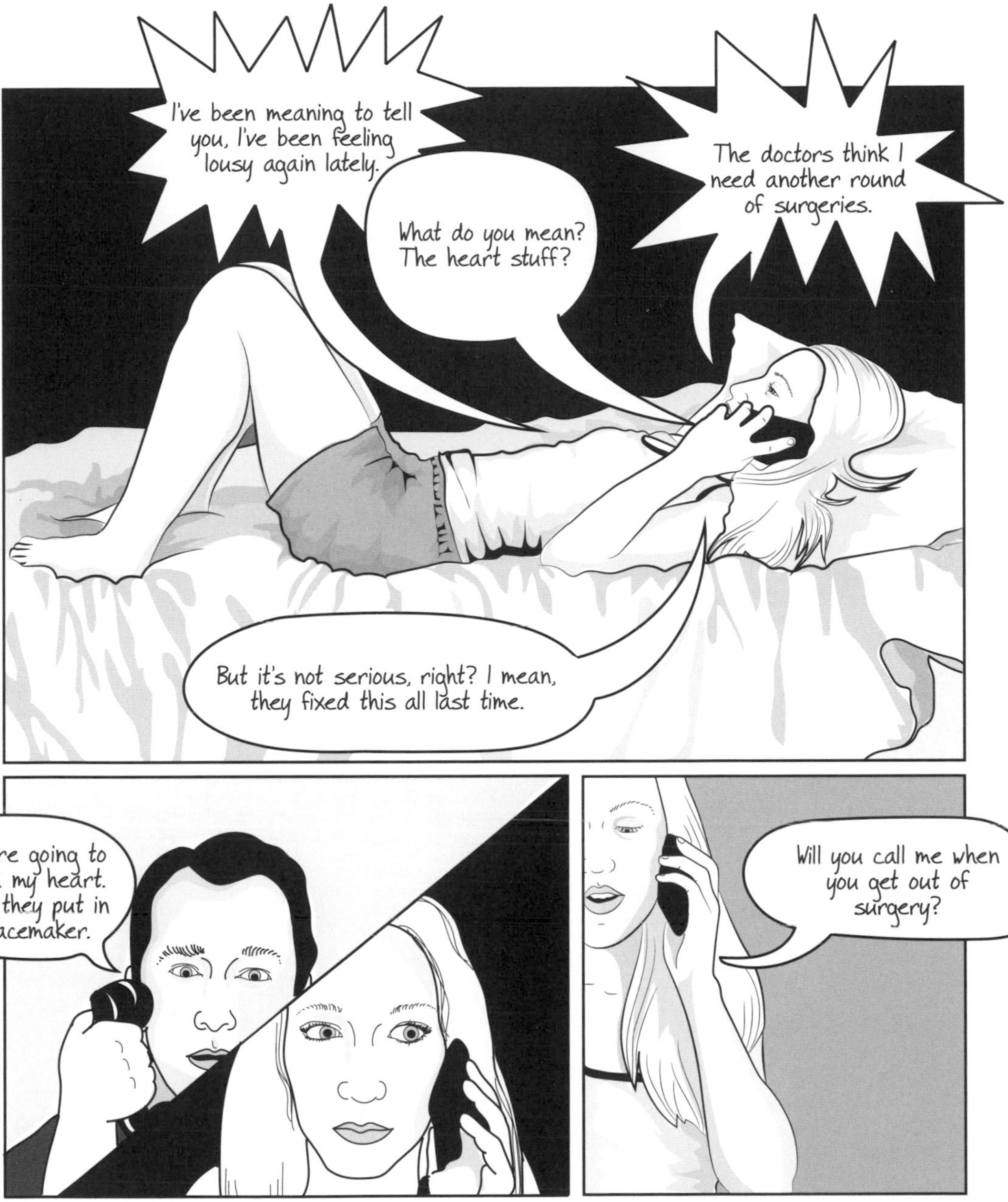
I've been meaning to tell you, I've been feeling lousy again lately.
What do you mean? The heart stuff?
The doctors think I need another round of surgeries.
But it's not serious, right? I mean, they fixed this all last time.
They're going to shock my heart. After they put in a pacemaker.
Will you call me when you get out of surgery?

I thought often about what it would be like to have your chest pulled open.

But I never connected the image to my uncle directly.

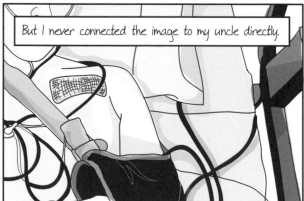

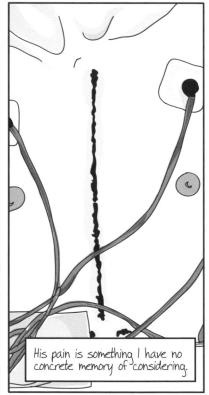

His pain is something I have no concrete memory of considering.

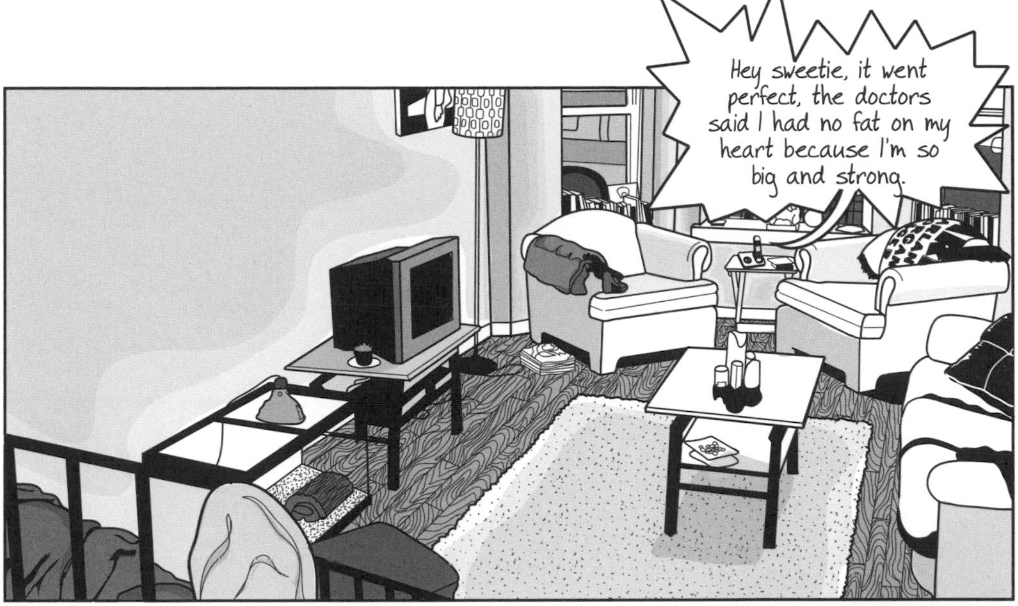
Hey sweetie, it went perfect, the doctors said I had no fat on my heart because I'm so big and strong.

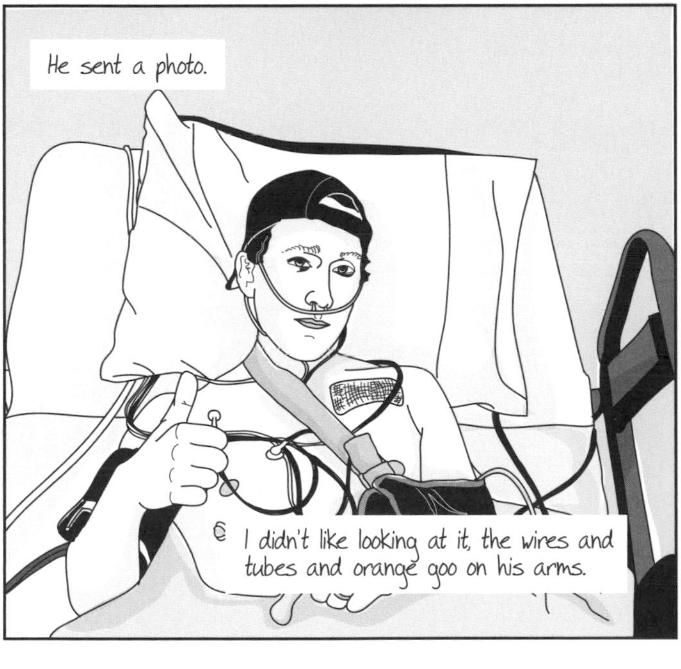
He sent a photo.
I didn't like looking at it, the wires and tubes and orange goo on his arms.

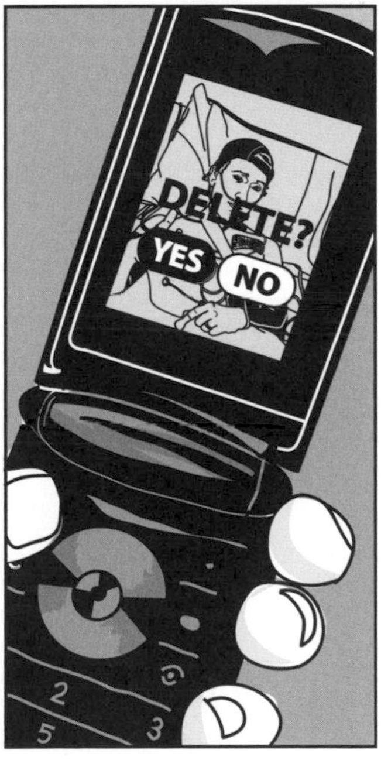
DELETE?
YES
NO
2
5
3

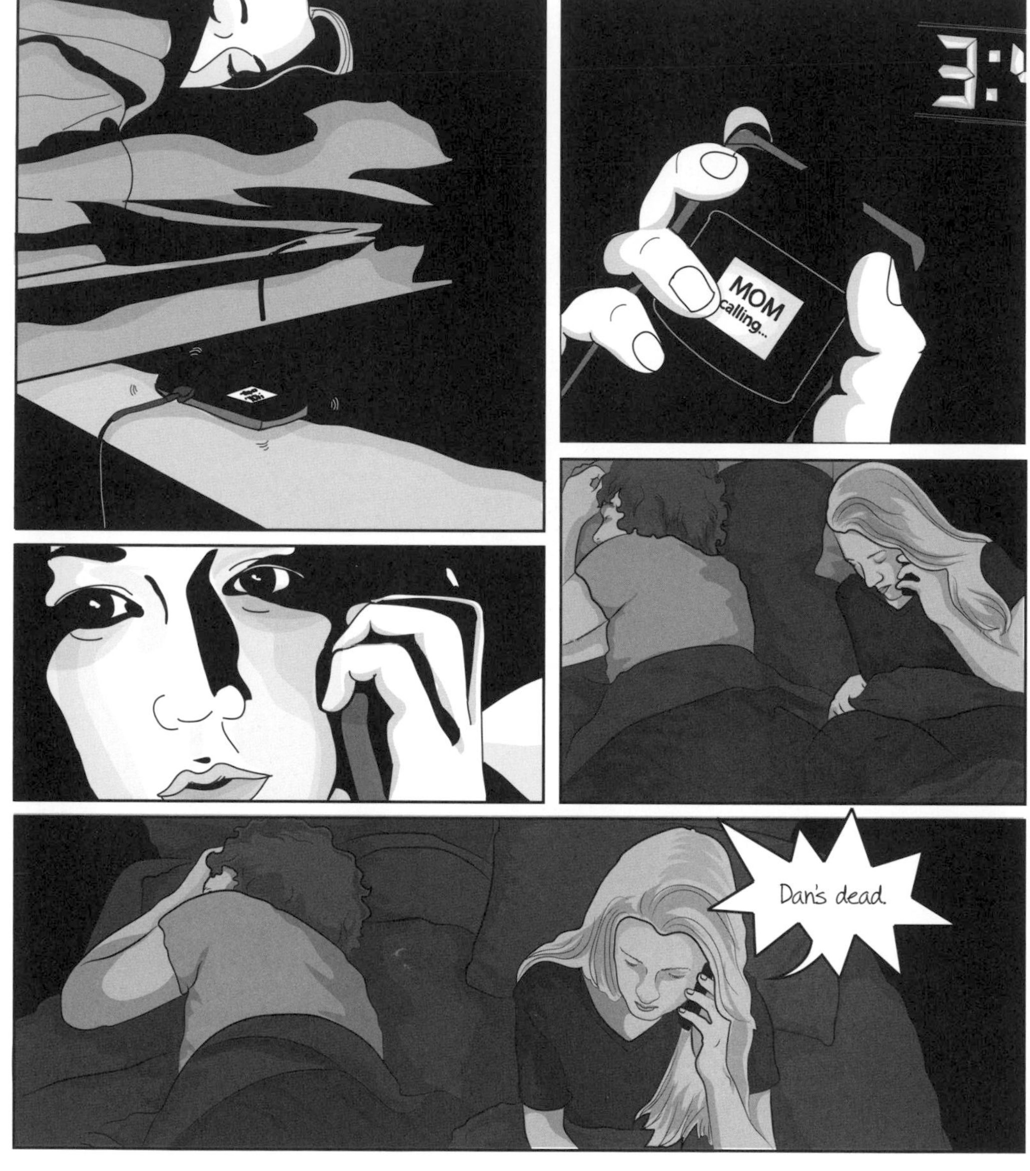
MOM
calling...
Dan's dead.

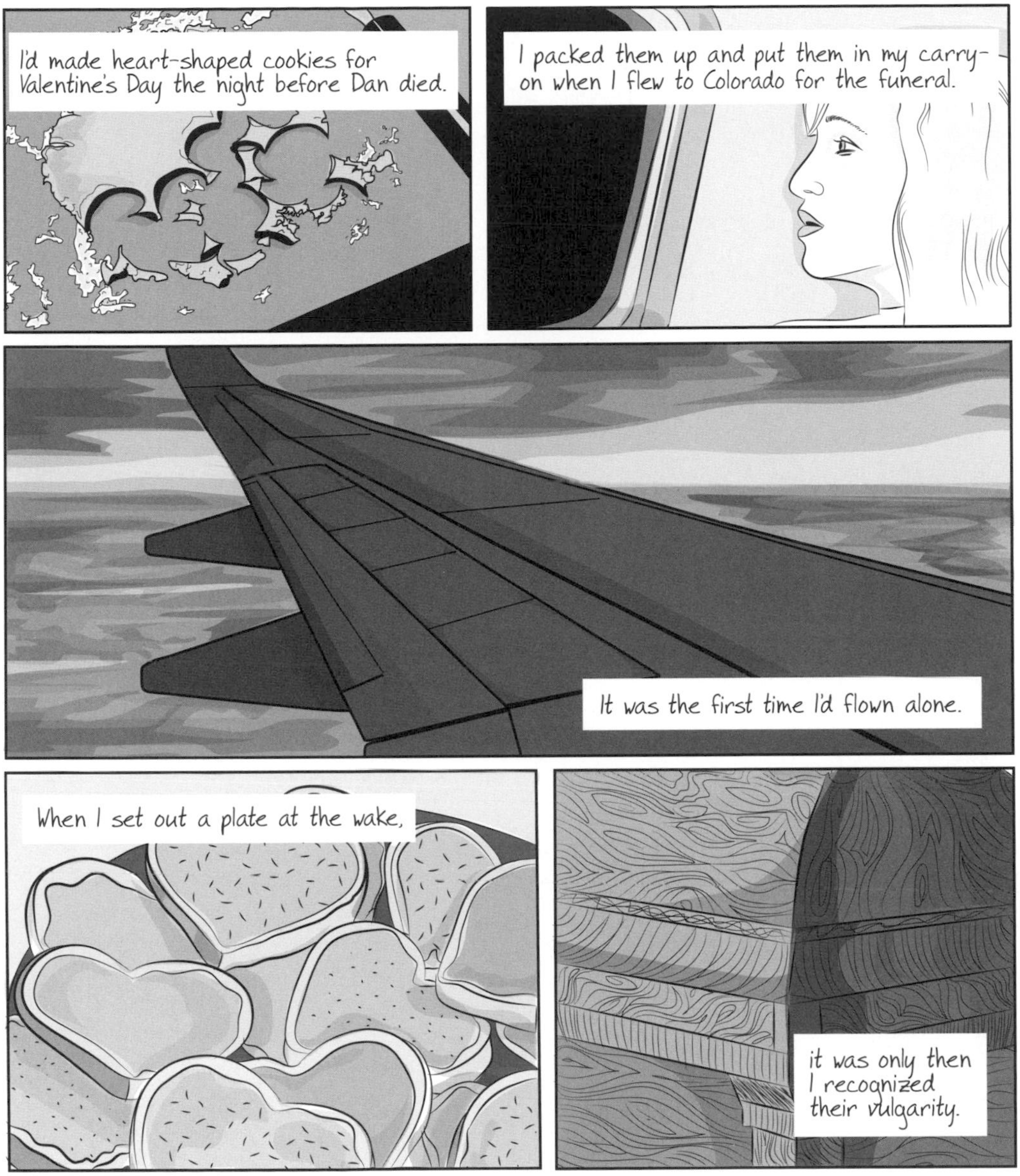
I'd made heart-shaped cookies for Valentine's Day the night before Dan died.
I packed them up and put them in my carry-on when I flew to Colorado for the funeral.
It was the first time I'd flown alone.
When I set out a plate at the wake,
it was only then I recognized their vulgarity.

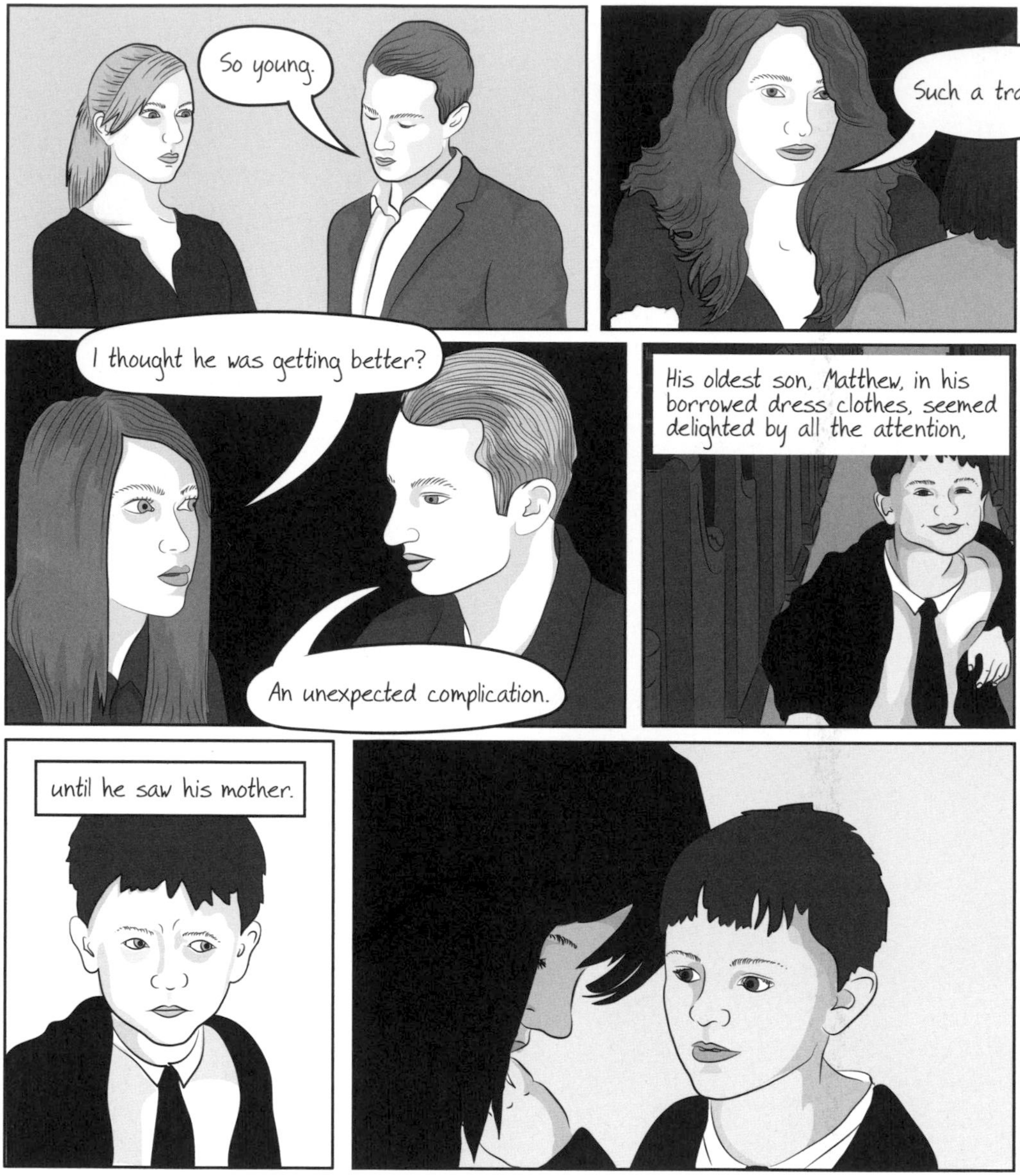
So young.
Such a tragedy.
I thought he was getting better?
An unexpected complication.
His oldest son, Matthew, in his borrowed dress clothes, seemed delighted by all the attention,
until he saw his mother.

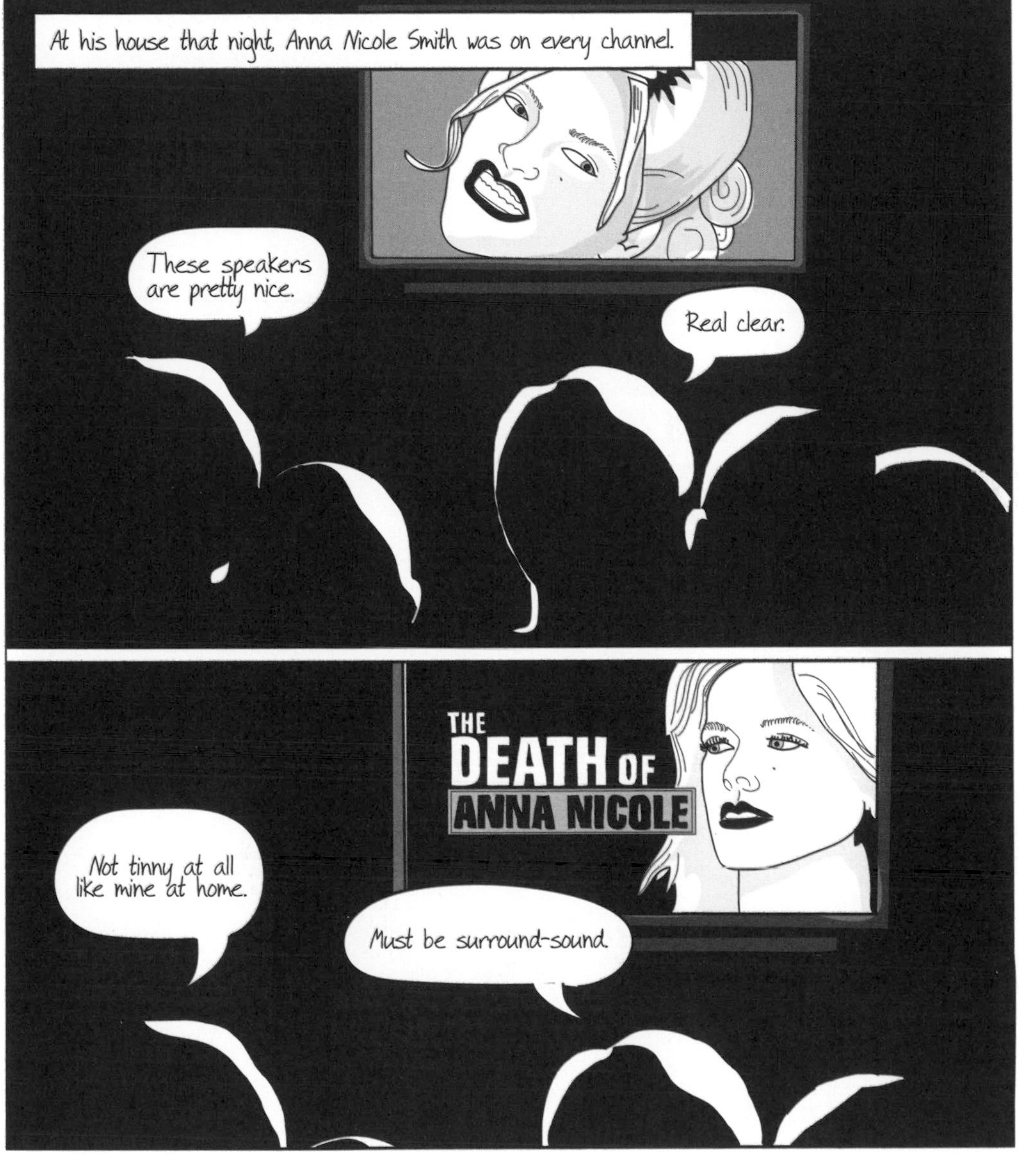
At his house that night, Anna Nicole Smith was on every channel.
These speakers are pretty nice.
Real clear.
THE DEATH OF ANNA NICOLE
Not tinny at all like mine at home.
Must be surround-sound.

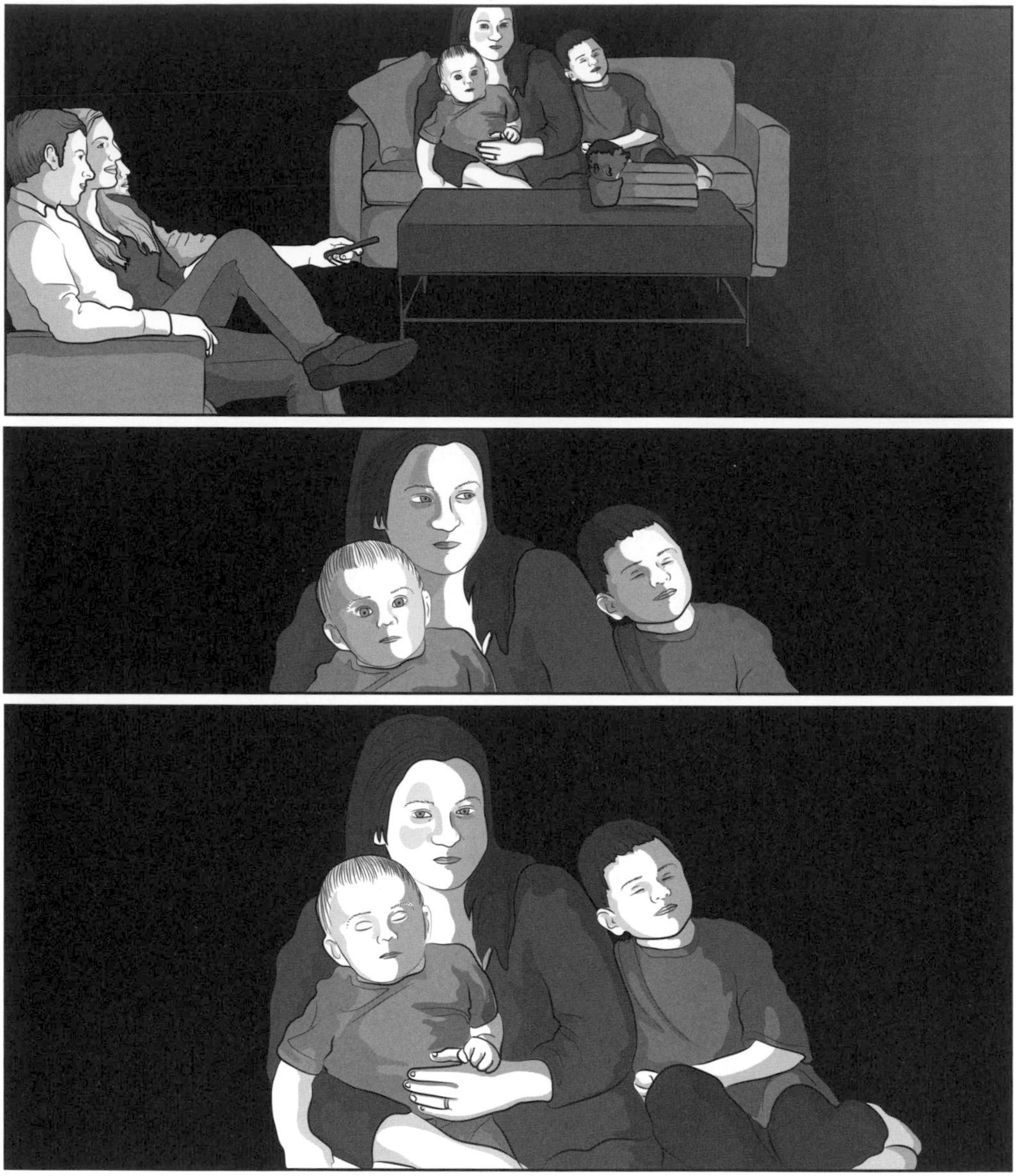

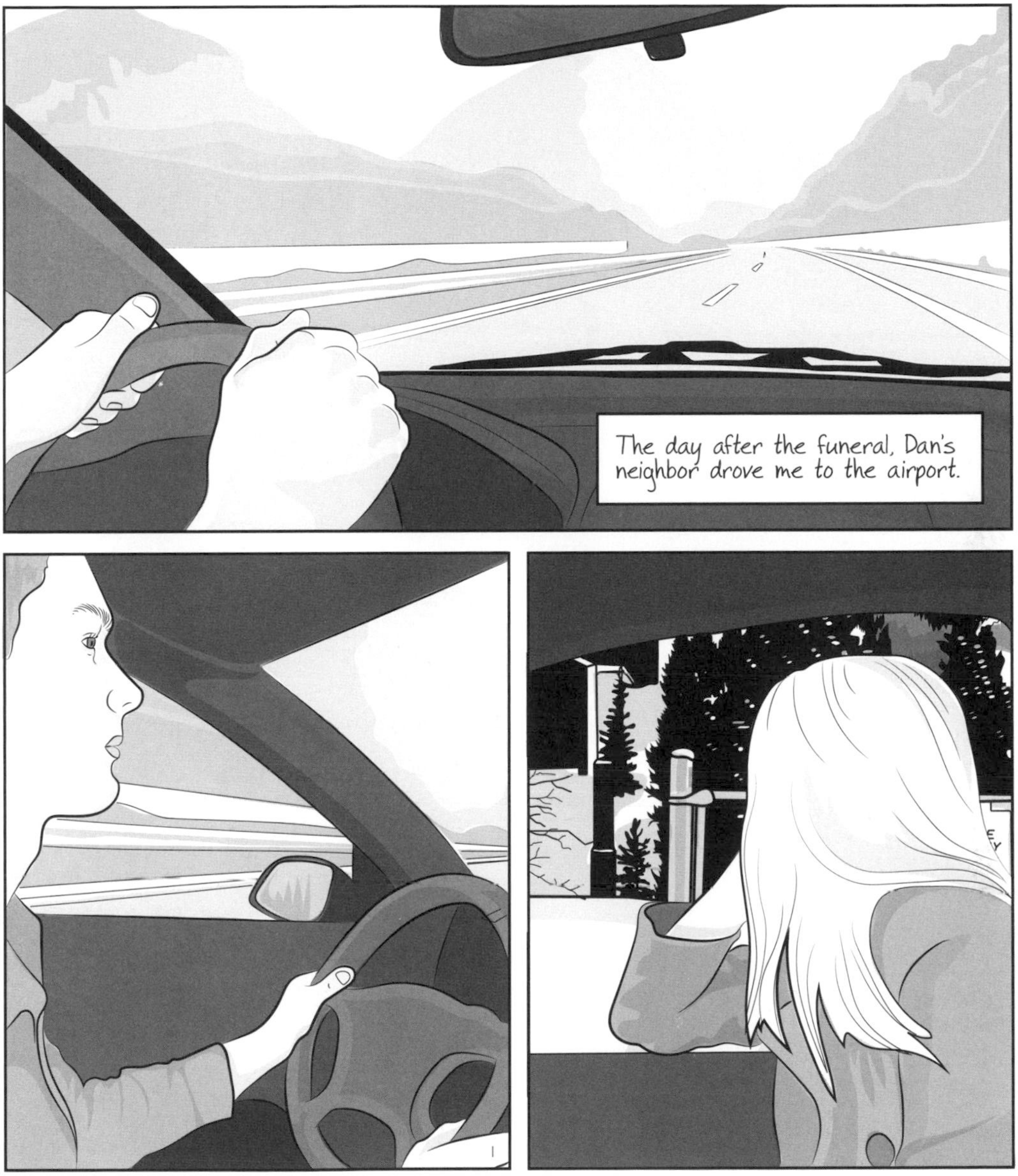
The day after the funeral, Dan's neighbor drove me to the airport.

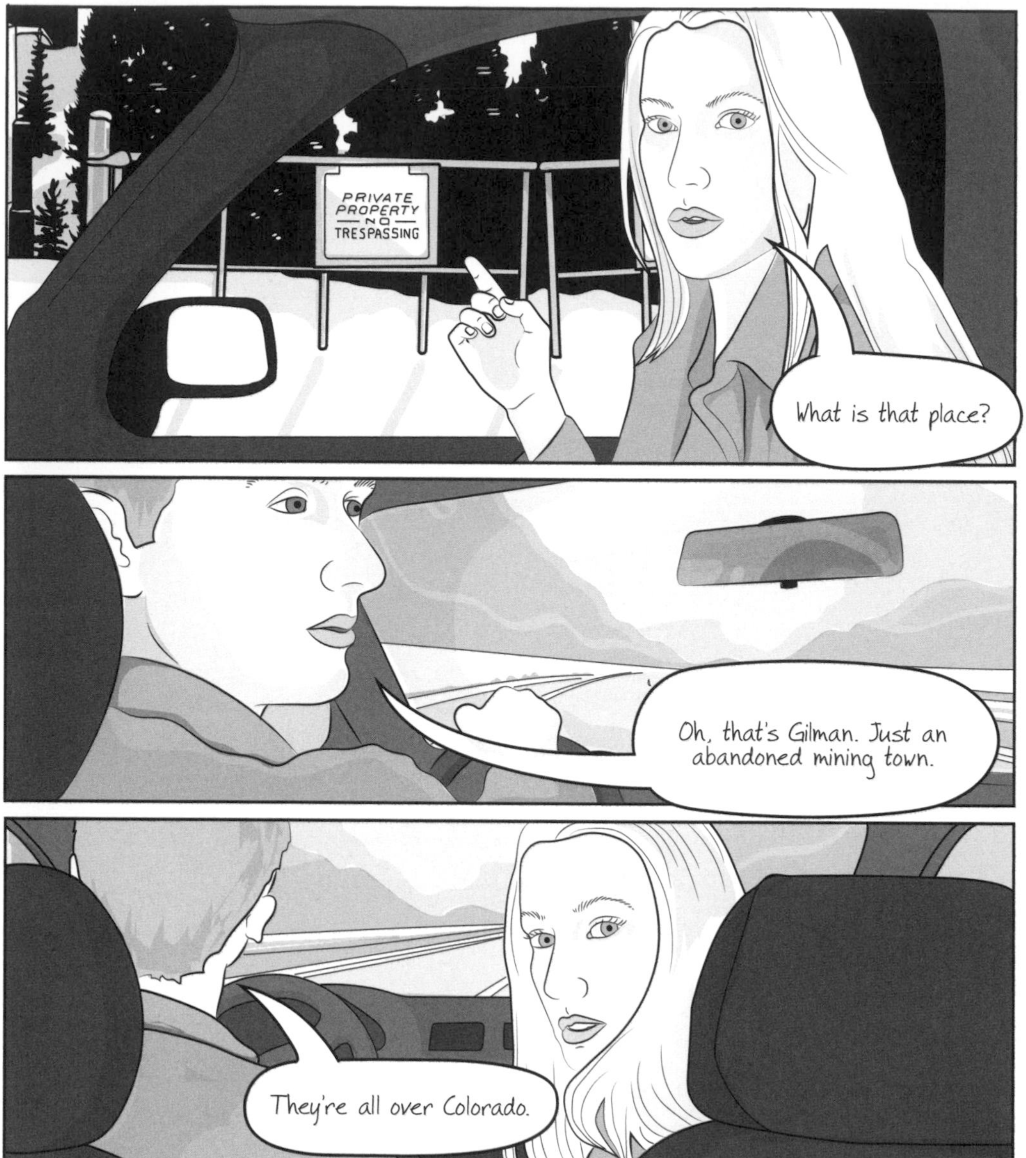
PRIVATE PROPERTY NO TRESPASSING
What is that place?
Oh, that's Gilman. Just an abandoned mining town.
They're all over Colorado.

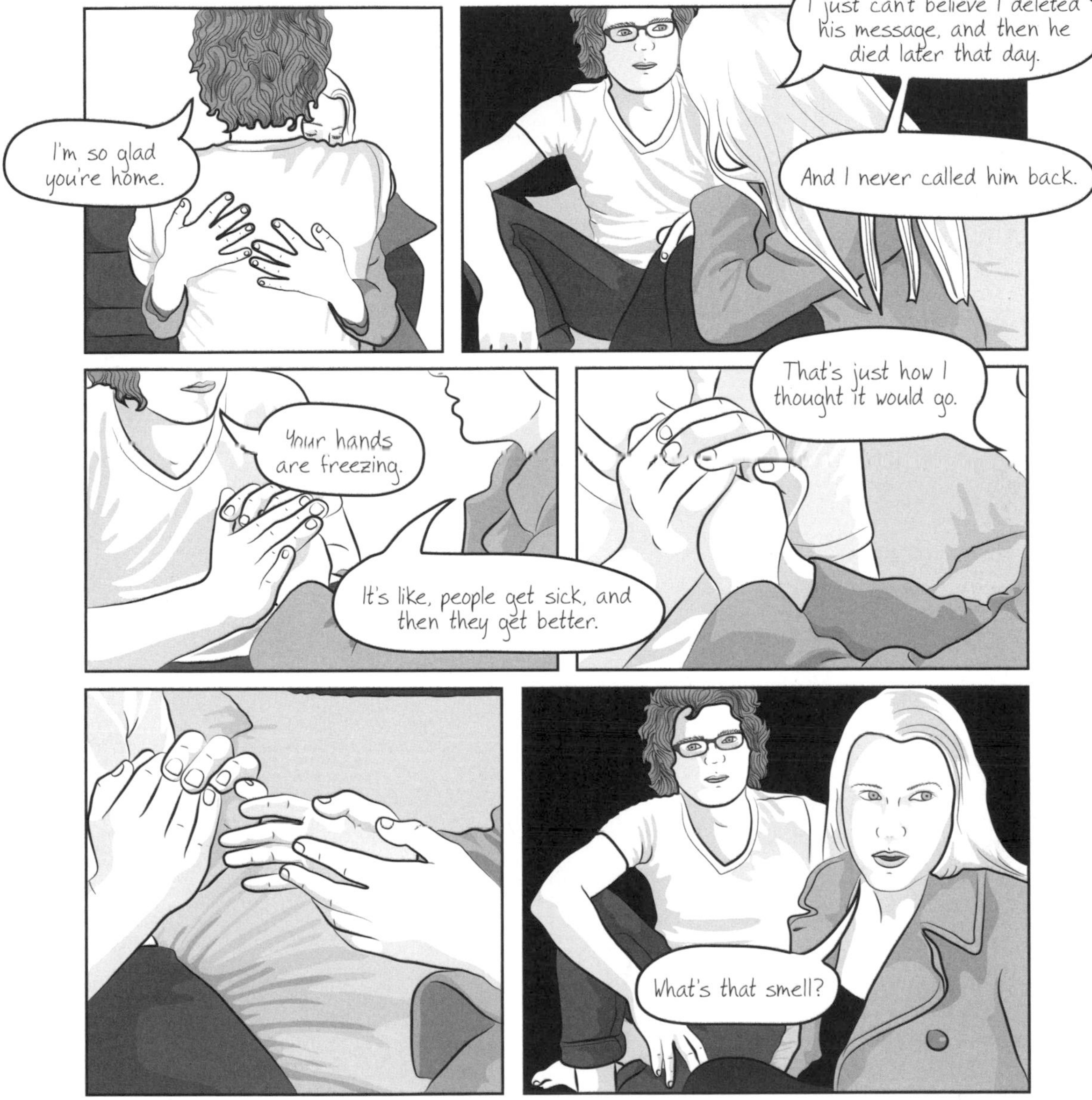
I'm so glad you're home.
I just can't believe I deleted his message, and then he died later that day.
And I never called him back.
Your hands are freezing.
It's like, people get sick, and then they get better.
That's just how I thought it would go.
What's that smell?

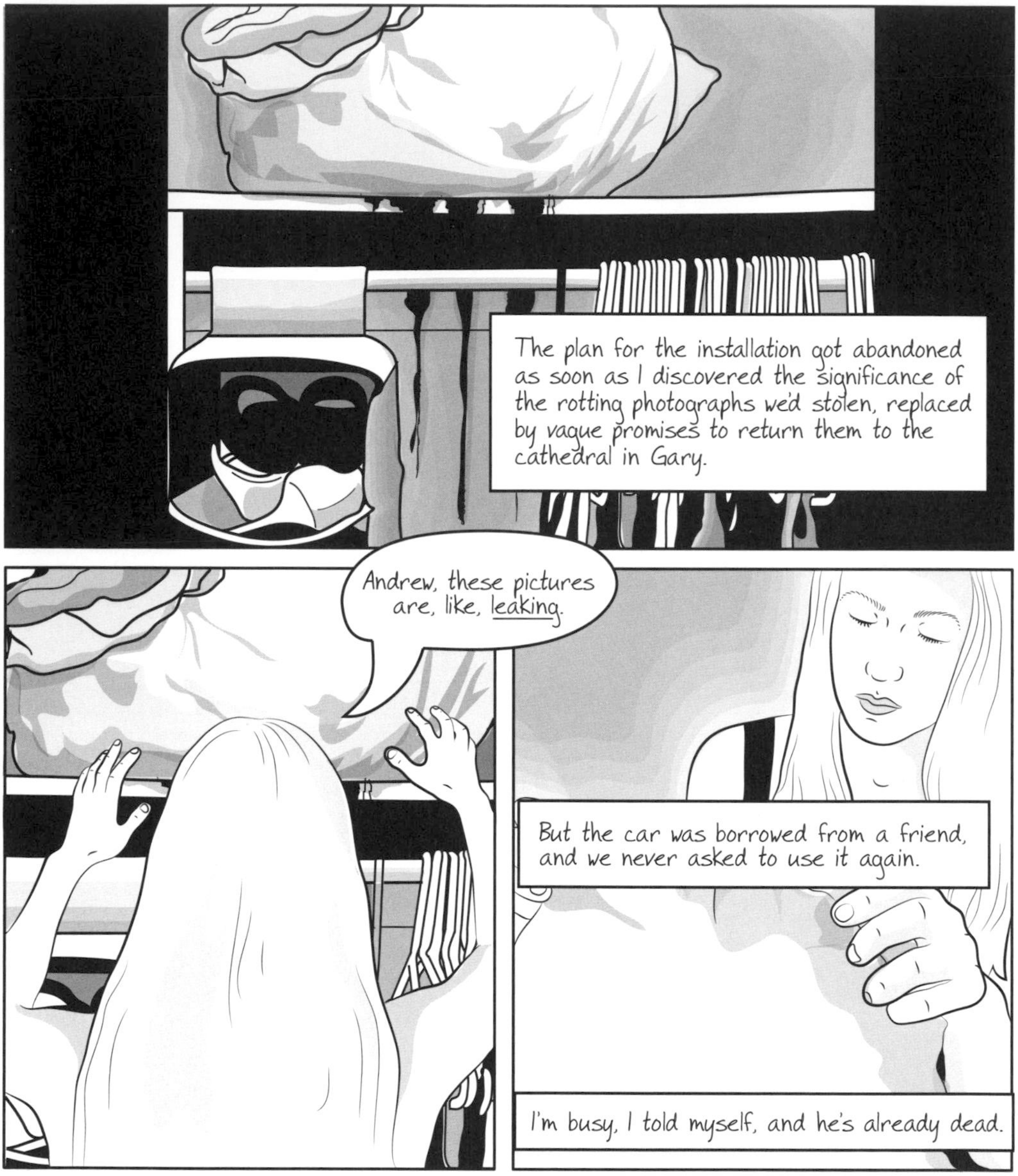
The plan for the installation got abandoned as soon as I discovered the significance of the rotting photographs we'd stolen, replaced by vague promises to return them to the cathedral in Gary.
Andrew, these pictures are, like, leaking.
But the car was borrowed from a friend, and we never asked to use it again.
I'm busy, I told myself, and he's already dead.

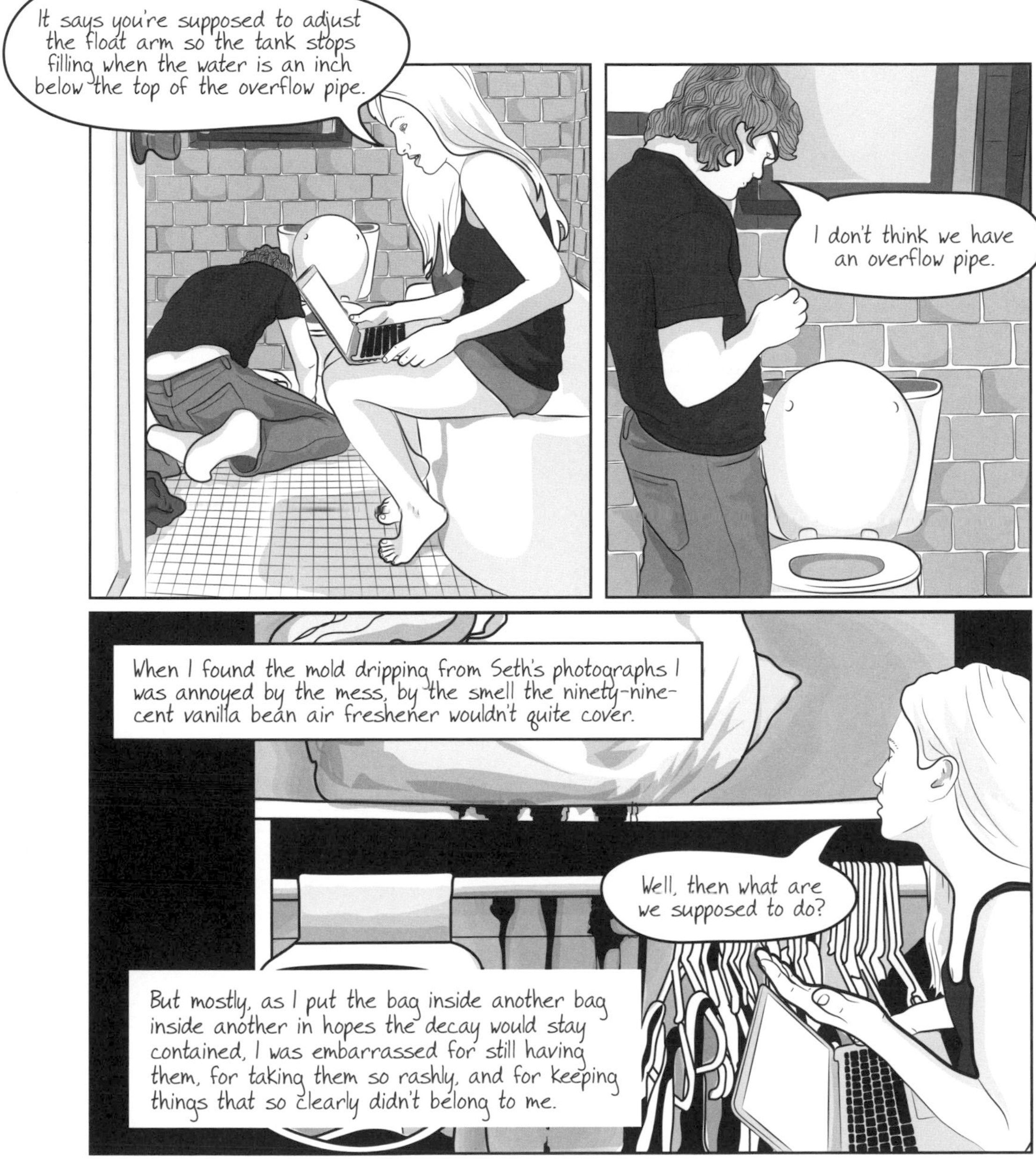
It says you're supposed to adjust the float arm so the tank stops filling when the water is an inch below the top of the overflow pipe.
I don't think we have an overflow pipe.
When I found the mold dripping from Seth's photographs I was annoyed by the mess, by the smell the ninety-nine-cent vanilla bean air freshener wouldn't quite cover.
Well, then what are we supposed to do?
But mostly, as I put the bag inside another bag inside another in hopes the decay would stay contained, I was embarrassed for still having them, for taking them so rashly, and for keeping things that so clearly didn't belong to me.

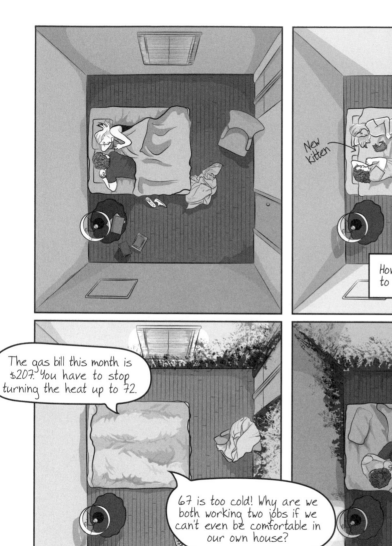

New Kitten

How unprepared we'd been to pretend we were adults.

The gas bill this month is $207. You have to stop turning the heat up to 72.

67 is too cold! Why are we both working two jobs if we can't even be comfortable in our own house?

The pipes froze that winter and we were without water for a week. We hadn't known to open the cabinets to warm the plumbing when Chicago dipped below zero.

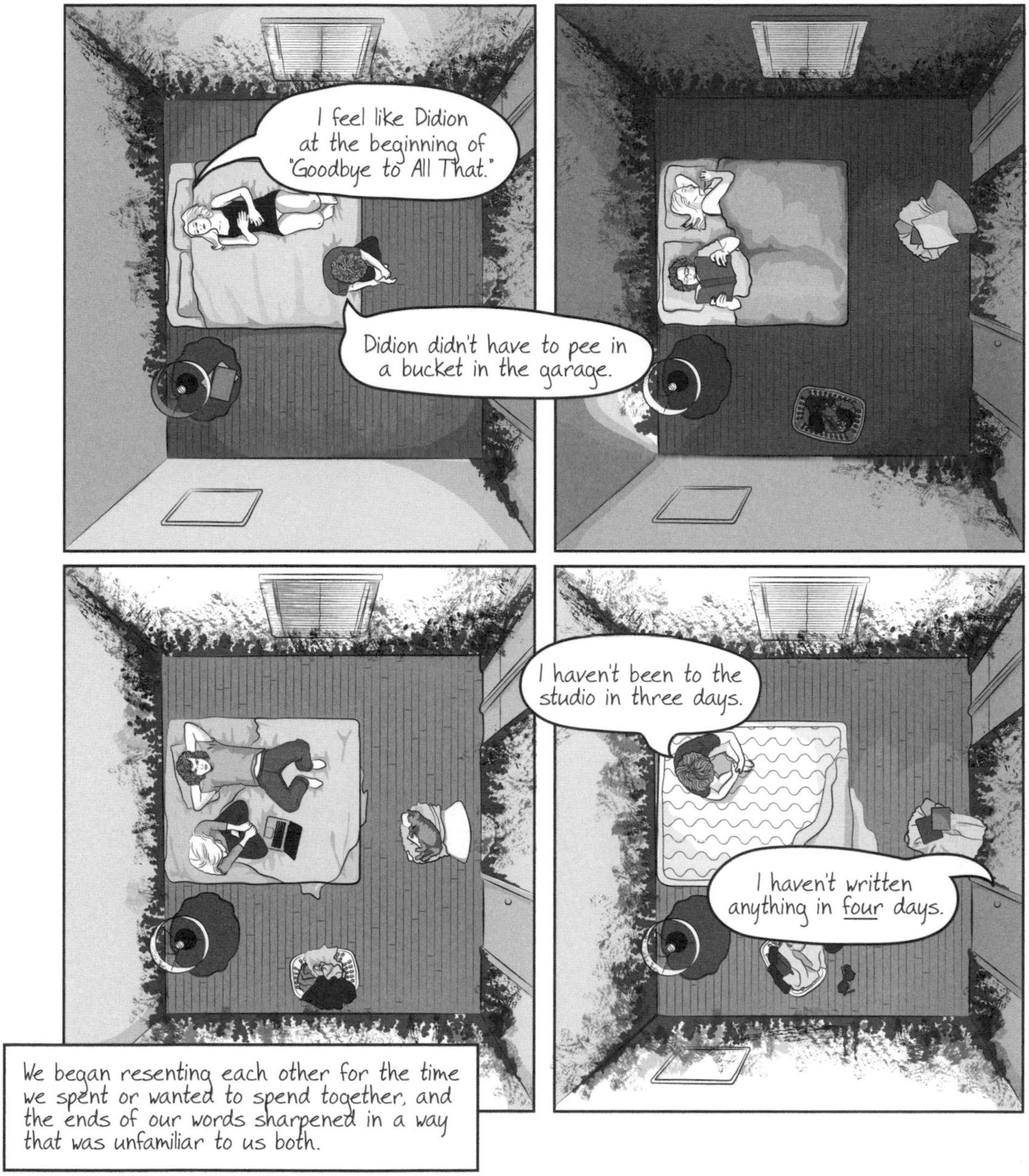
I feel like Didion at the beginning of "Goodbye to All That."
Didion didn't have to pee in a bucket in the garage.
I haven't been to the studio in three days.
I haven't written anything in four days.
We began resenting each other for the time we spent or wanted to spend together, and the ends of our words sharpened in a way that was unfamiliar to us both.

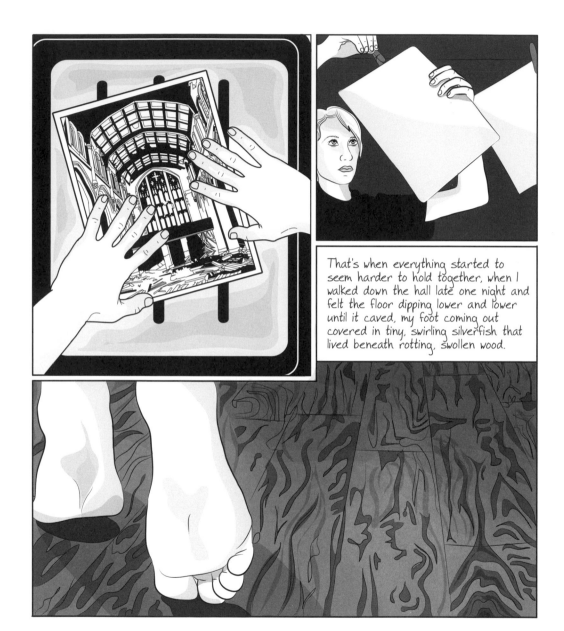

That's when everything started to seem harder to hold together, when I walked down the hall late one night and felt the floor dipping lower and lower until it caved, my foot coming out covered in tiny, swirling silverfish that lived beneath rotting, swollen wood.

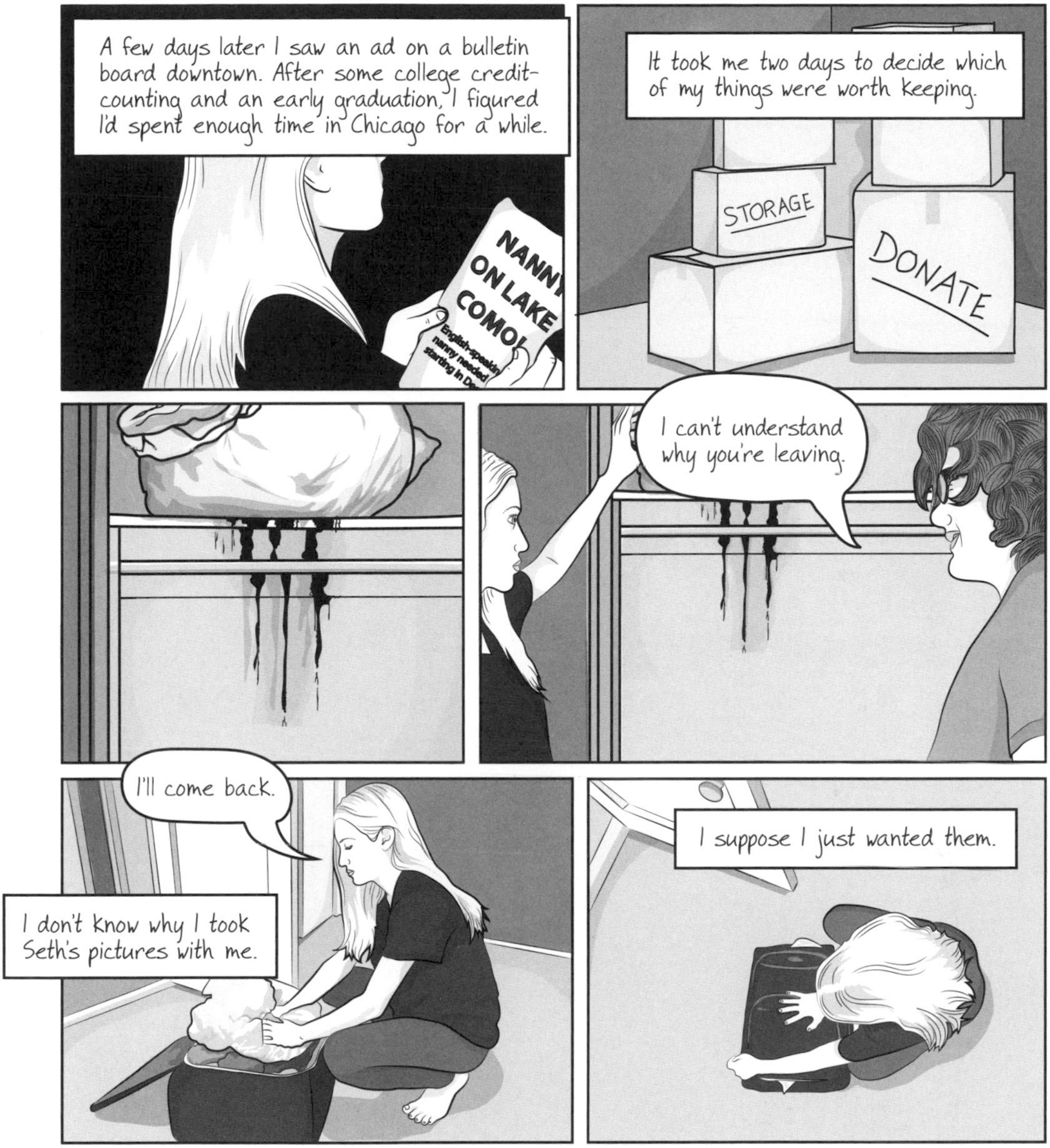

A few days later I saw an ad on a bulletin board downtown. After some college credit-counting and an early graduation, I figured I'd spent enough time in Chicago for a while.
It took me two days to decide which of my things were worth keeping.
STORAGE
DONATE
I can't understand why you're leaving.
I'll come back.
I don't know why I took Seth's pictures with me.
I suppose I just wanted them.

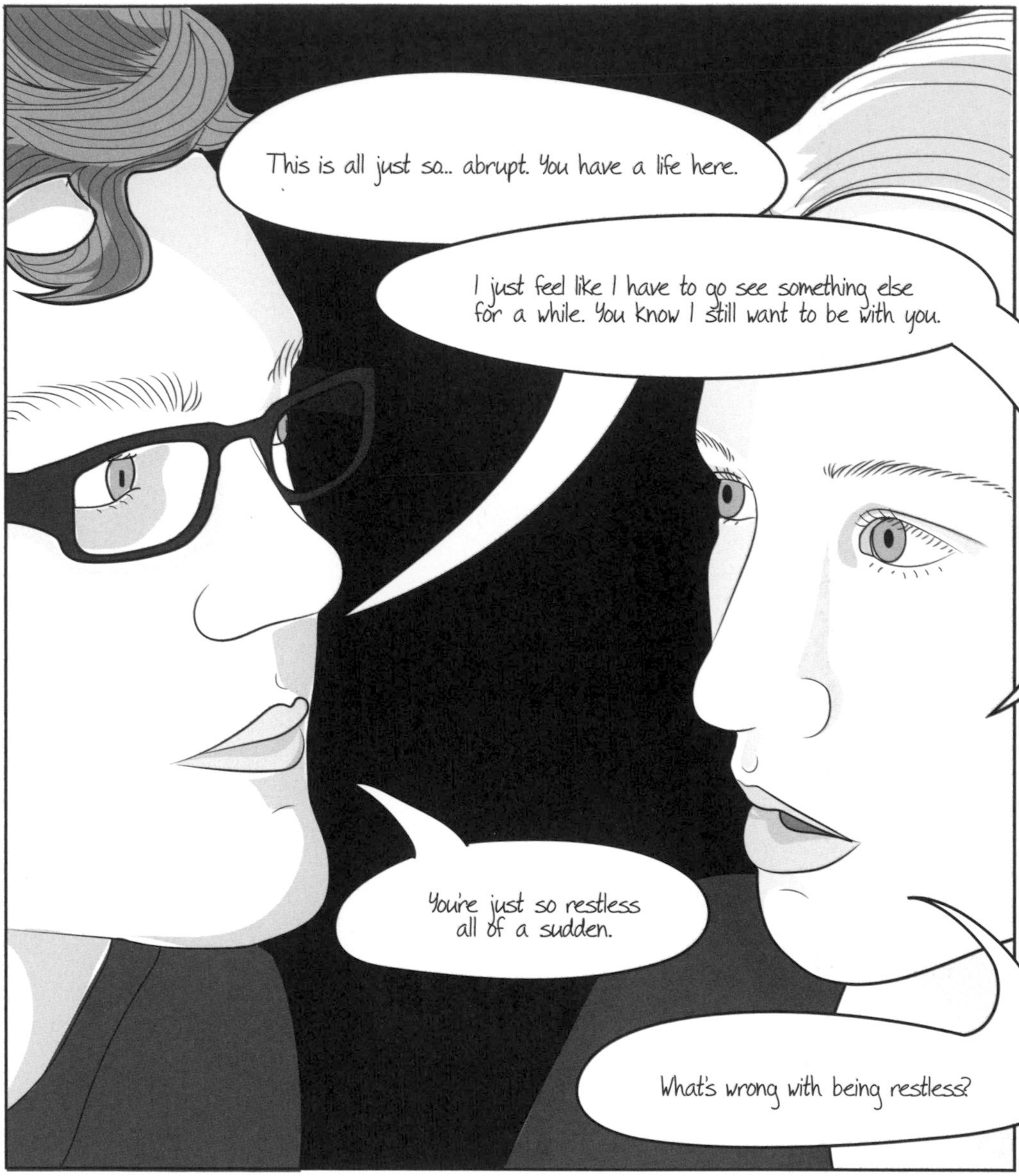
This is all just so.. abrupt. You have a life here.
I just feel like I have to go see something else for a while. You know I still want to be with you.
You're just so restless all of a sudden.
What's wrong with being restless?

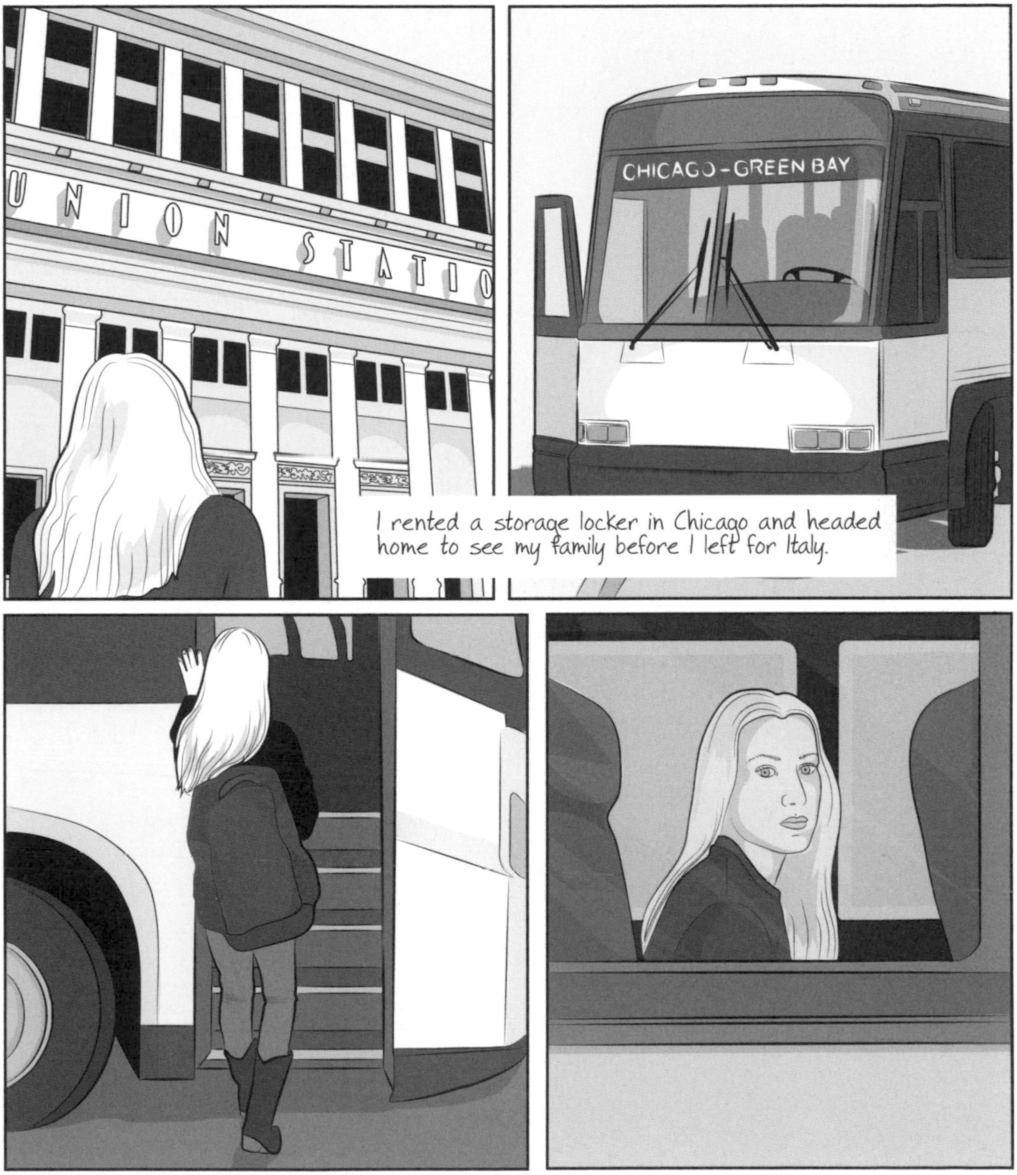
UNION STATIO
CHICAGO - GREEN BAY
I rented a storage locker in Chicago and headed home to see my family before I left for Italy.

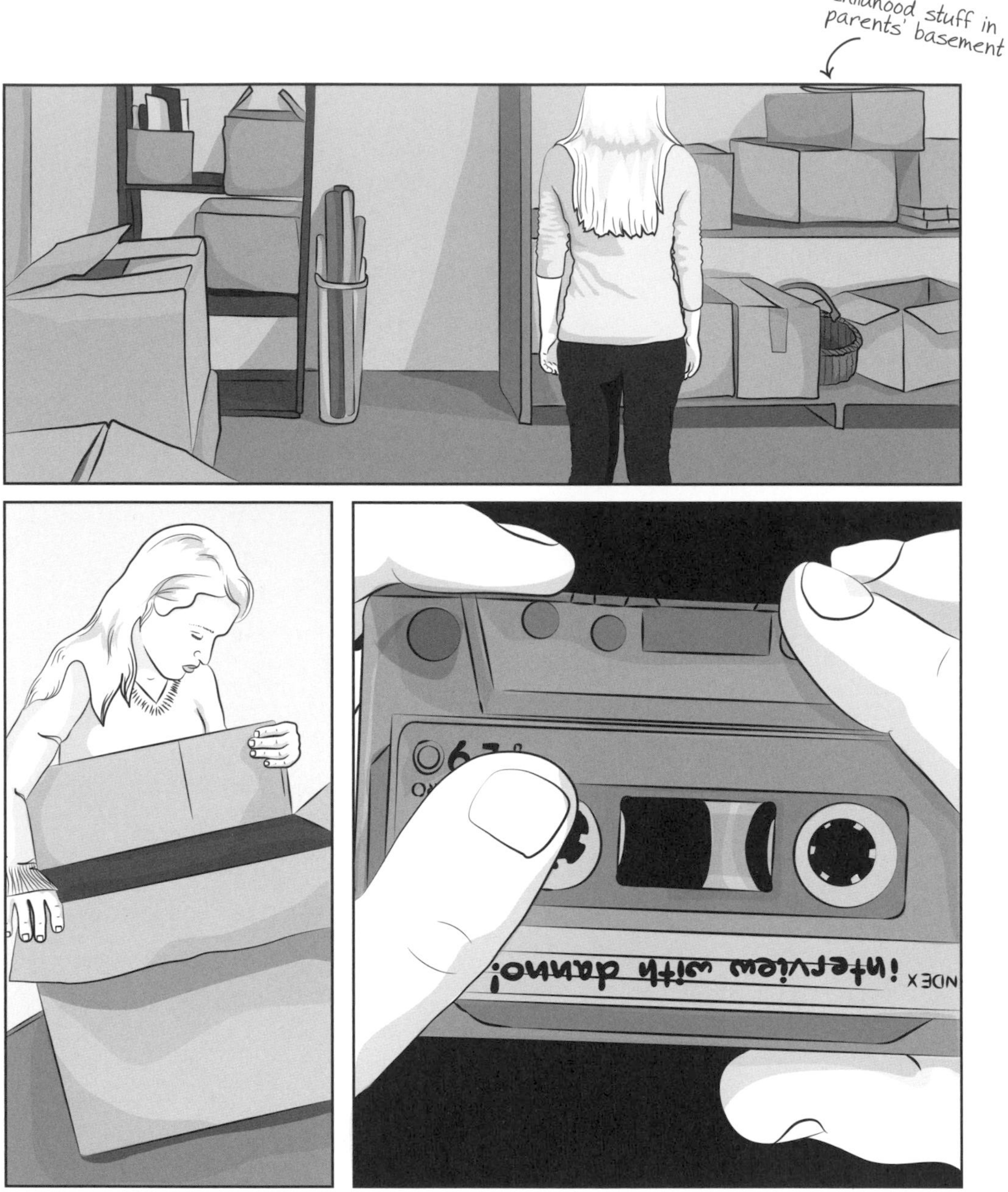
childhood stuff in parents' basement
interview with danno!

CHEVROLET

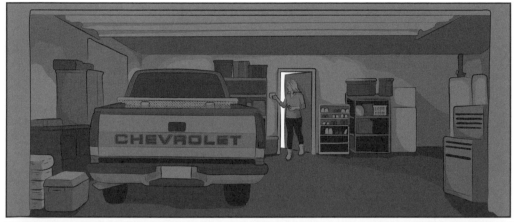

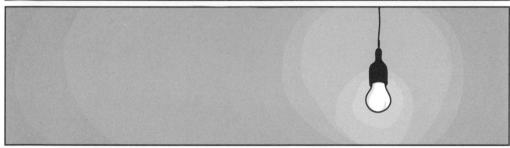

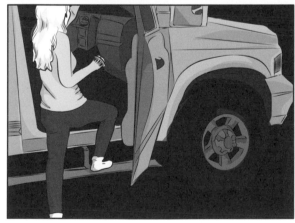

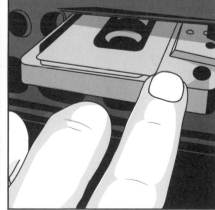

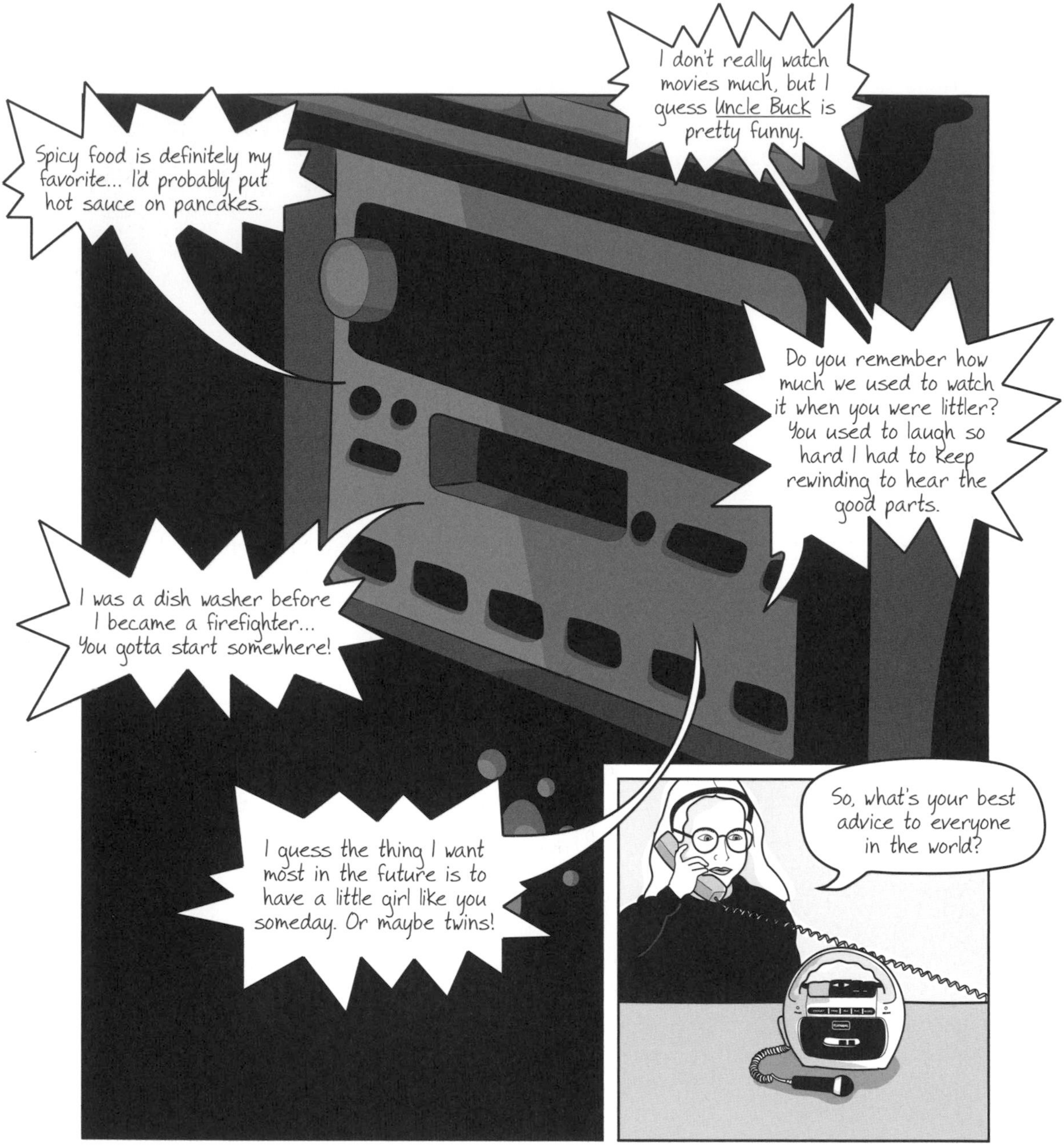
I don't really watch movies much, but I guess Uncle Buck is pretty funny.
Spicy food is definitely my favorite... I'd probably put hot sauce on pancakes.
Do you remember how much we used to watch it when you were littler? You used to laugh so hard I had to keep rewinding to hear the good parts.
I was a dish washer before I became a firefighter... You gotta start somewhere!
I guess the thing I want most in the future is to have a little girl like you someday. Or maybe twins!
So, what's your best advice to everyone in the world?

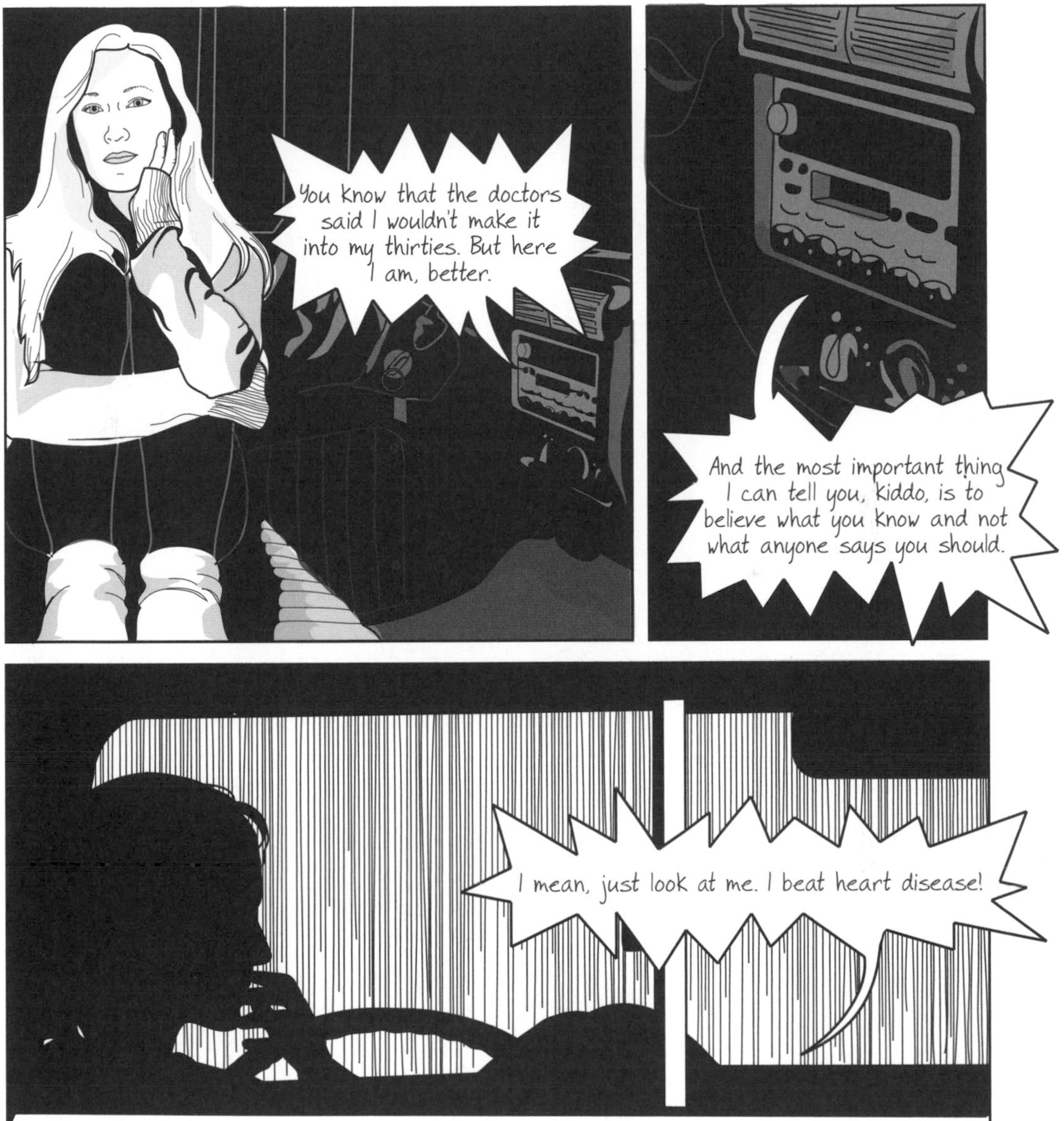
You know that the doctors said I wouldn't make it into my thirties. But here I am, better.
And the most important thing I can tell you, kiddo, is to believe what you know and not what anyone says you should.
I mean, just look at me. I beat heart disease!

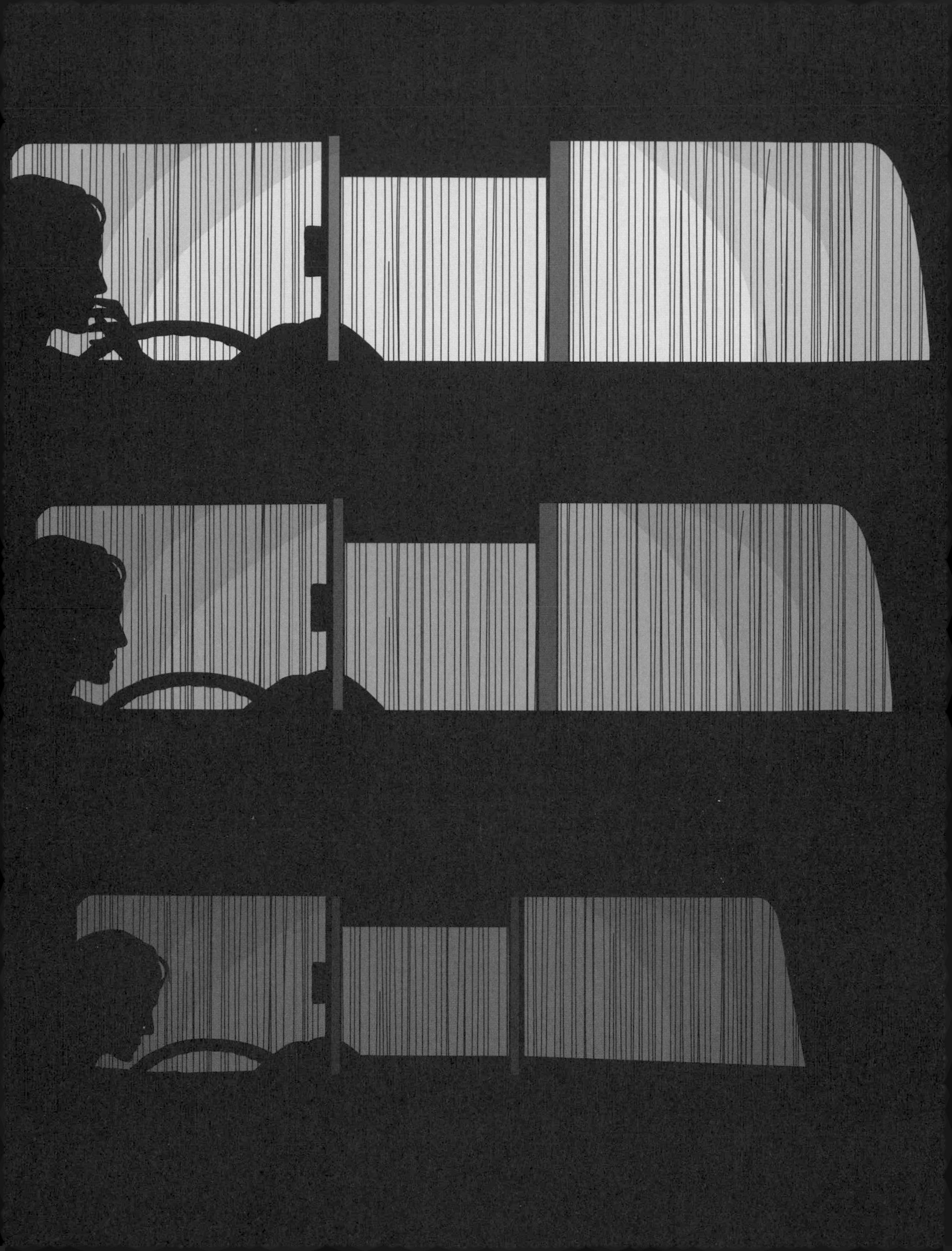

# Chapter 3

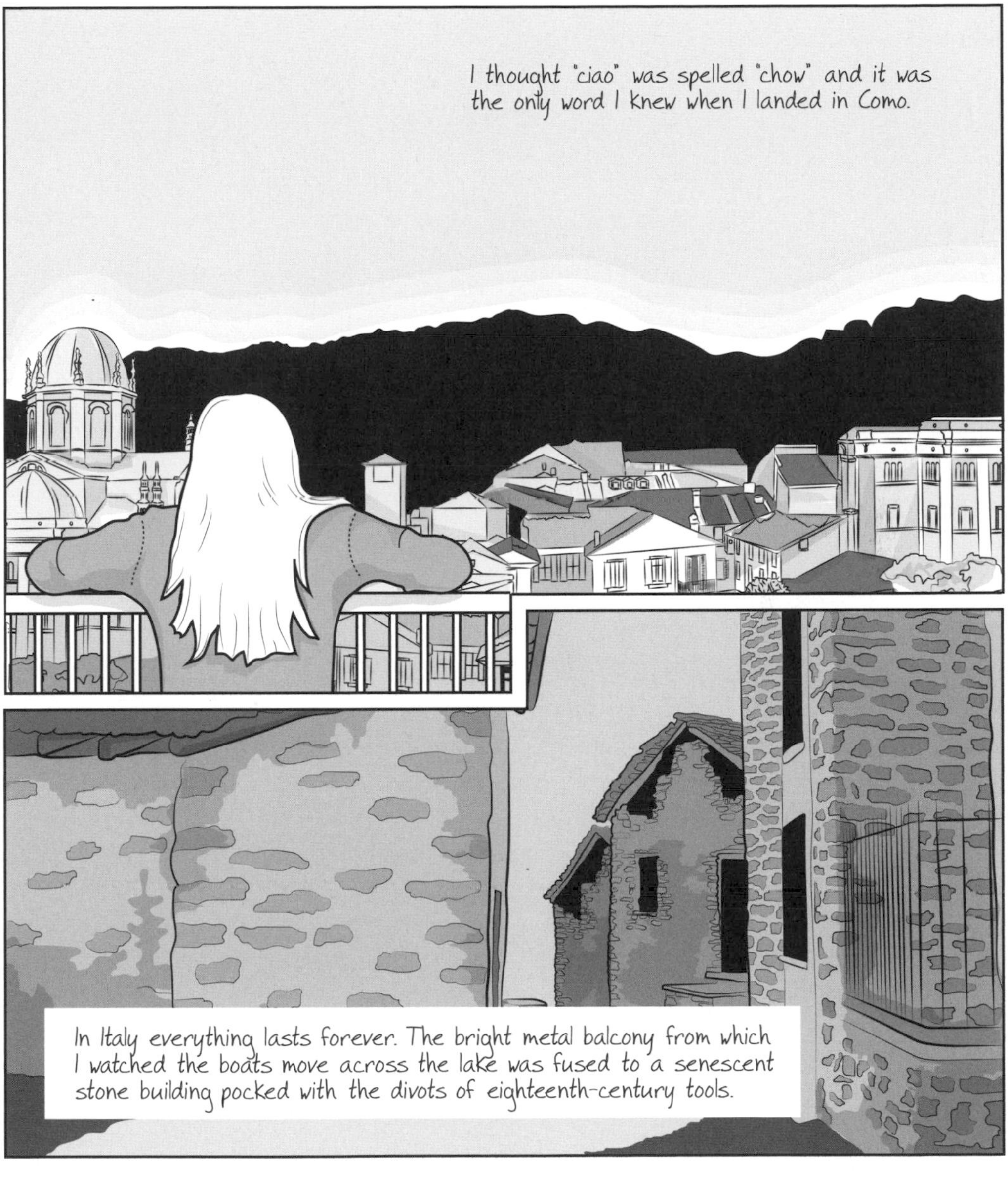
I thought "ciao" was spelled "chow" and it was the only word I knew when I landed in Como.
In Italy everything lasts forever. The bright metal balcony from which I watched the boats move across the lake was fused to a senescent stone building pocked with the divots of eighteenth-century tools.

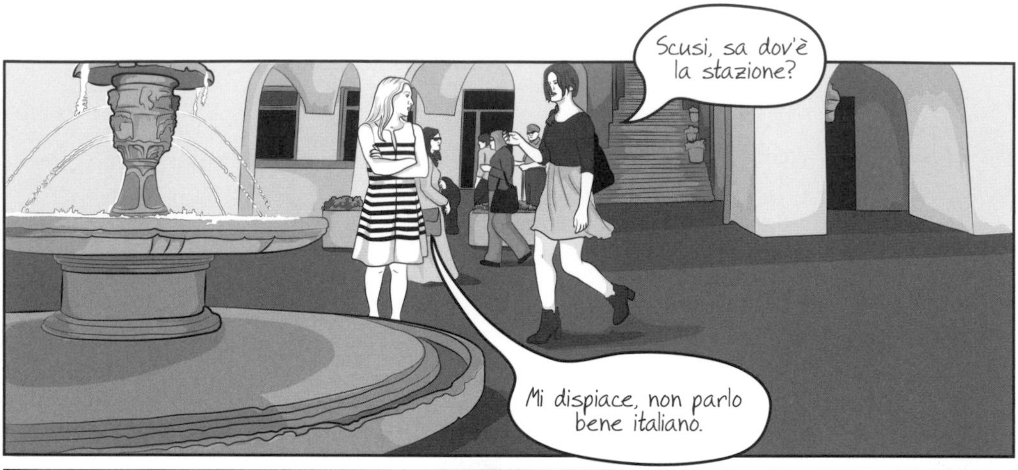
Scusi, sa dov'è la stazione?
Mi dispiace, non parlo bene italiano.

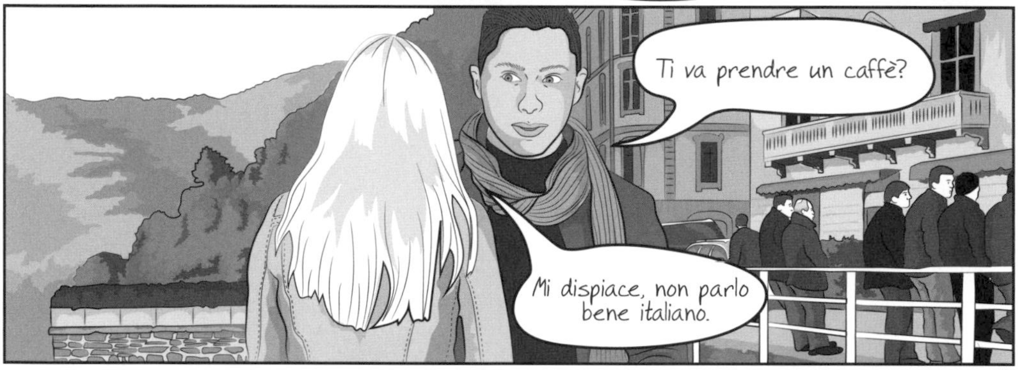
Ti va prendre un caffè?
Mi dispiace, non parlo bene italiano.

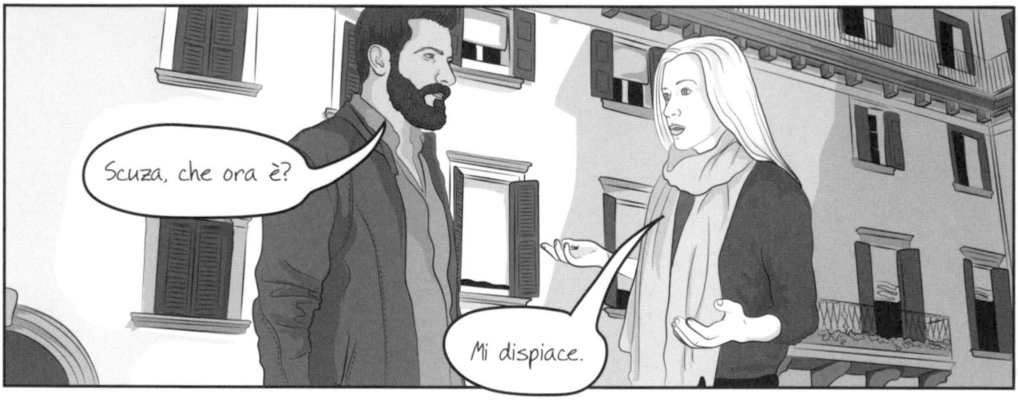
Scuza, che ora è?
Mi dispiace.

The town's cathedral was right outside my bedroom's balcony, and I liked the regularity of the tower's chimes, the static, unchanging nature of a church.

The rituals were familiar to me even without language, and I saved euro coins in a shoebox under my bed like a child hoarding an allowance, lighting candles to no one every night.

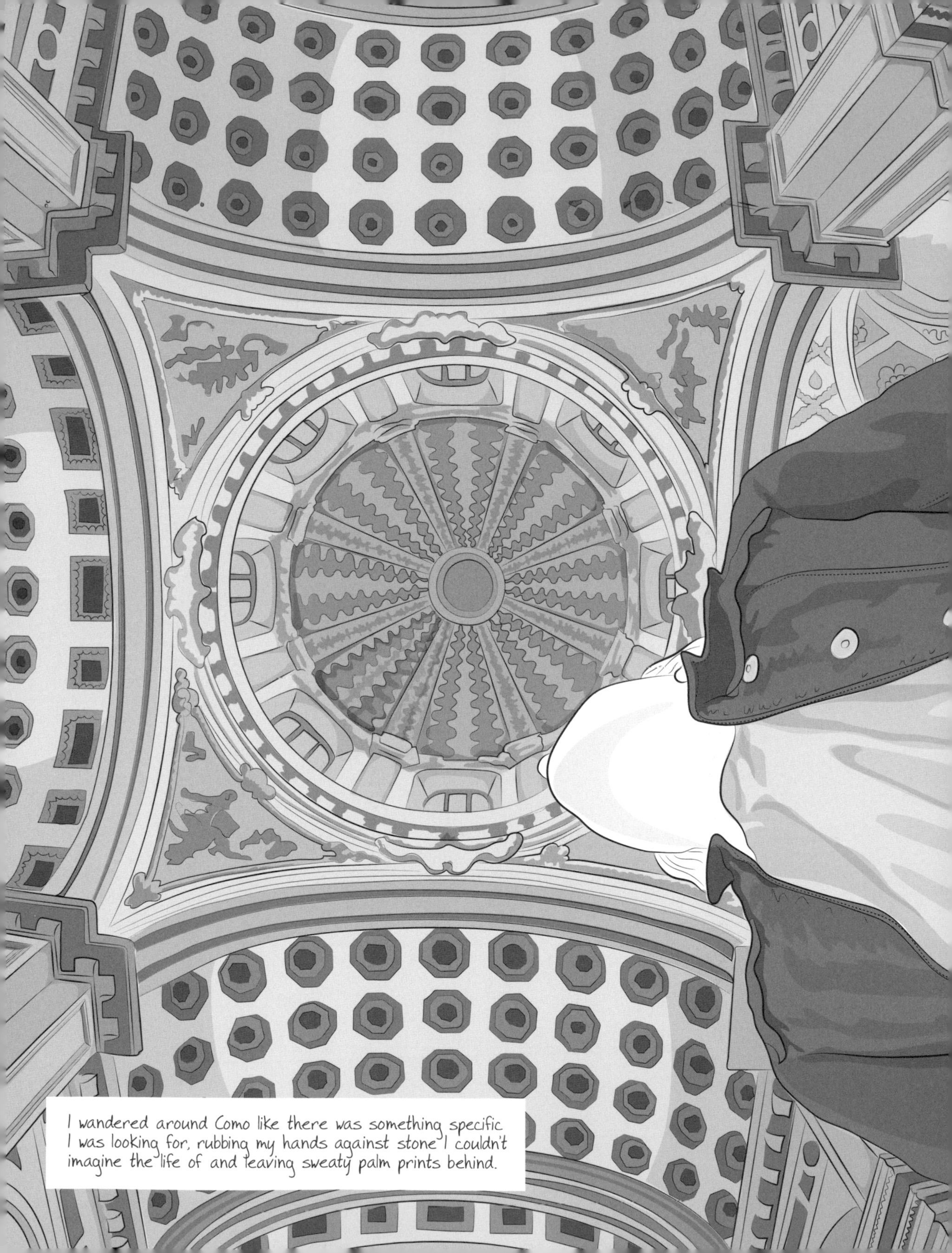
I wandered around Como like there was something specific I was looking for, rubbing my hands against stone I couldn't imagine the life of and leaving sweaty palm prints behind.

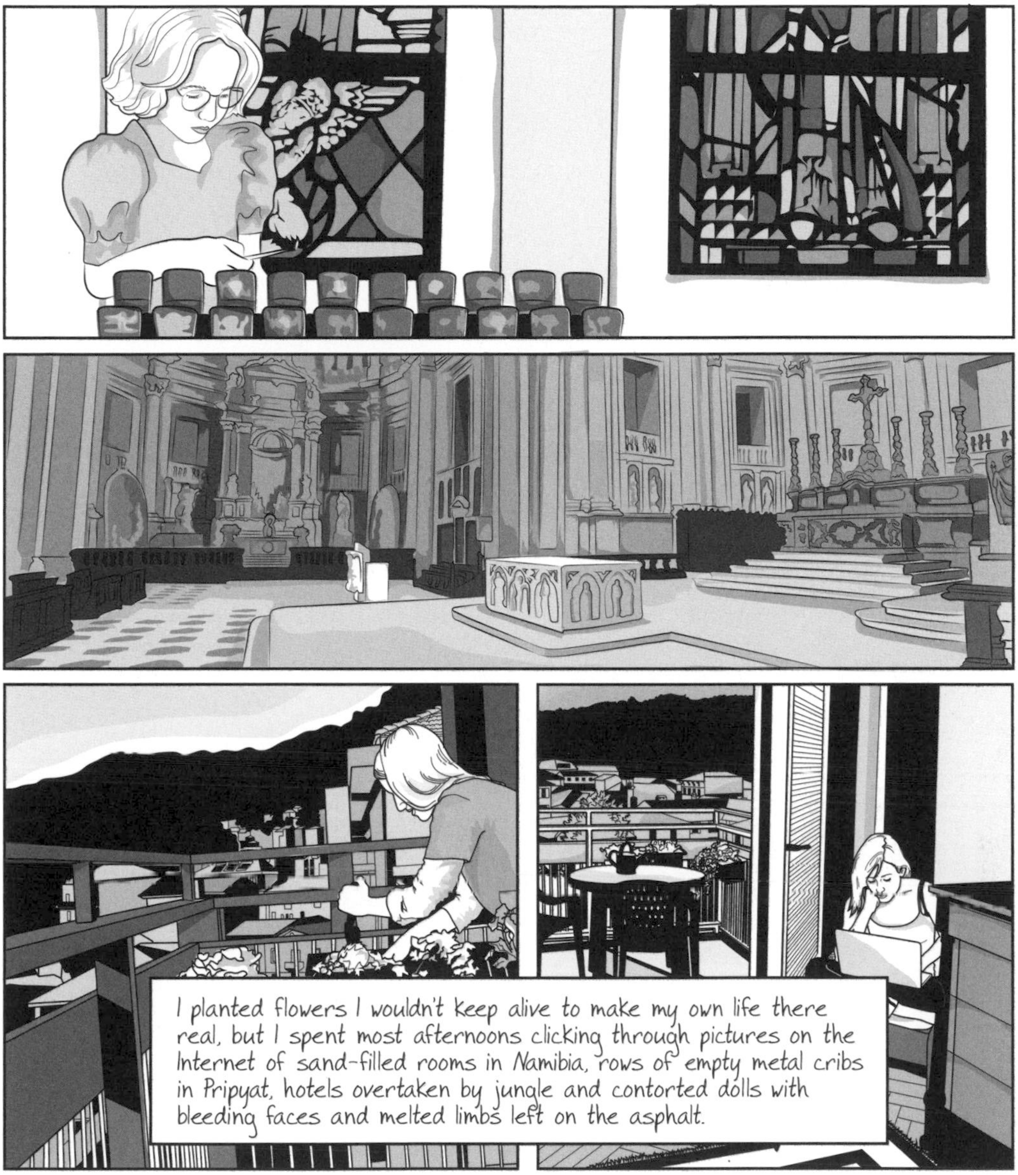
I planted flowers I wouldn't keep alive to make my own life there real, but I spent most afternoons clicking through pictures on the Internet of sand-filled rooms in Namibia, rows of empty metal cribs in Pripyat, hotels overtaken by jungle and contorted dolls with bleeding faces and melted limbs left on the asphalt.

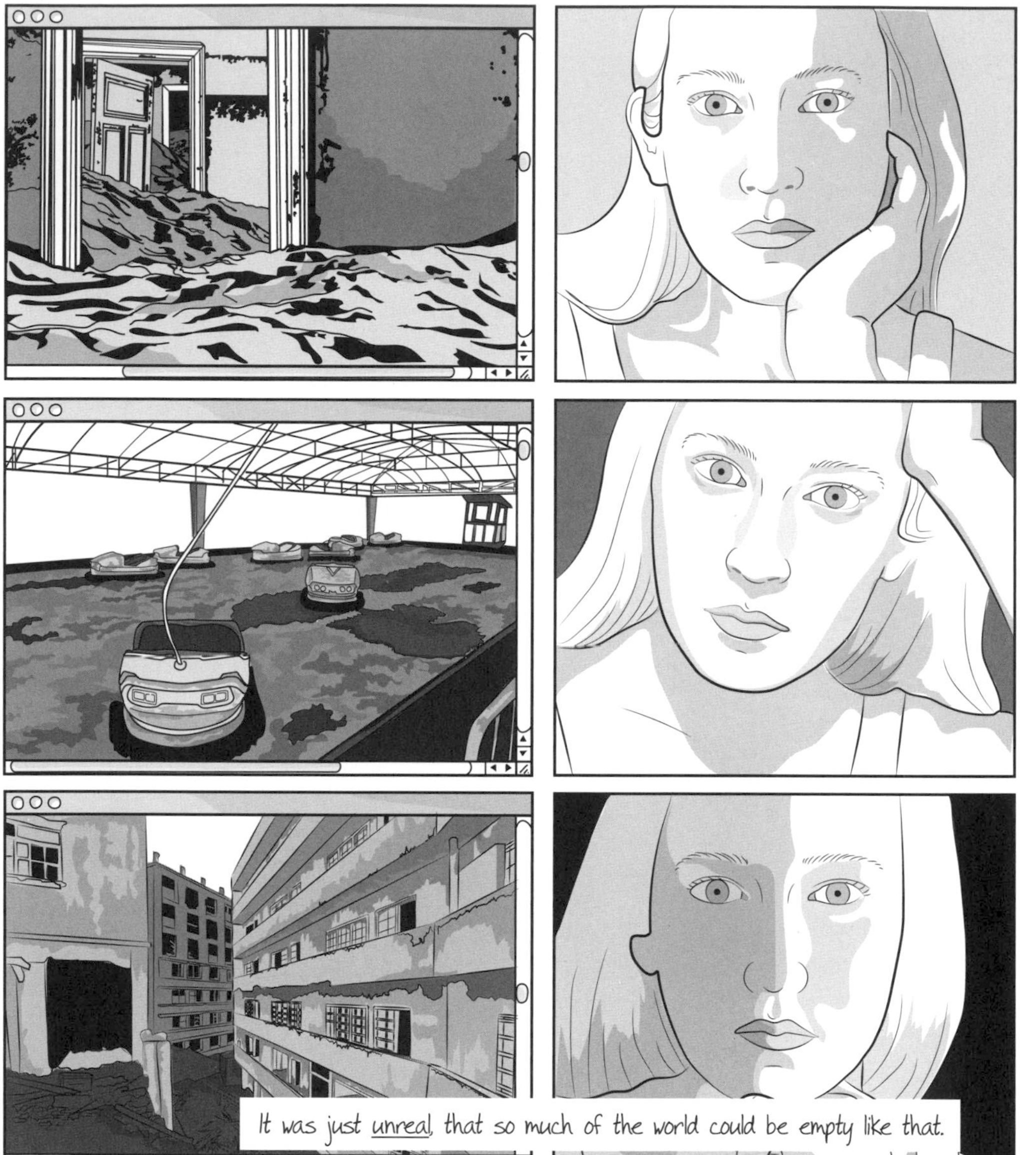
It was just unreal, that so much of the world could be empty like that.

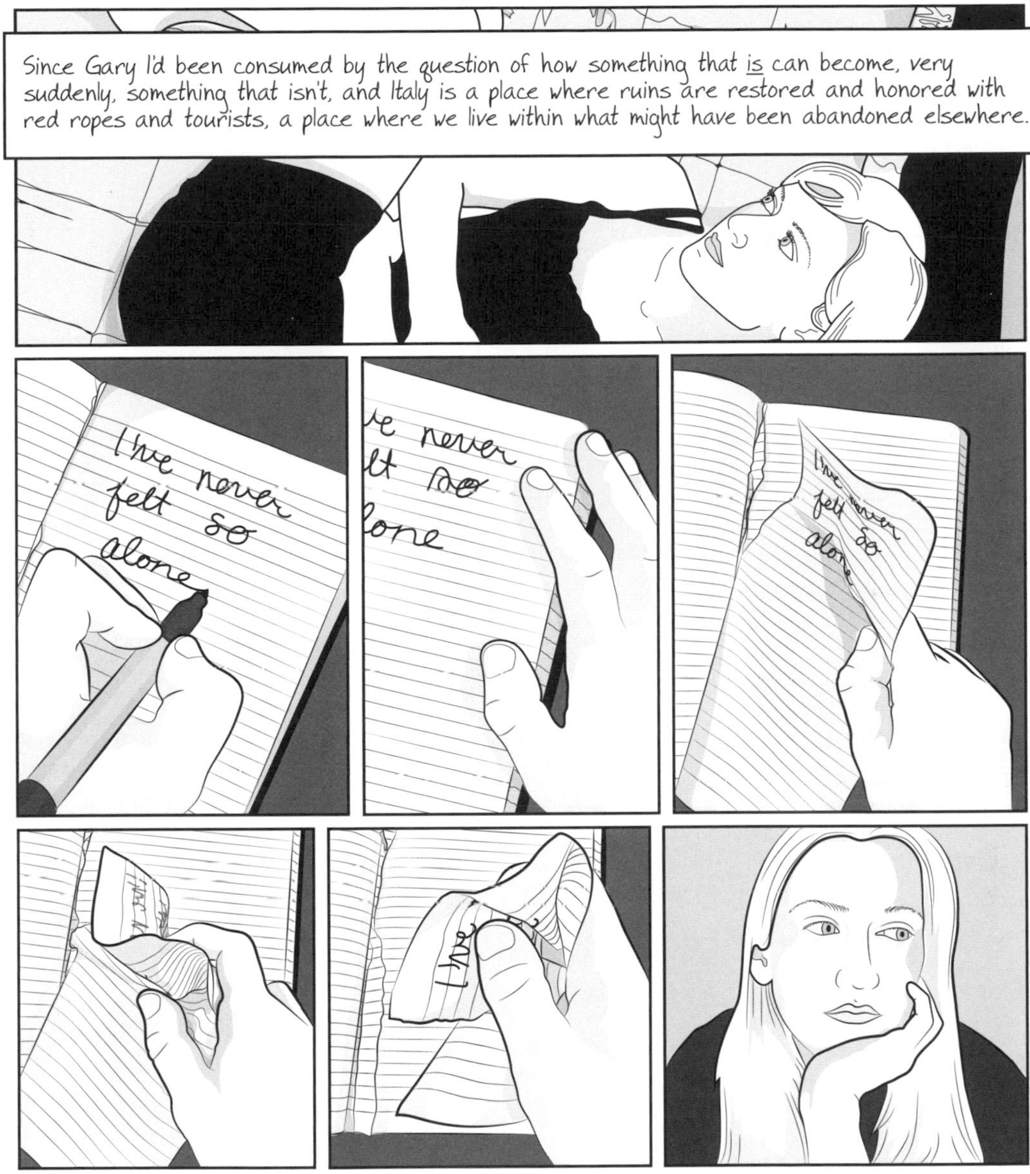
Since Gary I'd been consumed by the question of how something that is can become, very suddenly, something that isn't, and Italy is a place where ruins are restored and honored with red ropes and tourists, a place where we live within what might have been abandoned elsewhere.
I've never felt so alone

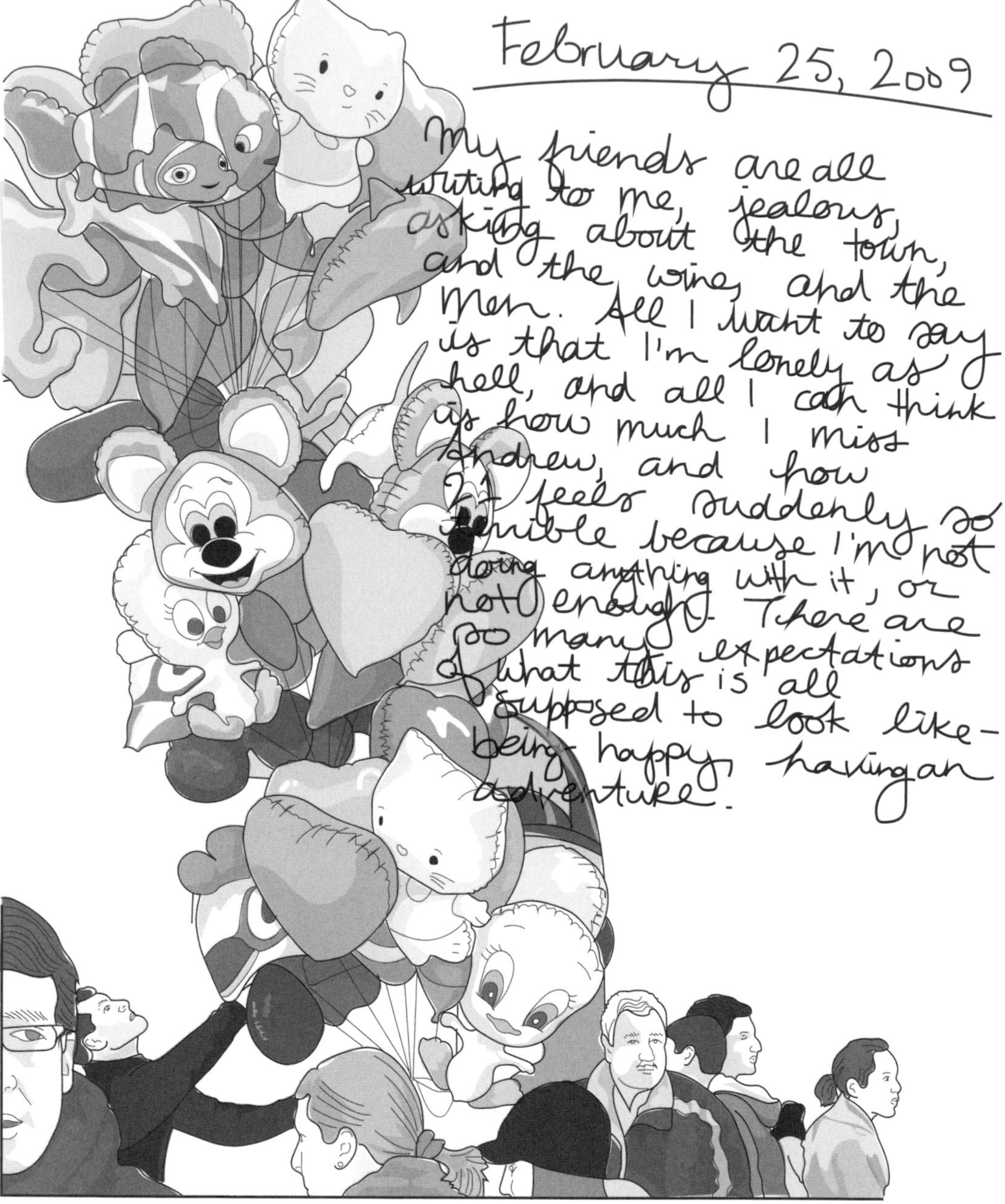
February 25, 2009
My friends are all writing to me, jealous, asking about the town, and the wine, and the men. All I want to say is that I'm lonely as hell, and all I can think is how much I miss Andrew, and how 27 feels suddenly so terrible because I'm not doing anything with it, or not enough. There are so many expectations of what this is all supposed to look like- being happy, having an adventure.

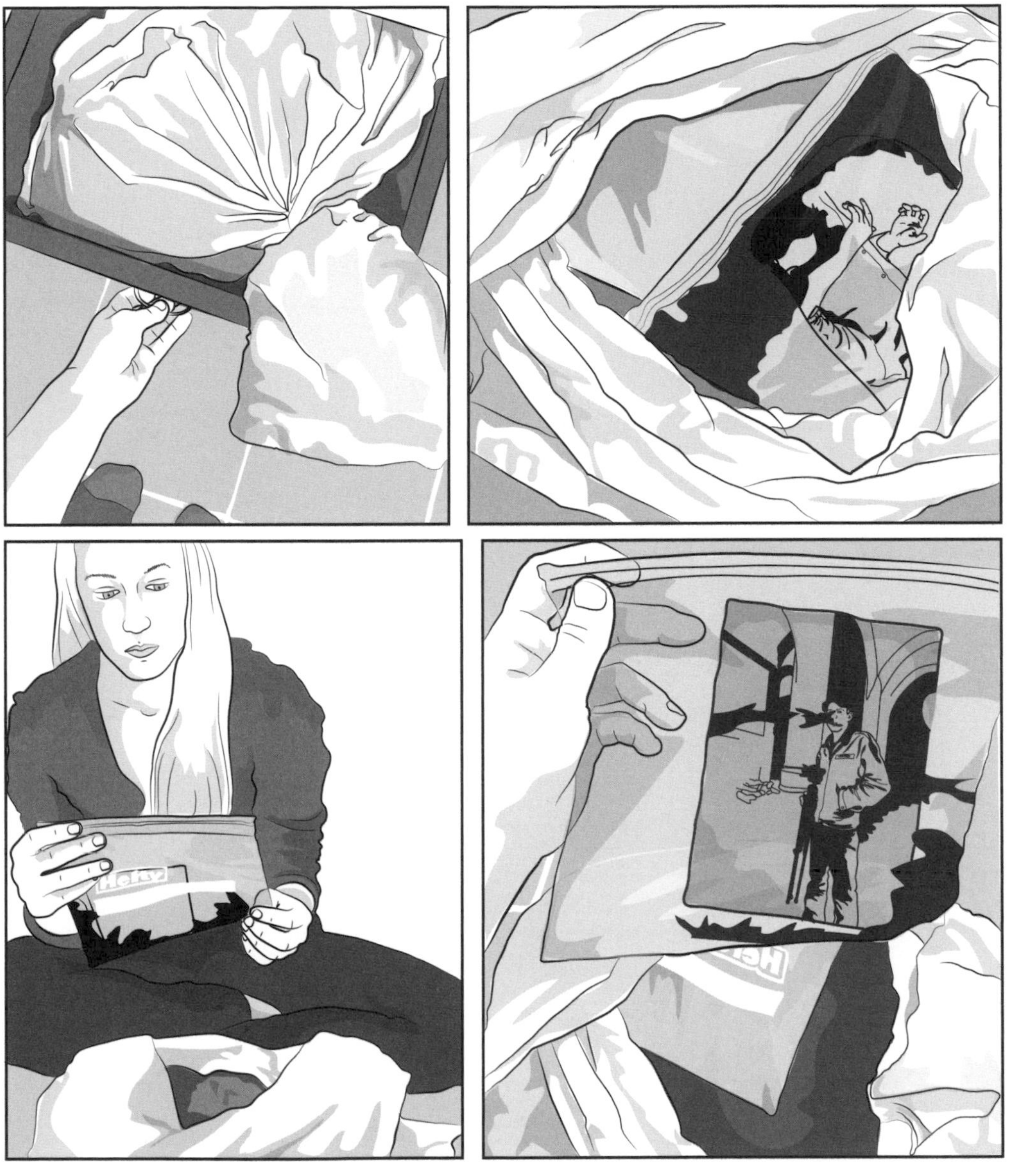
Hefty

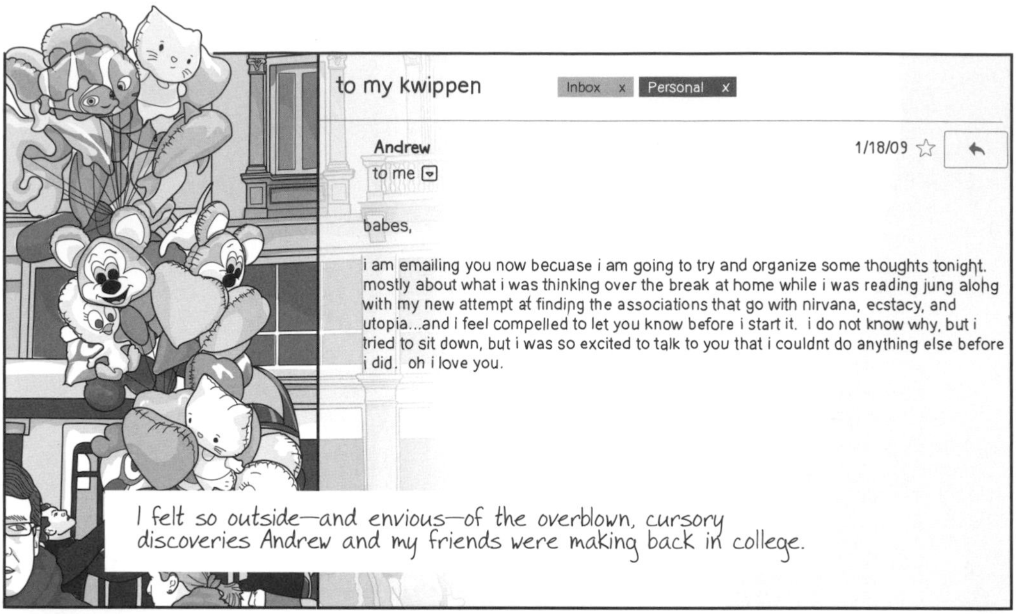
to my kwippen
Inbox x
Personal x
Andrew
to me
1/18/09
babes,
i am emailing you now becuase i am going to try and organize some thoughts tonight. mostly about what i was thinking over the break at home while i was reading jung alohg with my new attempt at finding the associations that go with nirvana, ecstacy, and utopia...and i feel compelled to let you know before i start it. i do not know why, but i tried to sit down, but i was so excited to talk to you that i couldnt do anything else before i did. oh i love you.
I felt so outside—and envious—of the overblown, cursory discoveries Andrew and my friends were making back in college.

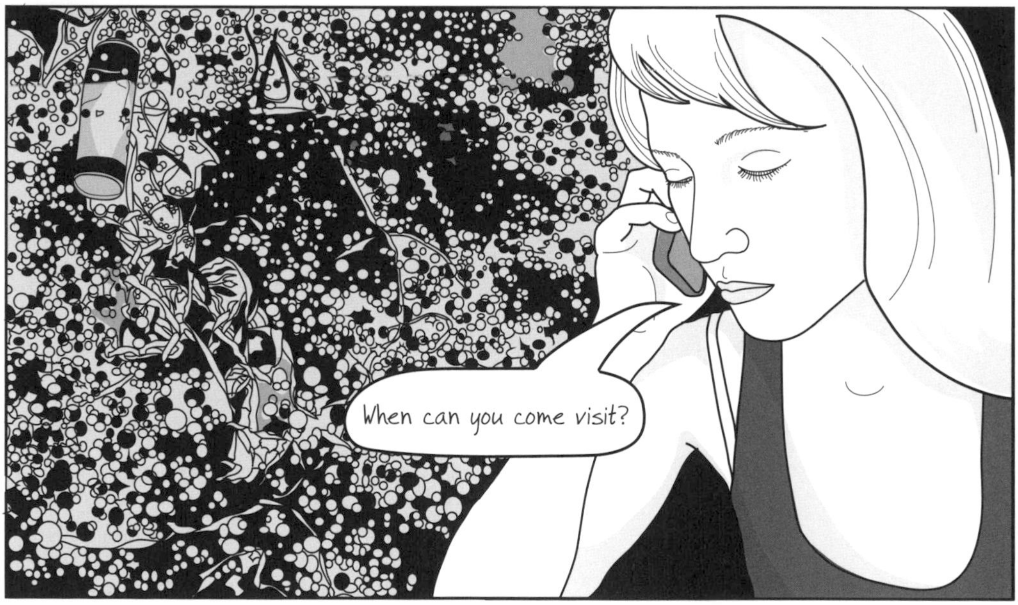
When can you come visit?

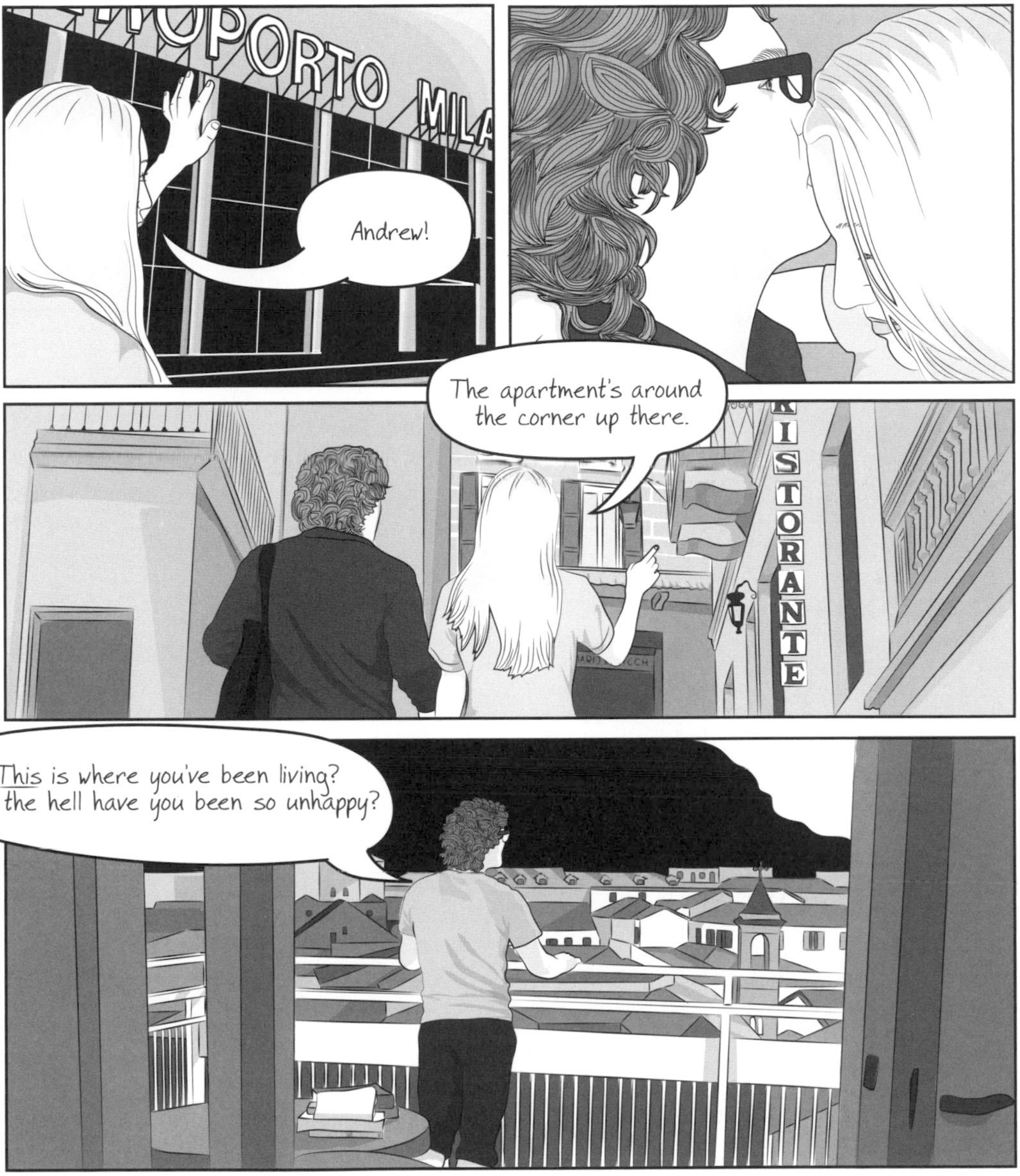
AEROPORTO MILA
Andrew!
The apartment's around the corner up there.
RISTORANTE
This is where you've been living? Why the hell have you been so unhappy?

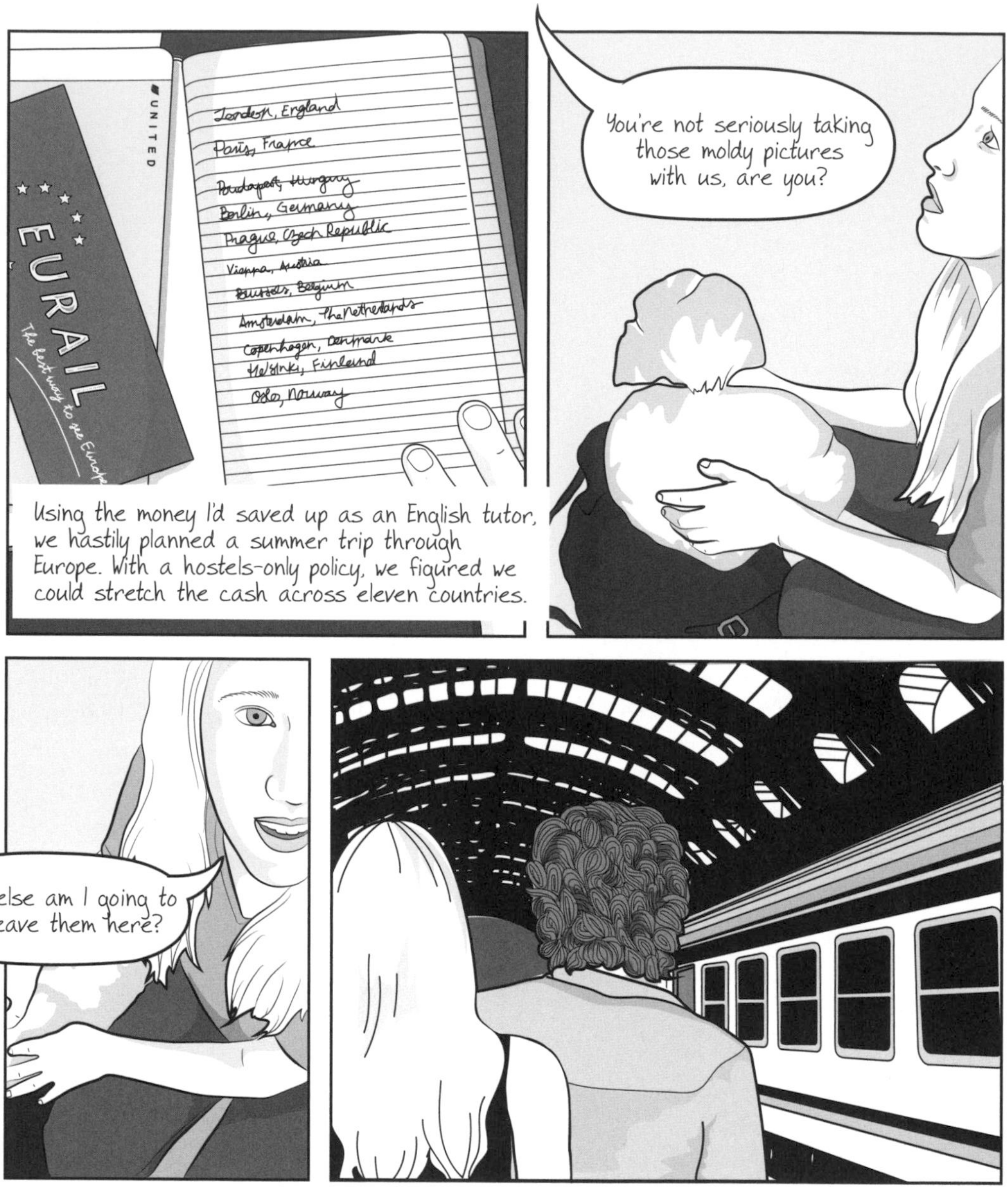
UNITED
EURAIL
London, England
Paris, France
Budapest, Hungary
Berlin, Germany
Prague, Czech Republic
Vienna, Austria
Brussels, Belgium
Amsterdam, The Netherlands
Copenhagen, Denmark
Helsinki, Finland
Oslo, Norway
Using the money I'd saved up as an English tutor, we hastily planned a summer trip through Europe. With a hostels-only policy, we figured we could stretch the cash across eleven countries.
You're not seriously taking those moldy pictures with us, are you?
What else am I going to do, leave them here?

Train to London

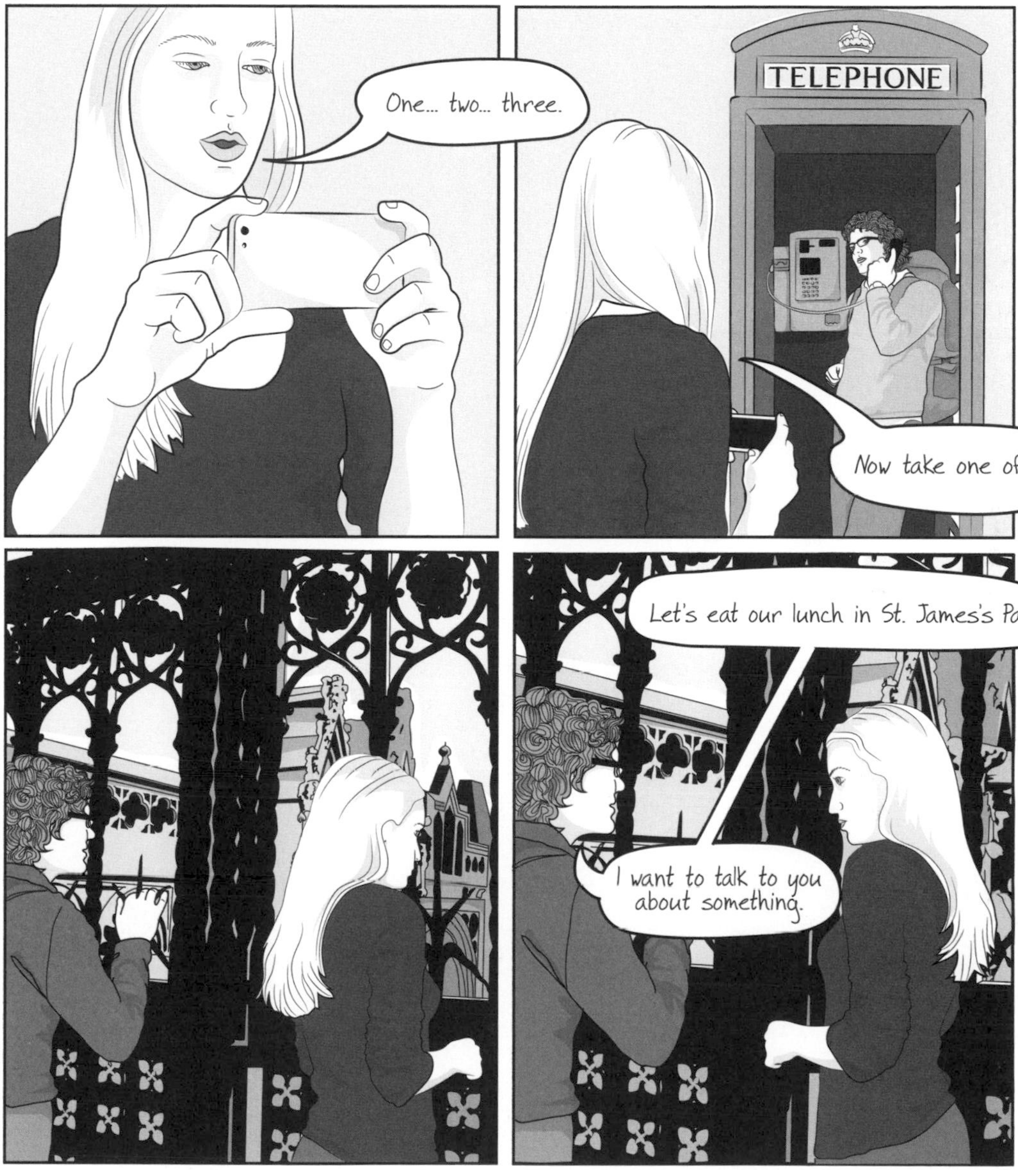
One... two... three.
TELEPHONE
Now take one of me.
Let's eat our lunch in St. James's Park.
I want to talk to you about something.

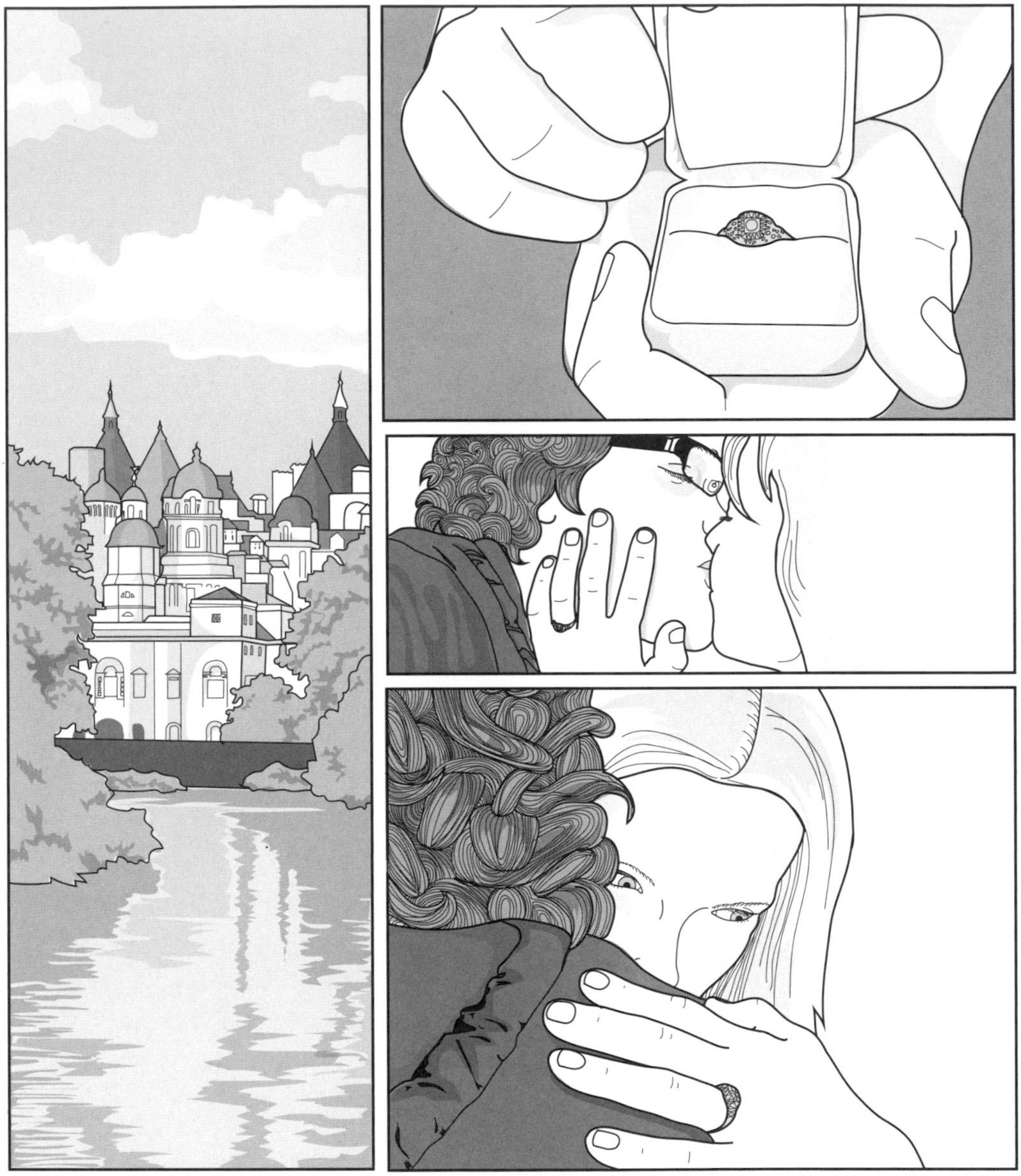

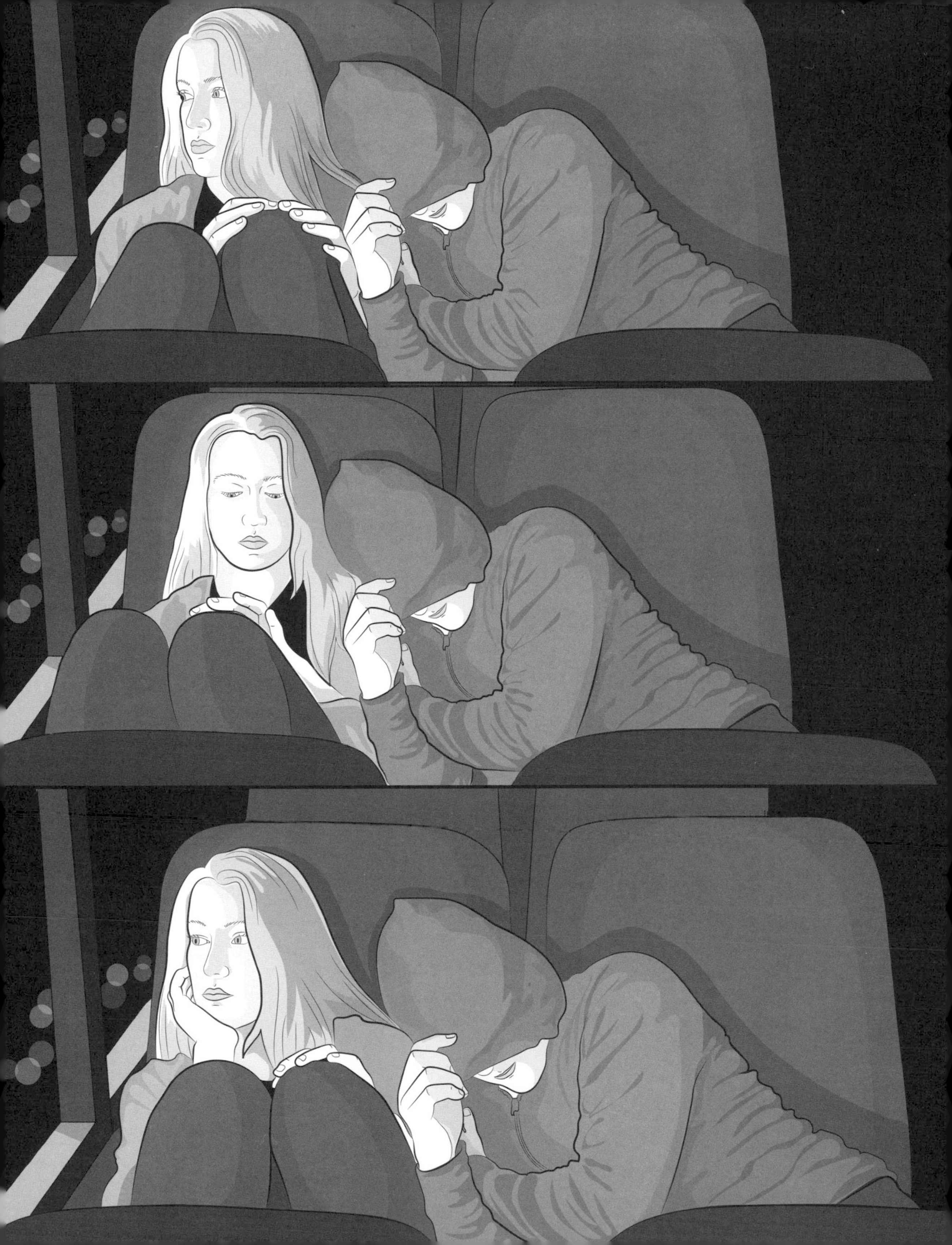

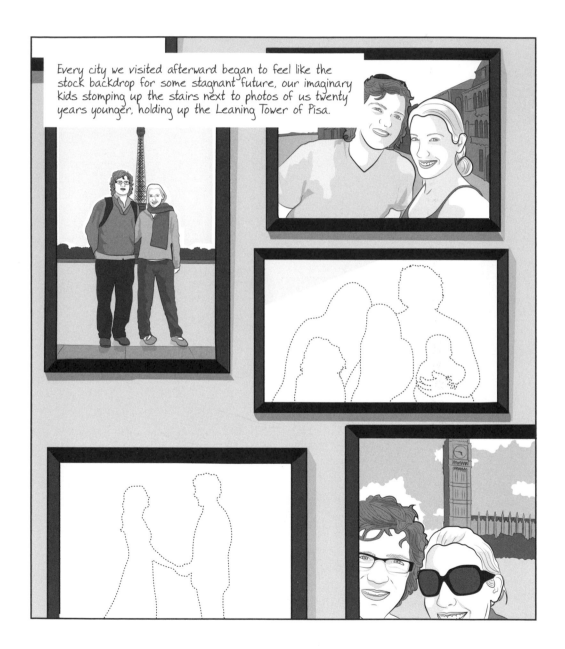

Every city we visited afterward began to feel like the stock backdrop for some stagnant future, our imaginary kids stomping up the stairs next to photos of us twenty years younger, holding up the Leaning Tower of Pisa.

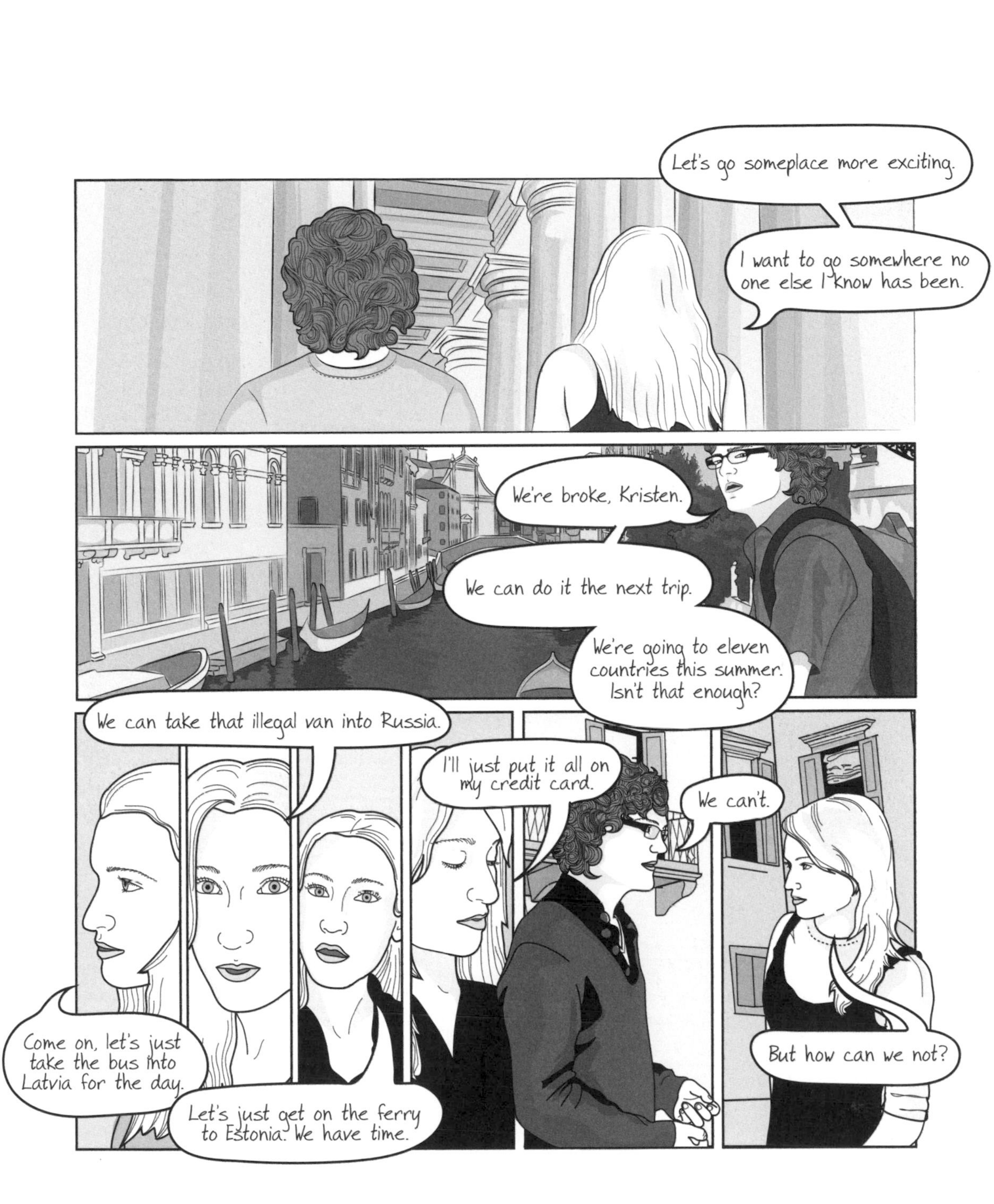
Let's go someplace more exciting.
I want to go somewhere no one else I know has been.
We're broke, Kristen.
We can do it the next trip.
We're going to eleven countries this summer. Isn't that enough?
We can take that illegal van into Russia.
Come on, let's just take the bus into Latvia for the day.
Let's just get on the ferry to Estonia. We have time.
I'll just put it all on my credit card.
We can't.
But how can we not?

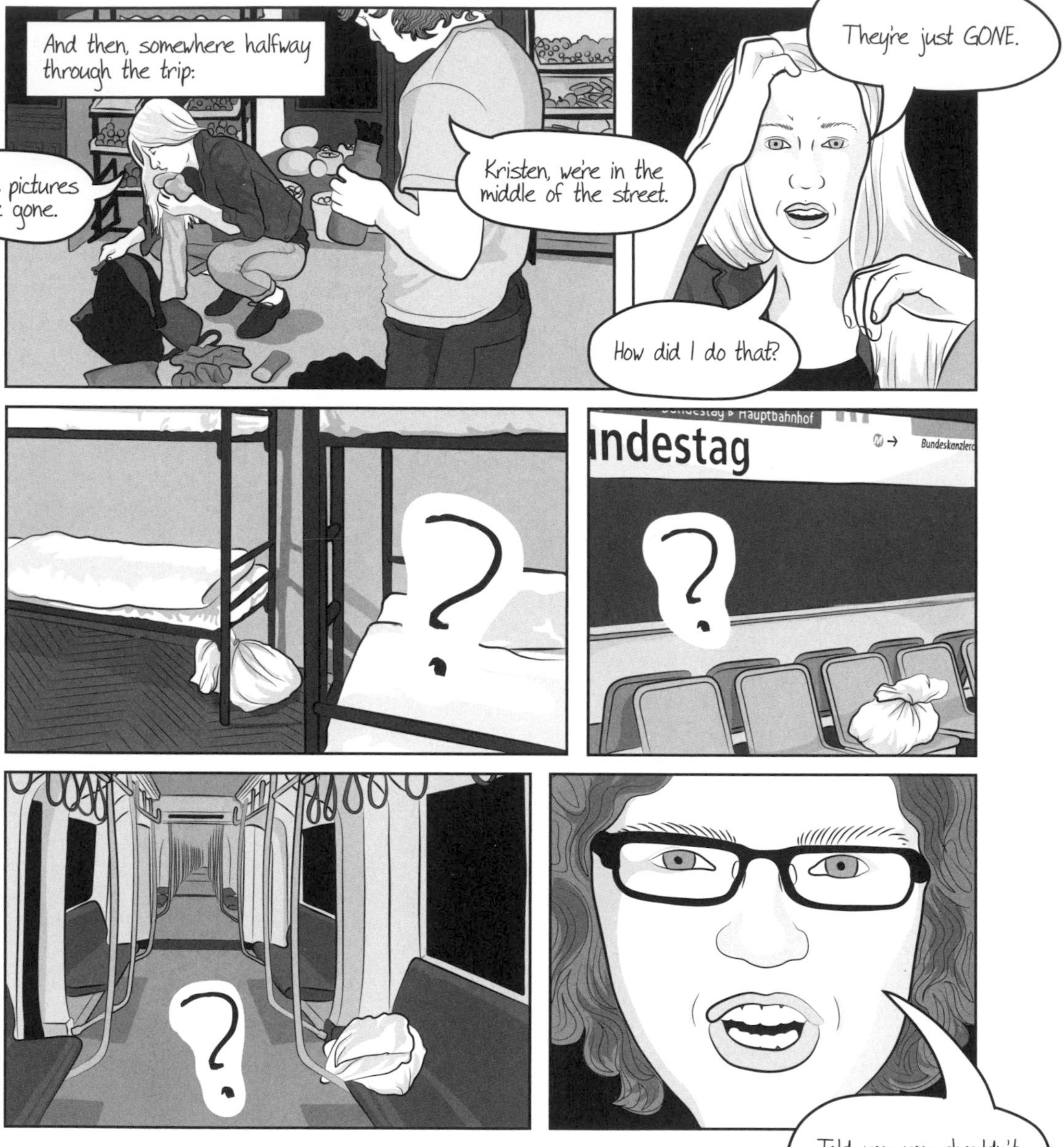
And then, somewhere halfway through the trip:
Seth's pictures are gone.
Kristen, we're in the middle of the street.
They're just GONE.
How did I do that?
Hauptbahnhof
?
?
?
Told you you shouldn't have taken them!

The Chicago house was the first place we'd lived away from our families' homes, our first pass at adulthood. I didn't understand how finite it was, or how quickly we would need to move on.

So instead of going back to Chicago, I loaded my storage locker into a U-Haul and headed to graduate school in Iowa City.

Andrew loyally documented the move.

He'd been awarded a yearlong painting fellowship in New York, and we planned to get married in Iowa when it was finished.

I'm buying a ticket to see you the minute I get my first paycheck.

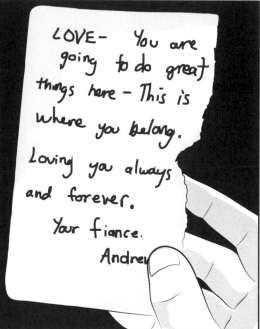

LOVE— You are going to do great things here — This is where you belong.

Loving you always and forever.

Your fiance.

Andrew

94

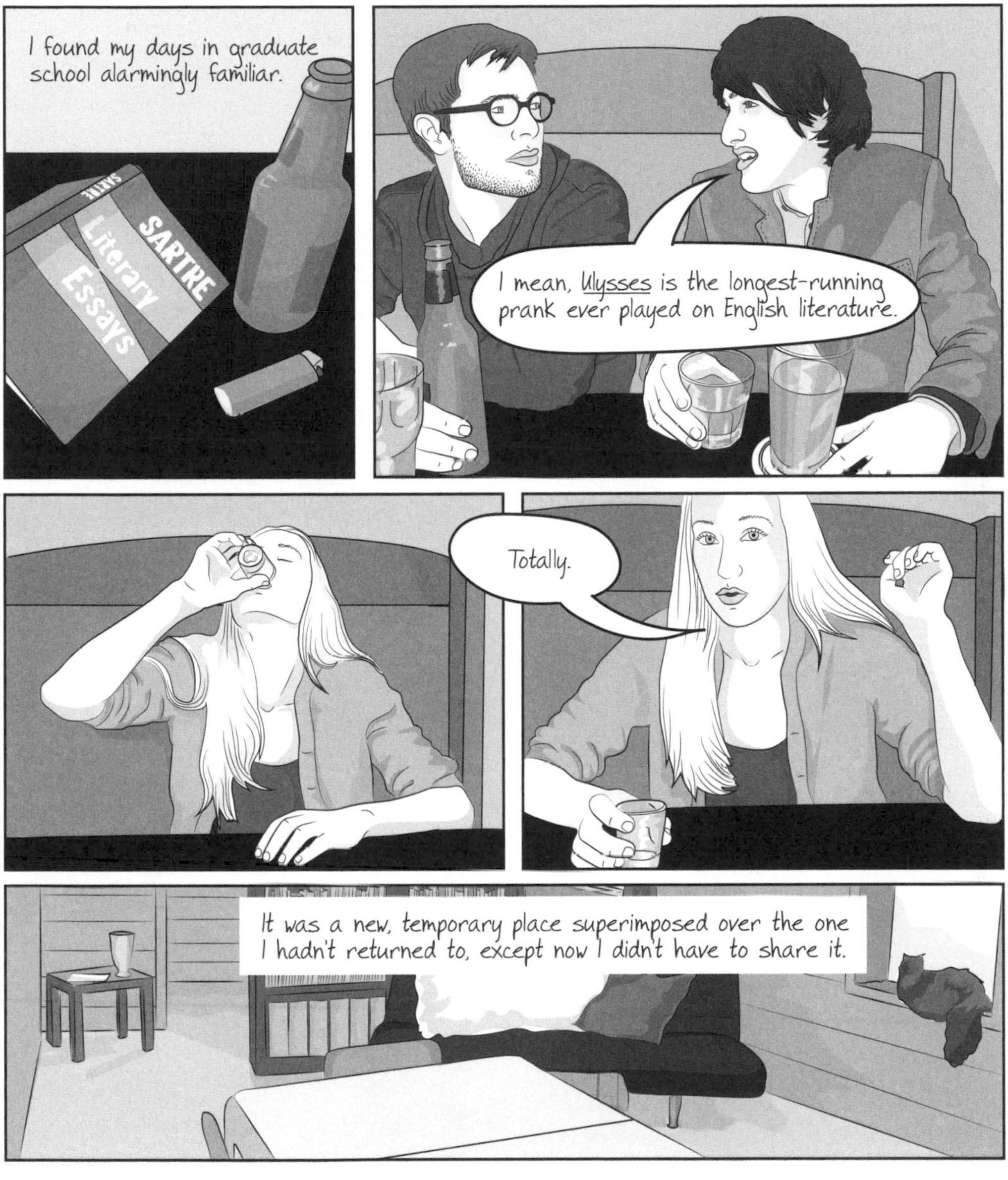
I found my days in graduate school alarmingly familiar.
SARTRE Literary Essays
I mean, Ulysses is the longest-running prank ever played on English literature.
Totally.
It was a new, temporary place superimposed over the one I hadn't returned to, except now I didn't have to share it.

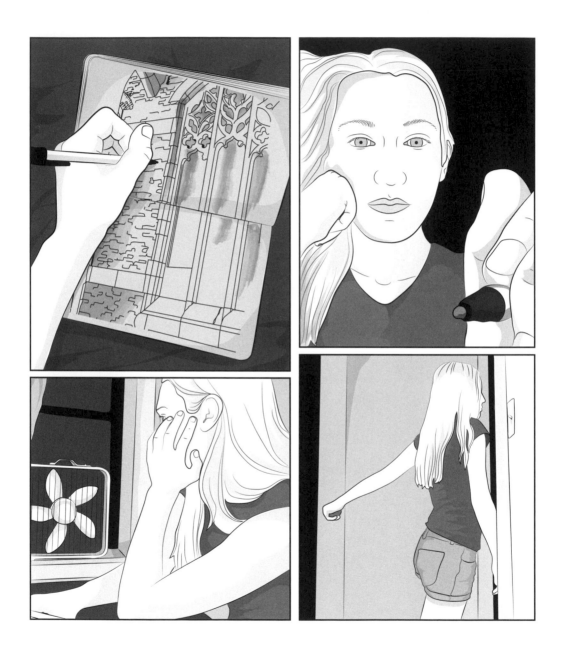

Like most small, liberal college towns, Iowa City is beautiful.

charming shops

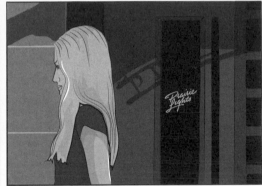

amazing bookstores

manicured lawns

historic buildings

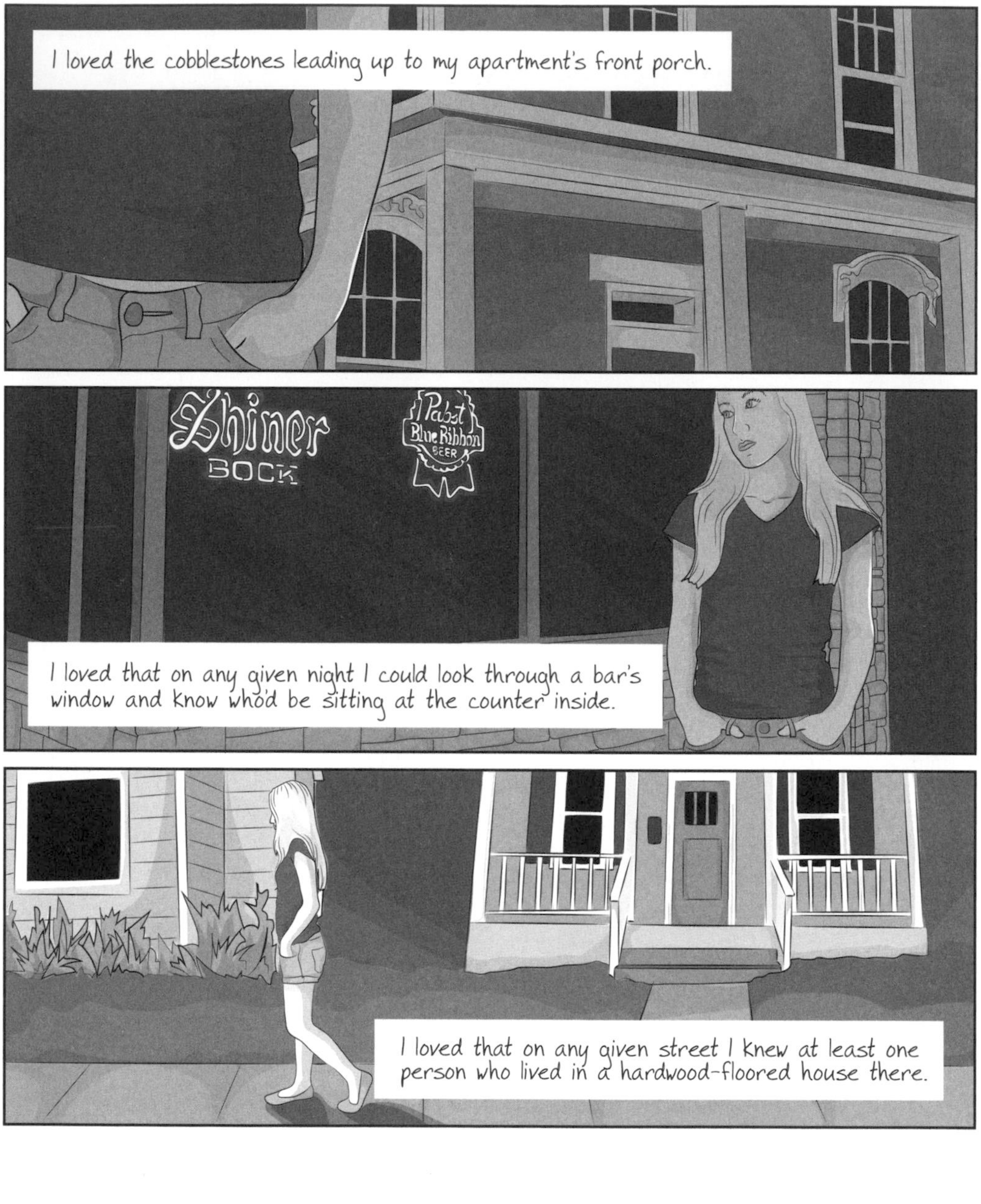
I loved the cobblestones leading up to my apartment's front porch.
Shiner
BOCK
Pabst
Blue Ribbon
BEER
I loved that on any given night I could look through a bar's window and know who'd be sitting at the counter inside.
I loved that on any given street I knew at least one person who lived in a hardwood-floored house there.

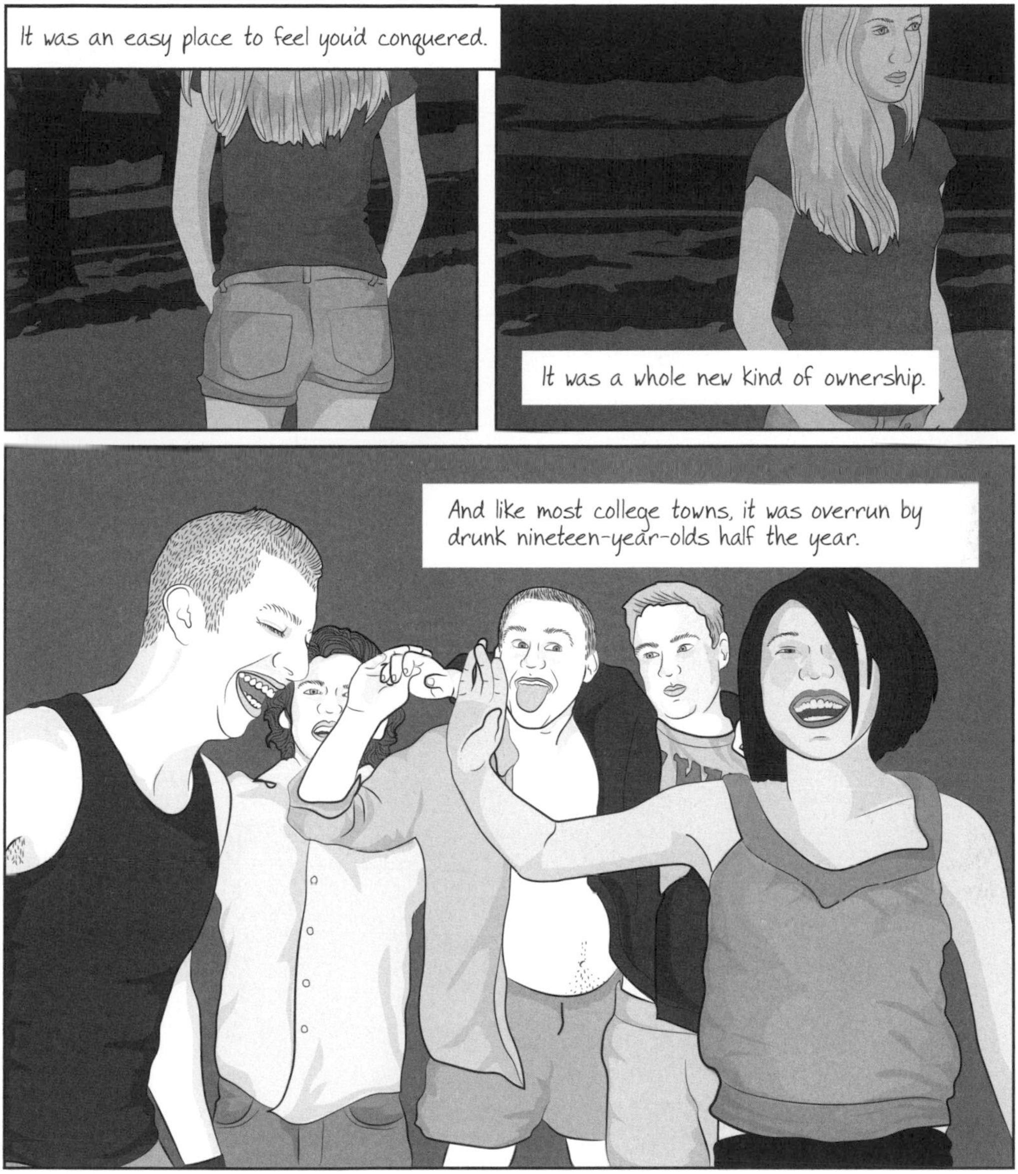
It was an easy place to feel you'd conquered.
It was a whole new kind of ownership.
And like most college towns, it was overrun by drunk nineteen-year-olds half the year.

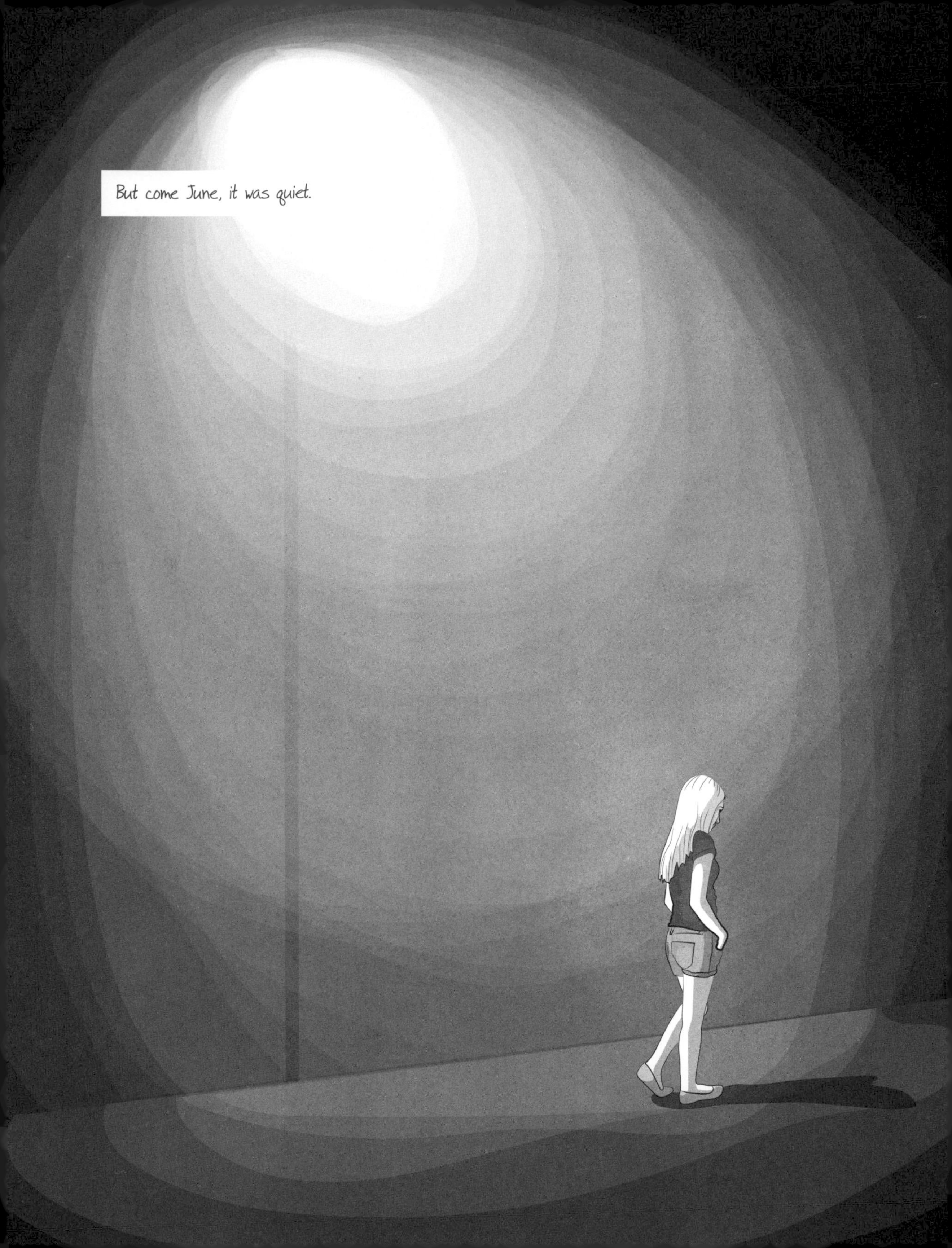
But come June, it was quiet.

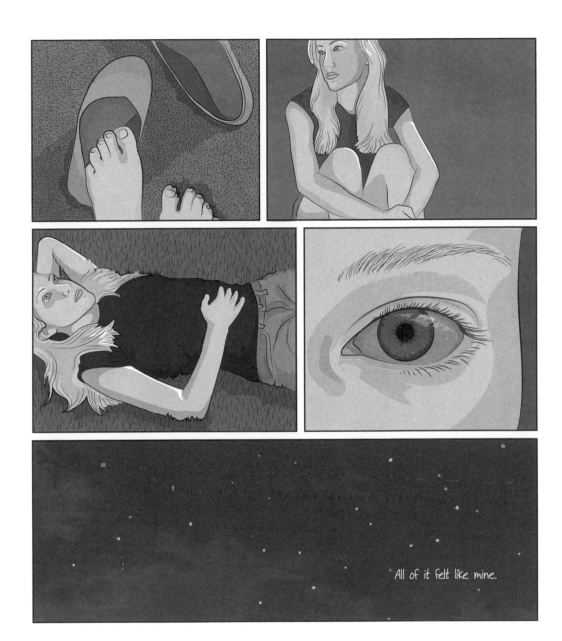

All of it felt like mine.

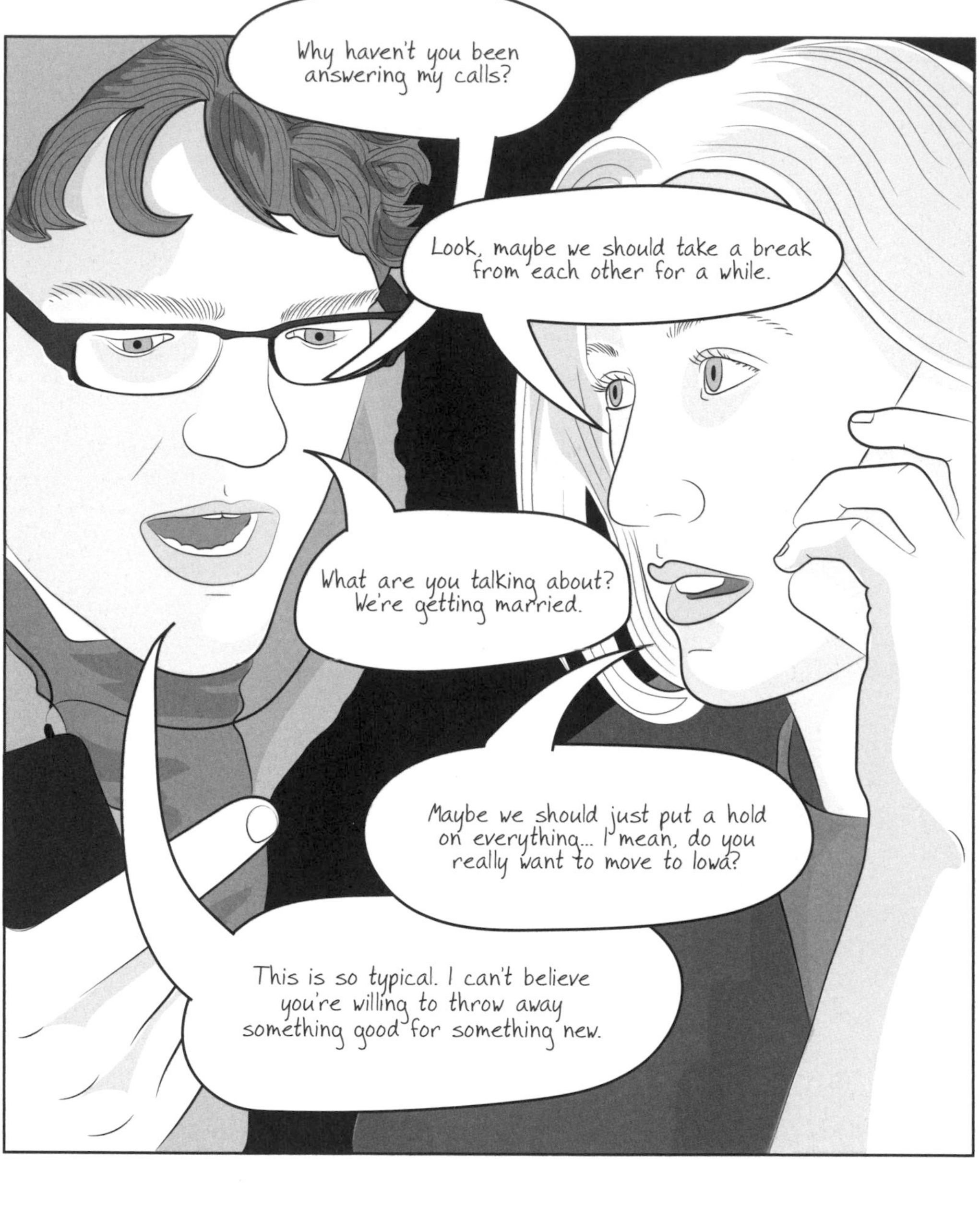
Why haven't you been answering my calls?
Look, maybe we should take a break from each other for a while.
What are you talking about? We're getting married.
Maybe we should just put a hold on everything... I mean, do you really want to move to Iowa?
This is so typical. I can't believe you're willing to throw away something good for something new.

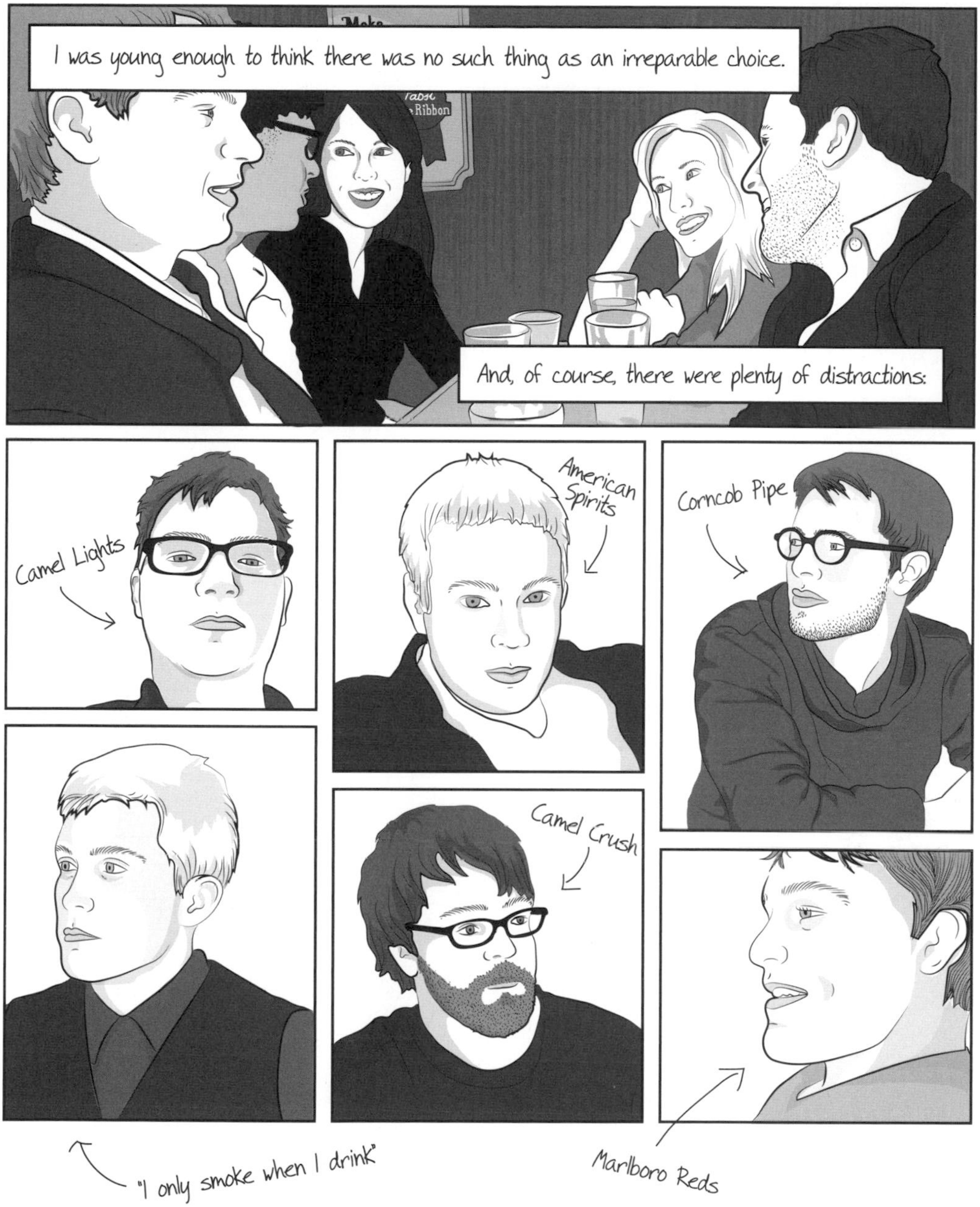
I was young enough to think there was no such thing as an irreparable choice.
And, of course, there were plenty of distractions:
Camel Lights
American Spirits
Corncob Pipe
Camel Crush
"I only smoke when I drink"
Marlboro Reds

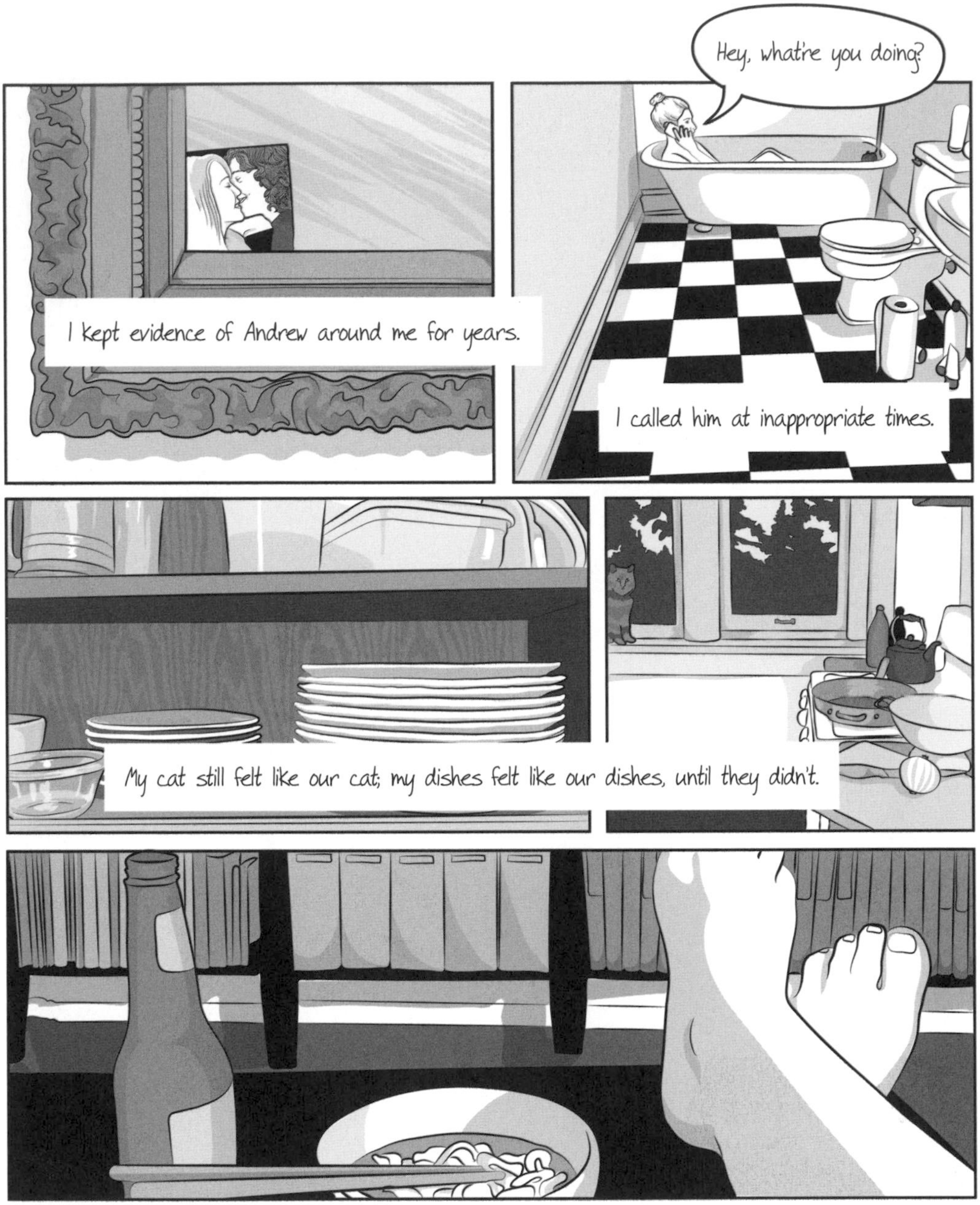
I kept evidence of Andrew around me for years.
Hey, what're you doing?
I called him at inappropriate times.
My cat still felt like our cat; my dishes felt like our dishes, until they didn't.

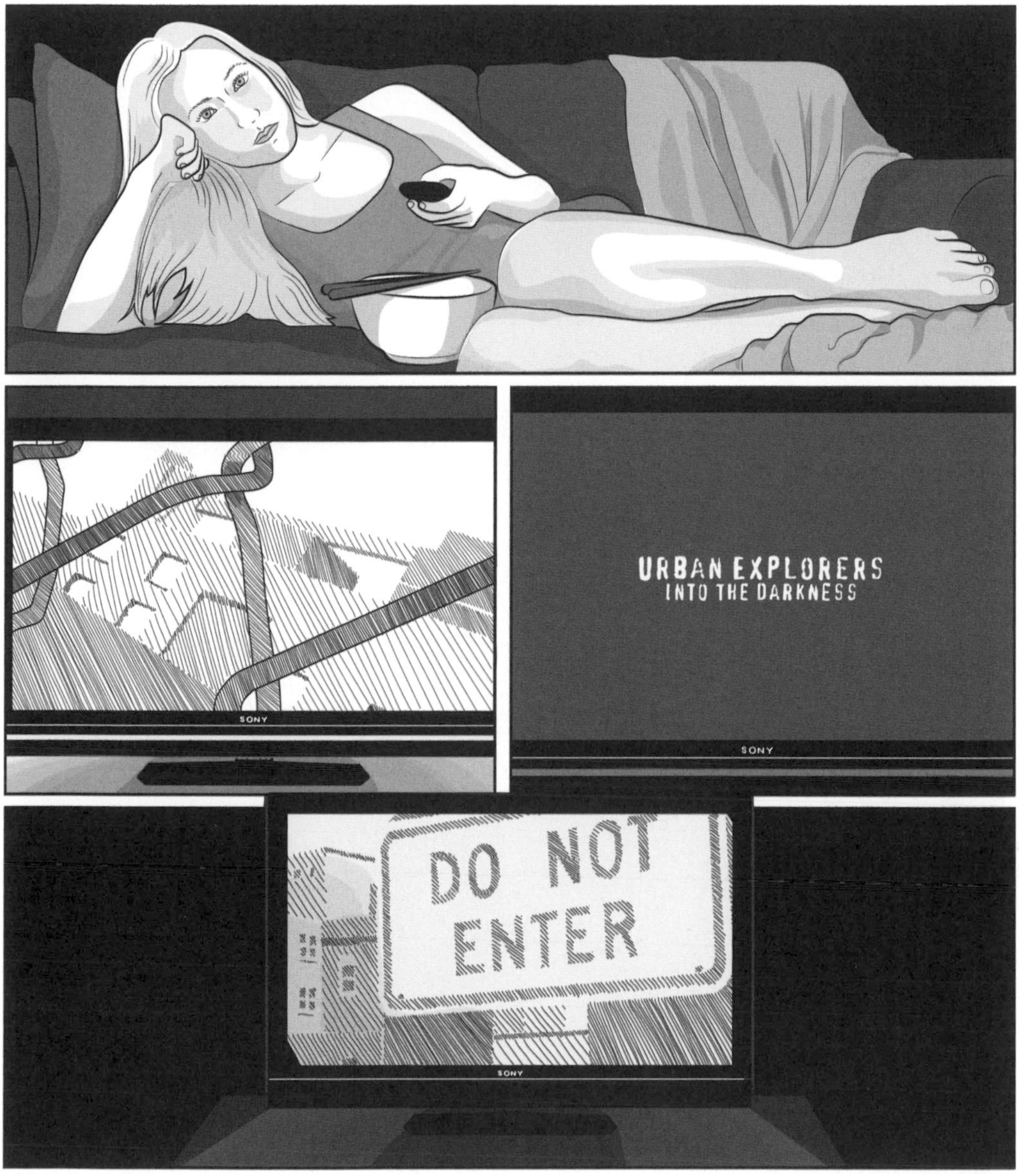
SONY
URBAN EXPLORERS
INTO THE DARKNESS
SONY
DO NOT
ENTER
SONY

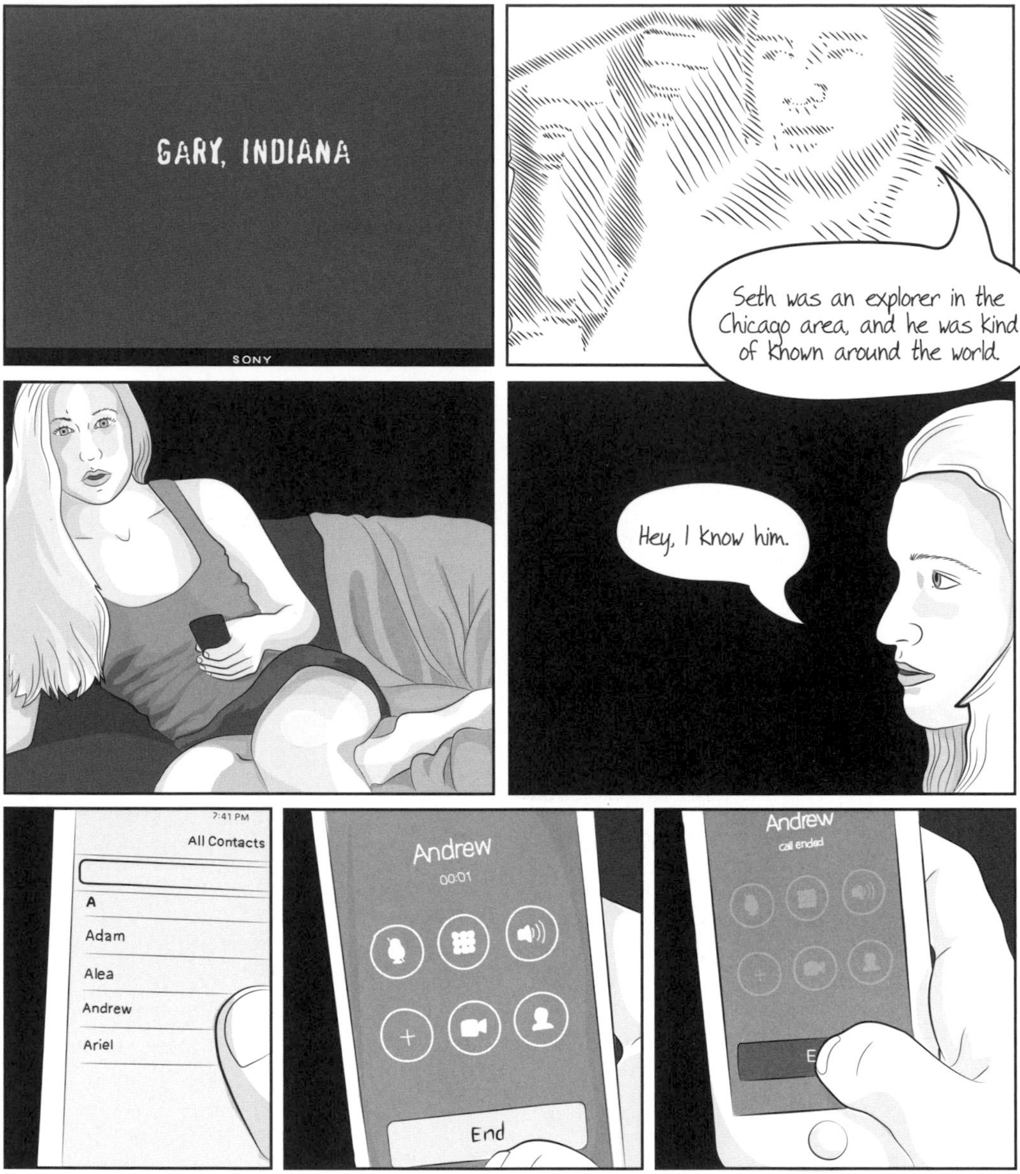
GARY, INDIANA
SONY
Seth was an explorer in the Chicago area, and he was kind of known around the world.
Hey, I know him.
7:41 PM
All Contacts
A
Adam
Alea
Andrew
Ariel
Andrew
00:01
End
Andrew
call ended

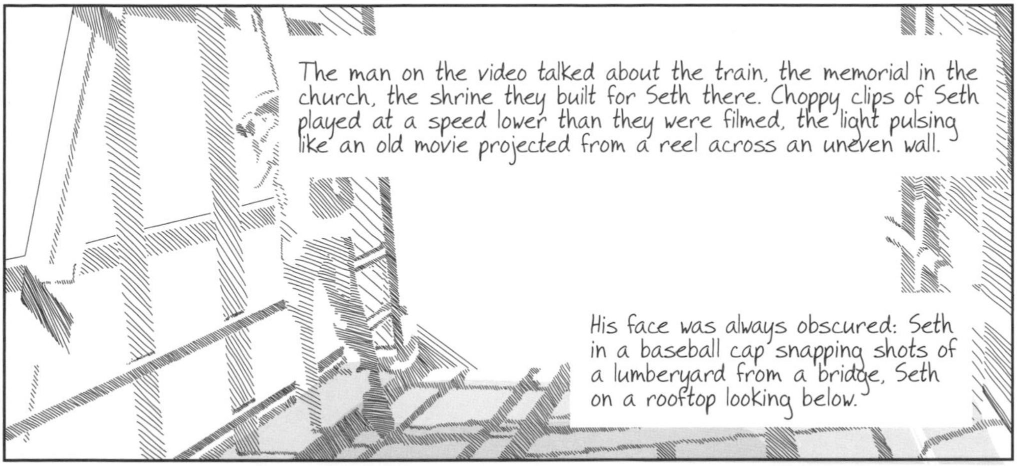
The man on the video talked about the train, the memorial in the church, the shrine they built for Seth there. Choppy clips of Seth played at a speed lower than they were filmed, the light pulsing like an old movie projected from a reel across an uneven wall.
His face was always obscured: Seth in a baseball cap snapping shots of a lumberyard from a bridge, Seth on a rooftop looking below.

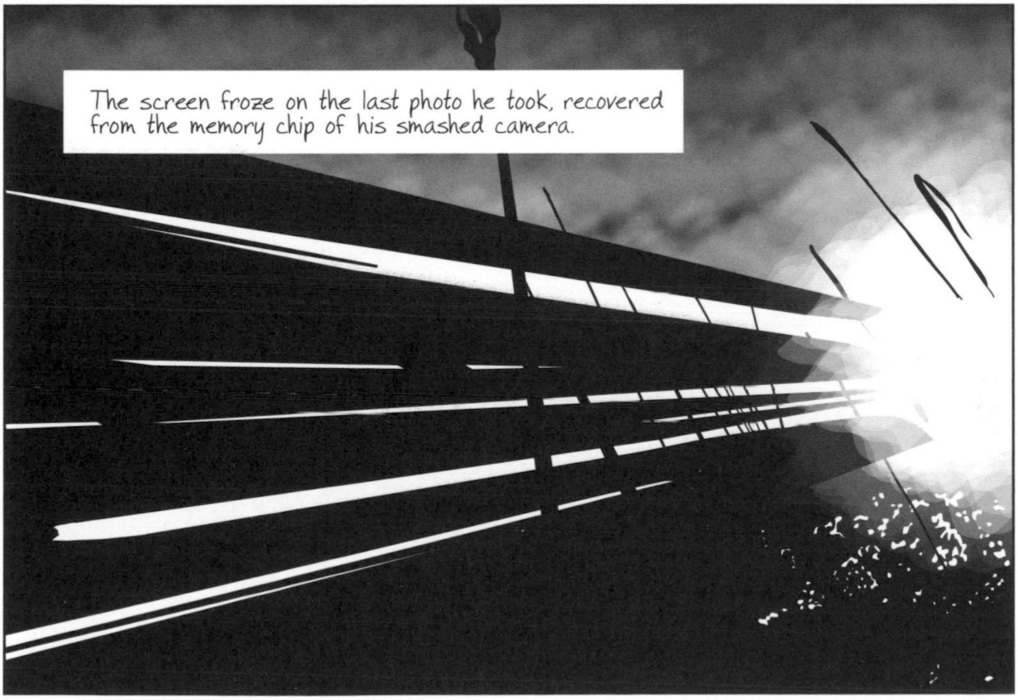
The screen froze on the last photo he took, recovered from the memory chip of his smashed camera.

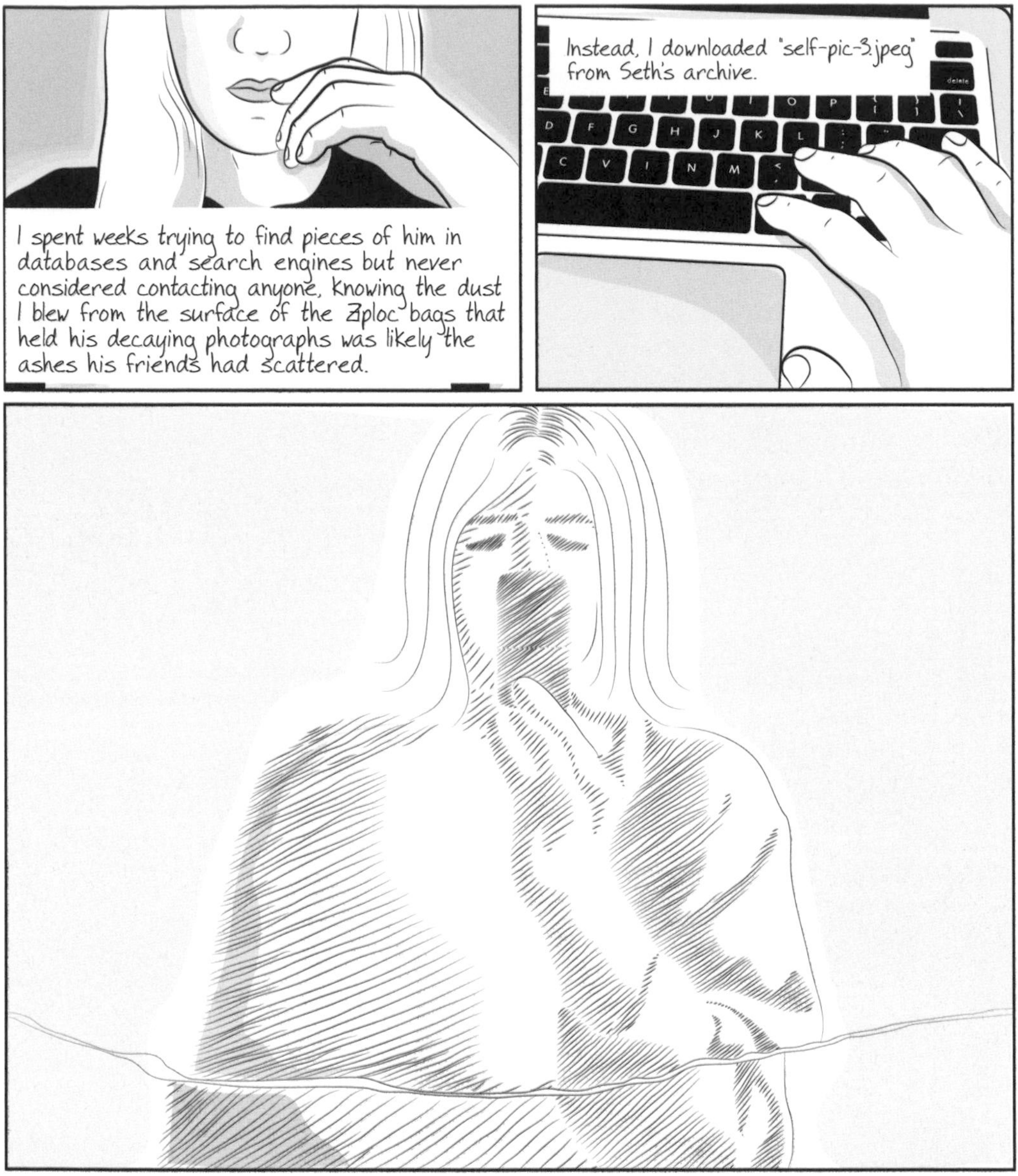
I spent weeks trying to find pieces of him in databases and search engines but never considered contacting anyone, knowing the dust I blew from the surface of the Ziploc bags that held his decaying photographs was likely the ashes his friends had scattered.
Instead, I downloaded "self-pic-3.jpeg" from Seth's archive.

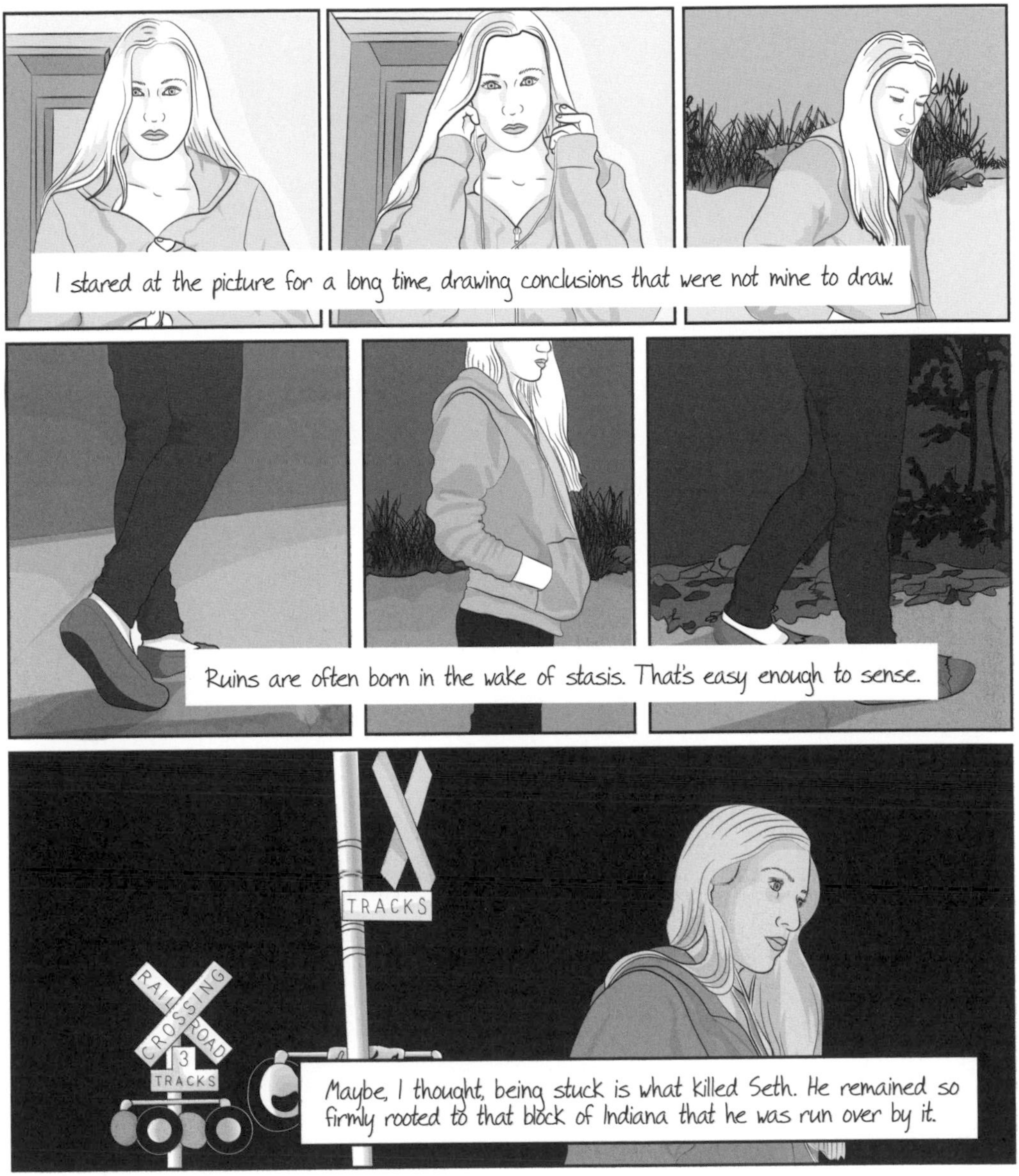
I stared at the picture for a long time, drawing conclusions that were not mine to draw.
Ruins are often born in the wake of stasis. That's easy enough to sense.
TRACKS
RAILROAD CROSSING
3 TRACKS
Maybe, I thought, being stuck is what killed Seth. He remained so firmly rooted to that block of Indiana that he was run over by it.

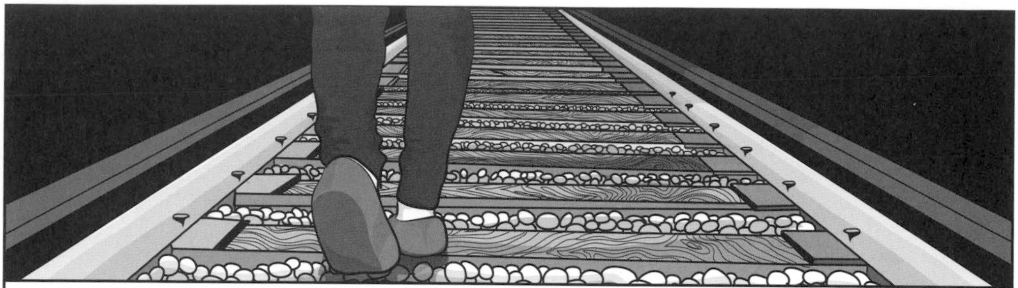

Iowa was a place I began leaving constantly to seek out and crawl through gutted mining towns and looted industrial buildings, bombed-out barracks and contaminated environmental zones in countries whose languages I couldn't speak, places that excrete warnings of the wars and quakes and depressions they've witnessed.

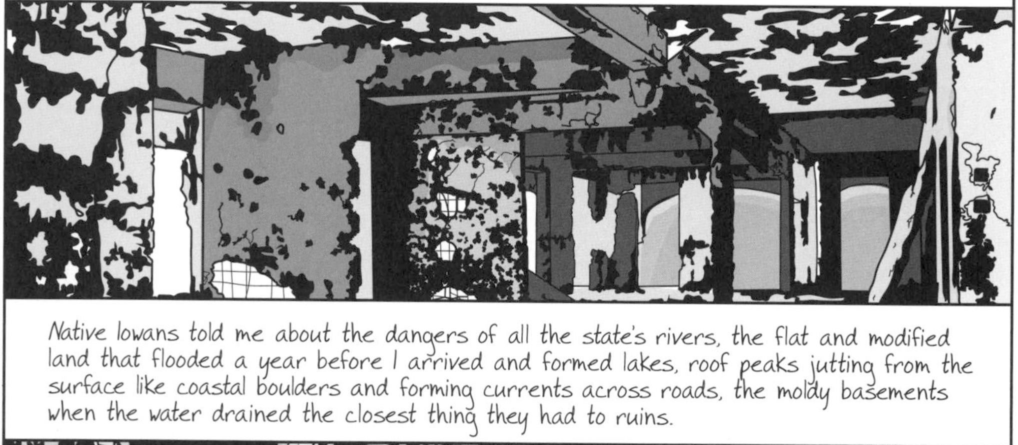

Native Iowans told me about the dangers of all the state's rivers, the flat and modified land that flooded a year before I arrived and formed lakes, roof peaks jutting from the surface like coastal boulders and forming currents across roads, the moldy basements when the water drained the closest thing they had to ruins.

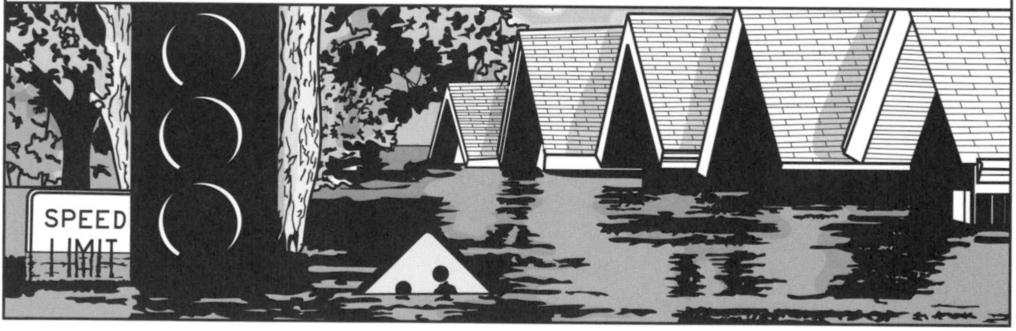
SPEED
LIMIT

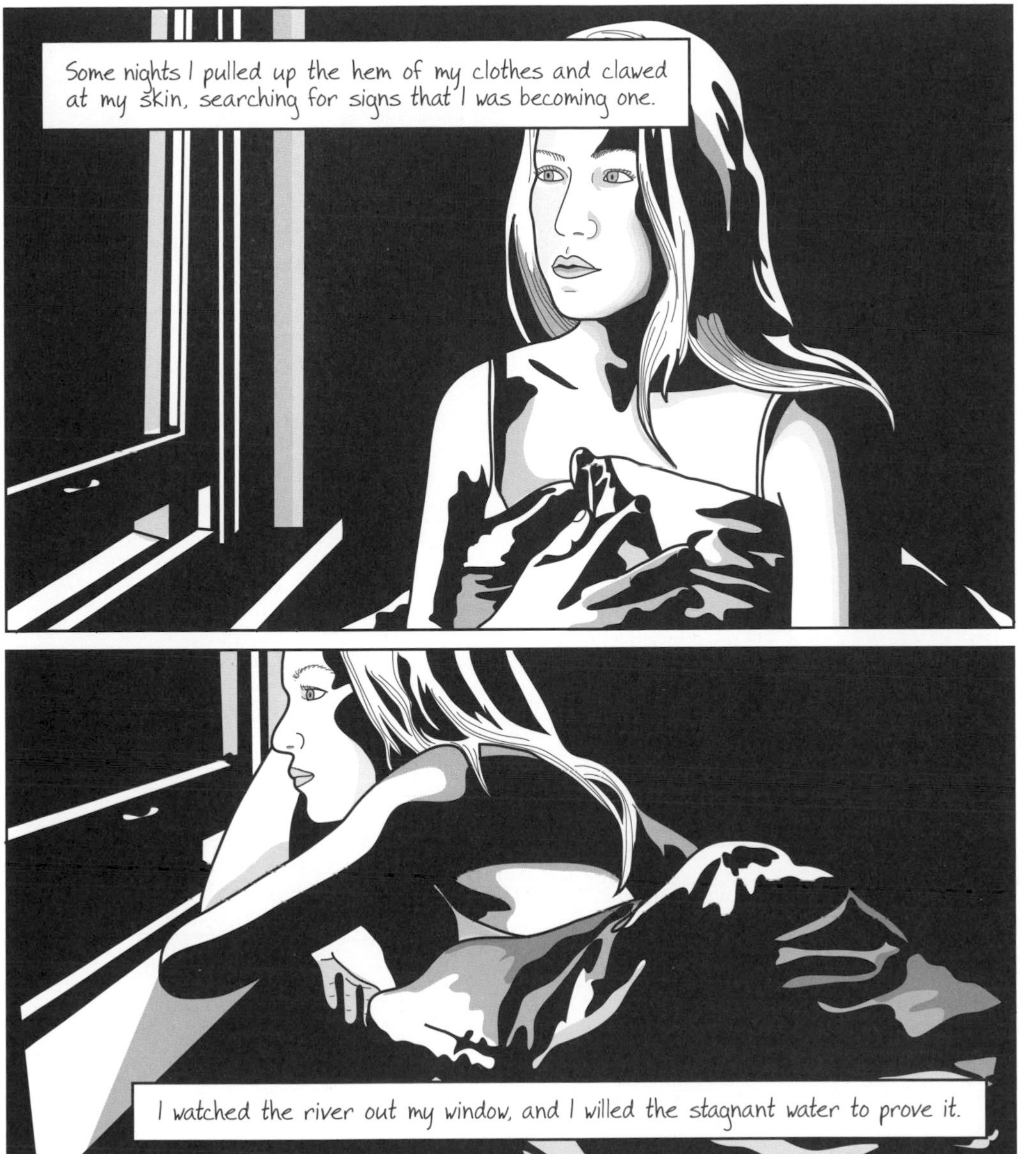
Some nights I pulled up the hem of my clothes and clawed at my skin, searching for signs that I was becoming one.
I watched the river out my window, and I willed the stagnant water to prove it.

# Chapter 4

Every few months I found myself looking again into the inscrutable heart defect that threaded through my family.

*Background* — Dilated cardiomyopathy is a form of heart muscle disease characterized by impaired systolic function and ventricular dilation. Familial transmission of the disease is frequently observed, and genetic heterogeneity is indicated by clinical and morphological variability in the disease phenotype. In the family MDDC1 reported here, the disease phenotype is severe and characterized by an autosomal dominant pattern of transmission. In addition, the majority of affected family members show signs of mild skeletal muscle involvement.

*Methods and Results* — On the basis of the clinical observation of both cardiac and skeletal muscle abnormalities in the MDDC1 family, the lamin A/C gene was examined in this kindred.

In the four years since Uncle Dan's death, everyone had begun enacting the natural progression of moving on.

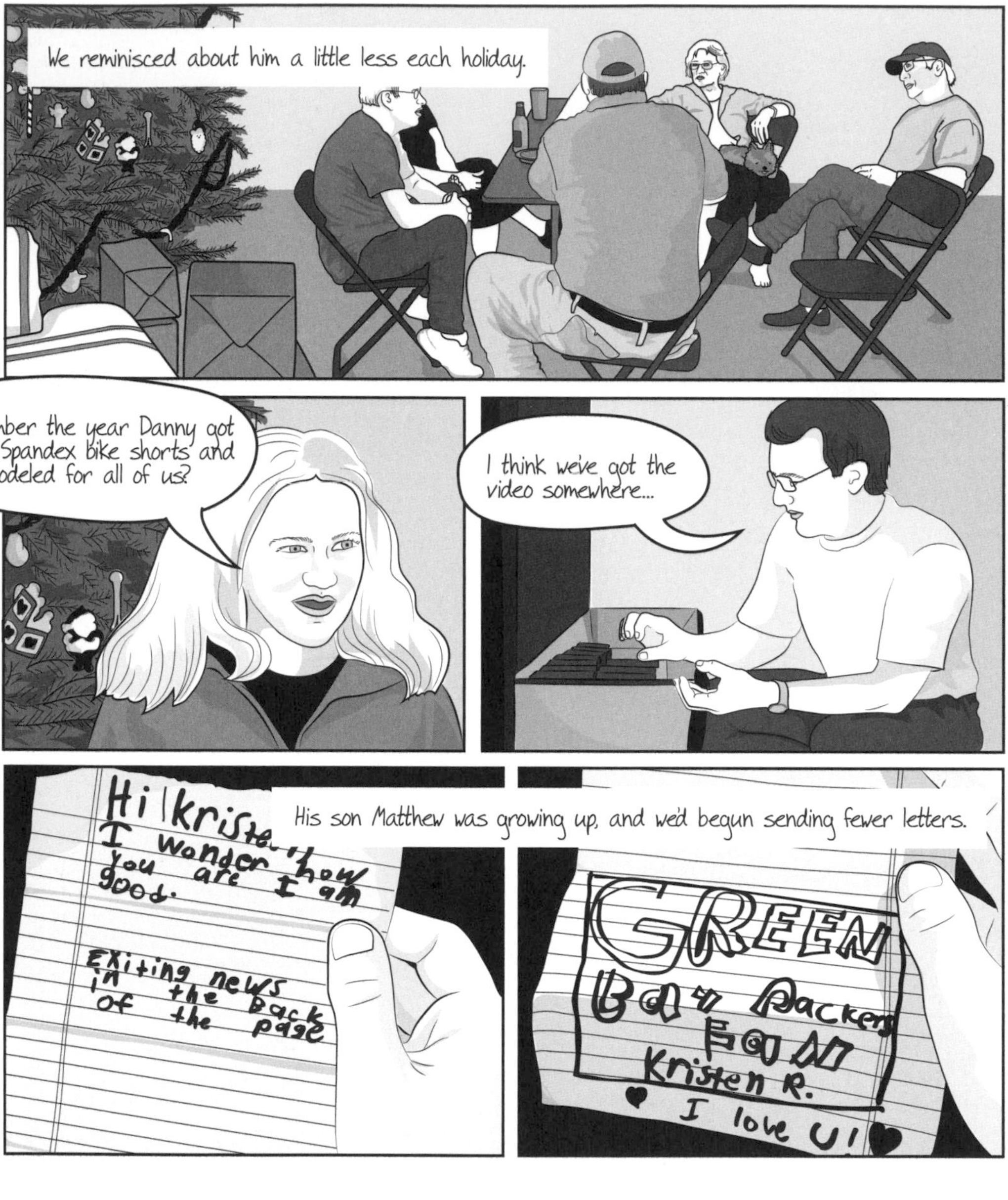
We reminisced about him a little less each holiday.
Remember the year Danny got those Spandex bike shorts and modeled for all of us?
I think we've got the video somewhere...
His son Matthew was growing up, and we'd begun sending fewer letters.
Hi! kristen, I wonder how you are I am good.
Exiting news in the back of the page
GREEN Bay Packers Fan Kristen R.
I love U!

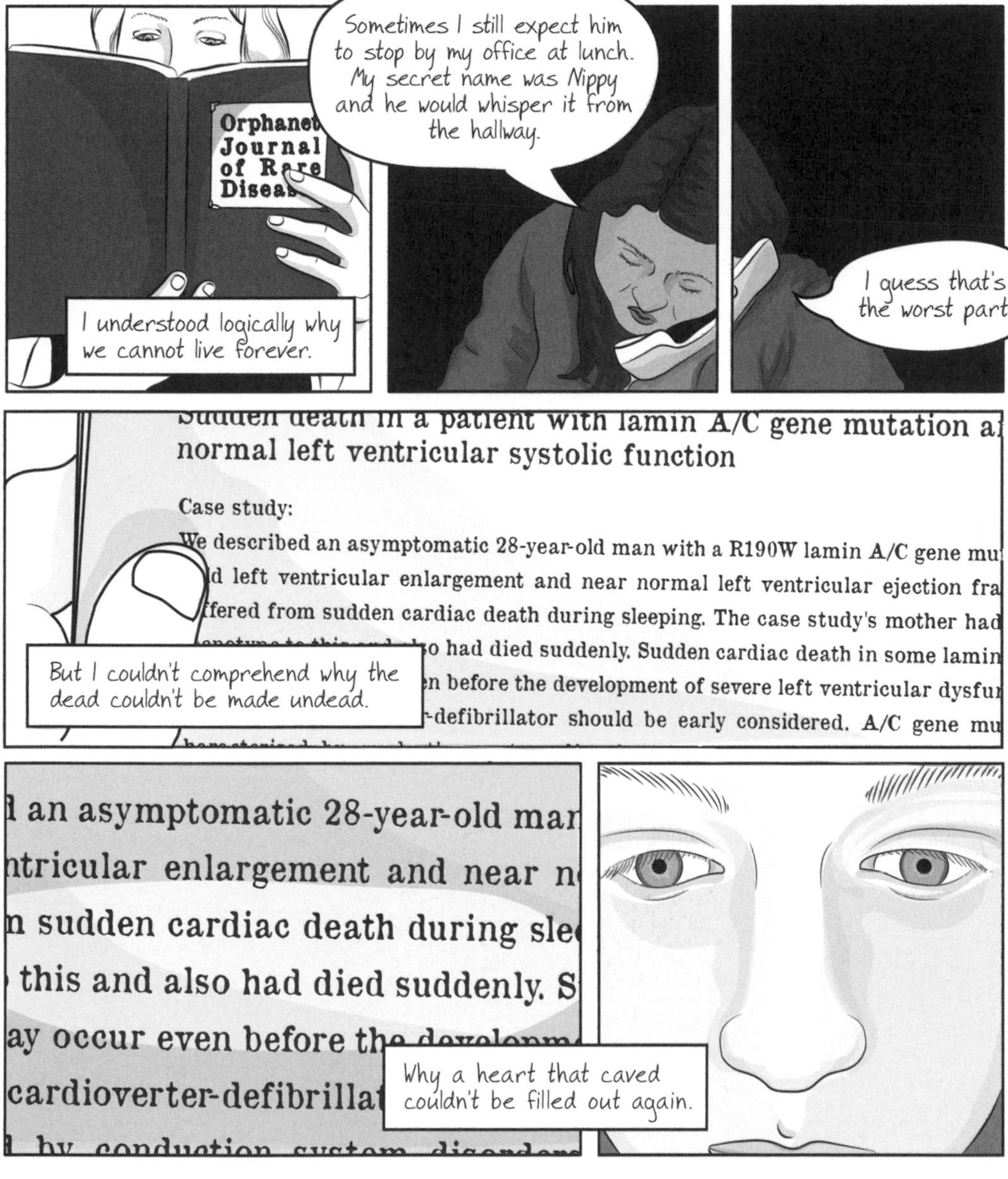
Orphanet Journal of Rare
I understood logically why we cannot live forever.
Sometimes I still expect him to stop by my office at lunch. My secret name was Nippy and he would whisper it from the hallway.
I guess that's the worst part.
normal left ventricular systolic function
Case study:
But I couldn't comprehend why the dead couldn't be made undead.
Why a heart that caved couldn't be filled out again.

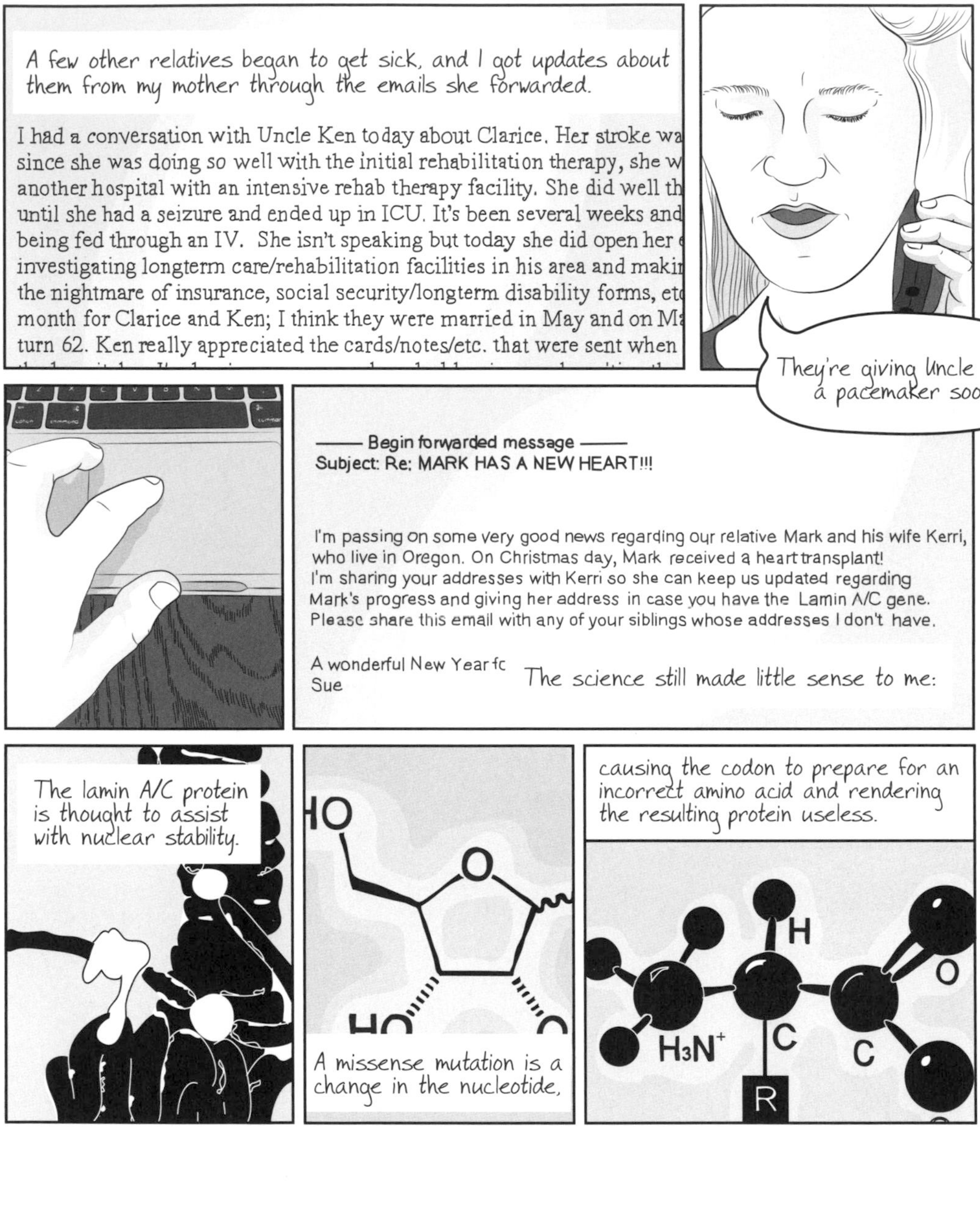

A few other relatives began to get sick, and I got updates about them from my mother through the emails she forwarded.

I had a conversation with Uncle Ken today about Clarice. Her stroke wa[s] since she was doing so well with the initial rehabilitation therapy, she w[ent to] another hospital with an intensive rehab therapy facility. She did well th[ere] until she had a seizure and ended up in ICU. It's been several weeks and [she's] being fed through an IV. She isn't speaking but today she did open her e[yes.] investigating longterm care/rehabilitation facilities in his area and makin[g] the nightmare of insurance, social security/longterm disability forms, etc[.] month for Clarice and Ken; I think they were married in May and on Ma[y] turn 62. Ken really appreciated the cards/notes/etc. that were sent when [...]

They're giving Uncle Roger a pacemaker soon...

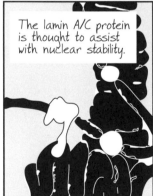

———— Begin forwarded message ————
Subject: Re: MARK HAS A NEW HEART!!!

I'm passing on some very good news regarding our relative Mark and his wife Kerri, who live in Oregon. On Christmas day, Mark received a heart transplant! I'm sharing your addresses with Kerri so she can keep us updated regarding Mark's progress and giving her address in case you have the Lamin A/C gene. Please share this email with any of your siblings whose addresses I don't have.

A wonderful New Year fo[r]
Sue

The science still made little sense to me:

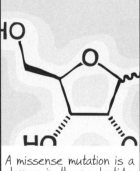

The lamin A/C protein is thought to assist with nuclear stability.

A missense mutation is a change in the nucleotide,

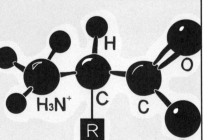

causing the codon to prepare for an incorrect amino acid and rendering the resulting protein useless.

$H_3N^+$

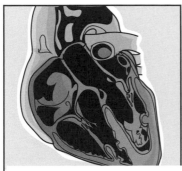  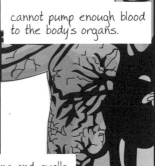

cannot pump enough blood to the body's organs.

When the mutation leads to dilated cardiomyopathy the heart weakens and swells,

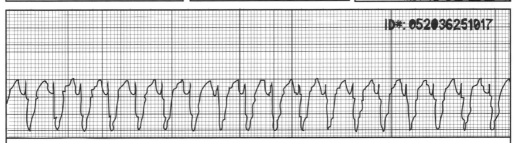

ID#: 052036251017

Ventricular tachycardia roots itself in a ventricle, speeding up its rhythm, causing it to quiver rather than contract. It misfires, moving nothing or not enough.

Hello, I'm trying to get in touch with a Dr. Keating about his paper on the lamin A/C gene?

If you're a current patient, I can take a message.

Hi, may I please speak with Dr. Vanderbeek?

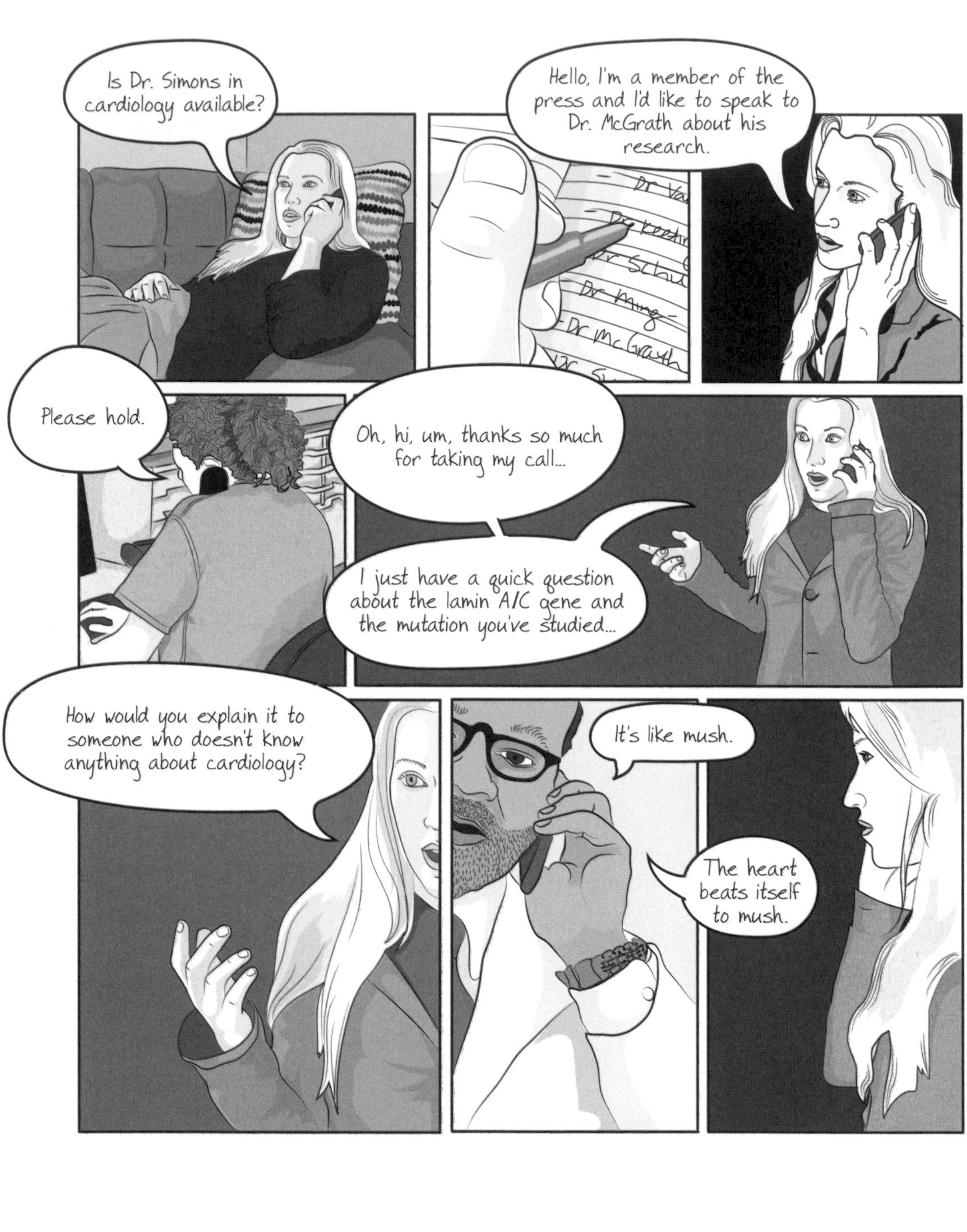

Is Dr. Simons in cardiology available?
Hello, I'm a member of the press and I'd like to speak to Dr. McGrath about his research.
Dr McGrath
Please hold.
Oh, hi, um, thanks so much for taking my call...
I just have a quick question about the lamin A/C gene and the mutation you've studied...
How would you explain it to someone who doesn't know anything about cardiology?
It's like mush.
The heart beats itself to mush.

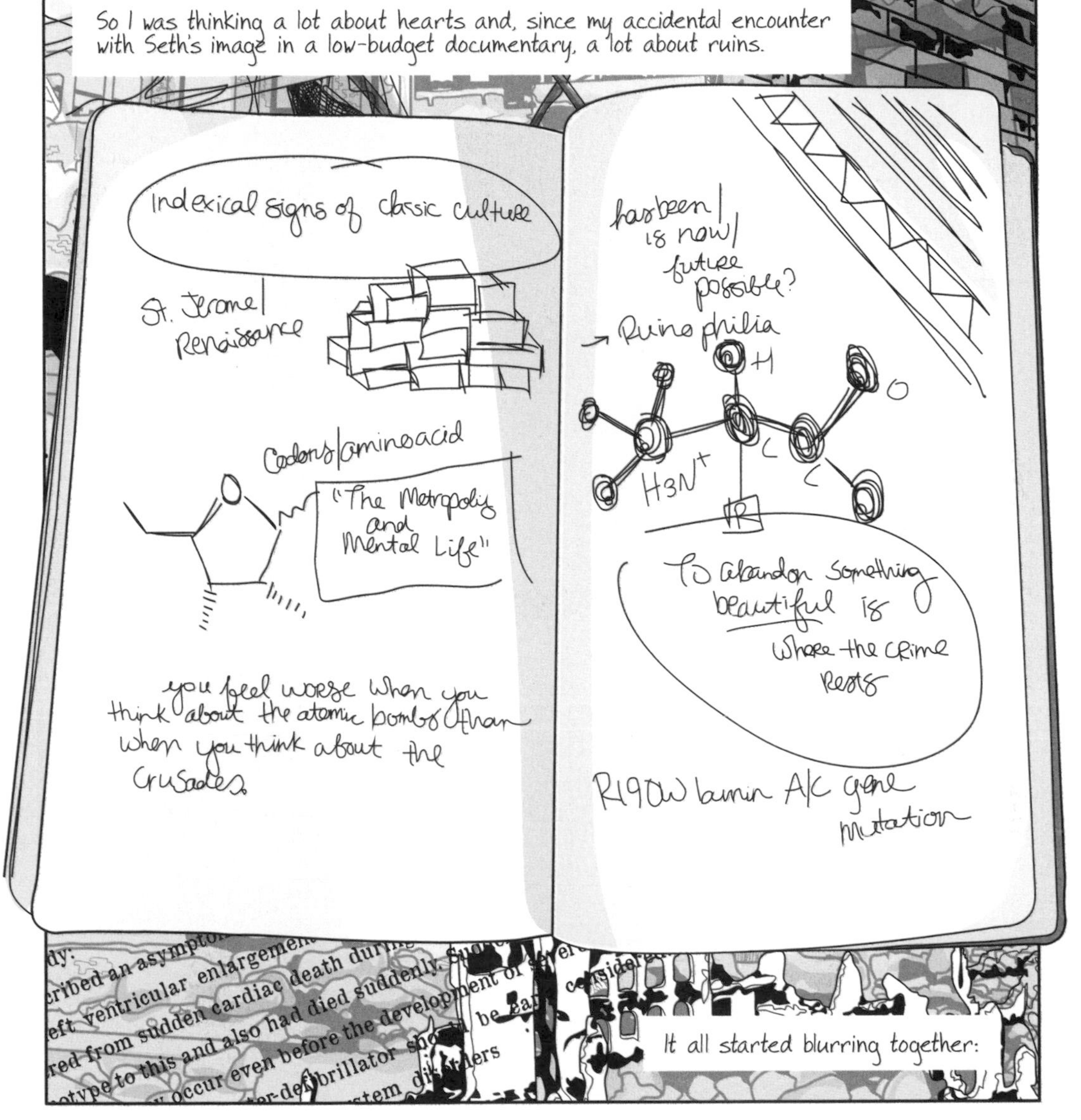
So I was thinking a lot about hearts and, since my accidental encounter with Seth's image in a low-budget documentary, a lot about ruins.
Indexical signs of classic culture
St. Jerome/ Renaissance
Codons/aminoacid
"The Metropolis and Mental Life"
you feel worse when you think about the atomic bombs than when you think about the crusades.
has been/ is now/ future possible?
→ Ruinophilia
H
O
H3N+
C
C
R
To abandon something beautiful is where the crime rests
R190W lamin A/C gene mutation
It all started blurring together:

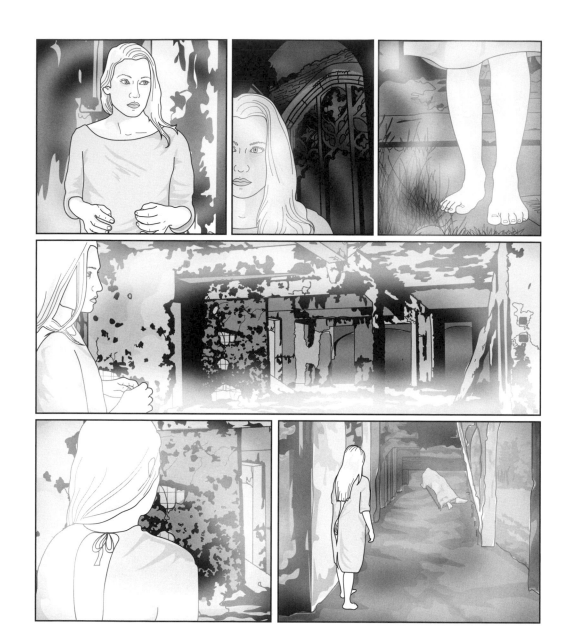

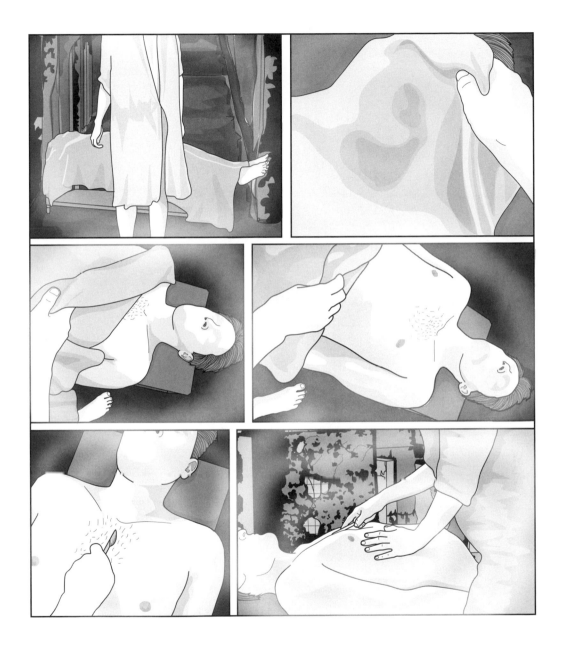

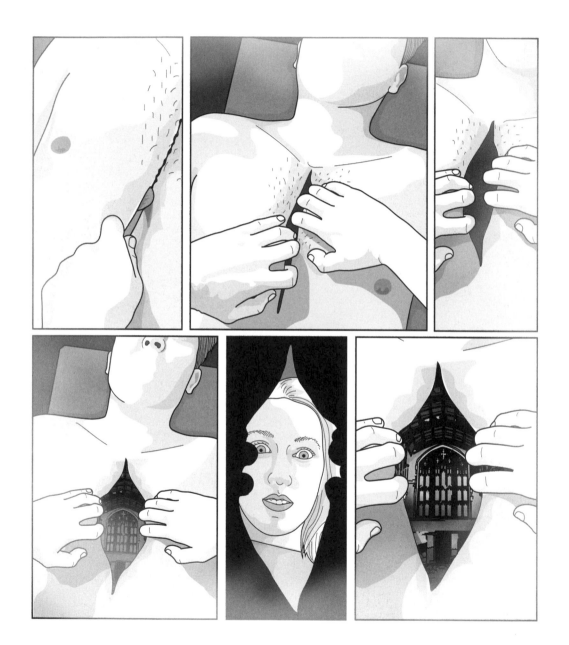

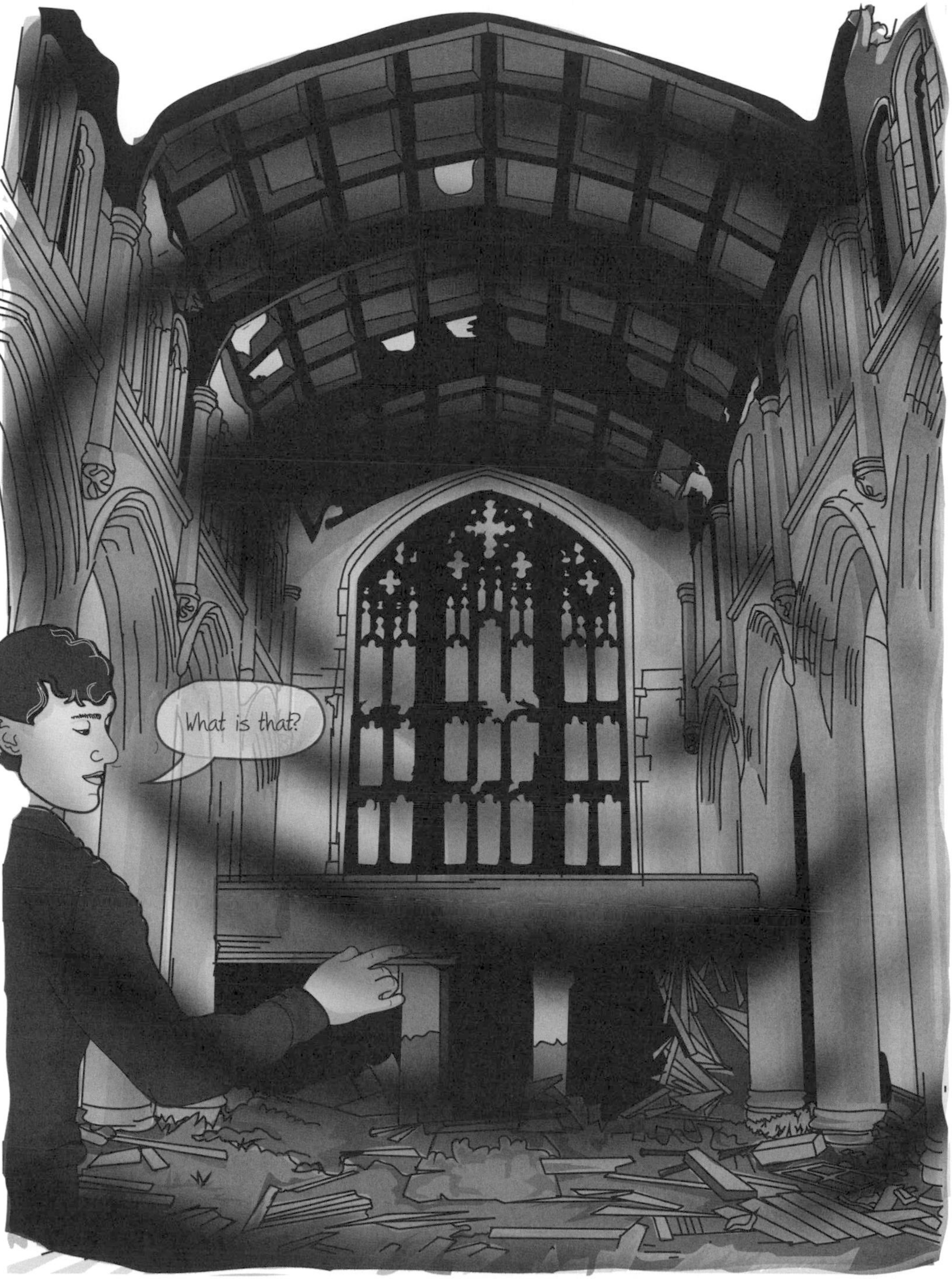
What is that?

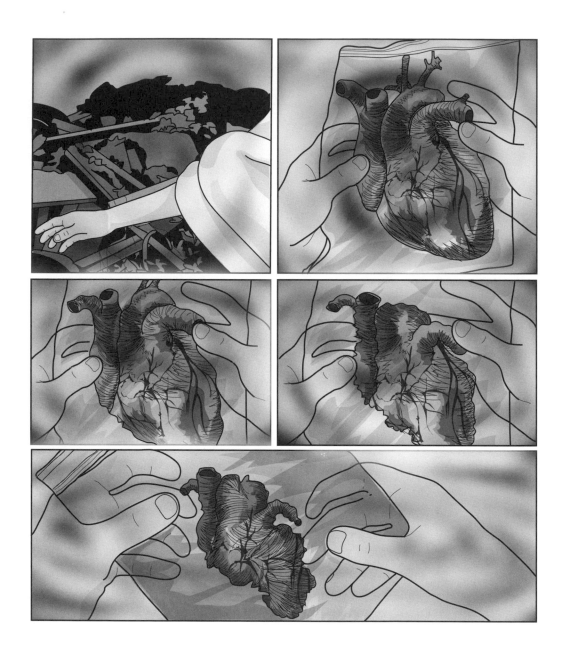

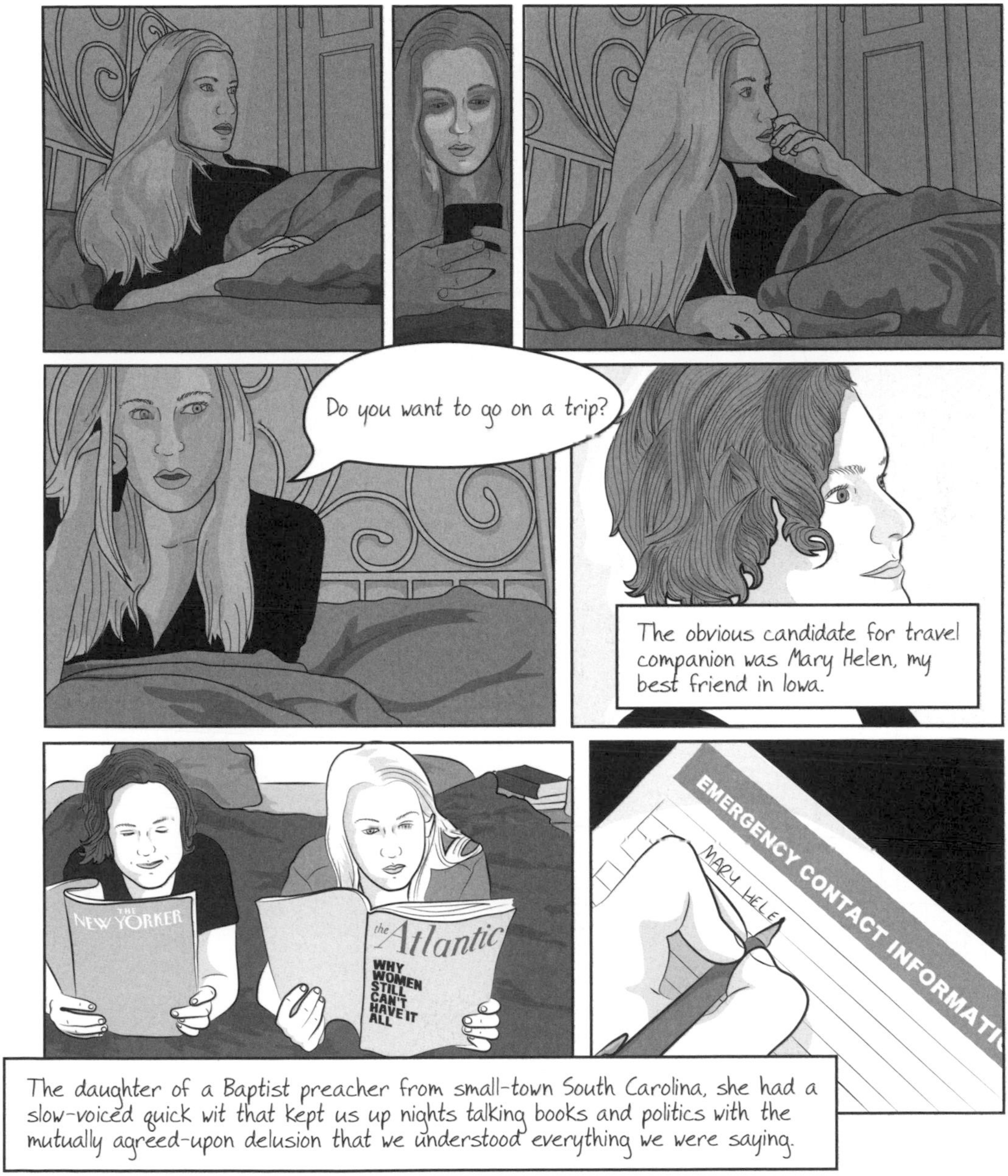
Do you want to go on a trip?
The obvious candidate for travel companion was Mary Helen, my best friend in Iowa.
THE NEW YORKER
the Atlantic
WHY WOMEN STILL CAN'T HAVE IT ALL
EMERGENCY CONTACT INFORMATI
MARY HELE
The daughter of a Baptist preacher from small-town South Carolina, she had a slow-voiced quick wit that kept us up nights talking books and politics with the mutually agreed-upon delusion that we understood everything we were saying.

Okay, so if we write a proposal we can get some funding from school.

| Traveler | | | eTicket Number | Frequ |
| ADTKE/KRISTENMS | | | 0052174721494 | |

FLIGHT INFORMATION
Day, Date

| Wed, 11MAY11 | CO6670² | W | CHICAGO OHARE (ORD) **8:05AM** | SAN F (SFO) |
| Wed, 11MAY11 | CO6019³ | L | SAN FRANCISCO (SFO) **12:40PM** | HONG (HKG) |
| Wed, 06JUL11 | CO6034⁴ | V | HONG KONG (HKG) **11:50AM** | CHICA (ORD) |

The goal was to see as many countries as possible and be away from home for as long as we could.

It felt like I had to see <u>everything</u>, as if it was the only way my life would count or matter. I didn't care where we were going as long as it was someplace new.

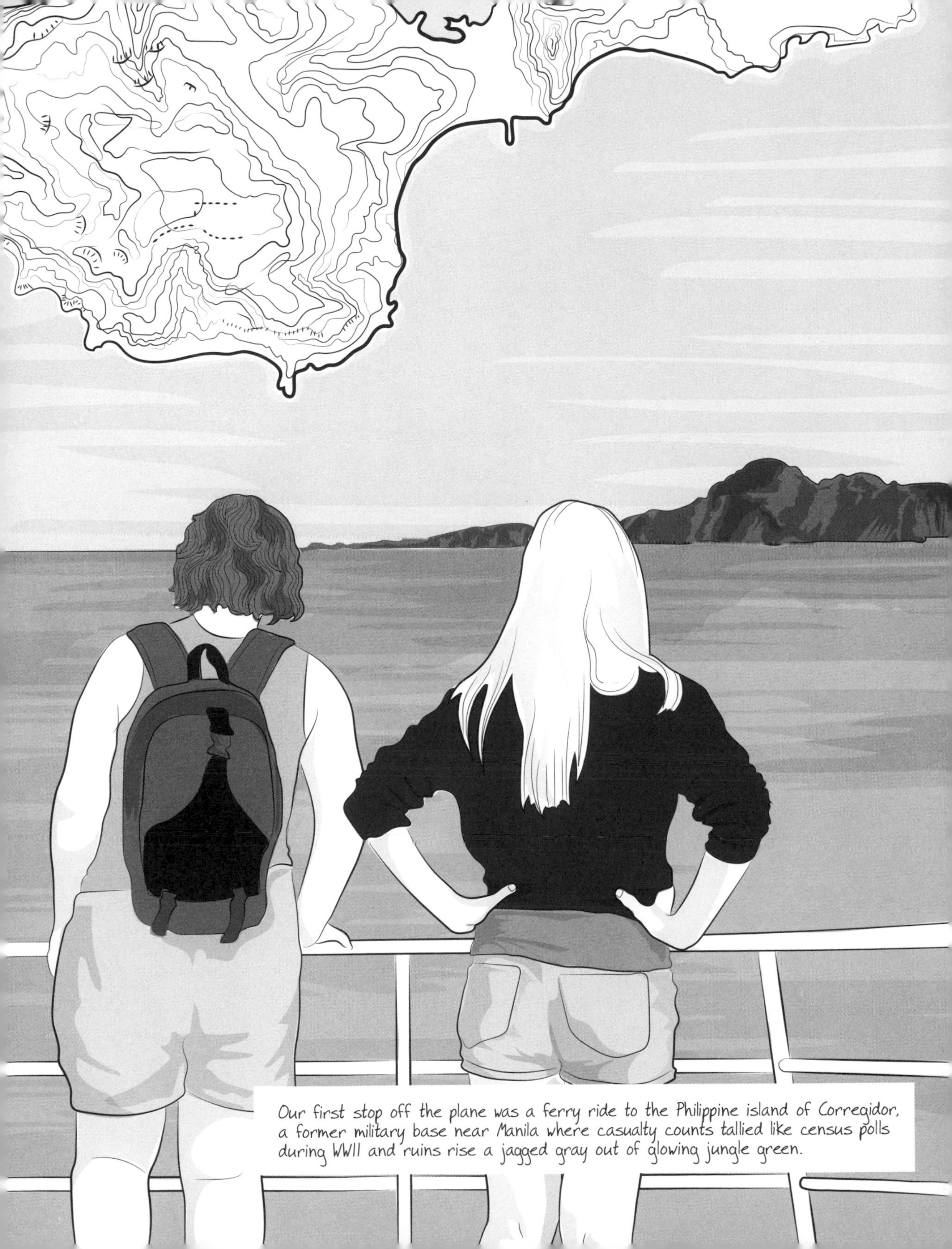
Our first stop off the plane was a ferry ride to the Philippine island of Corregidor, a former military base near Manila where casualty counts tallied like census polls during WWII and ruins rise a jagged gray out of glowing jungle green.

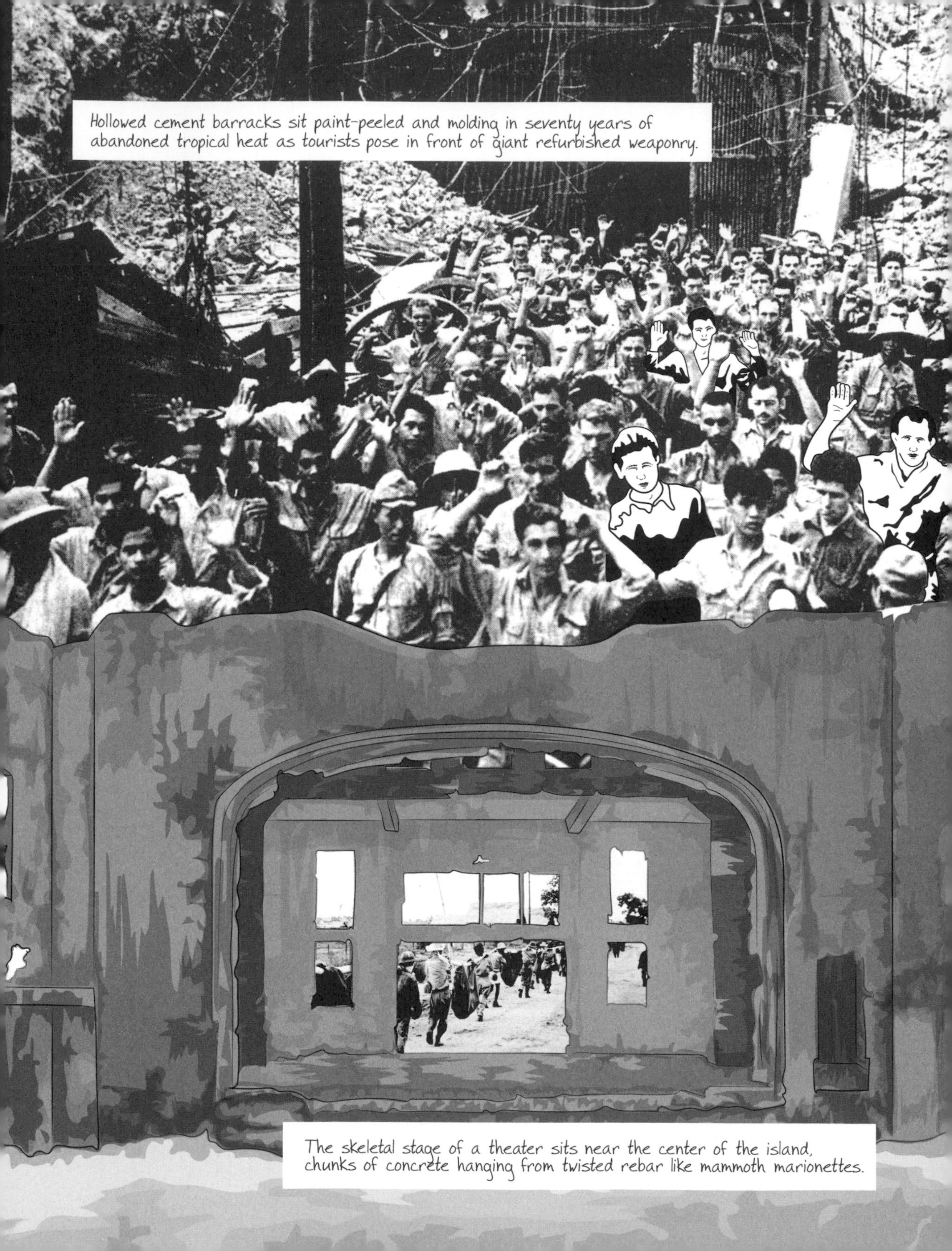
Hollowed cement barracks sit paint-peeled and molding in seventy years of abandoned tropical heat as tourists pose in front of giant refurbished weaponry.
The skeletal stage of a theater sits near the center of the island, chunks of concrete hanging from twisted rebar like mammoth marionettes.

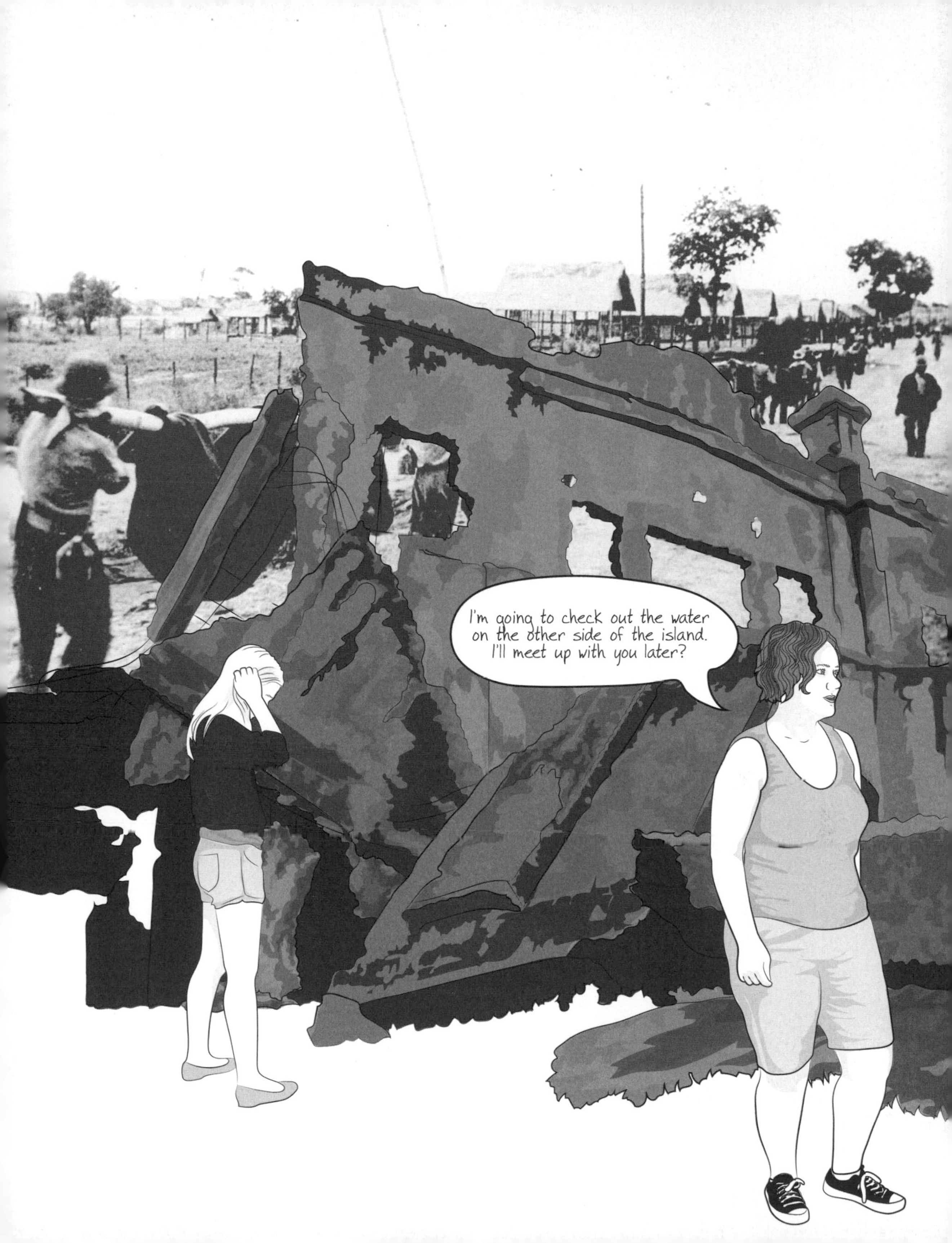
I'm going to check out the water on the other side of the island. I'll meet up with you later?

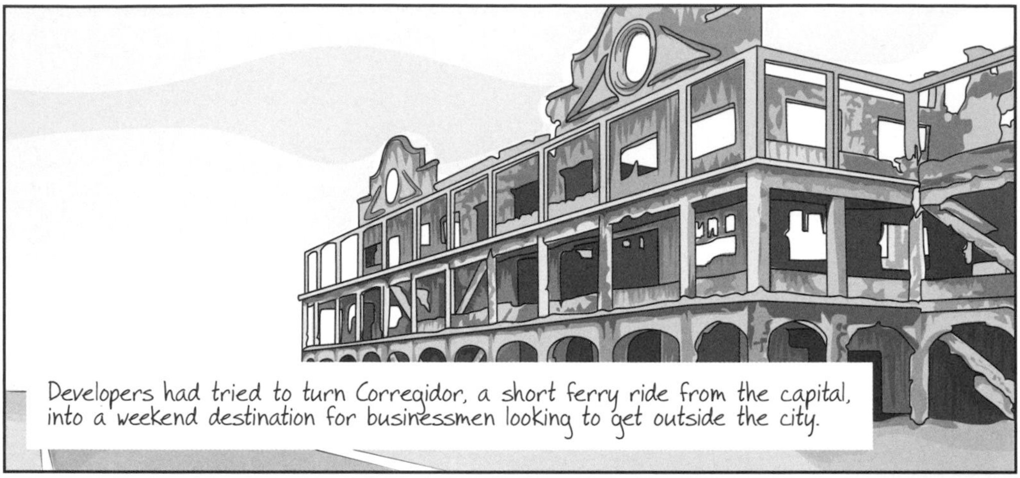
Developers had tried to turn Corregidor, a short ferry ride from the capital, into a weekend destination for businessmen looking to get outside the city.

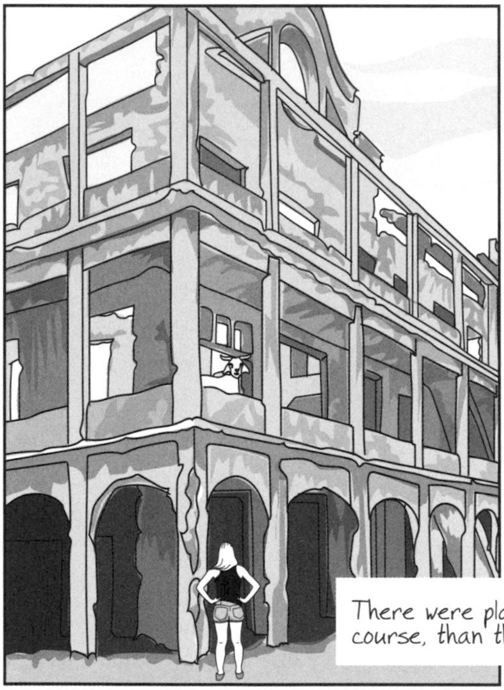

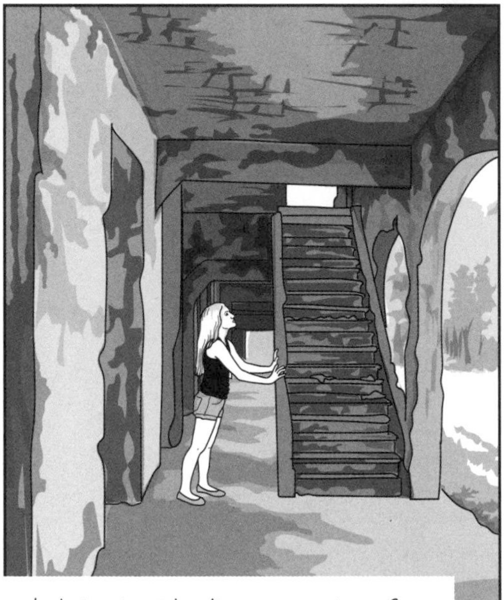
There were plans to bring in girls. More expensive, of course, than those across the bay in Manila, but worth it.

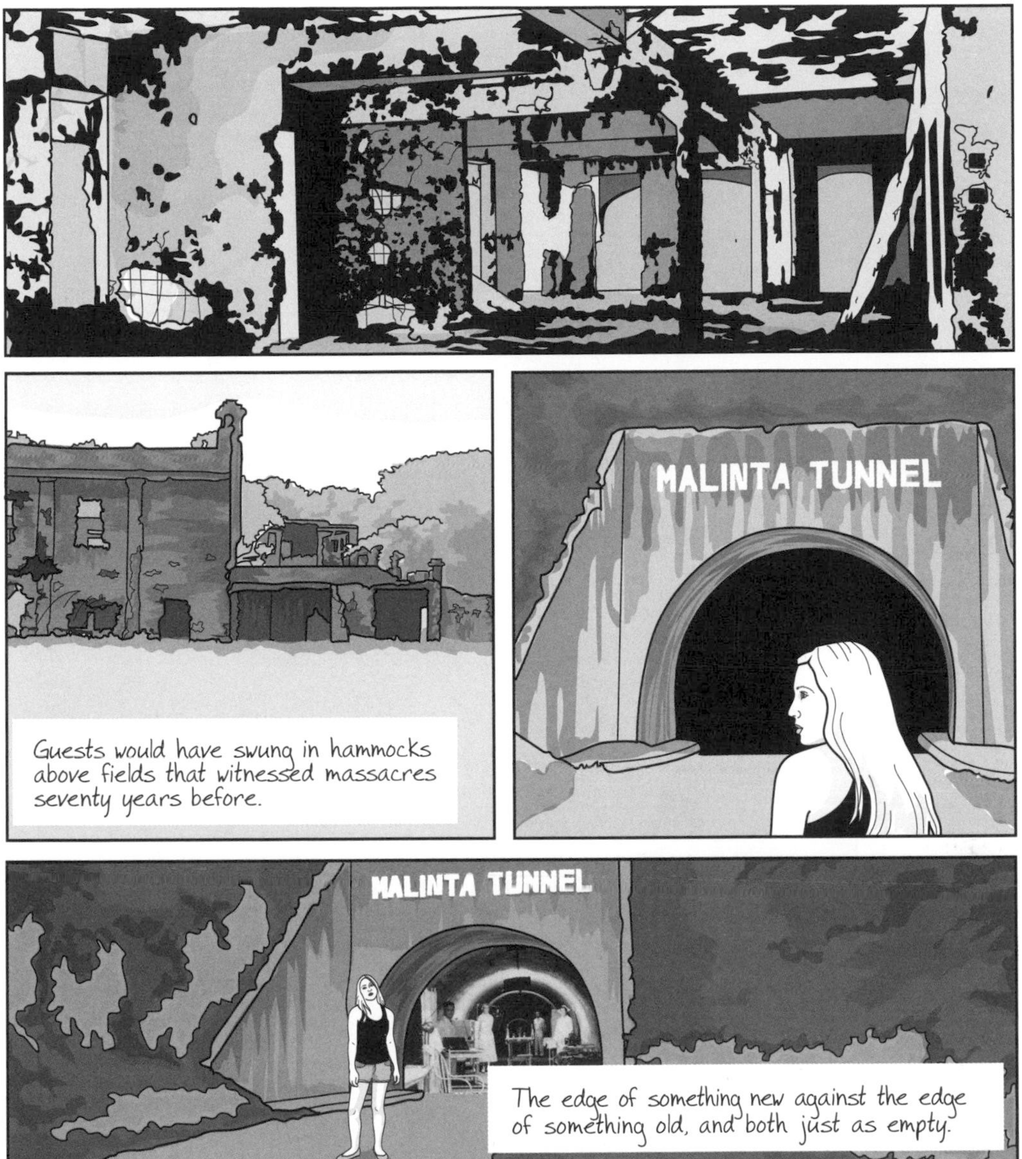
Guests would have swung in hammocks above fields that witnessed massacres seventy years before.
MALINTA TUNNEL
MALINTA TUNNEL
The edge of something new against the edge of something old, and both just as empty.

The Romantics saw ruins as symbolic of the art that came before them.

Aristocrats commissioned faux-collapsing temples across their estate lawns.

The Middle Ages, assumed to be the last before Christ's second coming, watched ruin as ominous reminders of more decay ahead.

Shakespeare, certainly, set many plays among them, and aging Greco-Roman statues litter the edges of Renaissance paintings by Roberti and Bellini.

When Lord Belvedere's wife moved in with his brother, Belvedere built a ruined monastery to obstruct the view of his failed marriage.

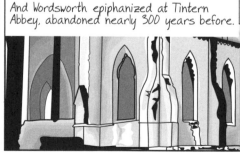

And Wordsworth epiphanized at Tintern Abbey, abandoned nearly 300 years before.

When a boy fell through a soft patch of dirt on the Esquiline hillside at the close of the 1600s, he accidentally discovered Emperor Nero's Domus Aurea, which successors had built on top of after Nero's suicide.

Raphael and Michelangelo were among those who crawled down to carve their names into the ancient Roman walls.

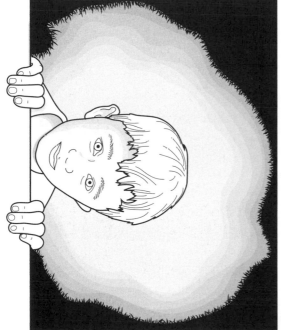

CASANOVA

MARQUIS DE SADE

DOMENICO GHIRLANDAIO

FILIPPINO LIPPI

And when archeologists began to uncover what'd been preserved for centuries in the underground's dampness, they put into motion the villa's slow decay.

Sociologist Georg Simmel saw ruins as representations of failing social structures and moral codes.

Rose Macaulay wrote of "ruin lust," chronicling a European fascination throughout the eighteenth and nineteenth centuries.

But in the 1940s, there was something distinctly less pleasing, she thought, about structures pulled apart by war.

Artist and scholar Svetlana Boym named this obsession "ruinophilia."

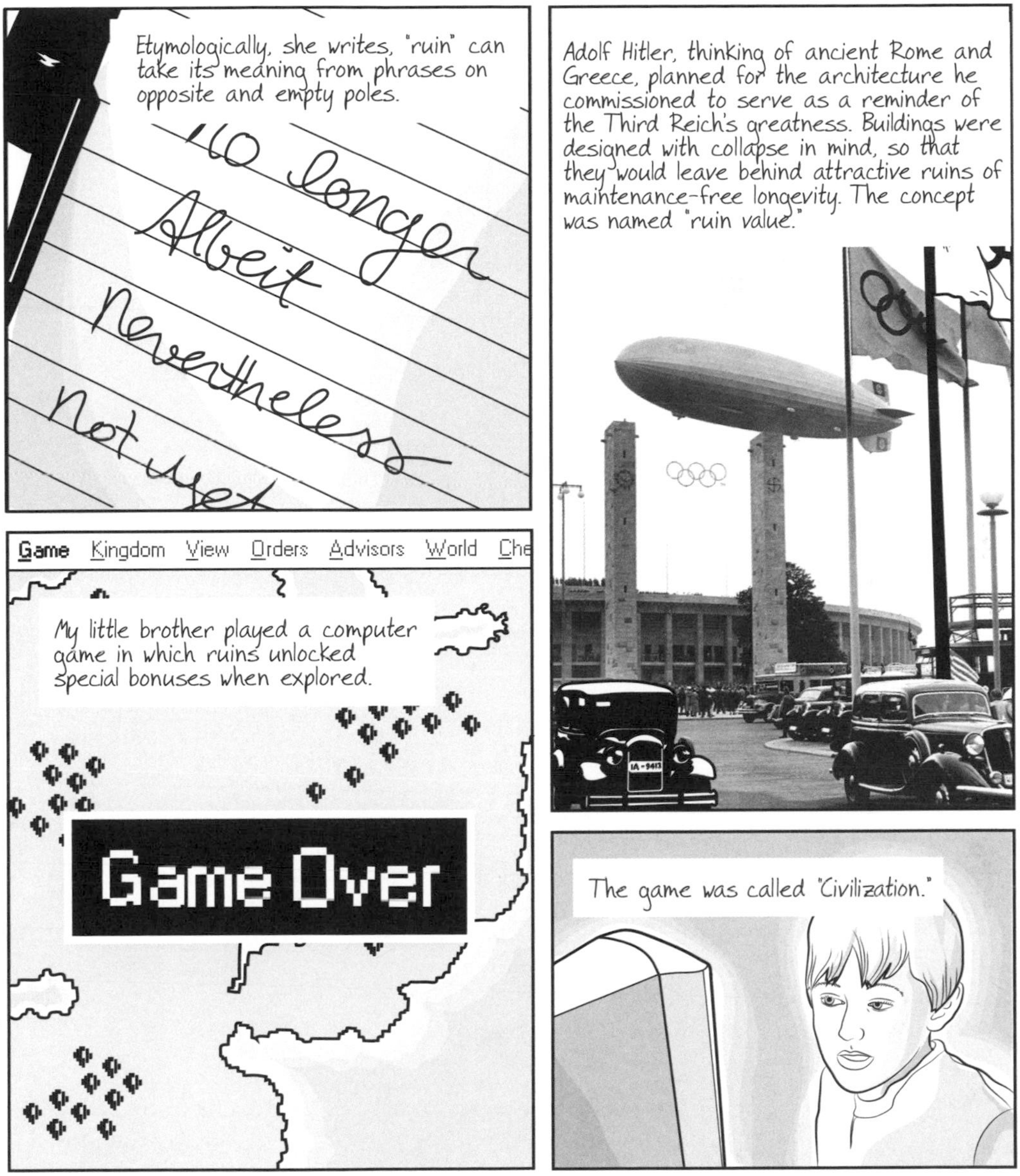
Etymologically, she writes, "ruin" can take its meaning from phrases on opposite and empty poles.
no longer
Albeit
Nevertheless
Not yet
Adolf Hitler, thinking of ancient Rome and Greece, planned for the architecture he commissioned to serve as a reminder of the Third Reich's greatness. Buildings were designed with collapse in mind, so that they would leave behind attractive ruins of maintenance-free longevity. The concept was named "ruin value."
Game Kingdom View Orders Advisors World Che
My little brother played a computer game in which ruins unlocked special bonuses when explored.
Game Over
The game was called "Civilization."

The house next door to my childhood home had column ruin sets in the garden, made of fiberglass and resin.

And at the bottom of my best friend's fish tank was a nearly identical model.

In 2013, Detroit housed over 70,000 abandoned properties.

DESOLATE DETROIT. THE FORSA...

NATIONAL PO...

WOULD THE LAST PERSON OUT DETROIT TURN OUT THE LIGHT...

Detroit's Beautiful, Horrible Decl...

TIME...

Empty art deco skyscrapers and turn-of-the-century train stations queued on street corners before traffic lights that hadn't lit in years.

Critics began naming this coverage "ruin porn."

"Exploitive," some have said. "Voyeuristic."

- **Misleading or falsified historical context.** This trend is common among today's dilettantish new generation of "urban exploration photographers," who display photographs of buildings - or even sets of photos from various buildings - under false names, with either absent or misleading contextual information. This exploits the genuine histories of real places, and also exploits the viewer's sensibilities.

(Ian Ference, <u>The Huffington Post</u>)

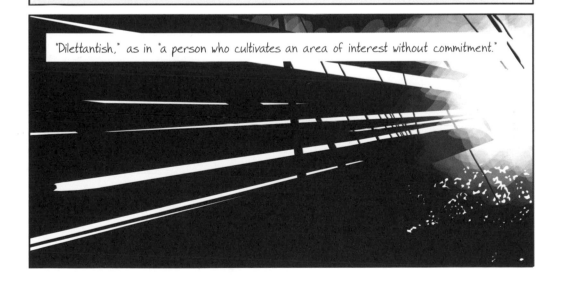

"Dilettantish," as in "a person who cultivates an area of interest without commitment."

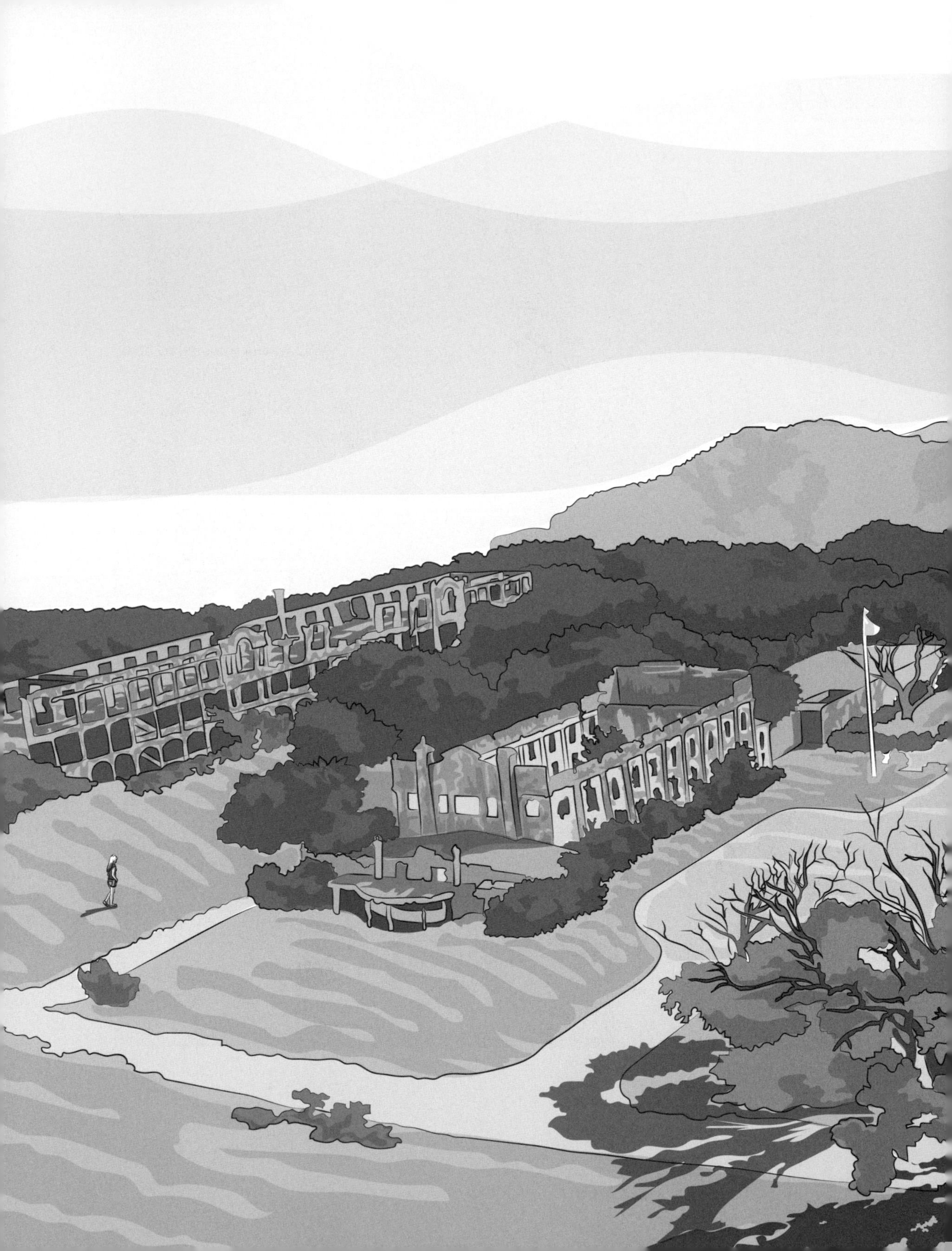

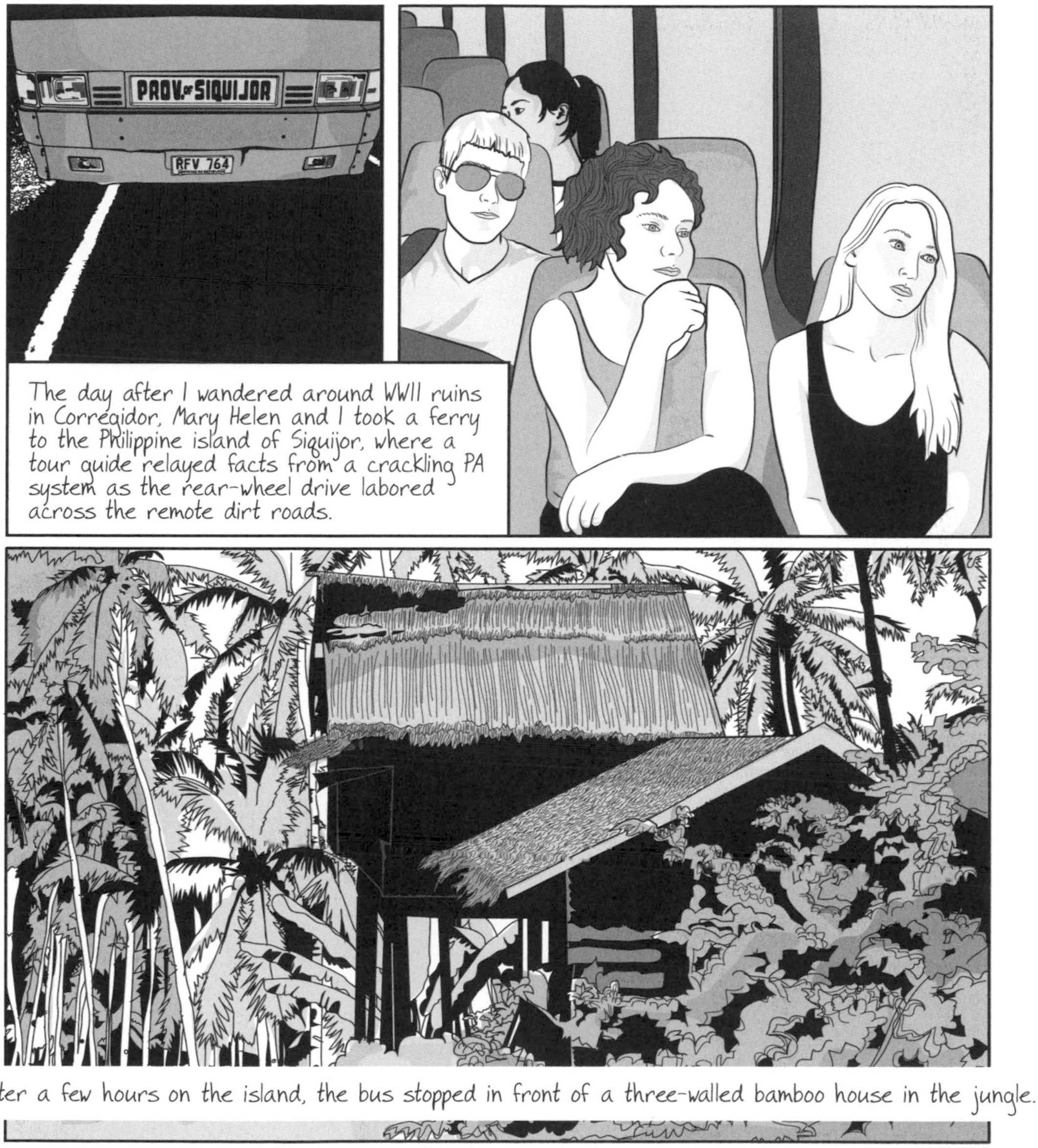
PROV. of SIQUIJOR
RFV 764
The day after I wandered around WWII ruins in Corregidor, Mary Helen and I took a ferry to the Philippine island of Siquijor, where a tour guide relayed facts from a crackling PA system as the rear-wheel drive labored across the remote dirt roads.
After a few hours on the island, the bus stopped in front of a three-walled bamboo house in the jungle.

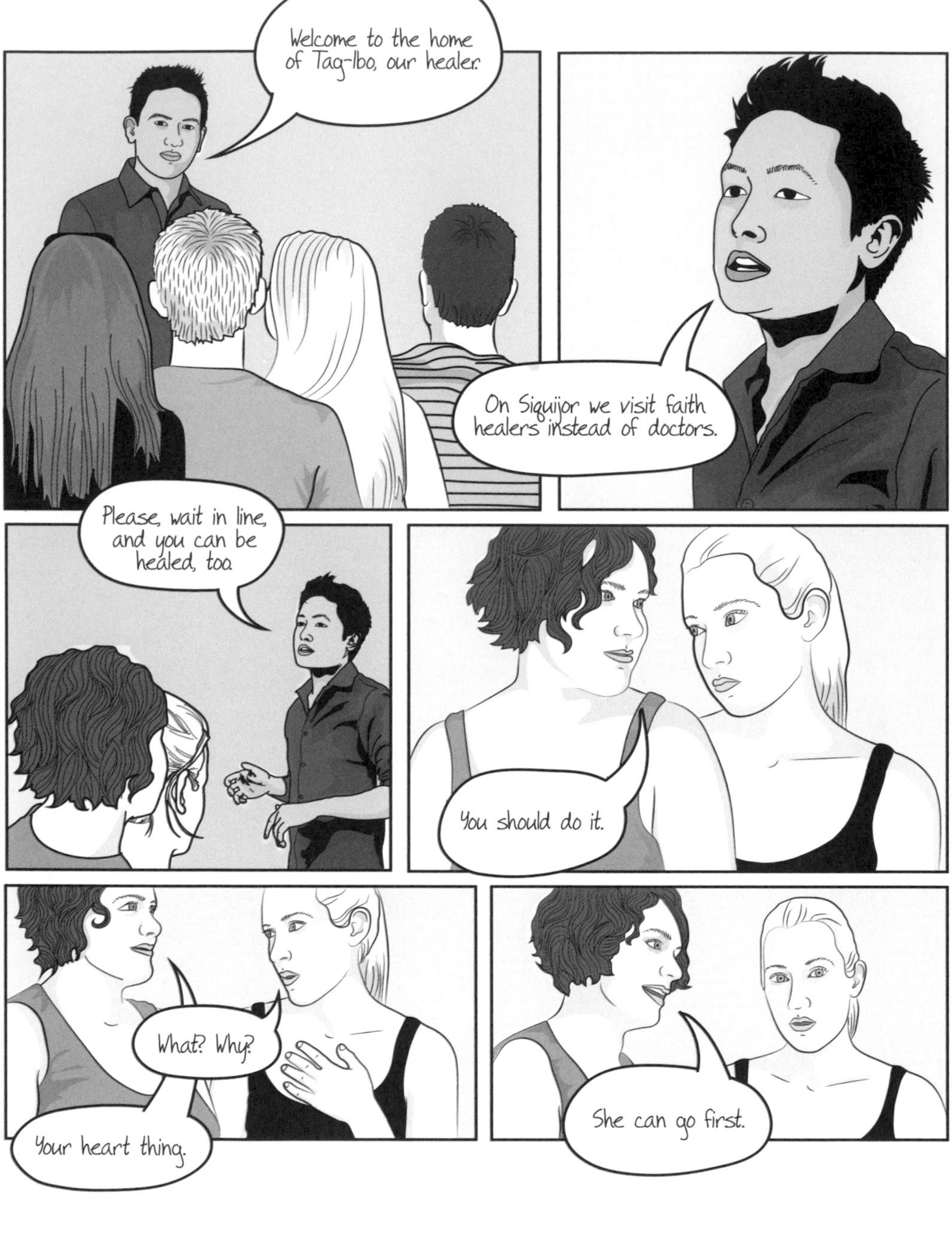
Welcome to the home of Tag-Ibo, our healer.
On Siquijor we visit faith healers instead of doctors.
Please, wait in line, and you can be healed, too.
You should do it.
What? Why?
Your heart thing.
She can go first.

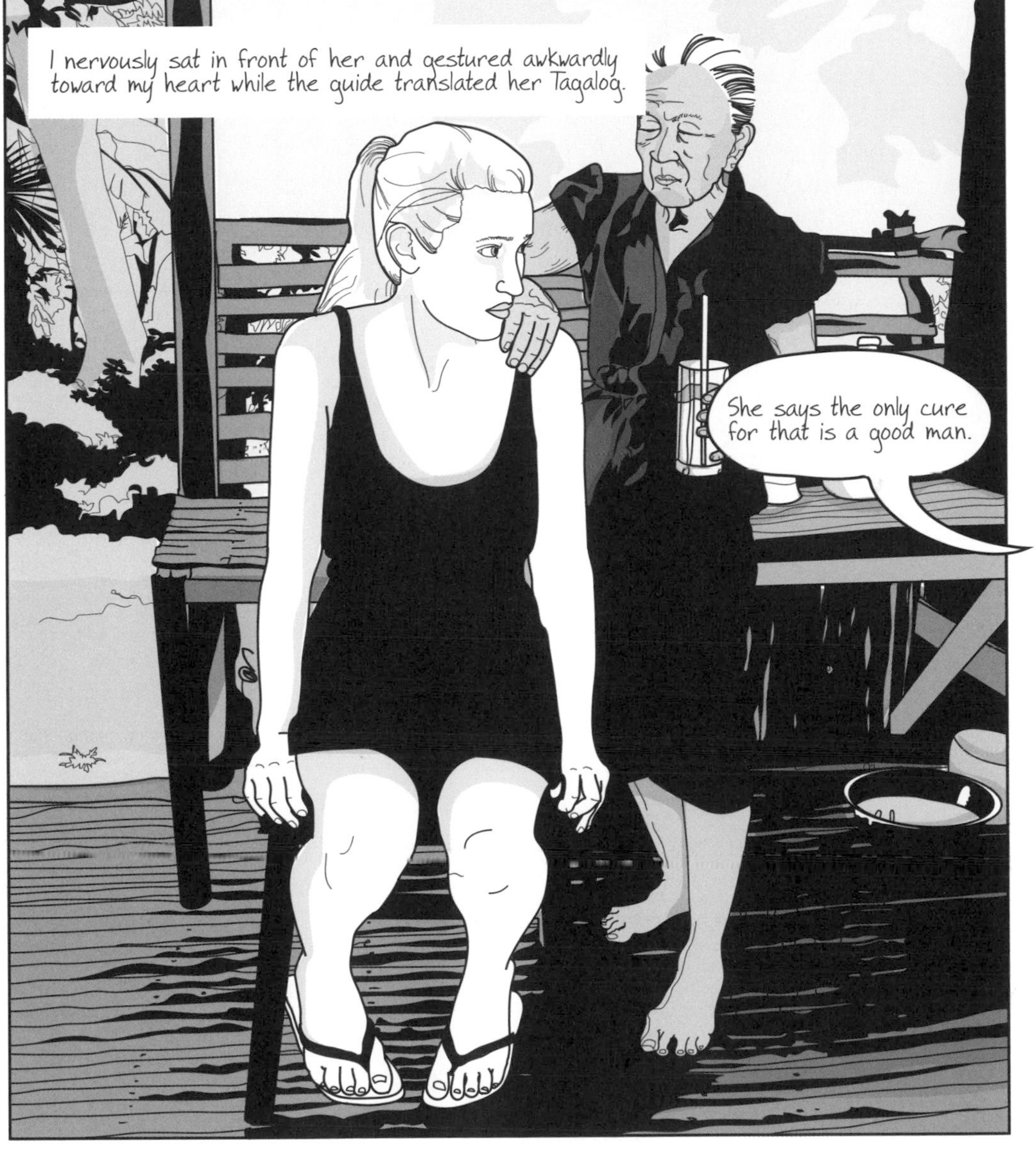
I nervously sat in front of her and gestured awkwardly toward my heart while the guide translated her Tagalog.
She says the only cure for that is a good man.

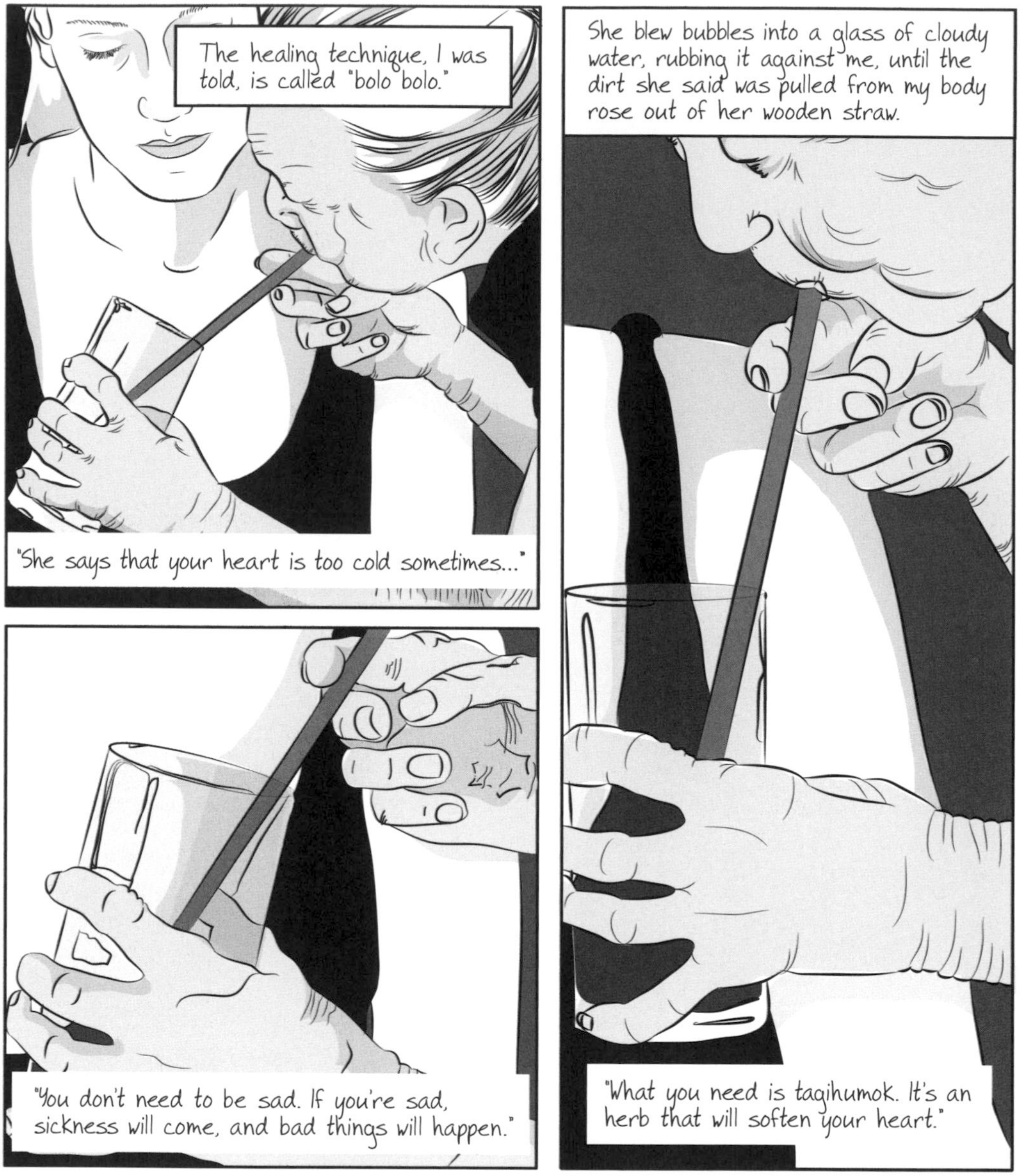
The healing technique, I was told, is called "bolo bolo."
"She says that your heart is too cold sometimes..."
She blew bubbles into a glass of cloudy water, rubbing it against me, until the dirt she said was pulled from my body rose out of her wooden straw.
"You don't need to be sad. If you're sad, sickness will come, and bad things will happen."
"What you need is tagihumok. It's an herb that will soften your heart."

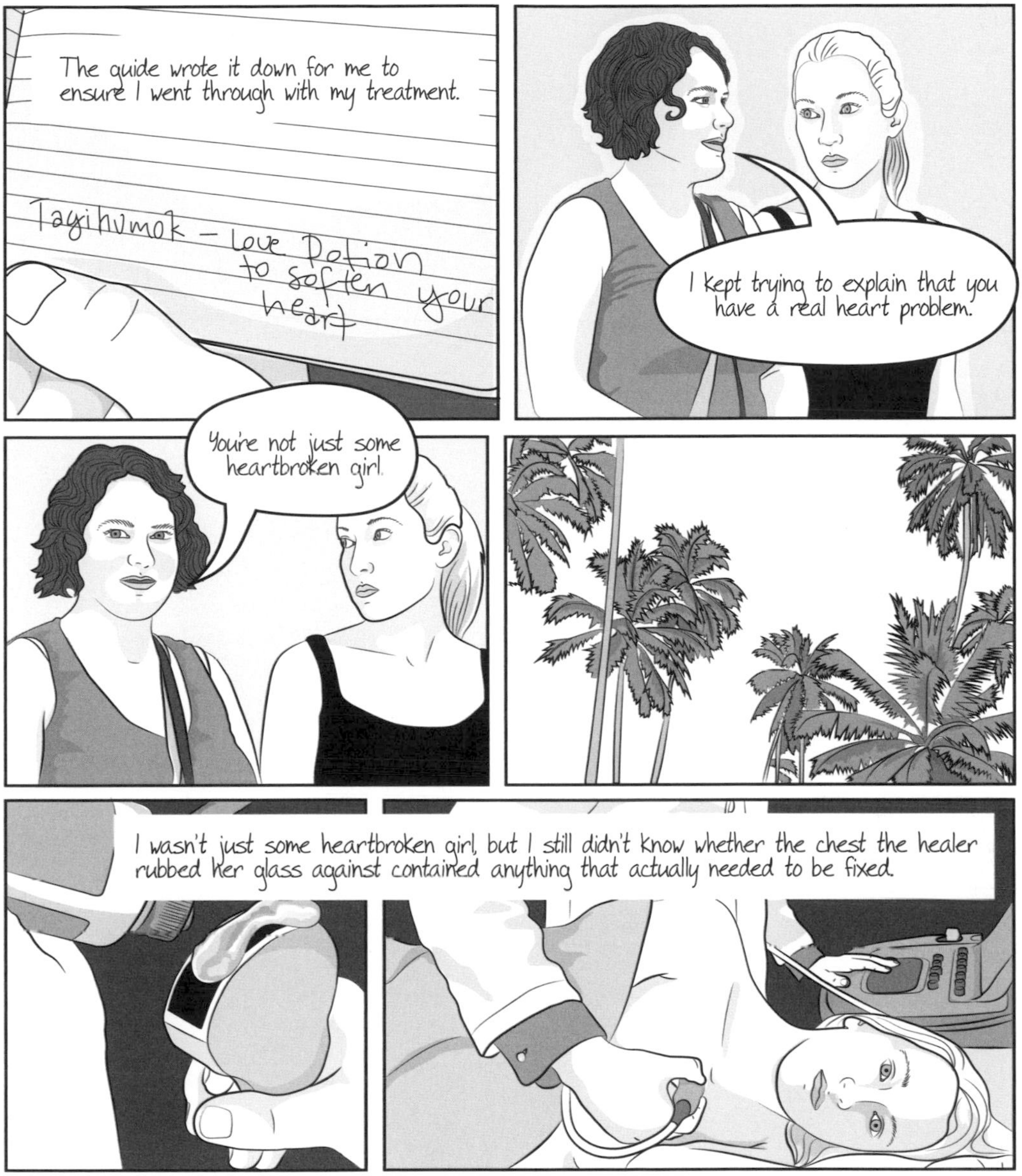
The guide wrote it down for me to ensure I went through with my treatment.
Tagihumok – love Potion to soften your heart
I kept trying to explain that you have a real heart problem.
You're not just some heartbroken girl.
I wasn't just some heartbroken girl, but I still didn't know whether the chest the healer rubbed her glass against contained anything that actually needed to be fixed.

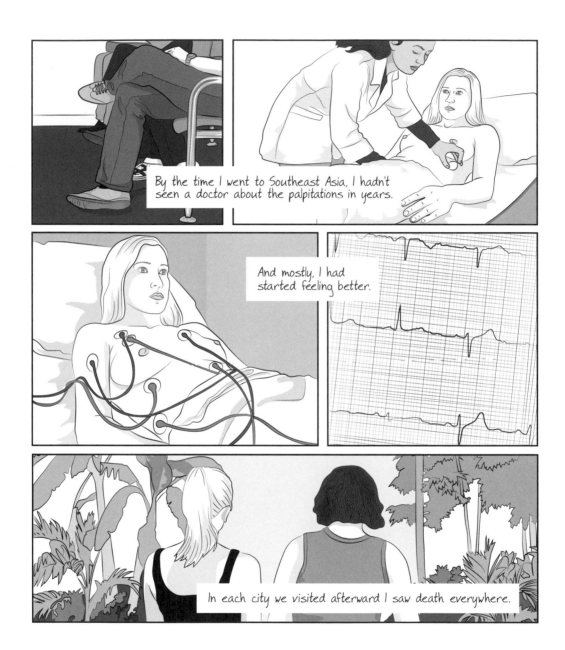

By the time I went to Southeast Asia, I hadn't seen a doctor about the palpitations in years.

And mostly, I had started feeling better.

In each city we visited afterward I saw death everywhere.

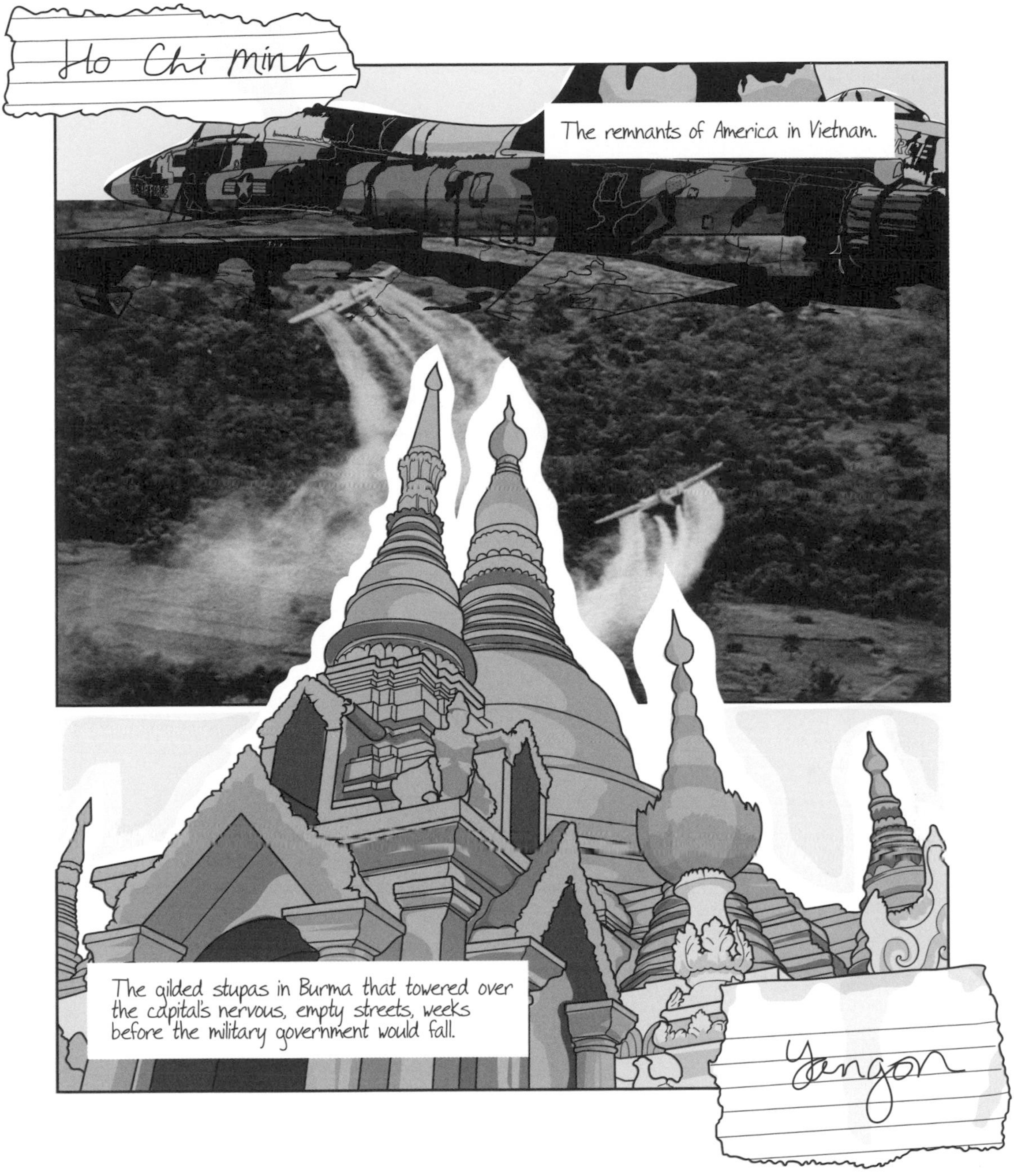
Ho Chi Minh
The remnants of America in Vietnam.
The gilded stupas in Burma that towered over the capital's nervous, empty streets, weeks before the military government would fall.
Yangon

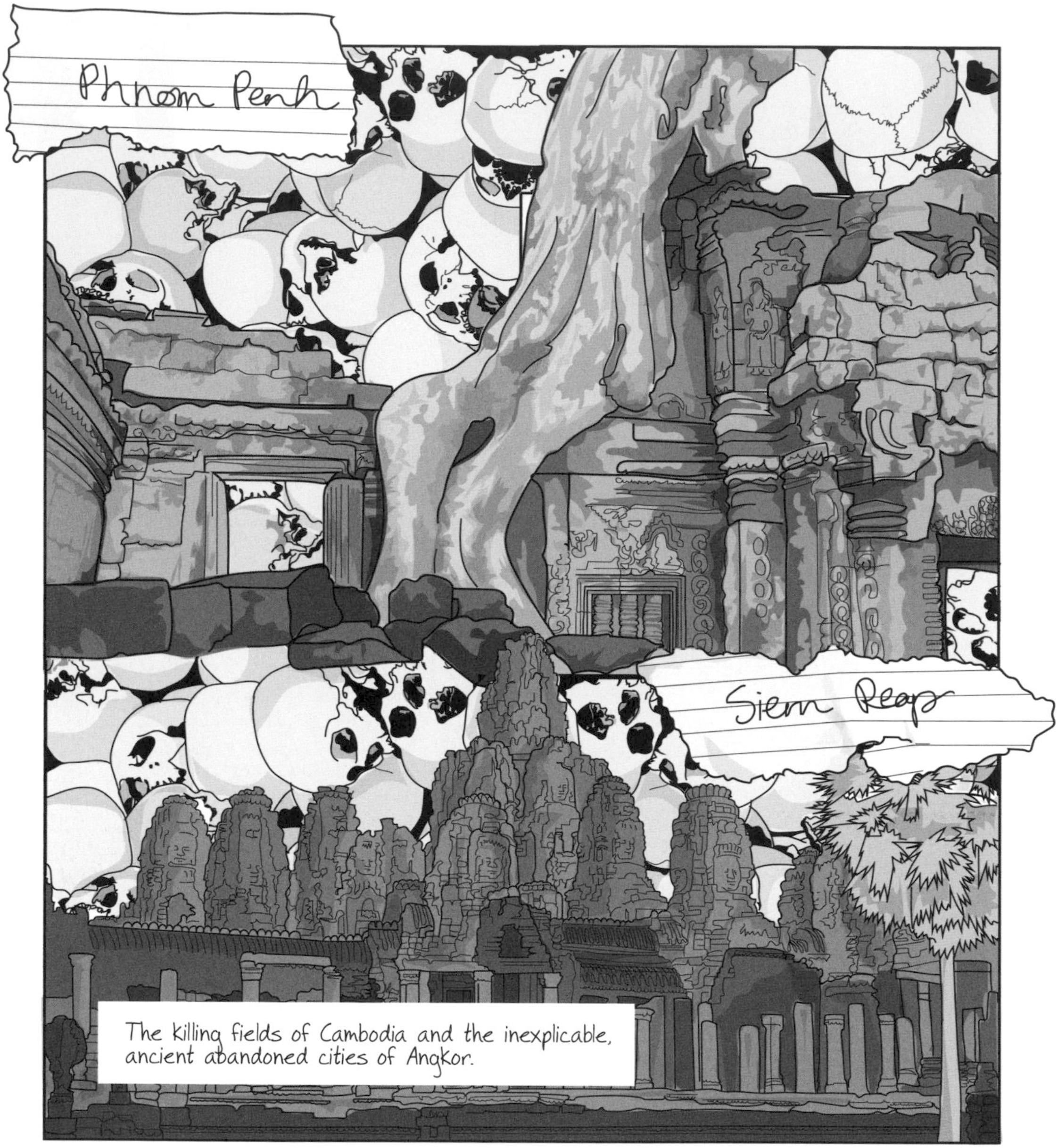
Phnom Penh
Siem Reap
The killing fields of Cambodia and the inexplicable, ancient abandoned cities of Angkor.

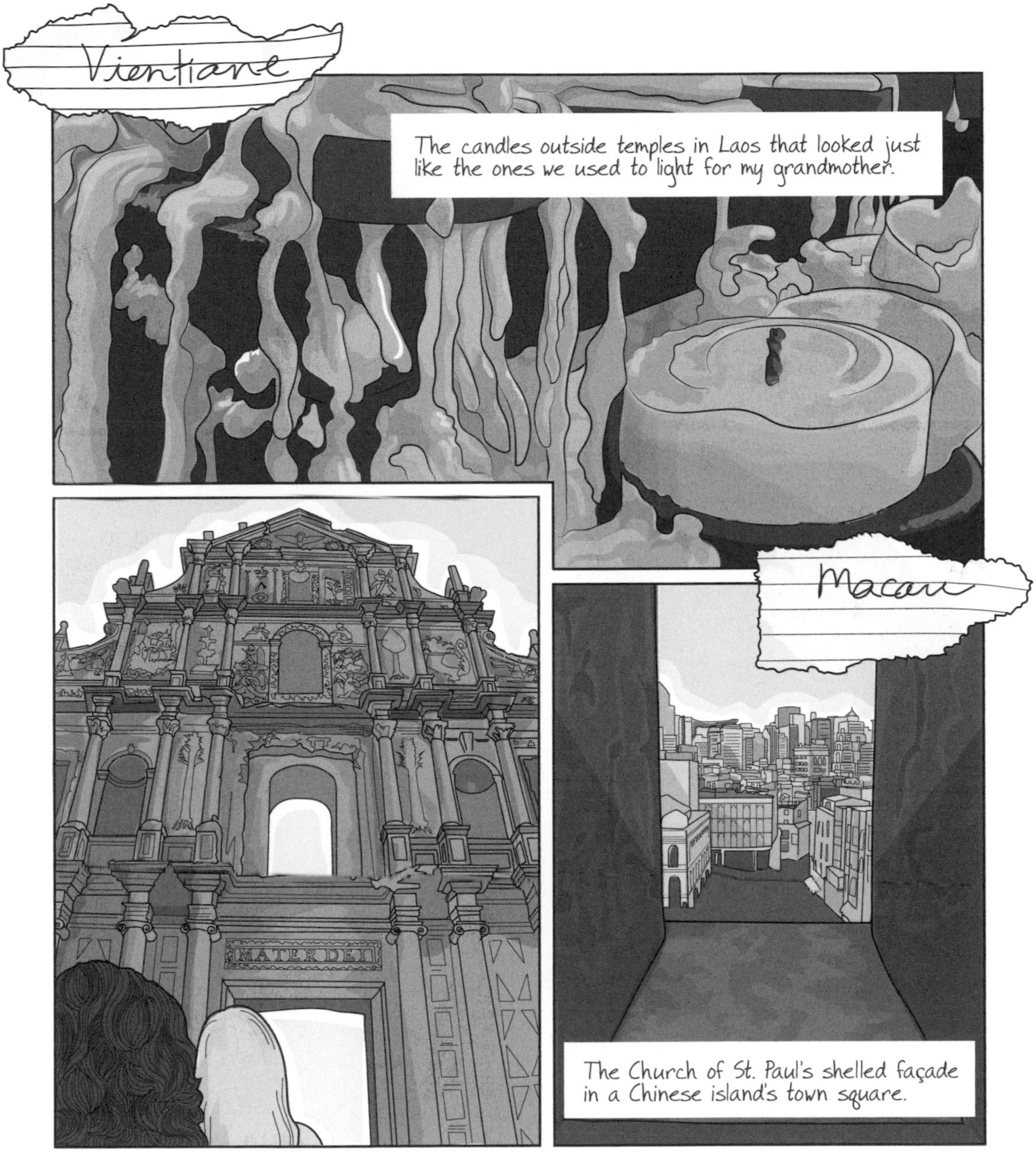
Vientiane
The candles outside temples in Laos that looked just like the ones we used to light for my grandmother.
MATER DEI
Macau
The Church of St. Paul's shelled façade in a Chinese island's town square.

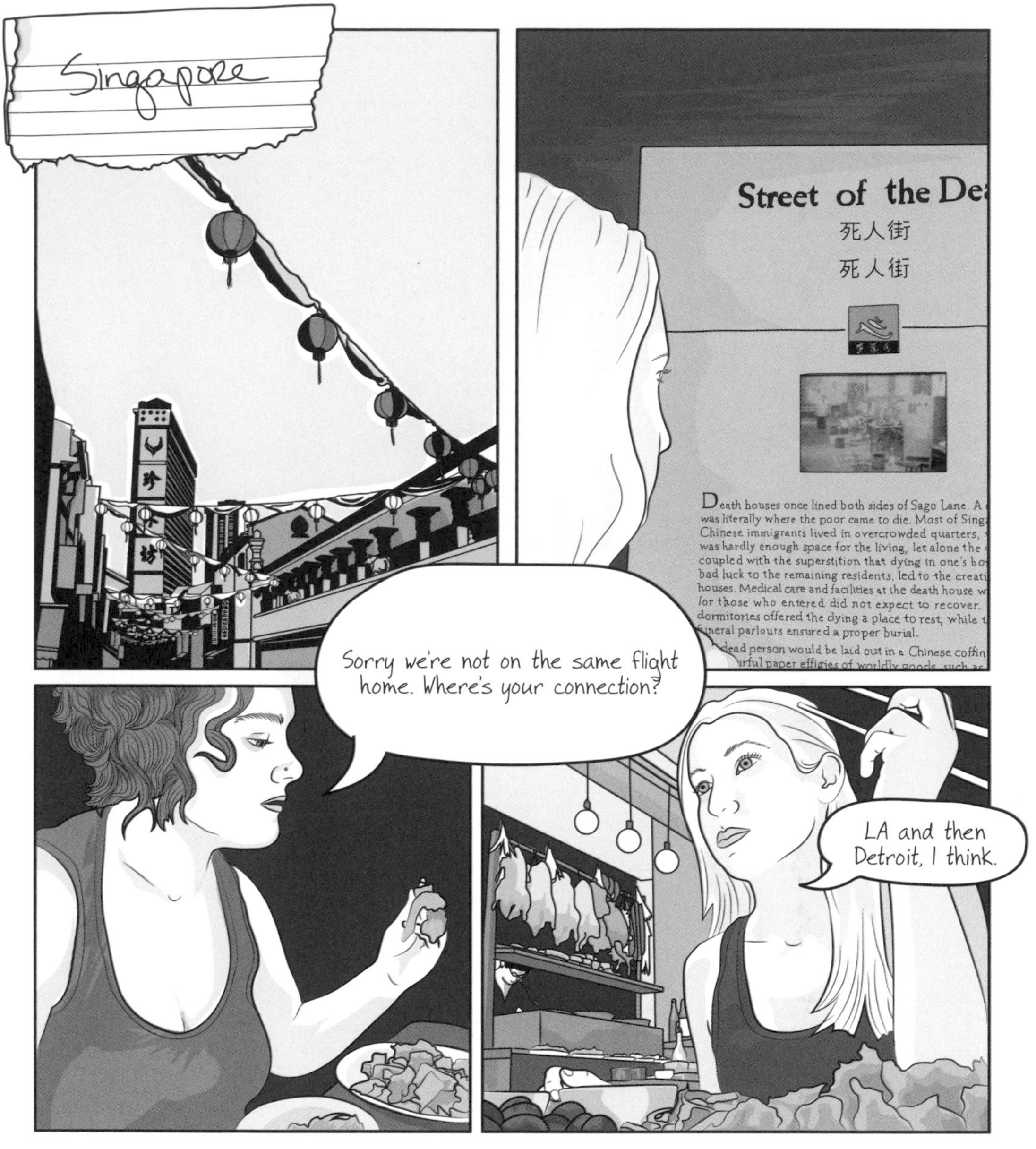
Singapore
Street of the De
死人街
死人街
Death houses once lined both sides of Sago Lane. A
was literally where the poor came to die. Most of Sing
Chinese immigrants lived in overcrowded quarters,
was hardly enough space for the living, let alone the
coupled with the superstition that dying in one's ho
bad luck to the remaining residents, led to the creati
houses. Medical care and facilities at the death house w
for those who entered did not expect to recover.
dormitories offered the dying a place to rest, while t
funeral parlours ensured a proper burial.
dead person would be laid out in a Chinese coffin
Sorry we're not on the same flight home. Where's your connection?
LA and then Detroit, I think.

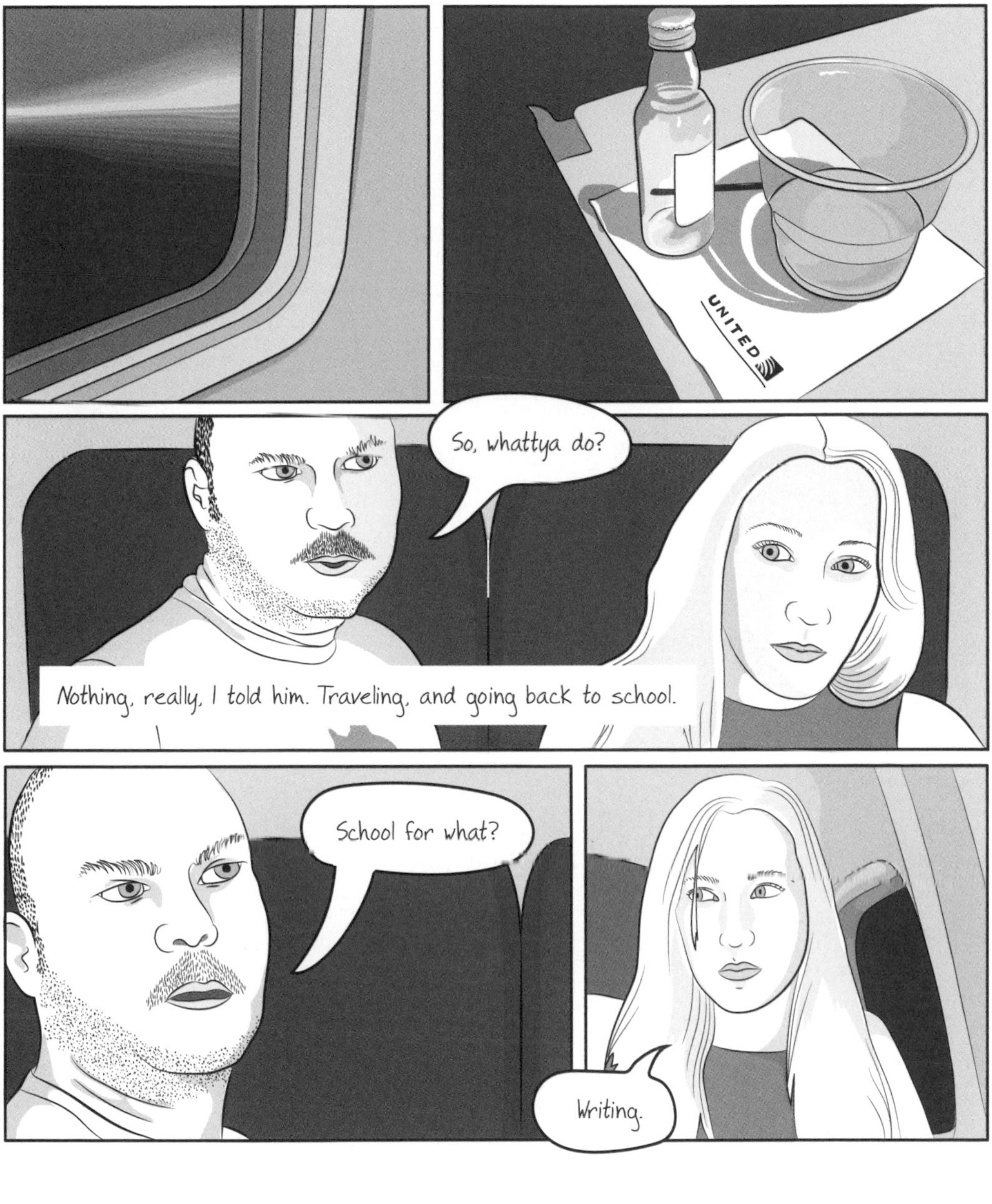
UNITED
So, whattya do?
Nothing, really, I told him. Traveling, and going back to school.
School for what?
Writing.

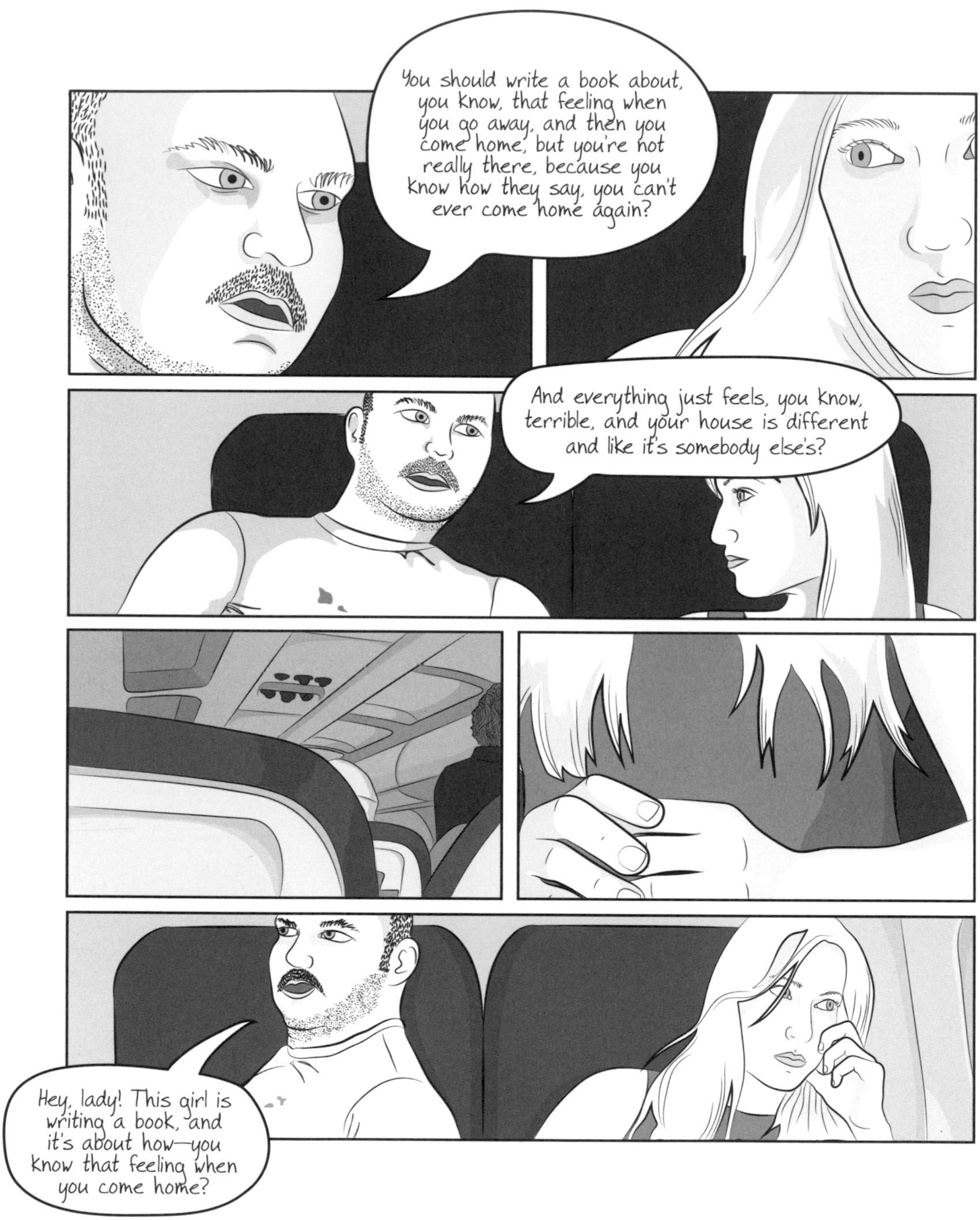
You should write a book about, you know, that feeling when you go away, and then you come home, but you're not really there, because you know how they say, you can't ever come home again?
And everything just feels, you know, terrible, and your house is different and like it's somebody else's?
Hey, lady! This girl is writing a book, and it's about how—you know that feeling when you come home?

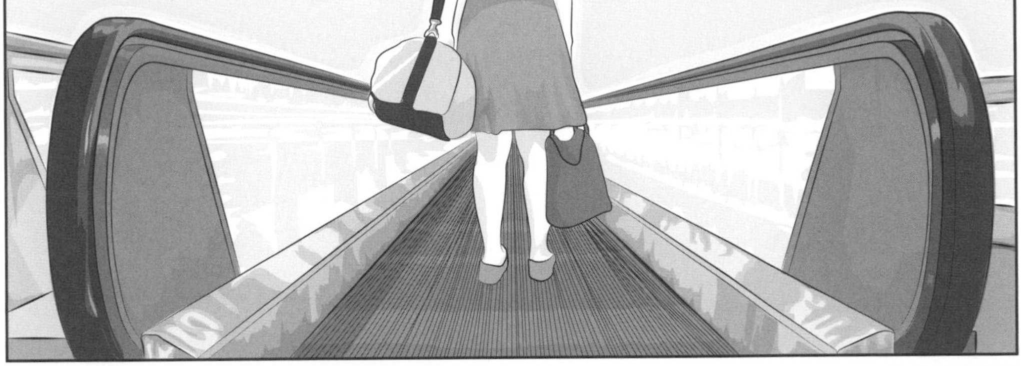

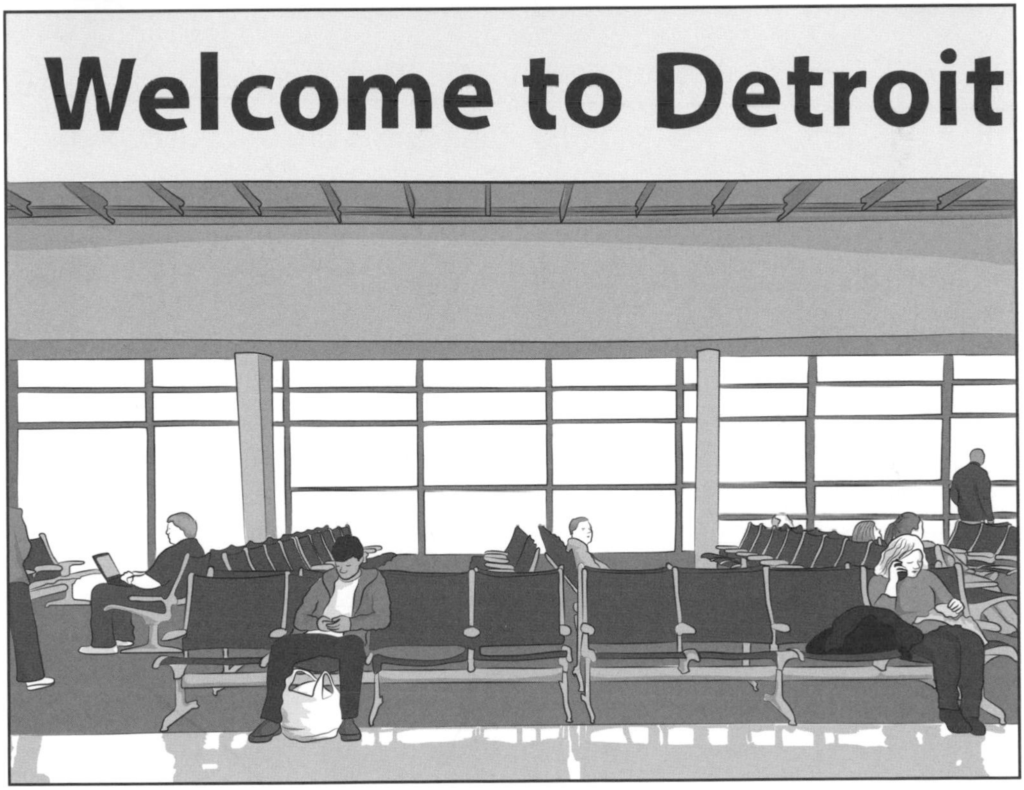
Welcome to Detroit

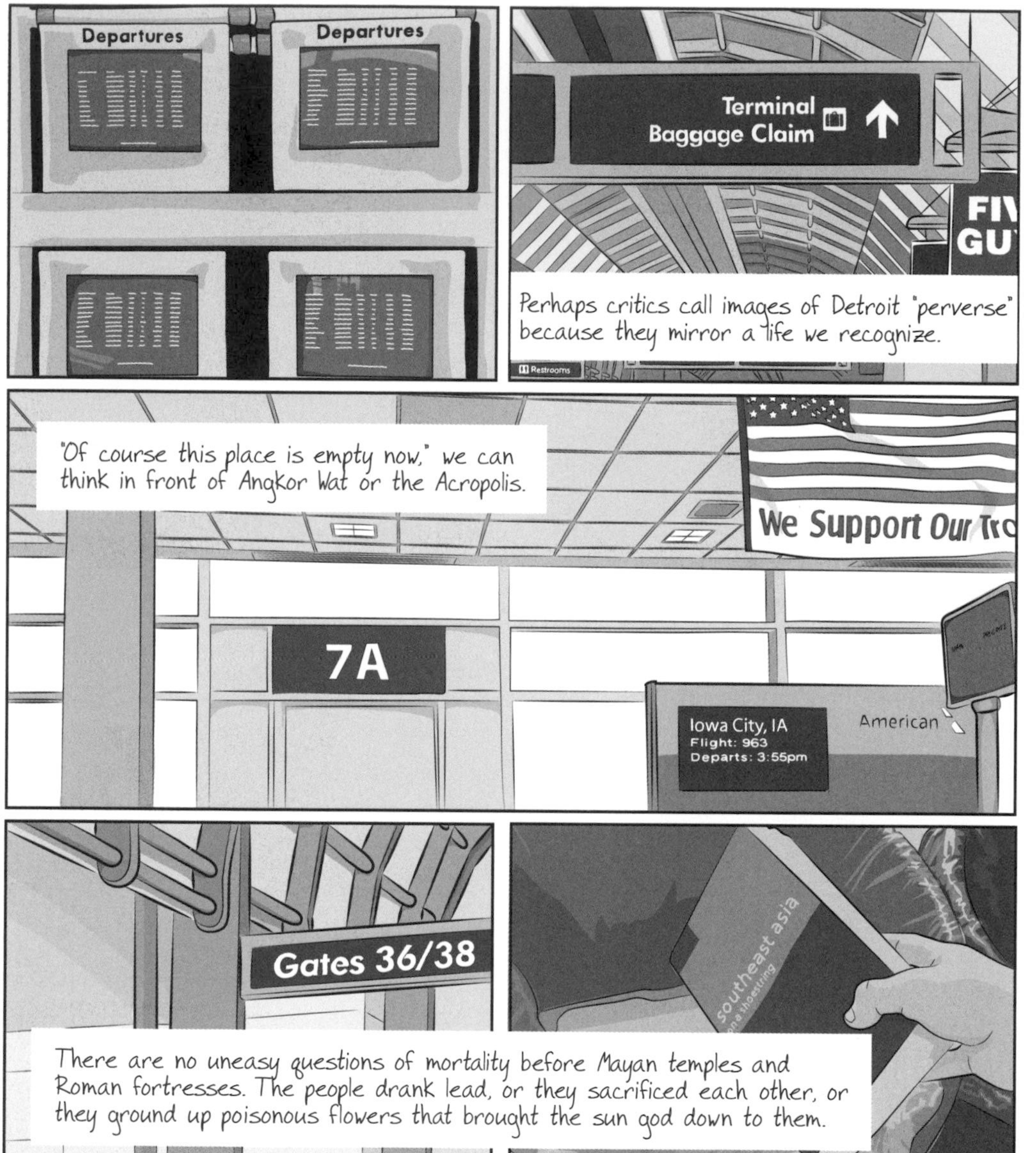
Departures
Departures
Terminal
Baggage Claim
Perhaps critics call images of Detroit "perverse" because they mirror a life we recognize.
Restrooms
"Of course this place is empty now," we can think in front of Angkor Wat or the Acropolis.
We Support Our
7A
Iowa City, IA
Flight: 963
Departs: 3:55pm
American
Gates 36/38
southeast asia
There are no uneasy questions of mortality before Mayan temples and Roman fortresses. The people drank lead, or they sacrificed each other, or they ground up poisonous flowers that brought the sun god down to them.

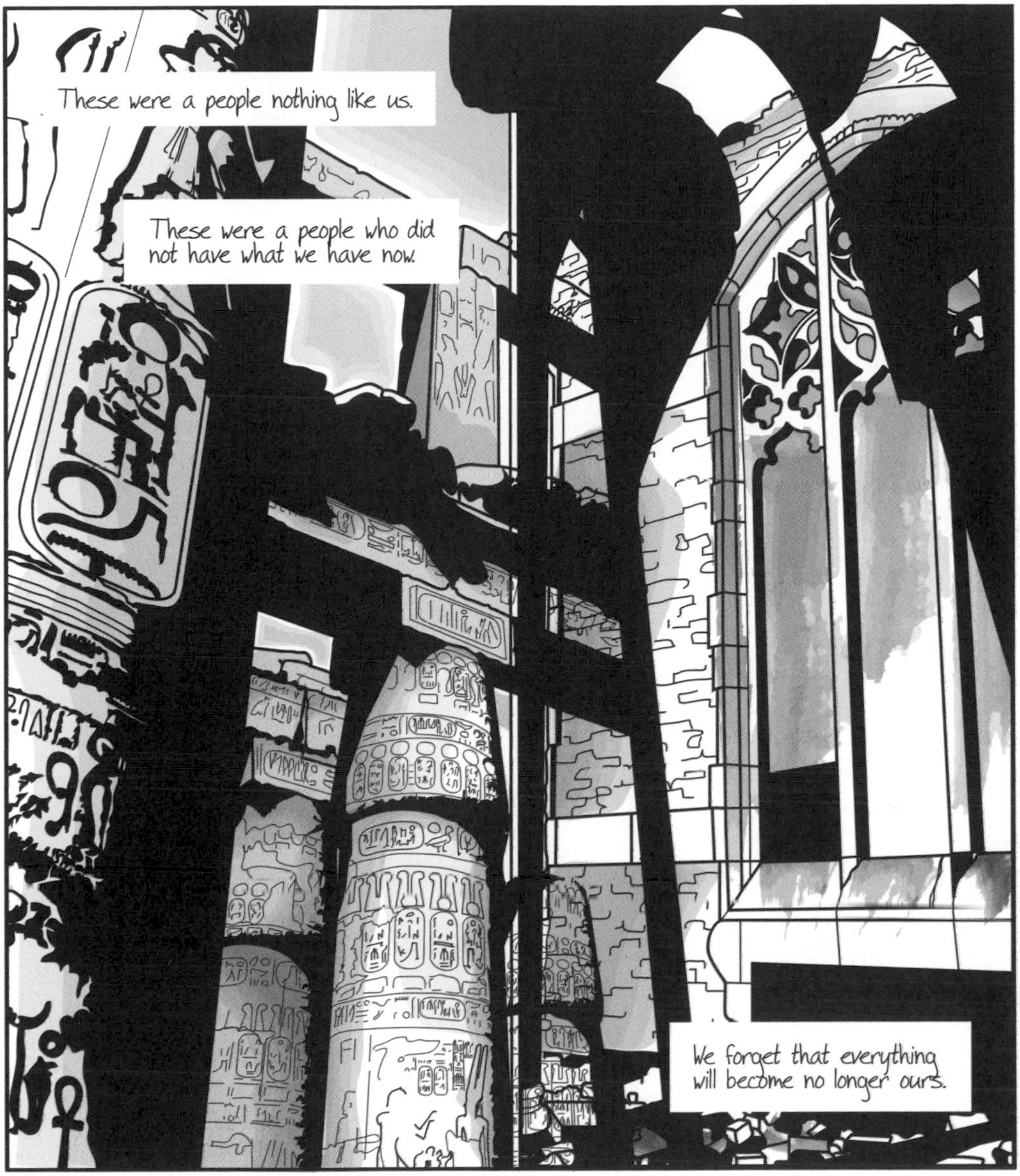
These were a people nothing like us.
These were a people who did not have what we have now.
We forget that everything will become no longer ours.

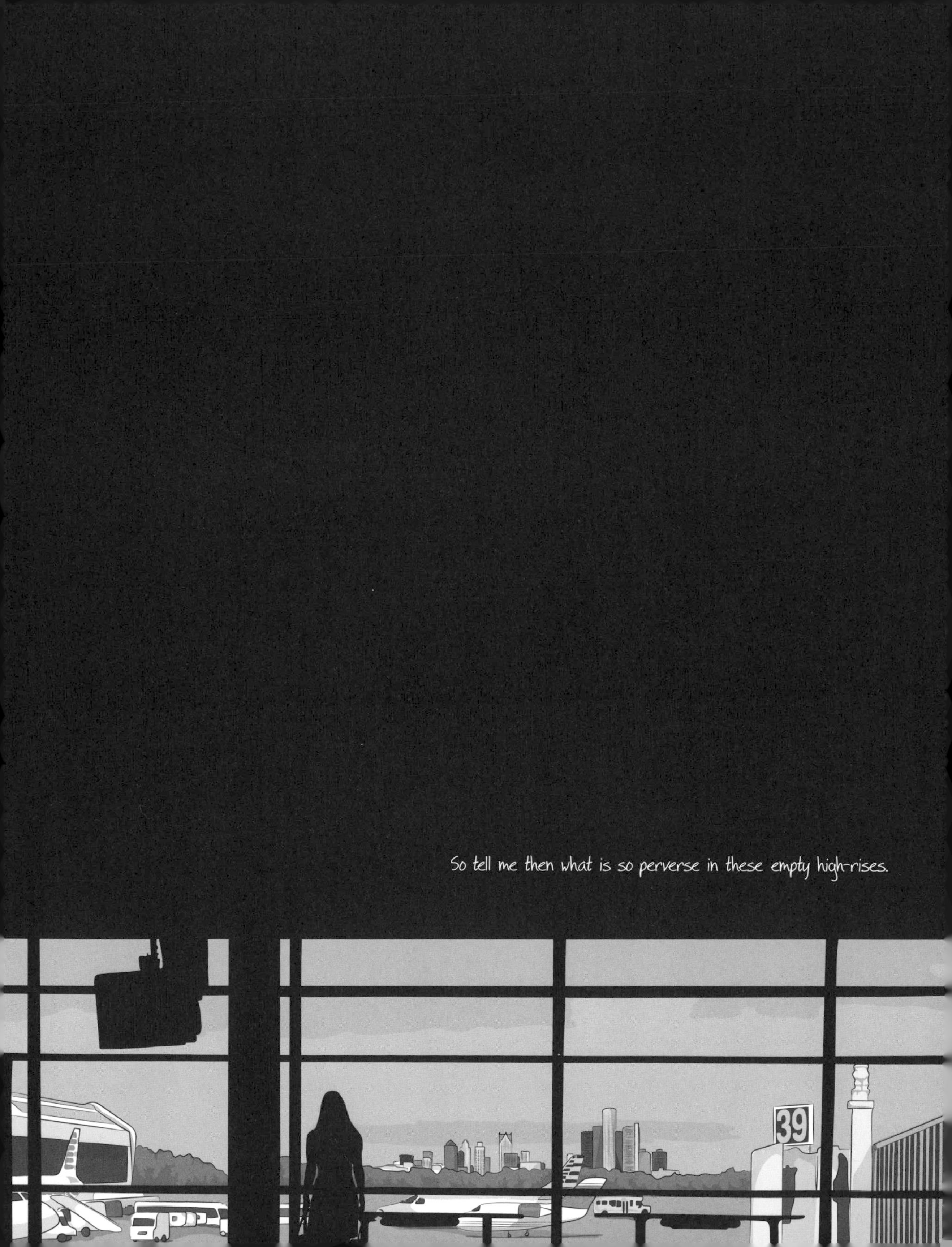
So tell me then what is so perverse in these empty high-rises.
39

In these calcifying rust-belt cities.

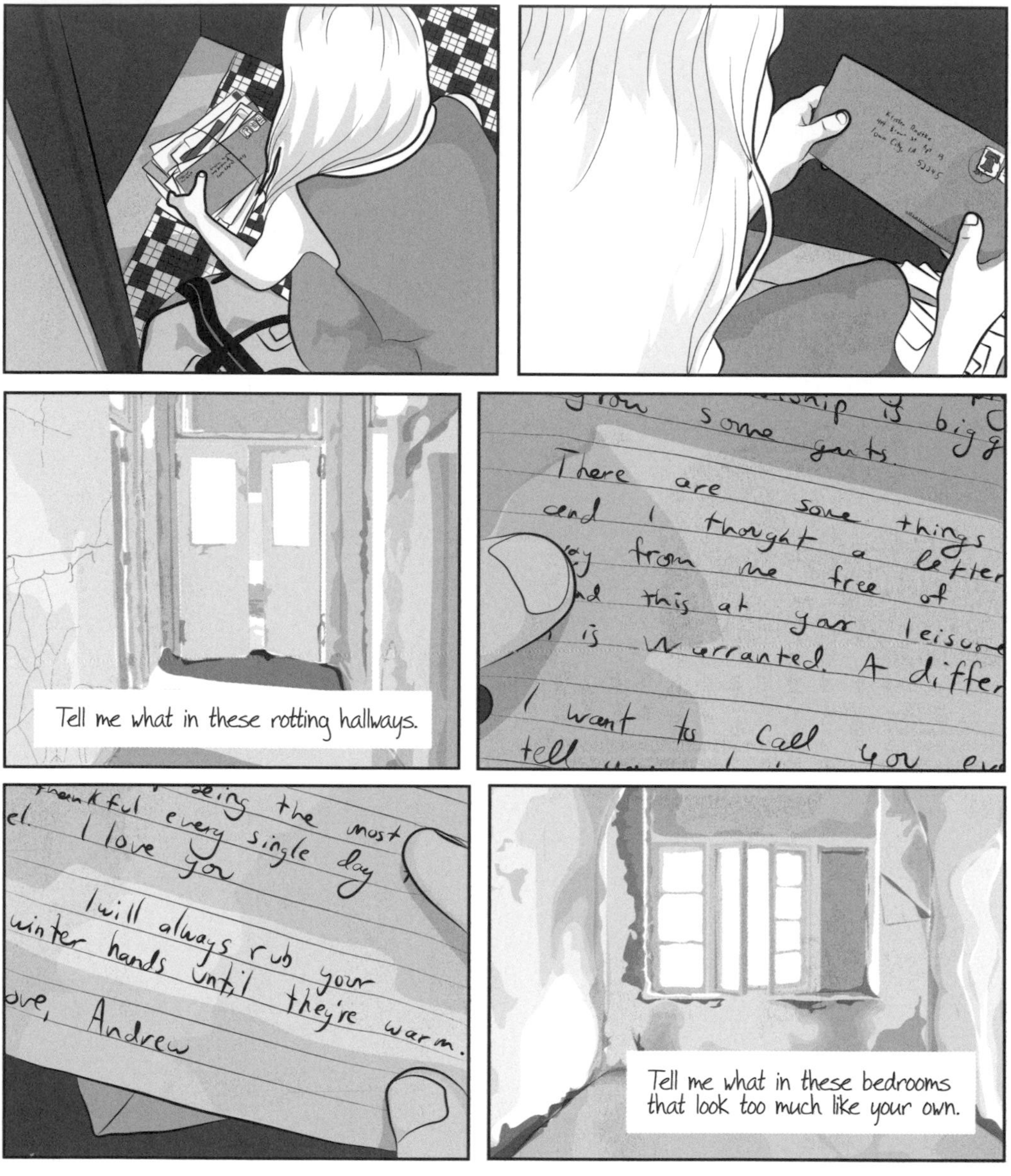
Tell me what in these rotting hallways.
some guts.
There are some things
and I thought a letter
from me free of
this at your leisure
is warranted. A differ
I want to call you
thankful every single day
I love you
I will always rub your
winter hands until they're warm.
Andrew
Tell me what in these bedrooms
that look too much like your own.

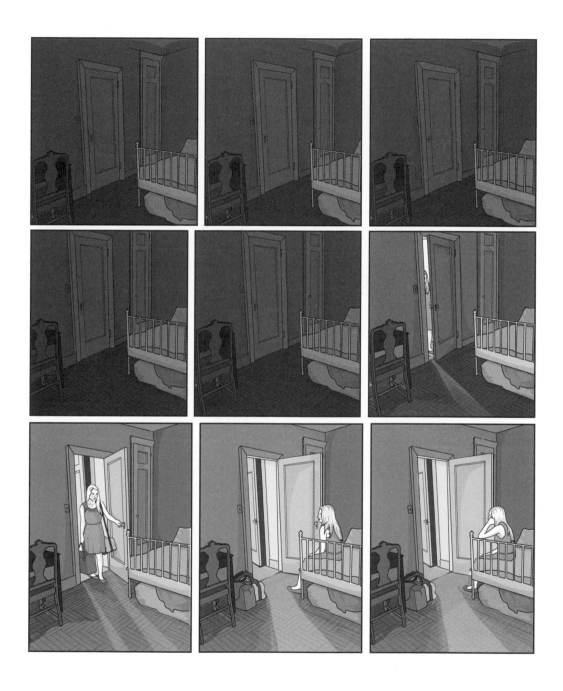

# Chapter 5

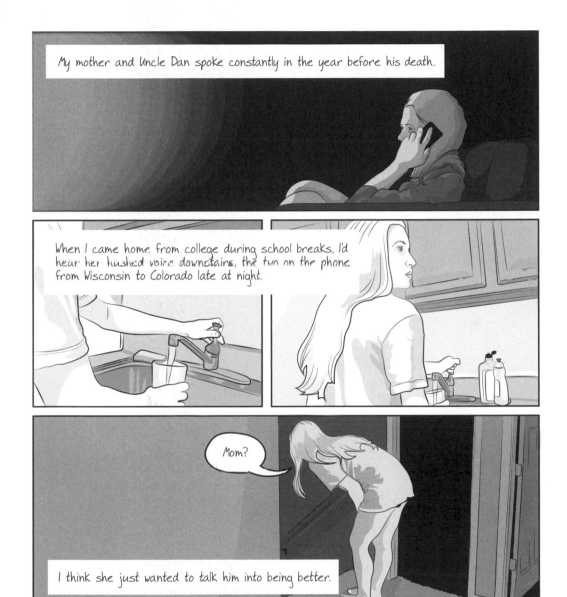

My mother and Uncle Dan spoke constantly in the year before his death.

When I came home from college during school breaks, I'd hear her hushed voice downstairs, the two on the phone from Wisconsin to Colorado late at night.

Mom?

I think she just wanted to talk him into being better.

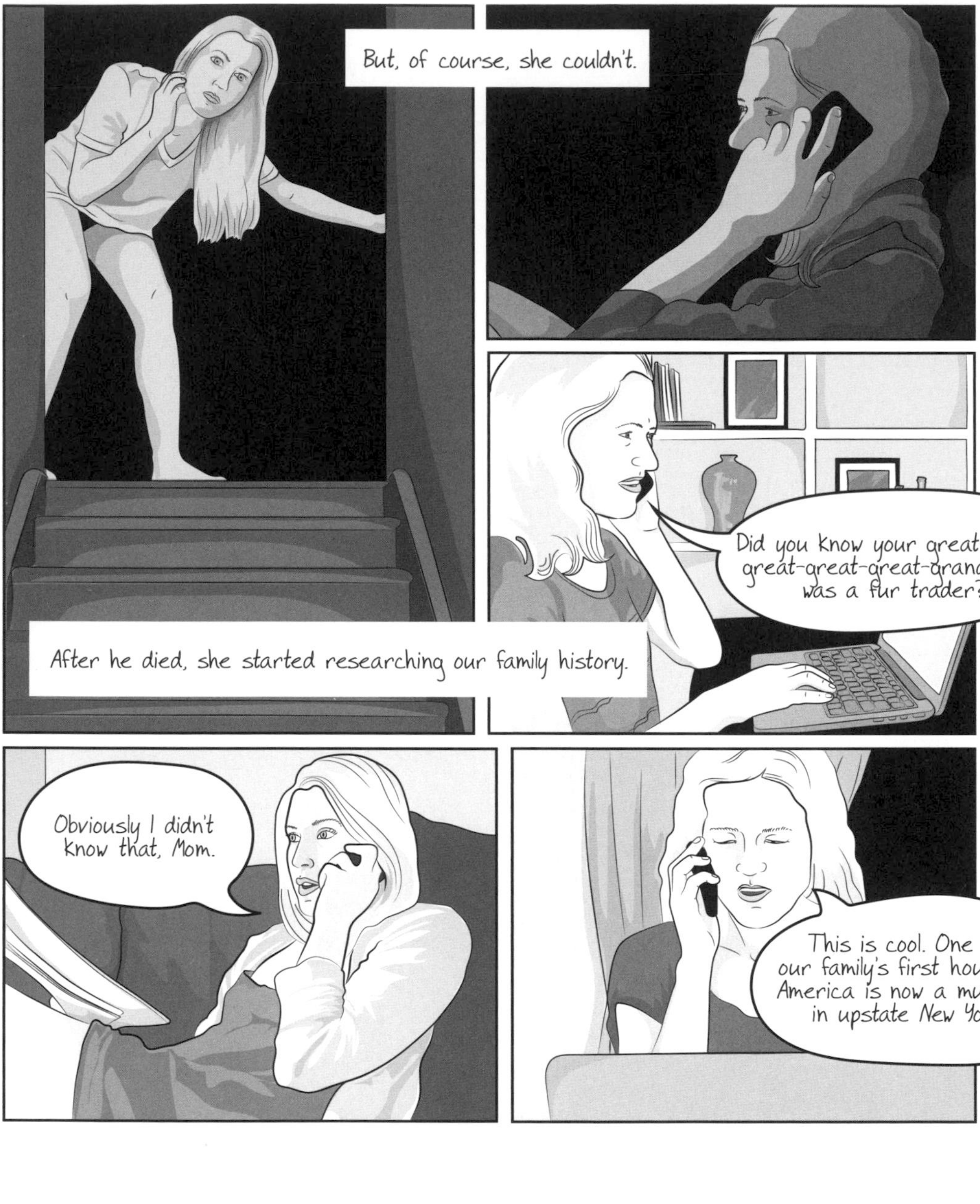
But, of course, she couldn't.
After he died, she started researching our family history.
Did you know your great-great-great-great-great-grandfather was a fur trader?
Obviously I didn't know that, Mom.
This is cool. One of our family's first houses in America is now a museum in upstate New York.

I never asked her whether it was Dan's dying that triggered her sudden interest in genealogy.

ST. MARTIN'S CEMETE

FRANK & CLEMENTINE
VANDENHOUTEN
BORN
SEPT. 25, 1901,
DIED
NOV. 30, 1902

Rest in peace

But I suppose a mysterious disease striking someone you love is a reasonable provocation to start looking for answers, or at least information.

FATHER    MOTHER

PROSPER
DUBOIS
JAN. 21 1858
MAY 18 1943

JULIA
DUBOIS
JUNE 5 19
OCT. 10

DUBOIS

RY
E OF
AMBEAU
20, 1883

I think she liked that the puzzles were solvable, the fact that she could search for a connection and find that connection marked in tangible, real-life stone.

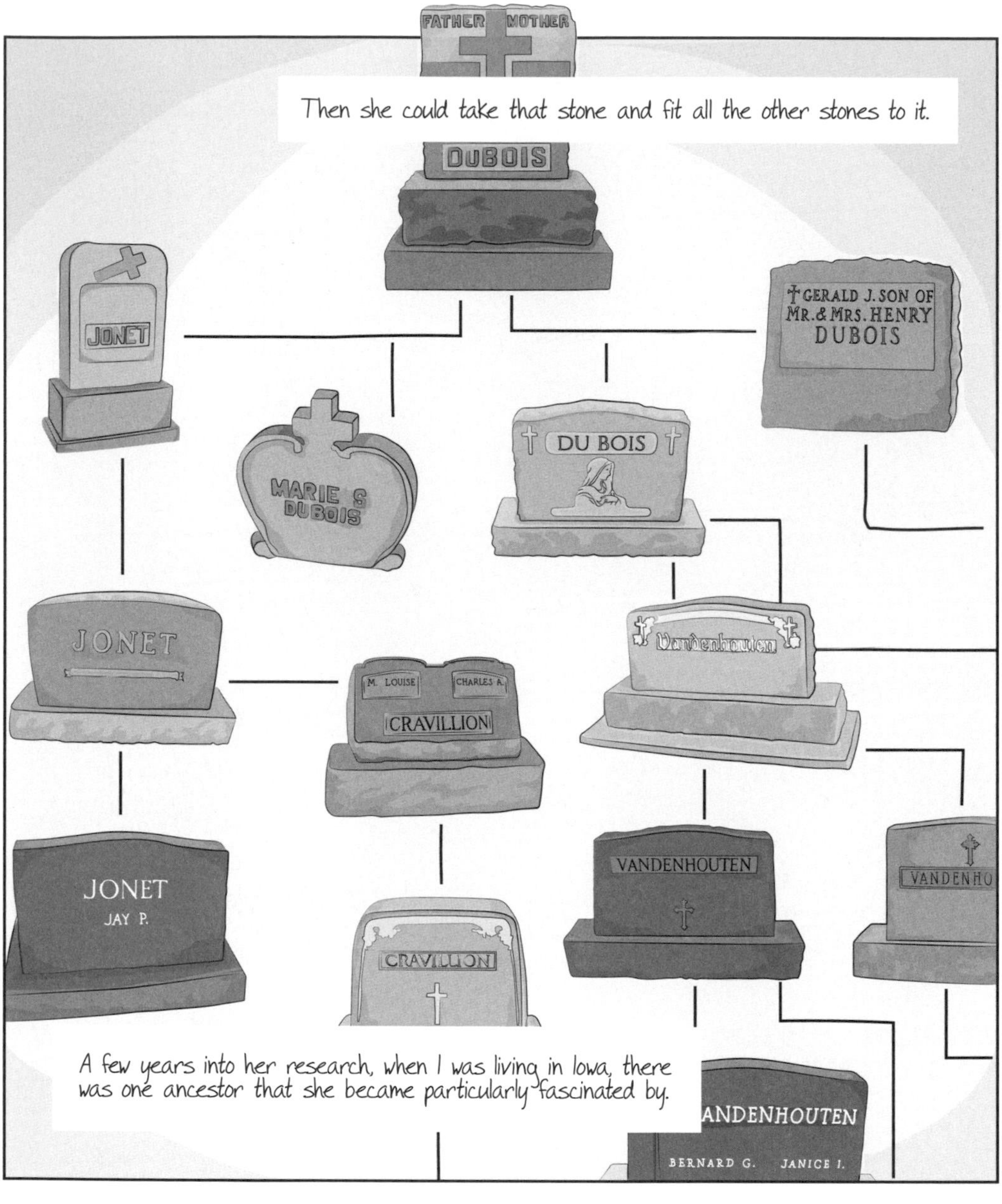
Then she could take that stone and fit all the other stones to it.
FATHER MOTHER
DUBOIS
JONET
GERALD J. SON OF MR. & MRS. HENRY DUBOIS
MARIE S DUBOIS
DU BOIS
JONET
M. LOUISE
CHARLES A.
CRAVILLION
Vandenhouten
JONET
JAY P.
CRAVILLION
VANDENHOUTEN
VANDENHO
A few years into her research, when I was living in Iowa, there was one ancestor that she became particularly fascinated by.
ANDENHOUTEN
BERNARD G.
JANICE I.

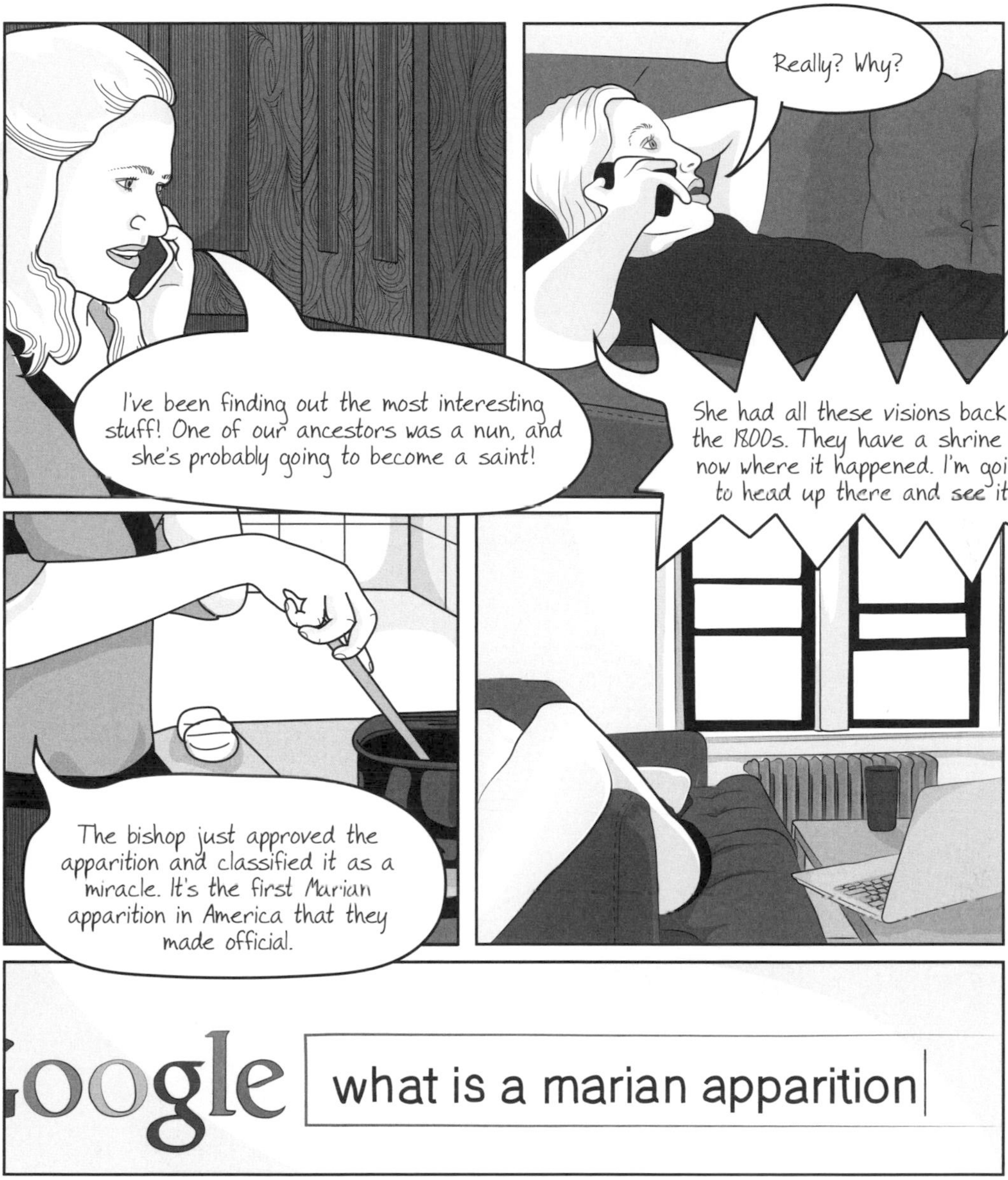
Really? Why?
I've been finding out the most interesting stuff! One of our ancestors was a nun, and she's probably going to become a saint!
She had all these visions back in the 1800s. They have a shrine up now where it happened. I'm going to head up there and see it.
The bishop just approved the apparition and classified it as a miracle. It's the first Marian apparition in America that they made official.
Google
what is a marian apparition

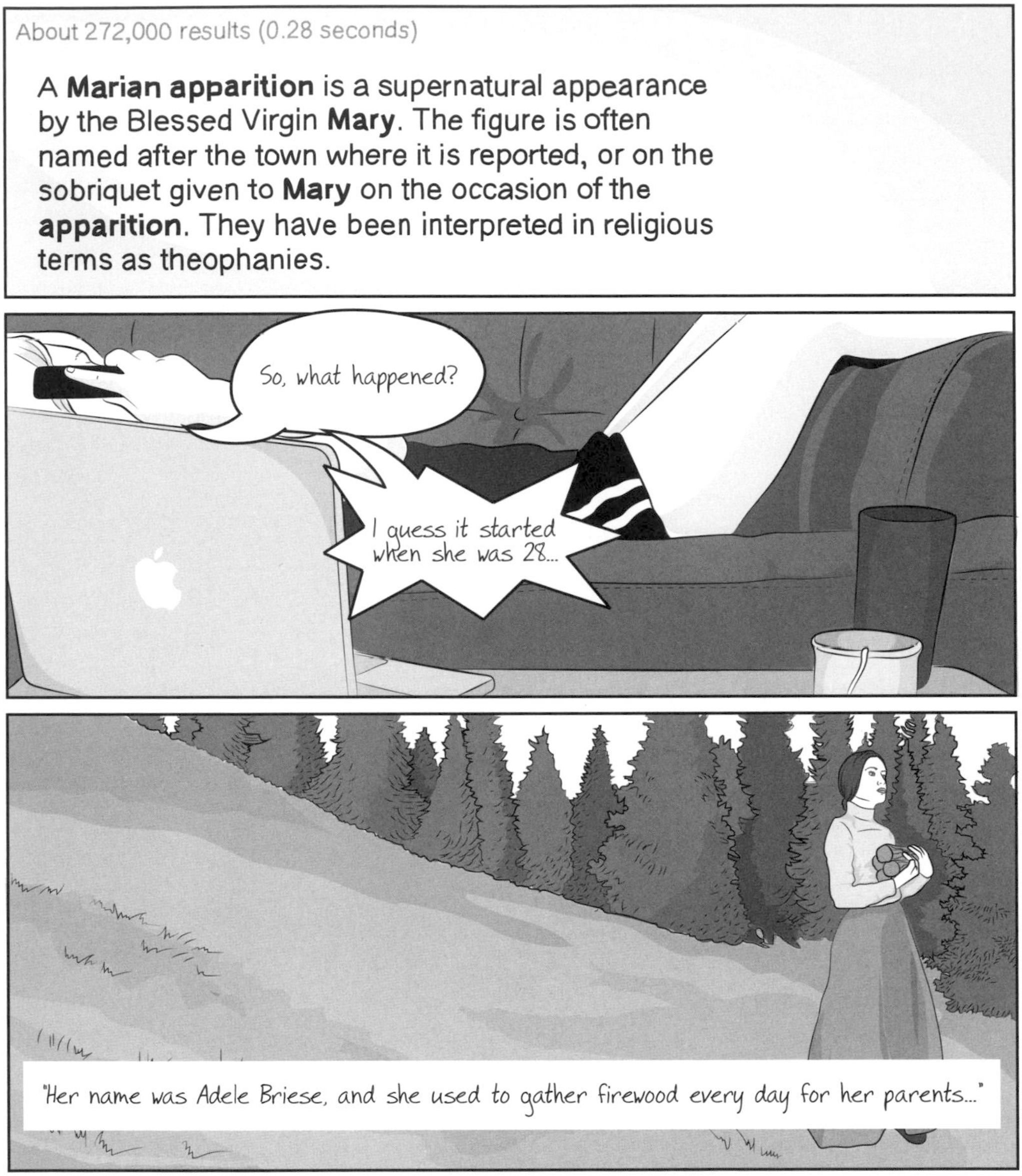
About 272,000 results (0.28 seconds)
A **Marian apparition** is a supernatural appearance by the Blessed Virgin **Mary**. The figure is often named after the town where it is reported, or on the sobriquet given to **Mary** on the occasion of the **apparition**. They have been interpreted in religious terms as theophanies.
So, what happened?
I guess it started when she was 28...
"Her name was Adele Briese, and she used to gather firewood every day for her parents..."

"And on her walk one day she looked up and saw this glowing, angelic woman.

"So obviously, she was terrified,

"And she dropped to the ground and started praying.

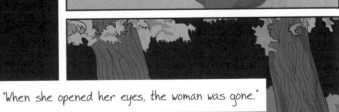

"When she opened her eyes, the woman was gone."

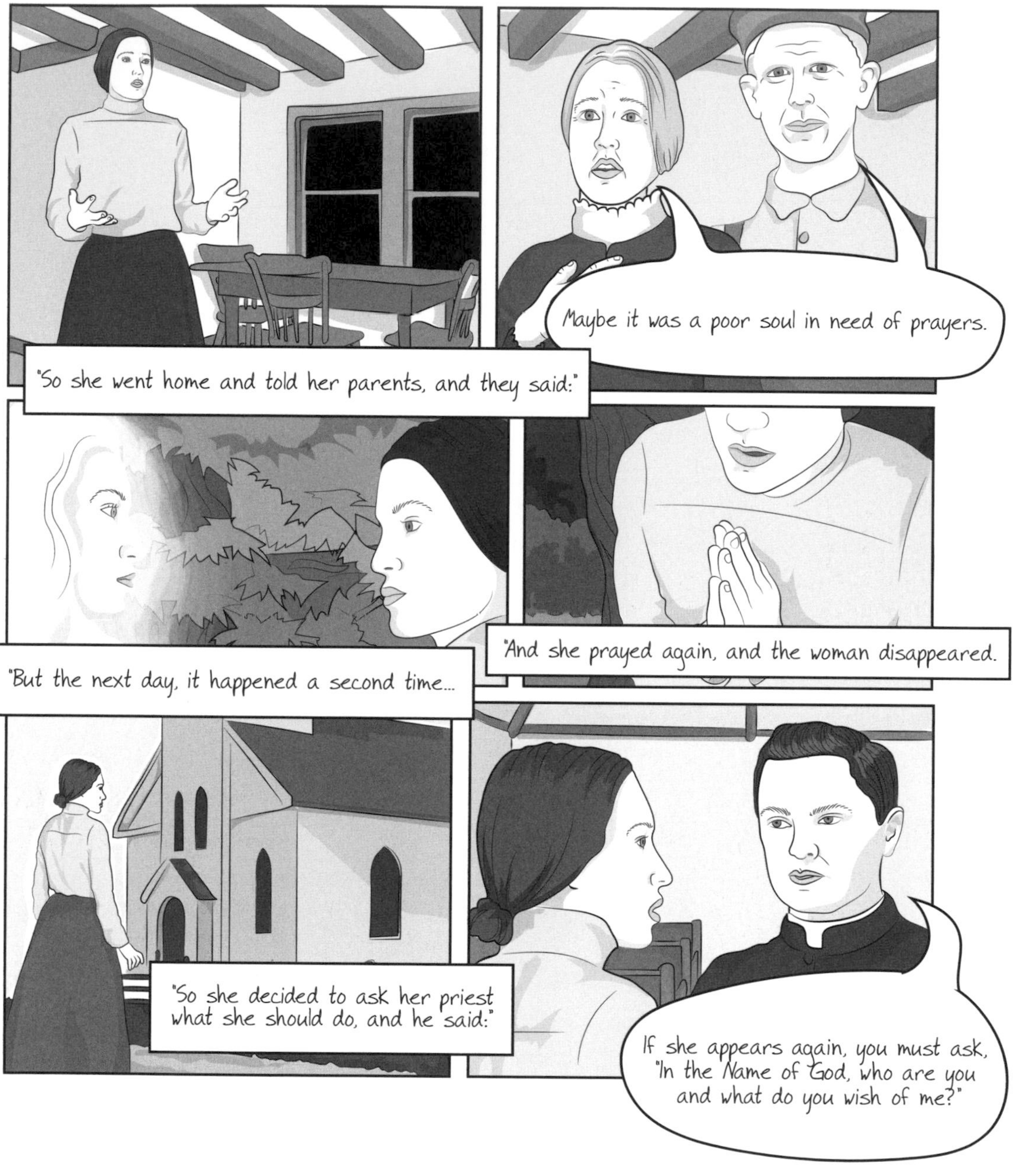
"So she went home and told her parents, and they said:"
Maybe it was a poor soul in need of prayers.
"But the next day, it happened a second time...
"And she prayed again, and the woman disappeared.
"So she decided to ask her priest what she should do, and he said:"
If she appears again, you must ask, "In the Name of God, who are you and what do you wish of me?"

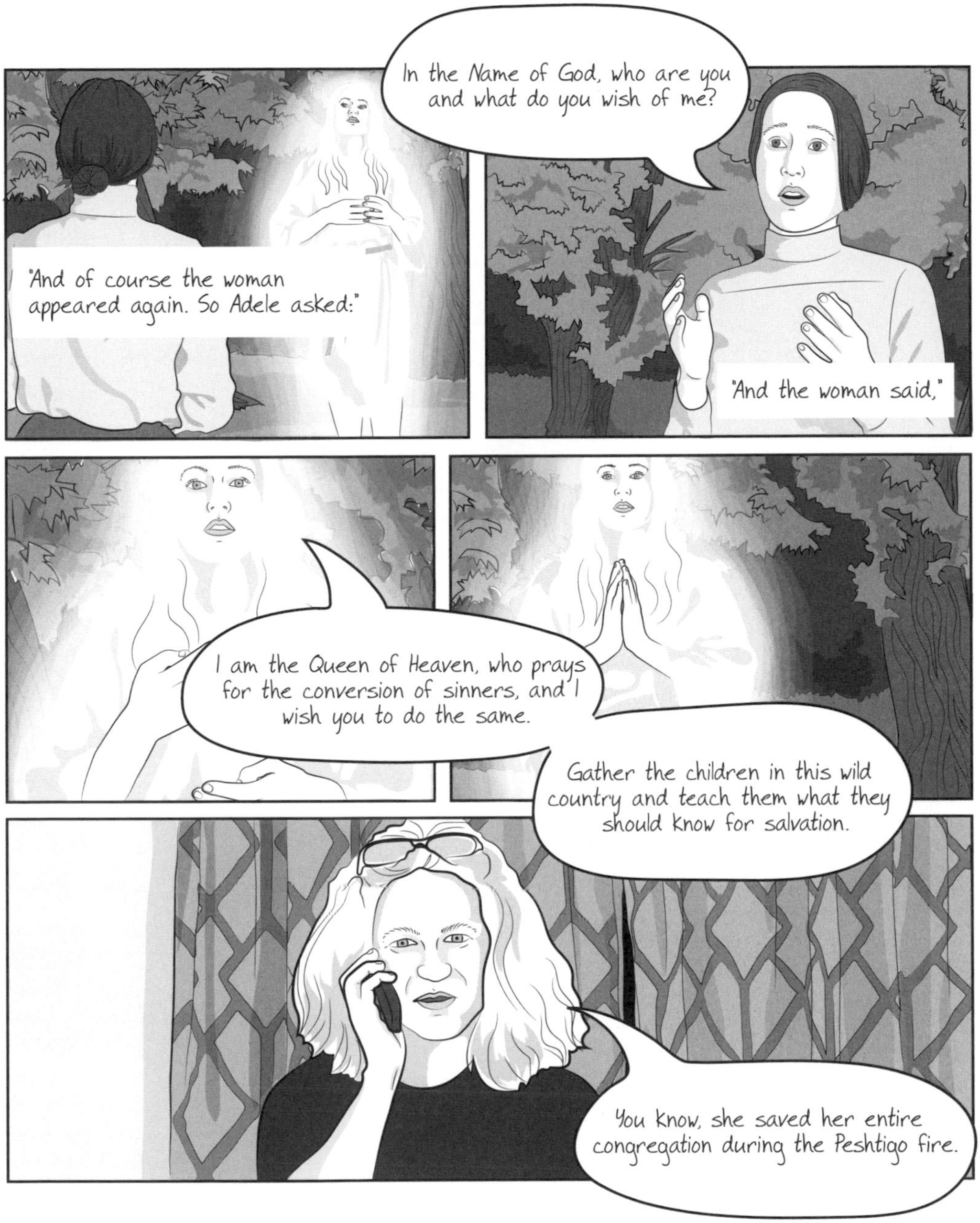
"And of course the woman appeared again. So Adele asked:"
In the Name of God, who are you and what do you wish of me?
"And the woman said,"
I am the Queen of Heaven, who prays for the conversion of sinners, and I wish you to do the same.
Gather the children in this wild country and teach them what they should know for salvation.
You know, she saved her entire congregation during the Peshtigo fire.

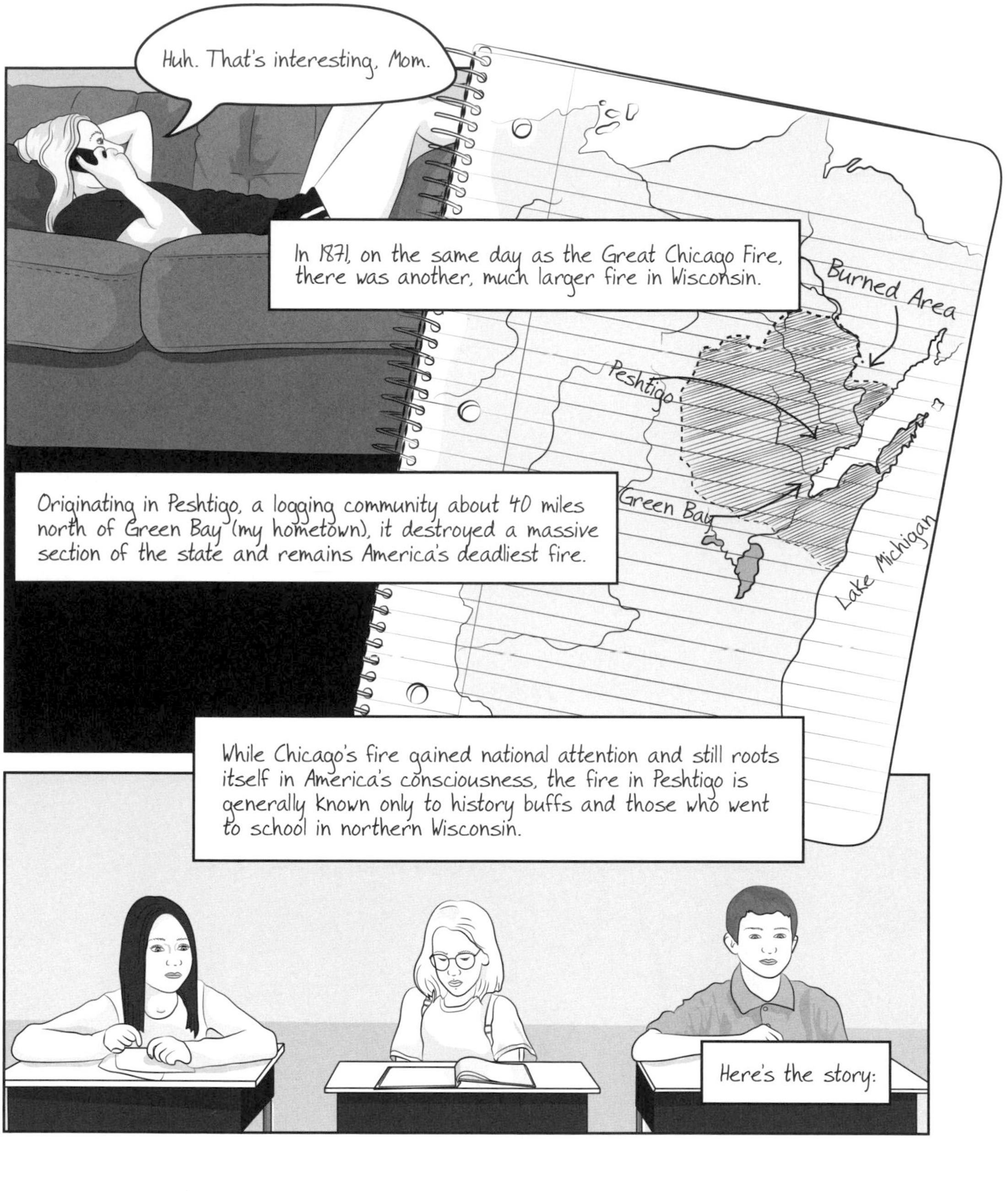

Huh. That's interesting, Mom.
In 1871, on the same day as the Great Chicago Fire, there was another, much larger fire in Wisconsin.
Burned Area
Peshtigo
Green Bay
Lake Michigan
Originating in Peshtigo, a logging community about 40 miles north of Green Bay (my hometown), it destroyed a massive section of the state and remains America's deadliest fire.
While Chicago's fire gained national attention and still roots itself in America's consciousness, the fire in Peshtigo is generally known only to history buffs and those who went to school in northern Wisconsin.
Here's the story:

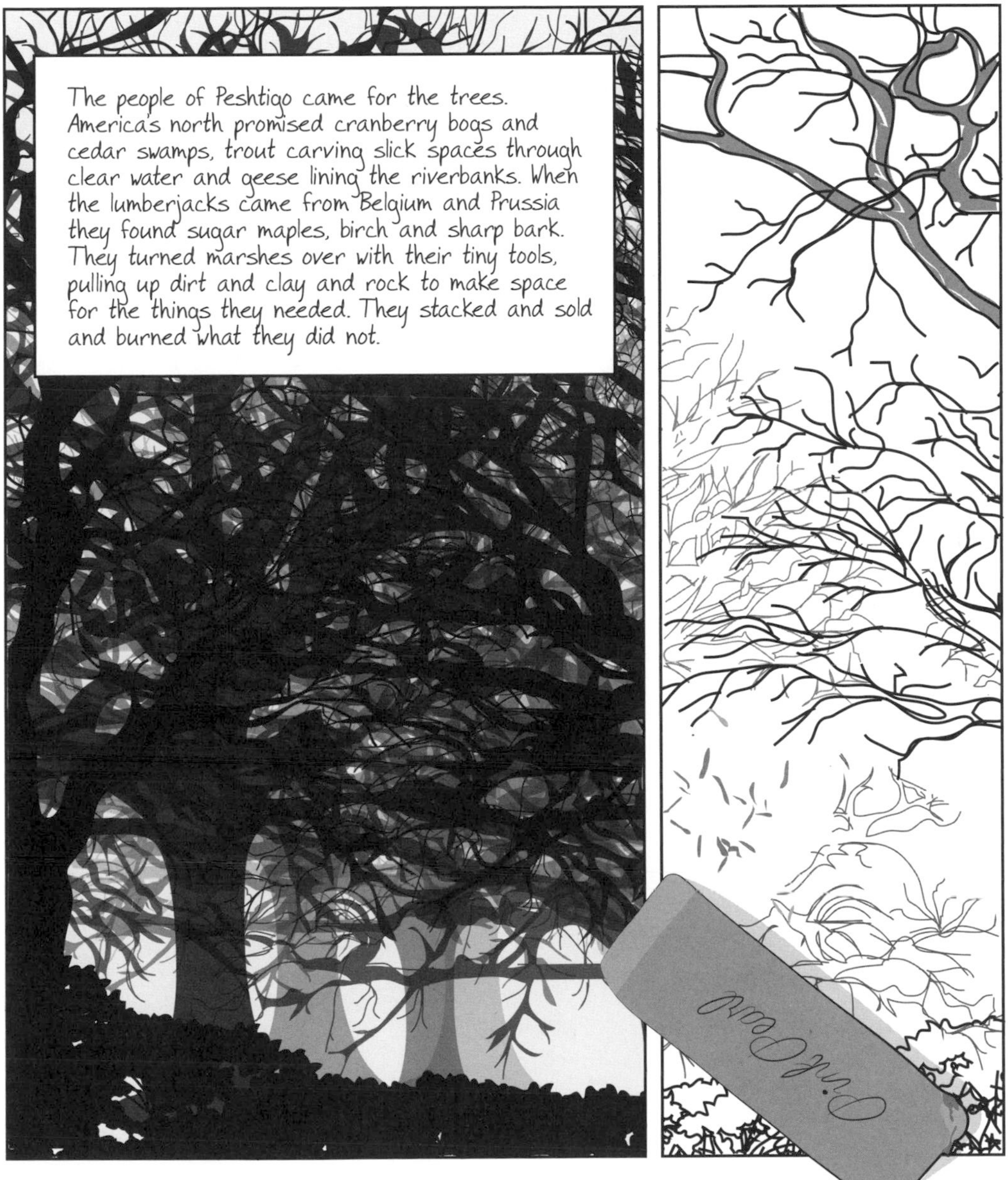
The people of Peshtigo came for the trees. America's north promised cranberry bogs and cedar swamps, trout carving slick spaces through clear water and geese lining the riverbanks. When the lumberjacks came from Belgium and Prussia they found sugar maples, birch and sharp bark. They turned marshes over with their tiny tools, pulling up dirt and clay and rock to make space for the things they needed. They stacked and sold and burned what they did not.

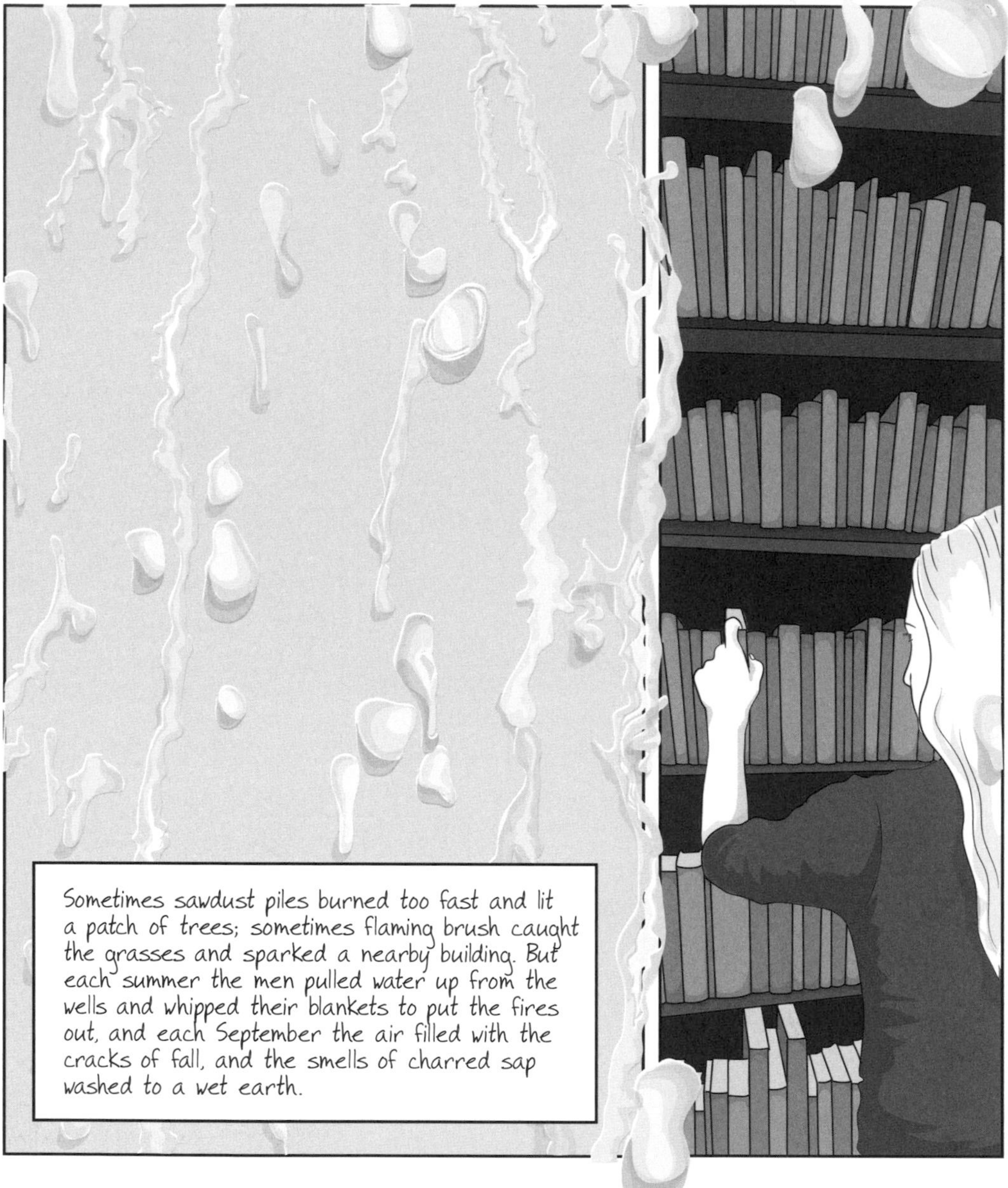
Sometimes sawdust piles burned too fast and lit a patch of trees; sometimes flaming brush caught the grasses and sparked a nearby building. But each summer the men pulled water up from the wells and whipped their blankets to put the fires out, and each September the air filled with the cracks of fall, and the smells of charred sap washed to a wet earth.

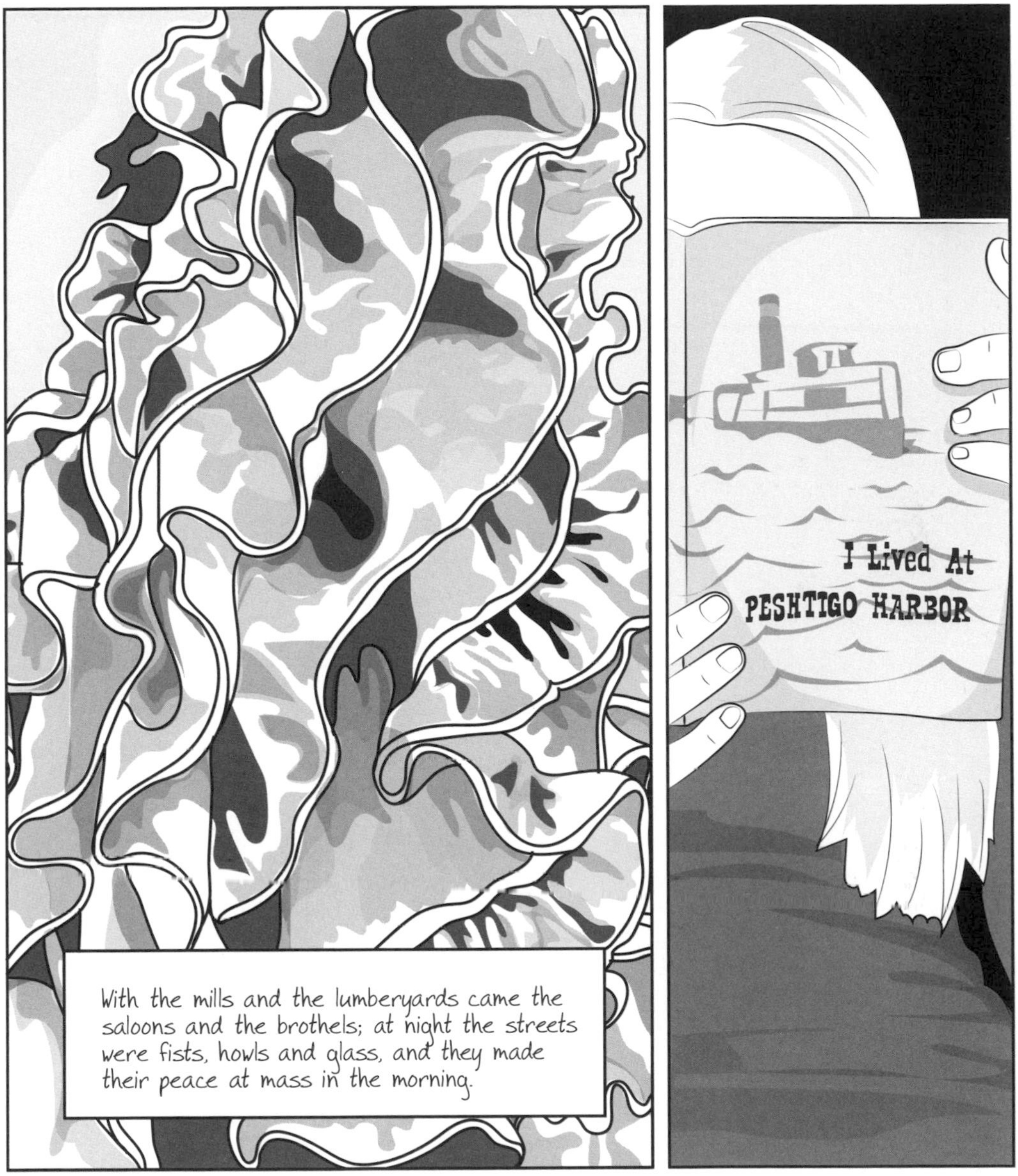
With the mills and the lumberyards came the saloons and the brothels; at night the streets were fists, howls and glass, and they made their peace at mass in the morning.
I Lived At PESHTIGO HARBOR

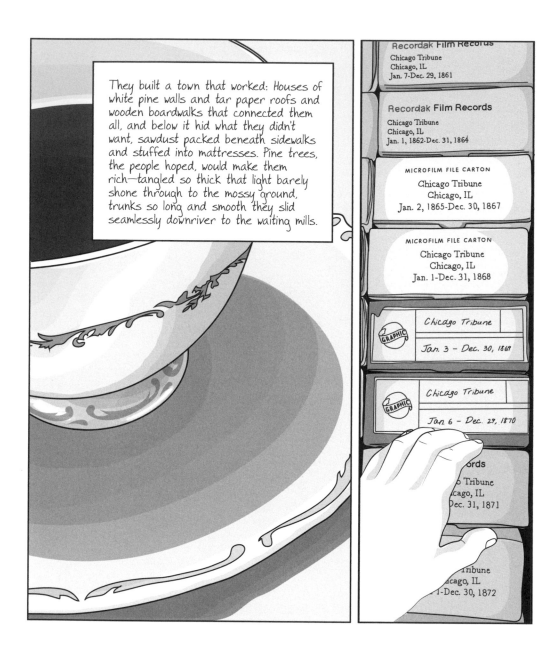

They built a town that worked: Houses of white pine walls and tar paper roofs and wooden boardwalks that connected them all, and below it hid what they didn't want, sawdust packed beneath sidewalks and stuffed into mattresses. Pine trees, the people hoped, would make them rich—tangled so thick that light barely shone through to the mossy ground, trunks so long and smooth they slid seamlessly downriver to the waiting mills.

Recordak Film Records
Chicago Tribune
Chicago, IL
Jan. 7-Dec. 29, 1861

Recordak Film Records
Chicago Tribune
Chicago, IL
Jan. 1, 1862-Dec. 31, 1864

MICROFILM FILE CARTON
Chicago Tribune
Chicago, IL
Jan. 2, 1865-Dec. 30, 1867

MICROFILM FILE CARTON
Chicago Tribune
Chicago, IL
Jan. 1-Dec. 31, 1868

GRAPHIC
Chicago Tribune
Jan. 3 – Dec. 30, 1869

GRAPHIC
Chicago Tribune
Jan. 6 – Dec. 29, 1870

...ords
...o Tribune
...icago, IL
...Dec. 31, 1871

...Tribune
...icago, IL
...1-Dec. 30, 1872

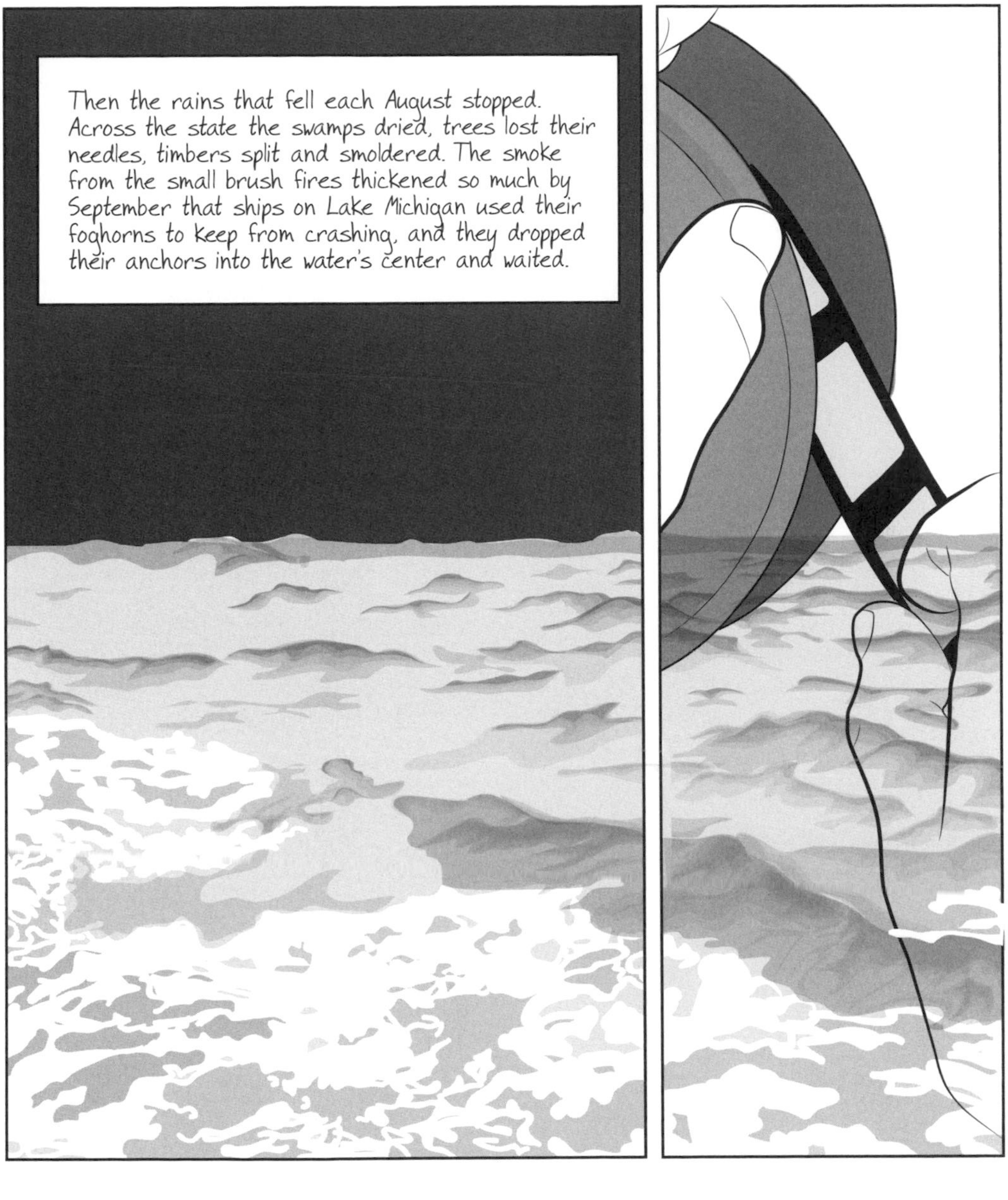
Then the rains that fell each August stopped. Across the state the swamps dried, trees lost their needles, timbers split and smoldered. The smoke from the small brush fires thickened so much by September that ships on Lake Michigan used their foghorns to keep from crashing, and they dropped their anchors into the water's center and waited.

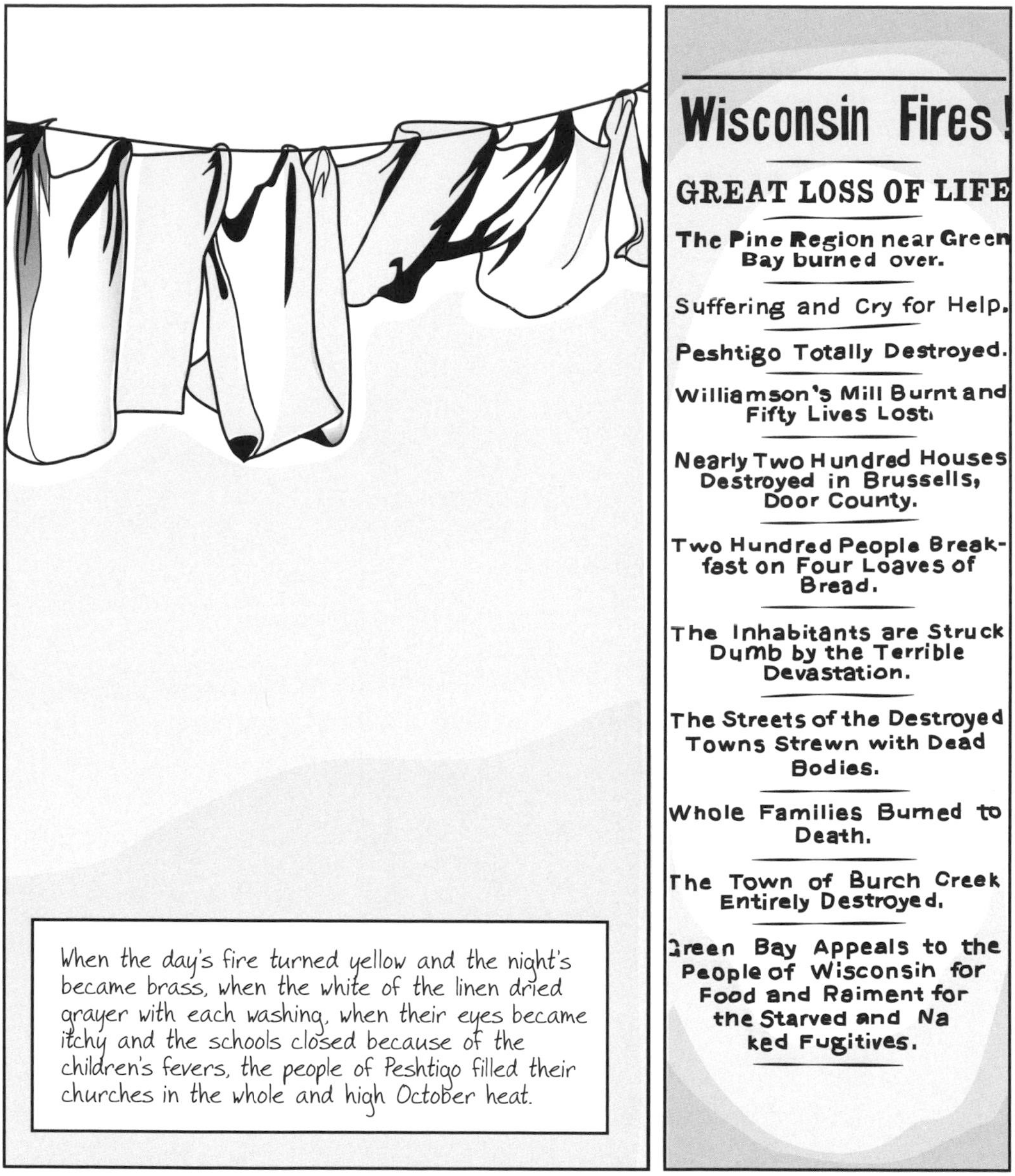
When the day's fire turned yellow and the night's became brass, when the white of the linen dried grayer with each washing, when their eyes became itchy and the schools closed because of the children's fevers, the people of Peshtigo filled their churches in the whole and high October heat.
Wisconsin Fires!
GREAT LOSS OF LIFE
The Pine Region near Green Bay burned over.
Suffering and Cry for Help.
Peshtigo Totally Destroyed.
Williamson's Mill Burnt and Fifty Lives Lost.
Nearly Two Hundred Houses Destroyed in Brussells, Door County.
Two Hundred People Breakfast on Four Loaves of Bread.
The Inhabitants are Struck Dumb by the Terrible Devastation.
The Streets of the Destroyed Towns Strewn with Dead Bodies.
Whole Families Burned to Death.
The Town of Burch Creek Entirely Destroyed.
Green Bay Appeals to the People of Wisconsin for Food and Raiment for the Starved and Naked Fugitives.

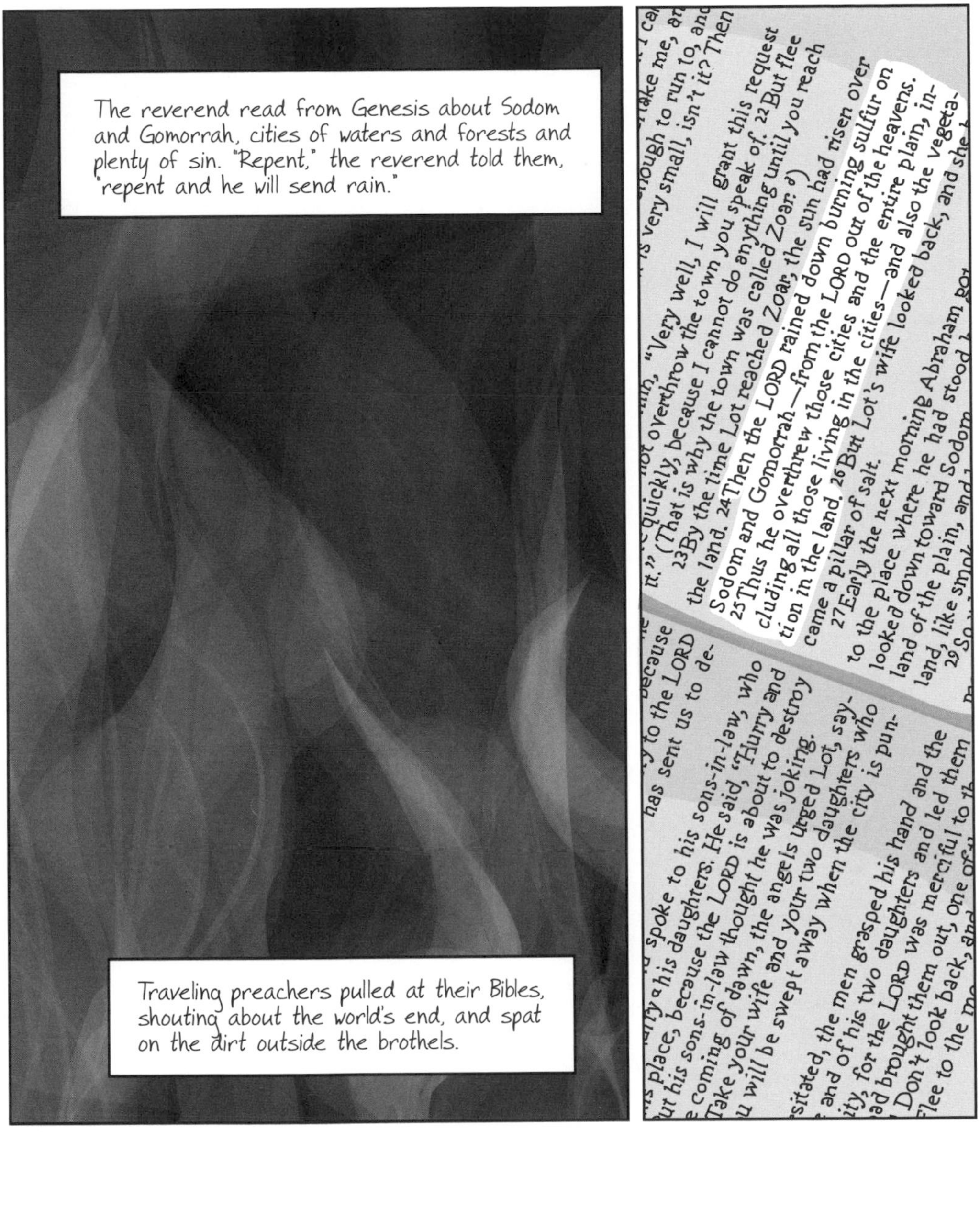
The reverend read from Genesis about Sodom and Gomorrah, cities of waters and forests and plenty of sin. "Repent," the reverend told them, "repent and he will send rain."
Sodom and Gomorrah—from the LORD out of the heavens.
25 Thus he overthrew those cities and the entire plain, including all those living in the cities—and also the vegeta-
tion in the land. 26 But Lot's wife looked back, and she
came a pillar of salt.
Traveling preachers pulled at their Bibles, shouting about the world's end, and spat on the dirt outside the brothels.

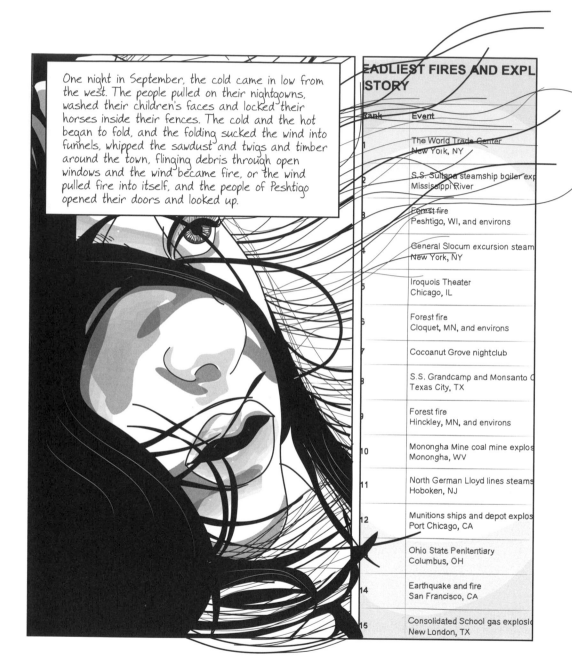

One night in September, the cold came in low from the west. The people pulled on their nightgowns, washed their children's faces and locked their horses inside their fences. The cold and the hot began to fold, and the folding sucked the wind into funnels, whipped the sawdust and twigs and timber around the town, flinging debris through open windows and the wind became fire, or the wind pulled fire into itself, and the people of Peshtigo opened their doors and looked up.

## EADLIEST FIRES AND EXPL[...] [...]STORY

| Rank | Event |
|---|---|
| 1 | The World Trade Center New York, NY |
| 2 | S.S. Sultana steamship boiler exp[...] Mississippi River |
| 3 | Forest fire Peshtigo, WI, and environs |
| 4 | General Slocum excursion steam[...] New York, NY |
| 5 | Iroquois Theater Chicago, IL |
| 6 | Forest fire Cloquet, MN, and environs |
| 7 | Cocoanut Grove nightclub |
| 8 | S.S. Grandcamp and Monsanto [...] Texas City, TX |
| 9 | Forest fire Hinckley, MN, and environs |
| 10 | Monongha Mine coal mine explos[...] Monongha, WV |
| 11 | North German Lloyd lines steams[...] Hoboken, NJ |
| 12 | Munitions ships and depot explos[...] Port Chicago, CA |
| 13 | Ohio State Penitentiary Columbus, OH |
| 14 | Earthquake and fire San Francisco, CA |
| 15 | Consolidated School gas explosio[...] New London, TX |

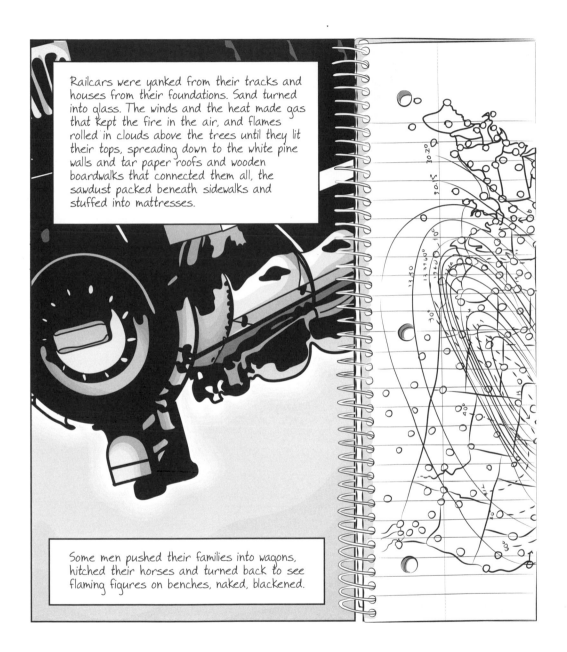

Railcars were yanked from their tracks and houses from their foundations. Sand turned into glass. The winds and the heat made gas that kept the fire in the air, and flames rolled in clouds above the trees until they lit their tops, spreading down to the white pine walls and tar paper roofs and wooden boardwalks that connected them all, the sawdust packed beneath sidewalks and stuffed into mattresses.

Some men pushed their families into wagons, hitched their horses and turned back to see flaming figures on benches, naked, blackened.

Those who were fast enough ran to the river and submerged themselves for hours, bobbing their heads to keep their hair from lighting, but the rapids were rough and the logs that had rolled from their stacks shot across the surface. Some people dropped into wells and fell into boiling water. The sky split and pulsed with the sound of fire, stalking, rolling. Horses stood burning, flames held up by hooves.

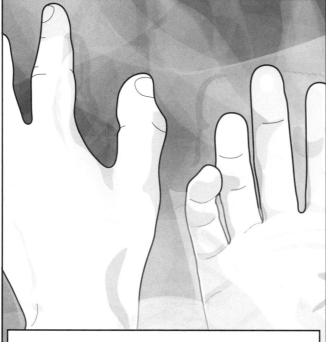

PESHTIGO

"The City Reborn from the Ashes of America's Most Disastrous Forest Fire October 8, 1871."

The Peshtigo Fire Museum is open from Memorial Weekend through October with hours from 10 a.m. to 4 p.m. d

Peshtigo
POPULATION        3537

The people remembered what the preachers had told them, and when they looked up to find fire that spun into cyclones, saw the sky spitting flames as the Bible had told them, some fell to the ground in their nightcaps and prayed for heaven rather than run.

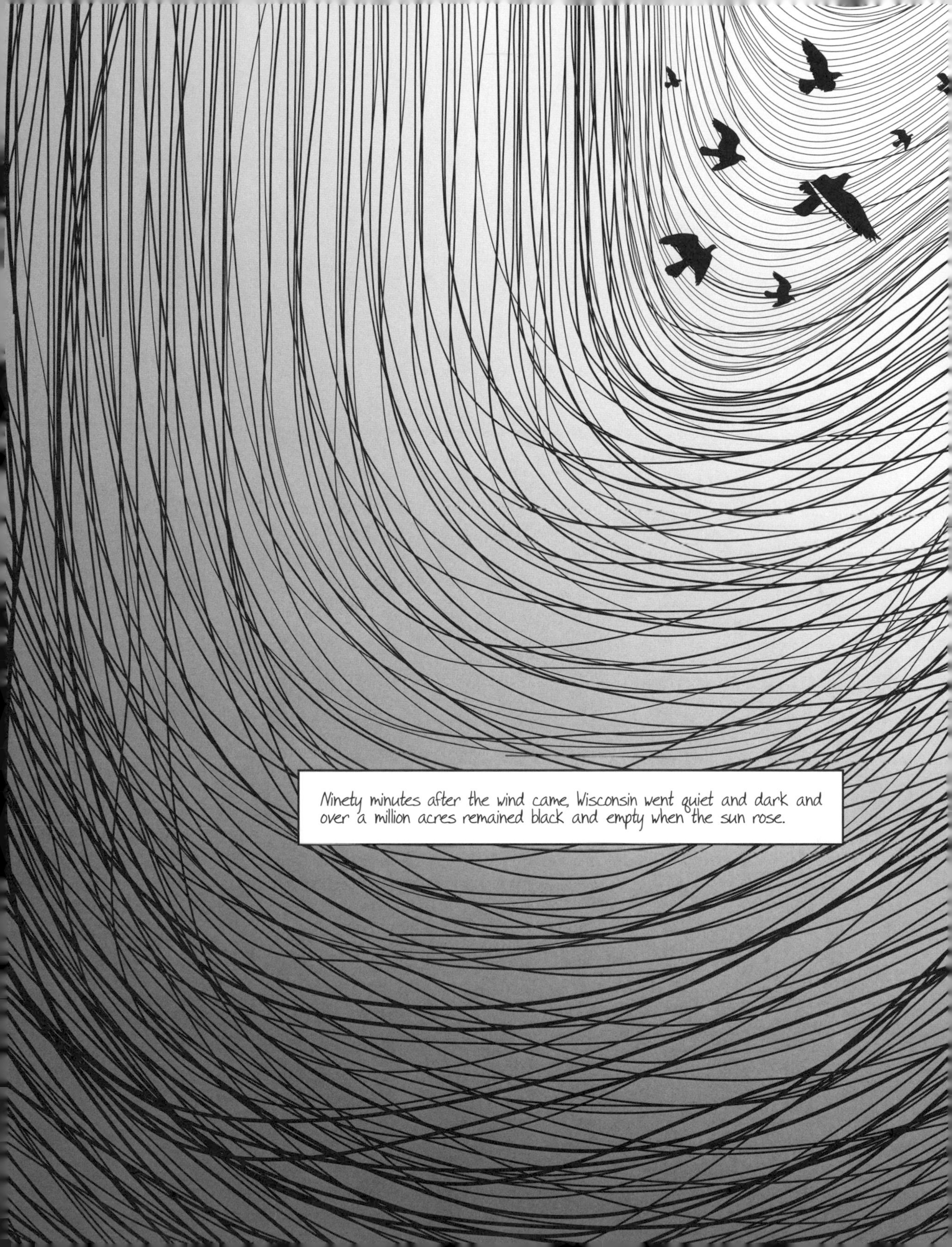
Ninety minutes after the wind came, Wisconsin went quiet and dark and over a million acres remained black and empty when the sun rose.

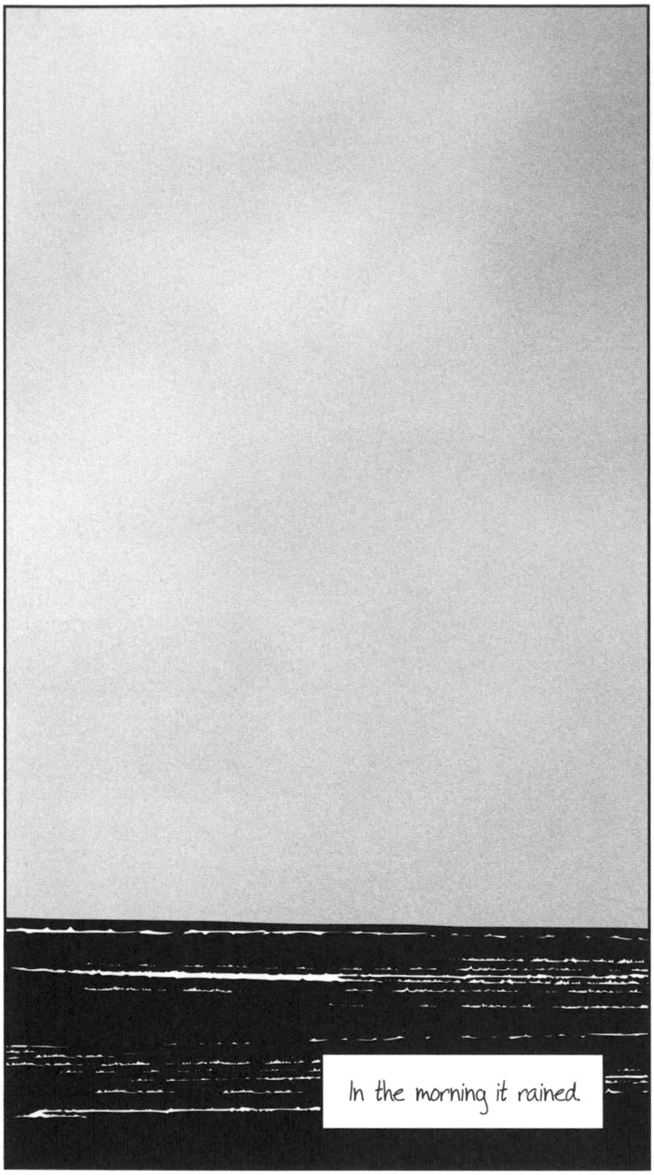
In the morning it rained.

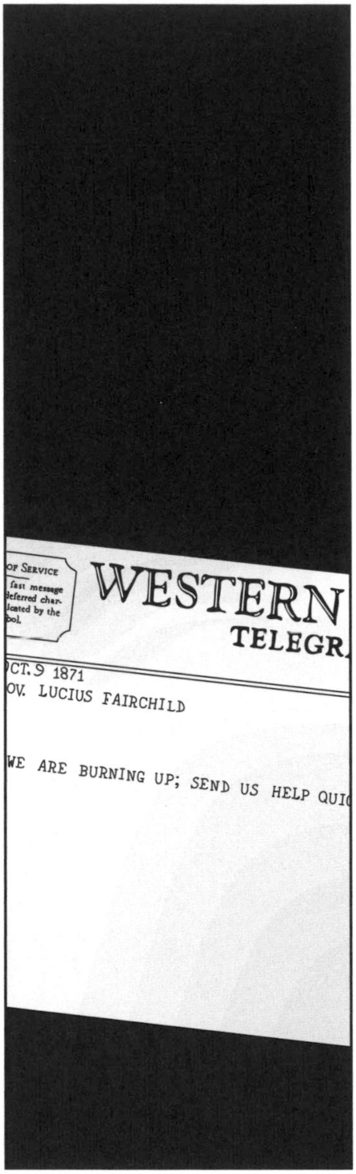
OF SERVICE
fast message
deferred char-
icated by the
bol.
WESTERN
TELEGR
OCT. 9 1871
OV. LUCIUS FAIRCHILD
WE ARE BURNING UP; SEND US HELP QUI

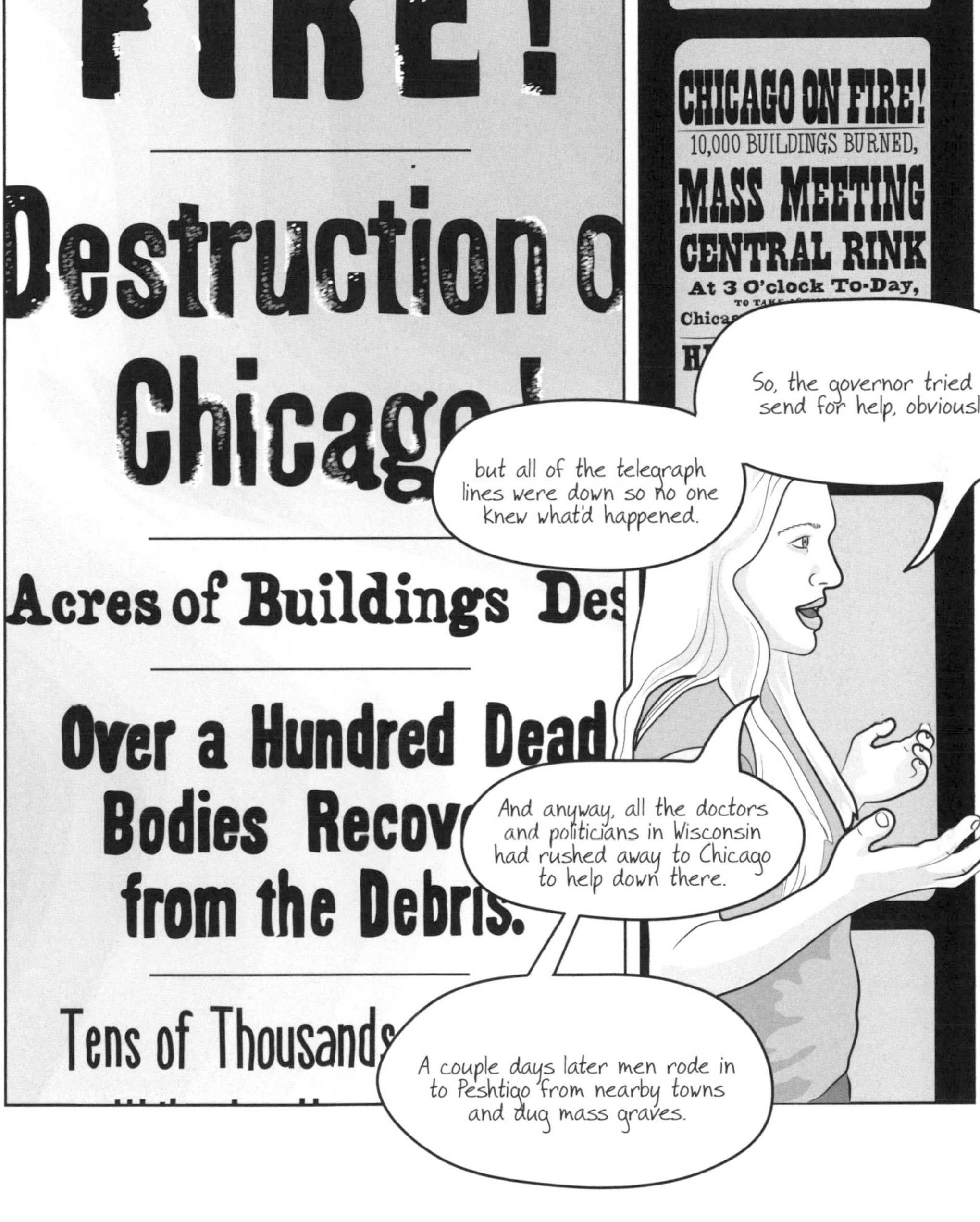

FIRE!
Destruction o
Chicago
Acres of Buildings Des
Over a Hundred Dead
Bodies Recove
from the Debris.
Tens of Thousands
CHICAGO ON FIRE!
10,000 BUILDINGS BURNED,
MASS MEETING
CENTRAL RINK
At 3 O'clock To-Day,
So, the governor tried to send for help, obviously,
but all of the telegraph lines were down so no one knew what'd happened.
And anyway, all the doctors and politicians in Wisconsin had rushed away to Chicago to help down there.
A couple days later men rode in to Peshtigo from nearby towns and dug mass graves.

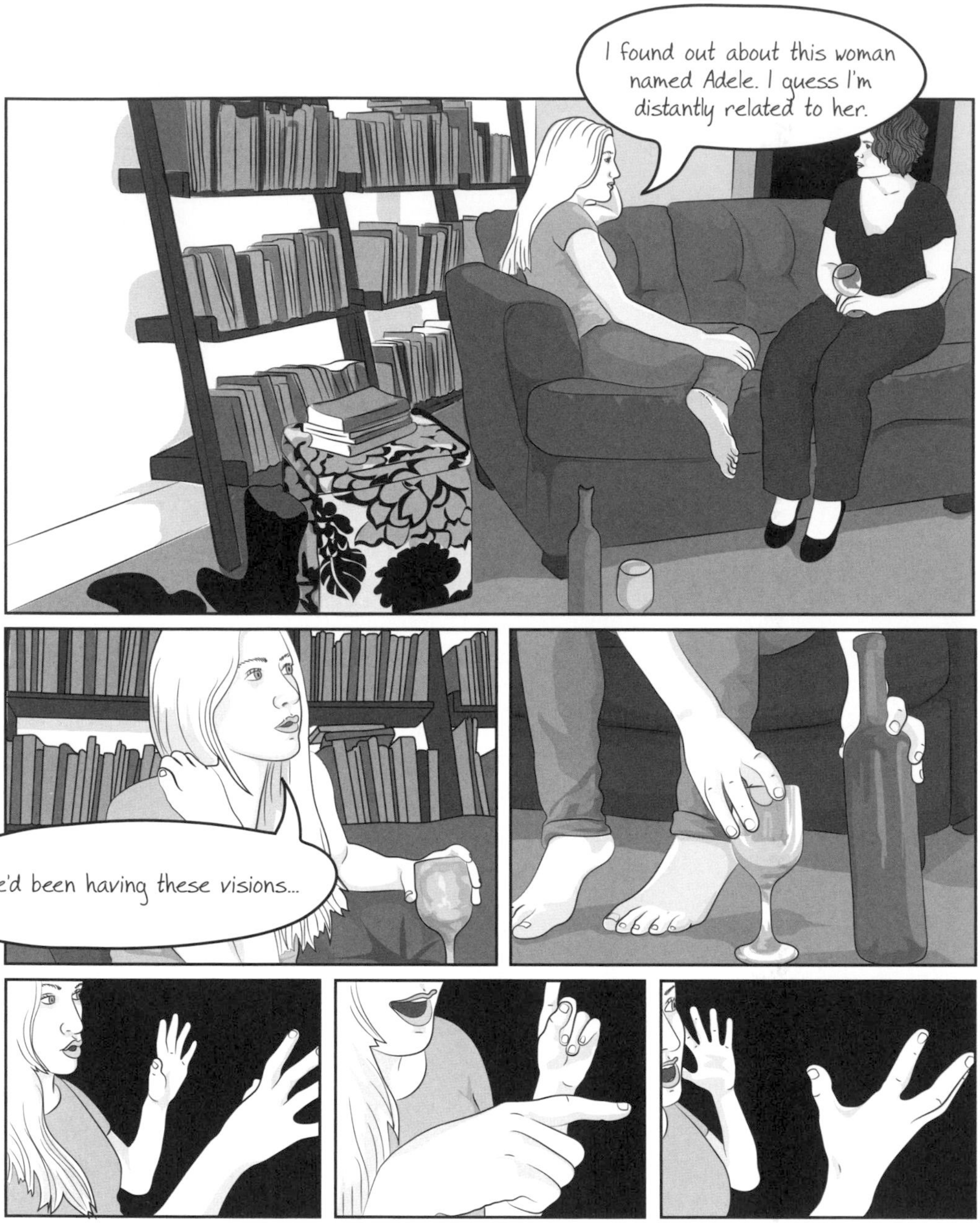
I found out about this woman named Adele. I guess I'm distantly related to her.
She'd been having these visions...

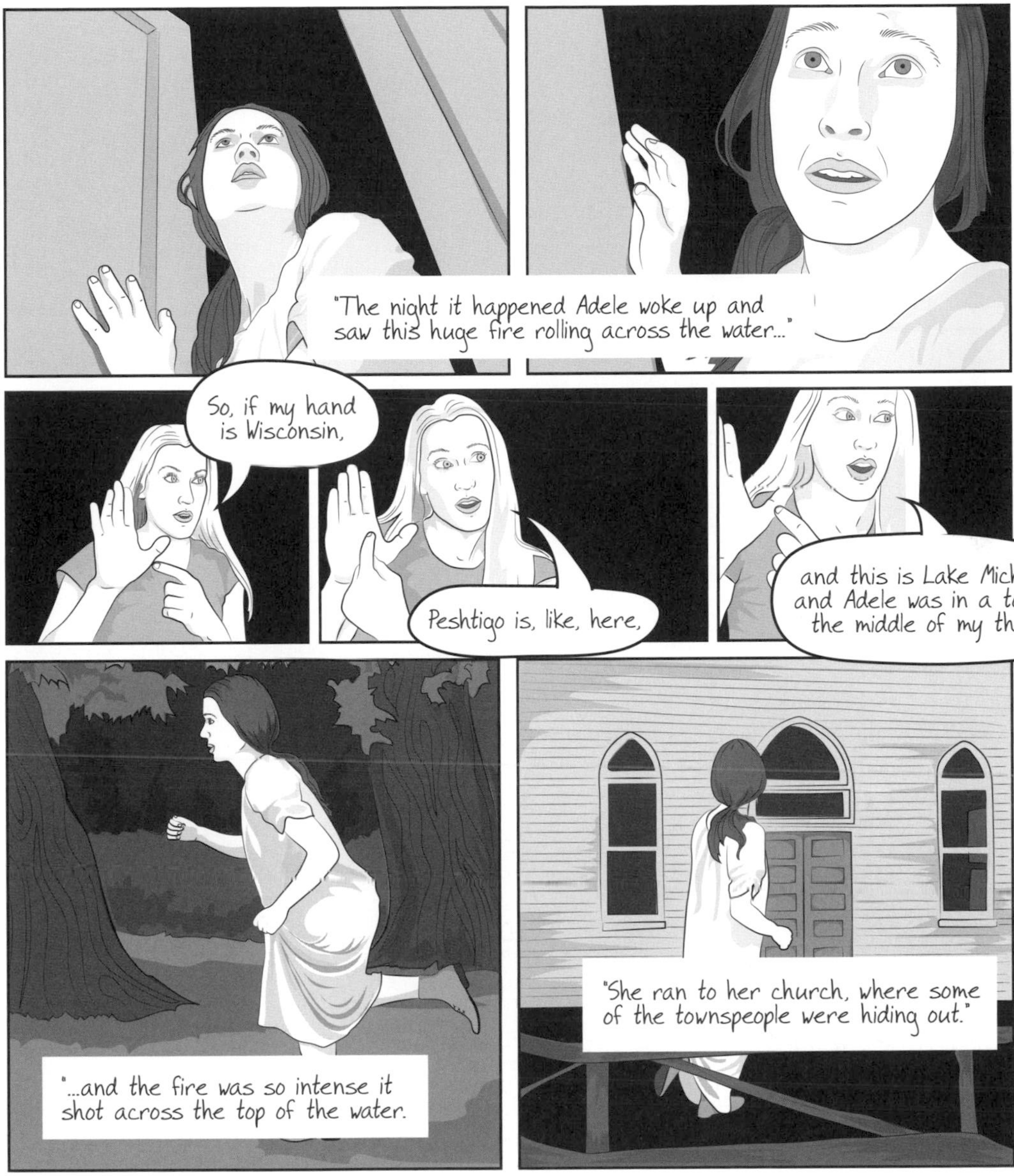
"The night it happened Adele woke up and saw this huge fire rolling across the water..."
So, if my hand is Wisconsin,
Peshtigo is, like, here,
and this is Lake Michigan, and Adele was in a town in the middle of my thumb,
"...and the fire was so intense it shot across the top of the water.
"She ran to her church, where some of the townspeople were hiding out."

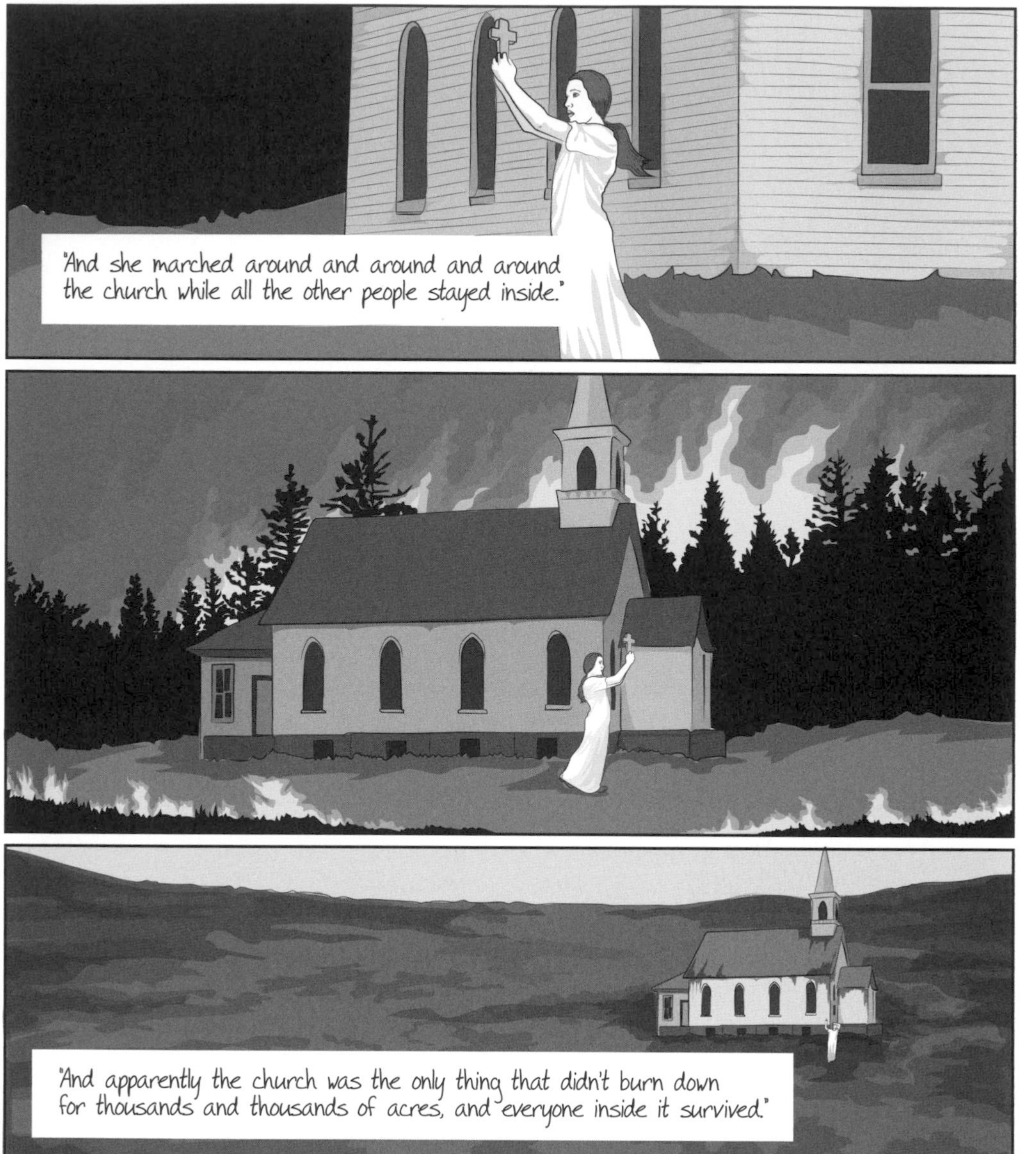
"And she marched around and around and around the church while all the other people stayed inside."
"And apparently the church was the only thing that didn't burn down for thousands and thousands of acres, and everyone inside it survived."

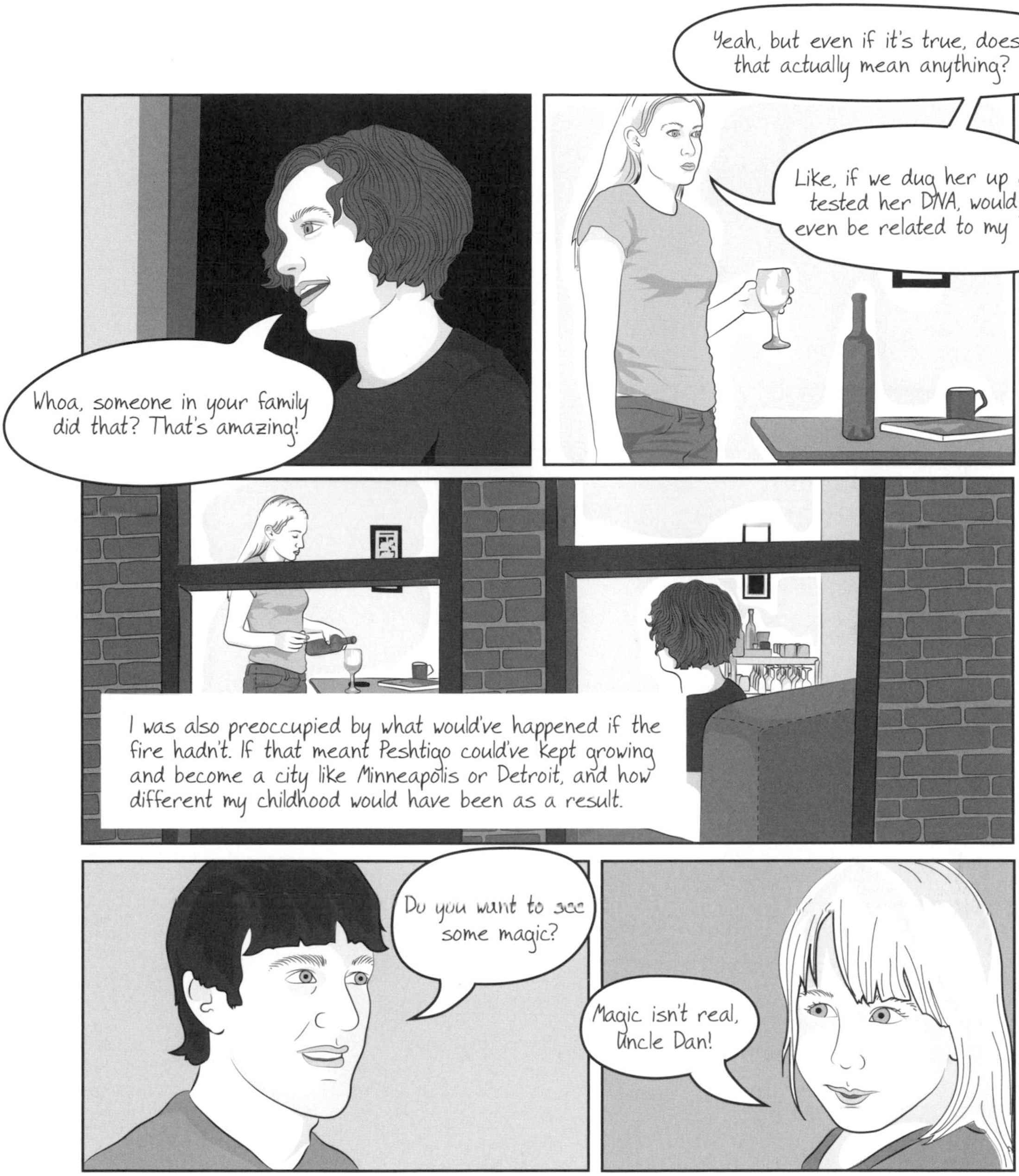
Whoa, someone in your family did that? That's amazing!
Yeah, but even if it's true, does that actually mean anything?
Like, if we dug her up and tested her DNA, would it even be related to my DNA?
I was also preoccupied by what would've happened if the fire hadn't. If that meant Peshtigo could've kept growing and become a city like Minneapolis or Detroit, and how different my childhood would have been as a result.
Do you want to see some magic?
Magic isn't real, Uncle Dan!

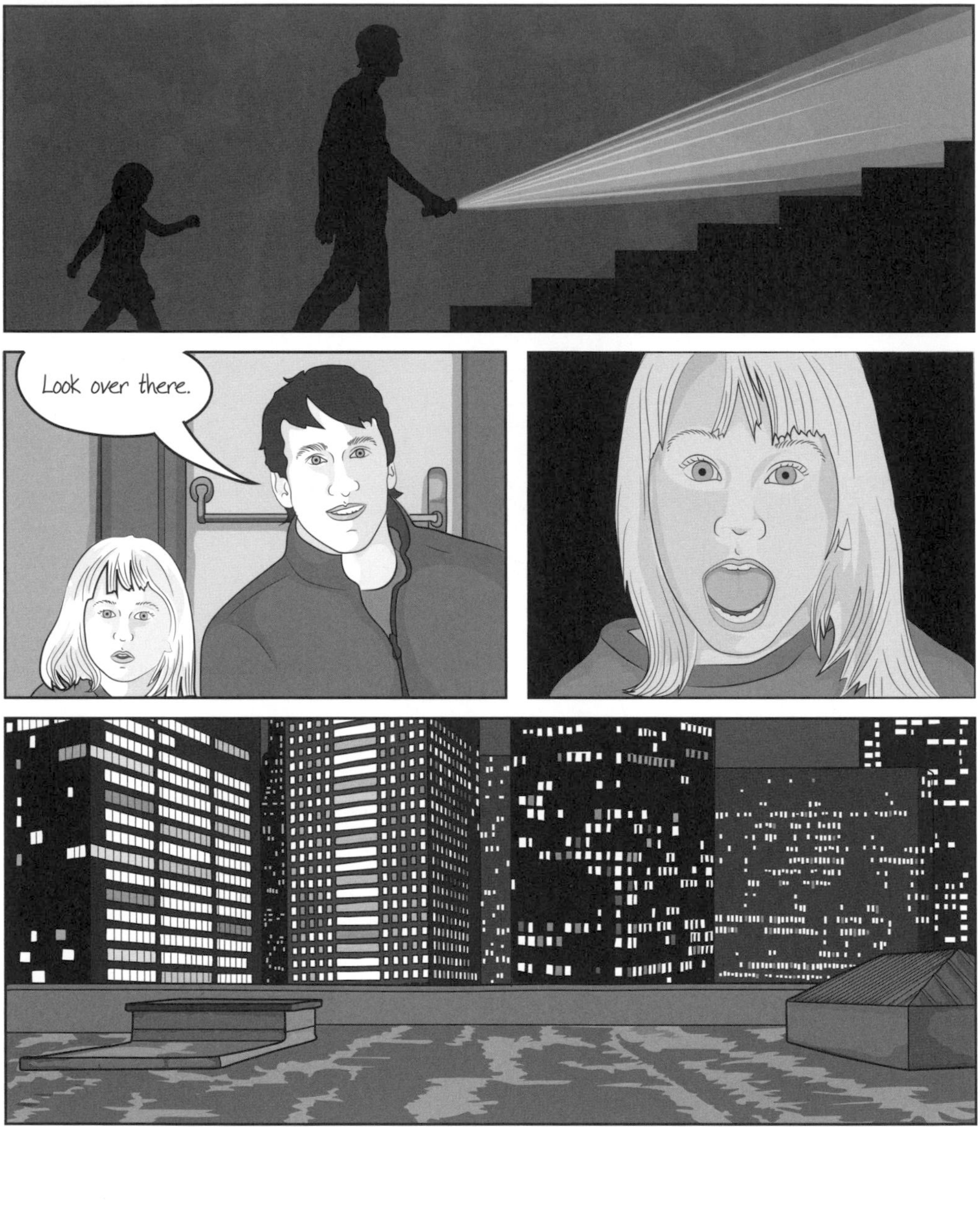
Look over there.

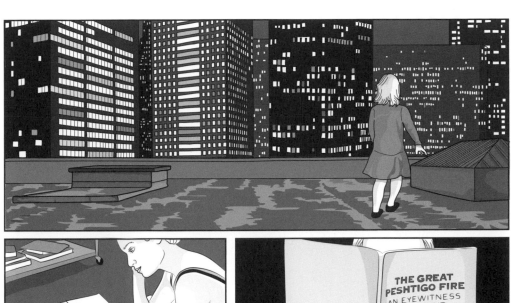

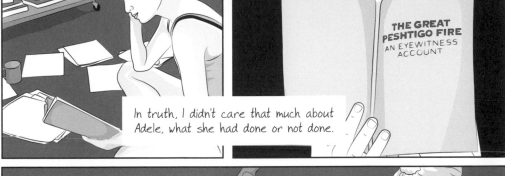

THE GREAT PESHTIGO FIRE
AN EYEWITNESS ACCOUNT
In truth, I didn't care that much about Adele, what she had done or not done.
But I loved the mythology of it all.
She gave me a connection to the fire that made me feel like I had some right to the story.

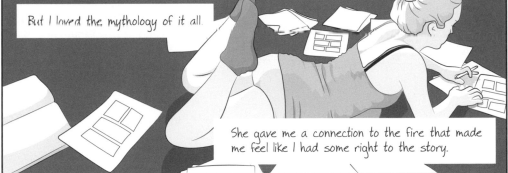

There wasn't much published about Peshtigo, which was not unexpected considering the limited attention it received after the fire itself.

Other than a handful of Xeroxed-and-stapled eyewitness accounts my mother had bought for me from the one-room museum in Peshtigo, there were only a few trade books that detailed the events.

Later, in 1941, Peshtigo would float up from its ghostly place

But I read one theory that came to bother me for years:

on, the U.S. military gathered all the information it could find to determine how to create the most devastating incendiary attacks on cities possible. Those responsible for planning the U.S. tactics in World War II would seek to understand how to create firestorm conditions using the information gathered from Peshtigo and other studies. Peshtigo was not only the first documented firestorm but it was the only firestorm

The combination of wind, topography and ignition sources that created the firestorm, primarily representing the conditions at the boundaries of human settlement and natural areas, is known as the Peshtigo Paradigm.[25] **The condition was closely studied by the American and British military during World War II to learn how to recreate firestorm conditions for bombing campaigns against cities in Germany and Japan.** The bombing of Dresden and the even more severe one of Tokyo by incendiary devices resulted in death tolls comparable to or exceeding those of the atomic bombings of

WARNING
RESTRICTED AREA

This area has been declared a Restricted Area by authority of the Commanding Officer, US Army Dugway Proving Ground, in accordance with the provisions of the directive issued by the Secretary of Defense on 20 August 1954, pursuant to the provisions of Section 21, Internal Security Act of 1950. Unauthorized entry is prohibited. All persons and vehicles entering hereon are liable for search. Photographing or making notes, drawings, maps, or graphic representations of this area, or its activities, is prohibited unless specifically authorized by the Commander. Any such material found in the possession of unauthorized persons shall be confiscated.

USE OF DEADLY FORCE
AUTHORIZED

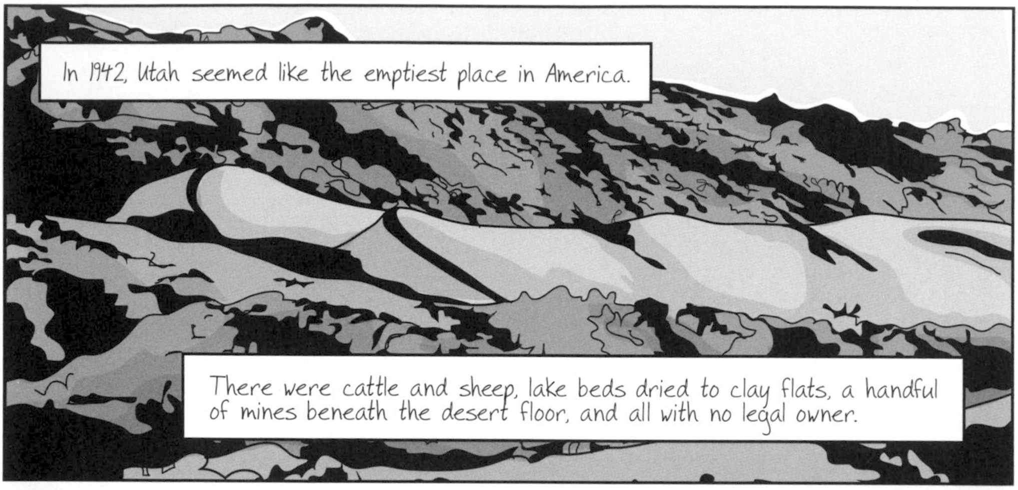
In 1942, Utah seemed like the emptiest place in America.
There were cattle and sheep, lake beds dried to clay flats, a handful of mines beneath the desert floor, and all with no legal owner.

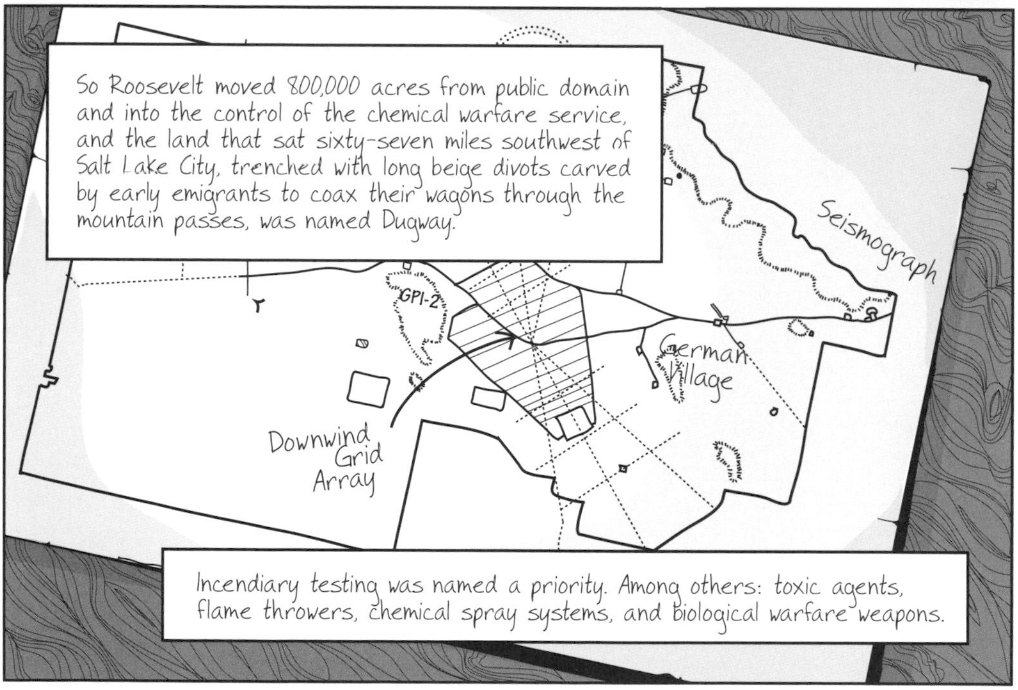
So Roosevelt moved 800,000 acres from public domain and into the control of the chemical warfare service, and the land that sat sixty-seven miles southwest of Salt Lake City, trenched with long beige divots carved by early emigrants to coax their wagons through the mountain passes, was named Dugway.
Seismograph
GPI-2
German Village
Downwind Grid Array
Incendiary testing was named a priority. Among others: toxic agents, flame throwers, chemical spray systems, and biological warfare weapons.

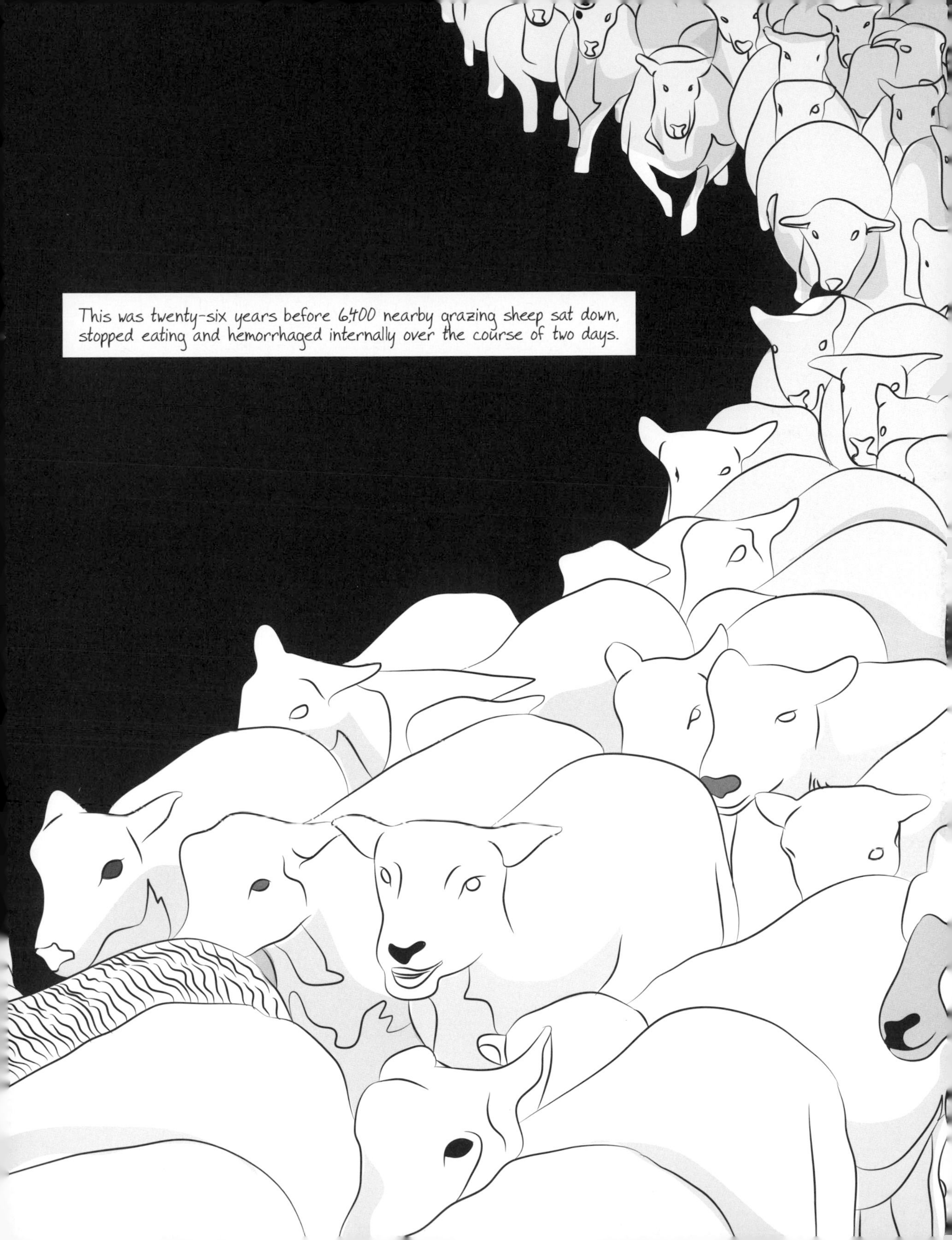
This was twenty-six years before 6,400 nearby grazing sheep sat down, stopped eating and hemorrhaged internally over the course of two days.

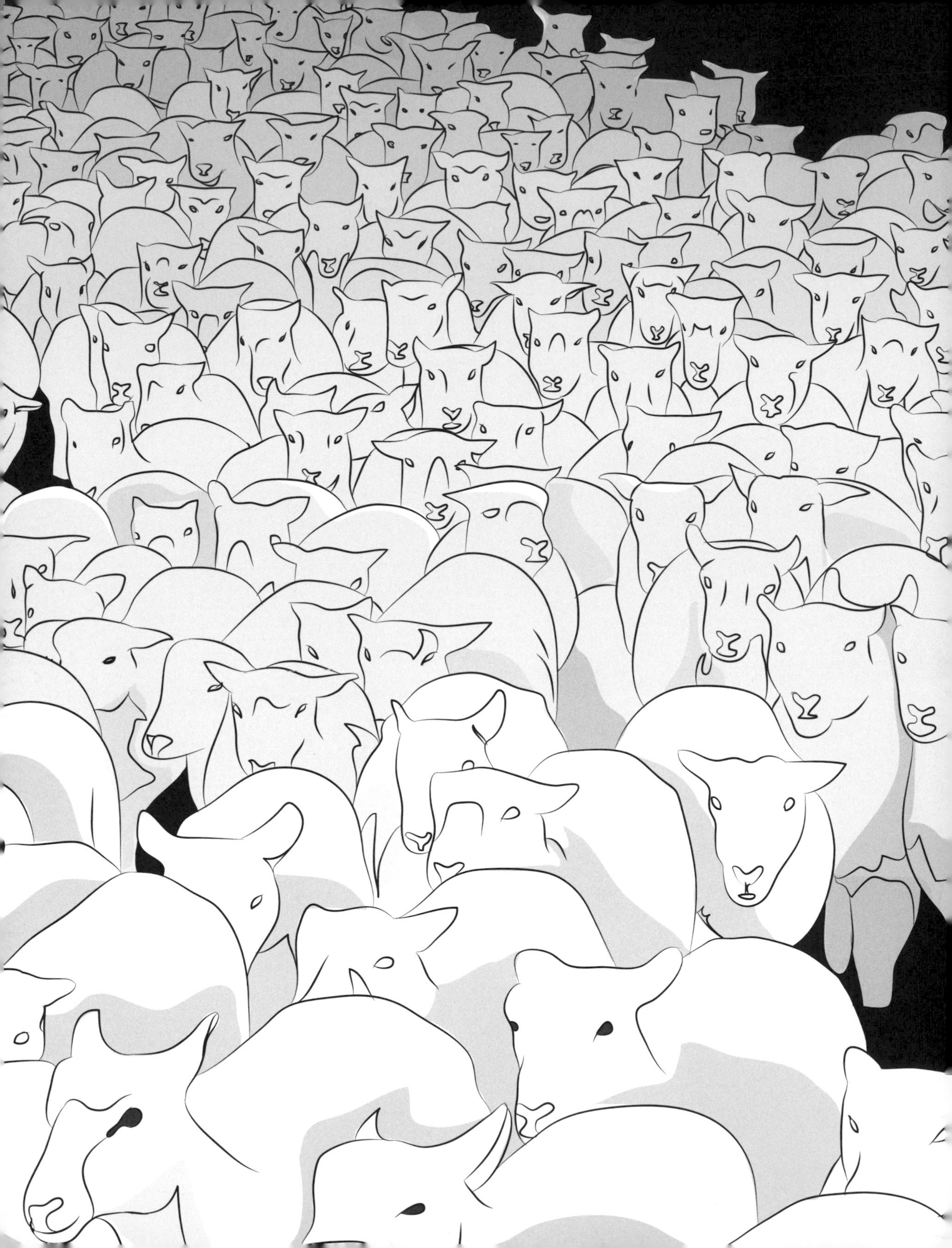

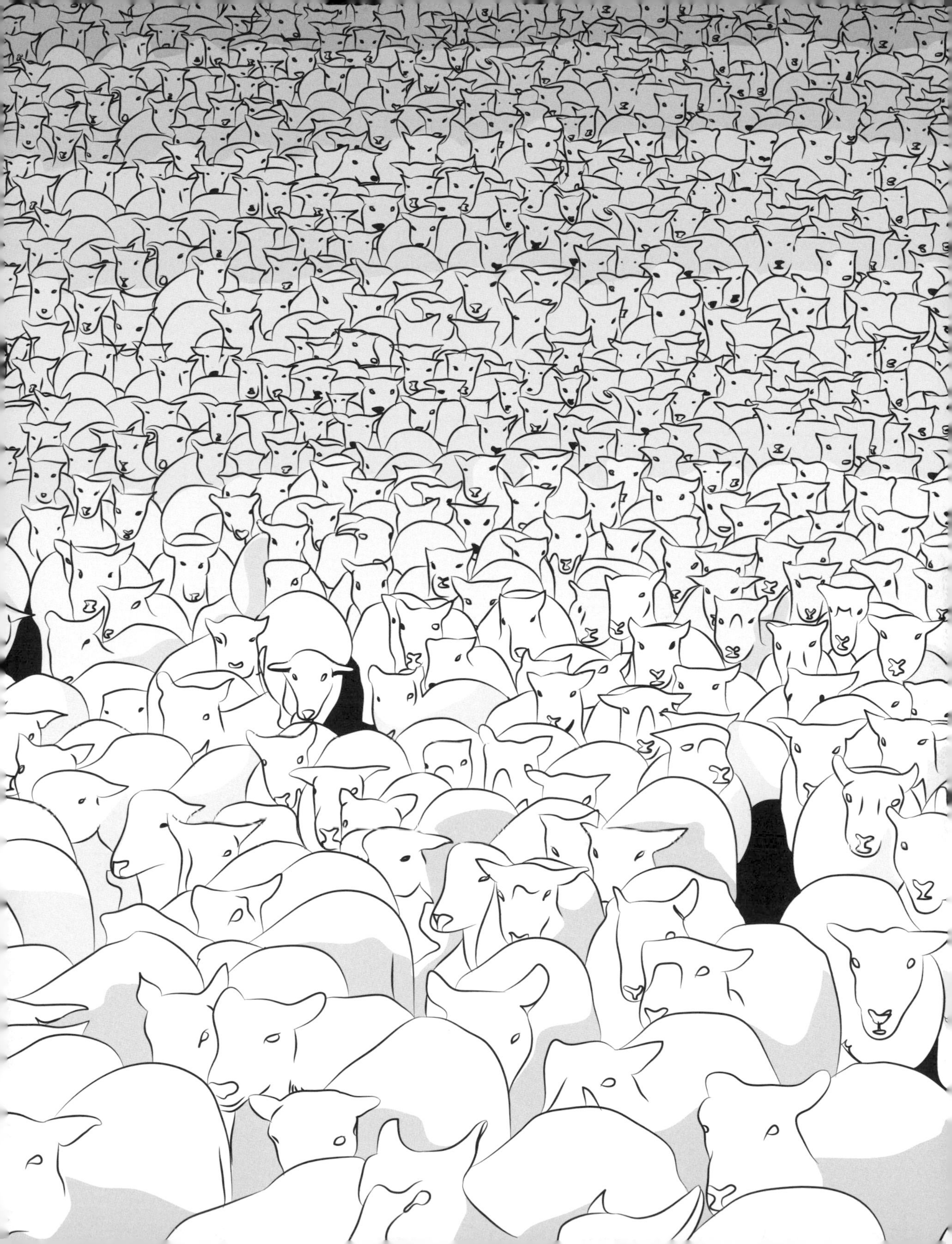

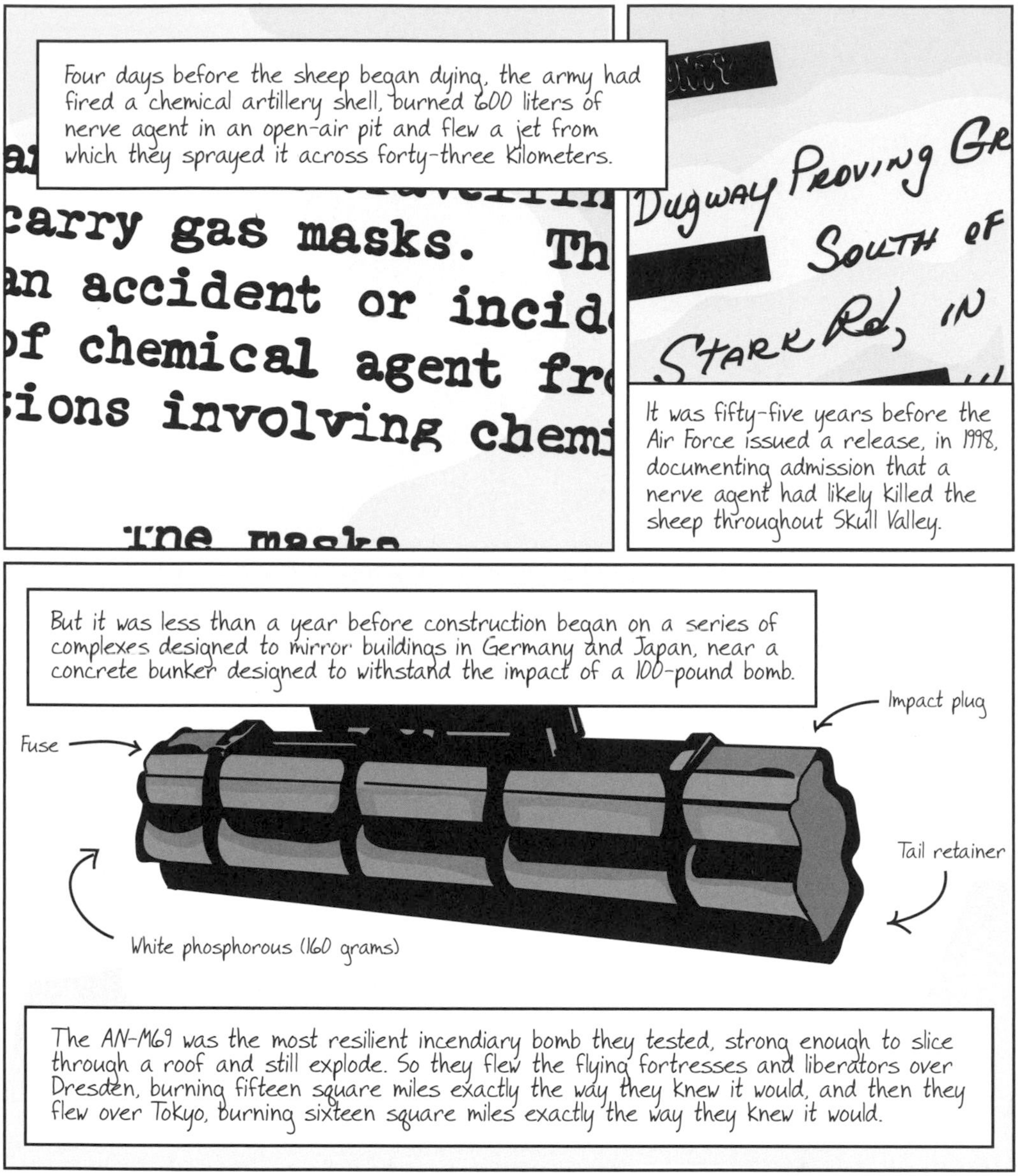

Four days before the sheep began dying, the army had fired a chemical artillery shell, burned 600 liters of nerve agent in an open-air pit and flew a jet from which they sprayed it across forty-three kilometers.

carry gas masks. Th

an accident or incide

of chemical agent fro

sions involving chemi

ine masks

Dugway Proving Gr

South of

Stark Rd, IN

It was fifty-five years before the Air Force issued a release, in 1998, documenting admission that a nerve agent had likely killed the sheep throughout Skull Valley.

But it was less than a year before construction began on a series of complexes designed to mirror buildings in Germany and Japan, near a concrete bunker designed to withstand the impact of a 100-pound bomb.

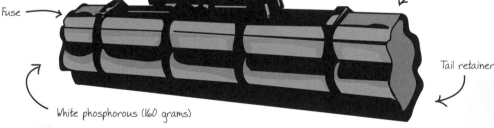

Fuse

Impact plug

Tail retainer

White phosphorous (160 grams)

The AN-M69 was the most resilient incendiary bomb they tested, strong enough to slice through a roof and still explode. So they flew the flying fortresses and liberators over Dresden, burning fifteen square miles exactly the way they knew it would, and then they flew over Tokyo, burning sixteen square miles exactly the way they knew it would.

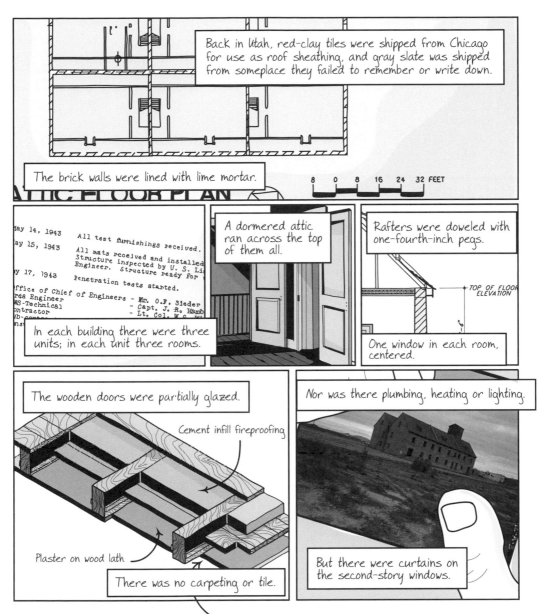

Back in Utah, red-clay tiles were shipped from Chicago for use as roof sheathing, and gray slate was shipped from someplace they failed to remember or write down.

The brick walls were lined with lime mortar.

8  0  8  16  24  32 FEET

ATTIC FLOOR PLAN

May 14, 1943    All test furnishings received.
May 15, 1943    All mats received and installed.
                Structure inspected by U. S. Li
                Engineer.  Structure ready for
May 17, 1943    Penetration tests started.

Office of Chief of Engineers - Mr. O.F. Sieder
Area Engineer
WS-Technical                  - Capt. J. R. Hamb
Contractor                    - Lt. Col. W. C. Wi
Wb-contra

In each building there were three units; in each unit three rooms.

A dormered attic ran across the top of them all.

Rafters were doweled with one-fourth-inch pegs.

TOP OF FLOOR ELEVATION

One window in each room, centered.

The wooden doors were partially glazed.

Cement infill fireproofing

Plaster on wood lath

There was no carpeting or tile.

Nor was there plumbing, heating or lighting.

But there were curtains on the second-story windows.

Secured tongue-and-groove, fastened by two nails

199

This is where Peshtigo comes in: There are some reports that say Allied scientists studied the only firestorm ever documented to learn what they could about fire.

They found stacks of seventy-year-old maps with circular wind patterns drawn across them, confused letters meteorologists had drafted to each other about the air they did not understand.

*repared from reports made by U.S. Army Signal Service observers at :35 P.M. Central Standard time, October 8, 1877, course of cyclonic stor*

It was the gas, scientists found, carbureted hydrogen, that made everything burn so hot—produced faster than it could be consumed, and so it rose, and the fire pulled itself higher and wider, a mile high and five long in 2,000-degree air.

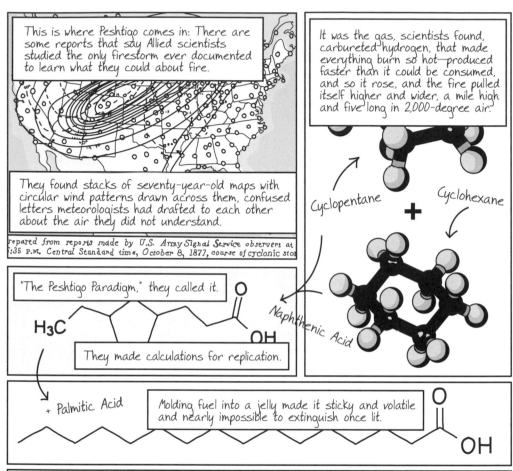

Cyclopentane

+

Cyclohexane

Naphthenic Acid

"The Peshtigo Paradigm," they called it.

$H_3C$

OH

They made calculations for replication.

+ Palmitic Acid

Molding fuel into a jelly made it sticky and volatile and nearly impossible to extinguish once lit.

OH

nd munitions under temperate zone conditions. Researchers dropped phos yanogen chloride, and hydrogen cyanide bombs ranging in size from 100 000 pounds from different altitudes under different meteorological condit. o estimate the quantity of munitions required to lay down a lethal concentrati f gas upon a given area. Gas and smoke clouds were also tested under metec onditions

In Utah, eighteen pieces of furniture were bought or built for each apartment.

nd chem

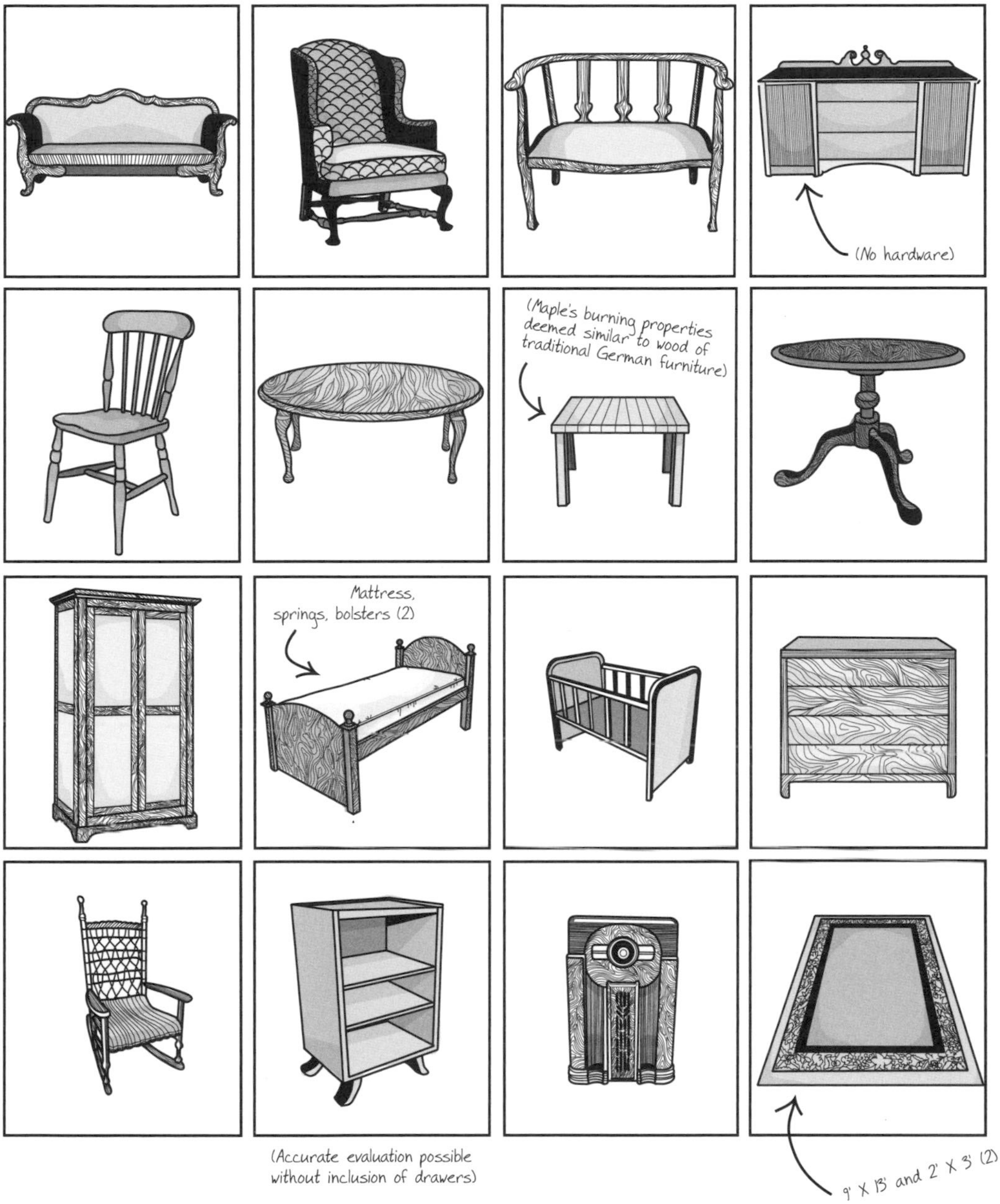
(No hardware)
(Maple's burning properties deemed similar to wood of traditional German furniture)
Mattress, springs, bolsters (2)
(Accurate evaluation possible without inclusion of drawers)
9' X 13' and 2' X 3' (2)

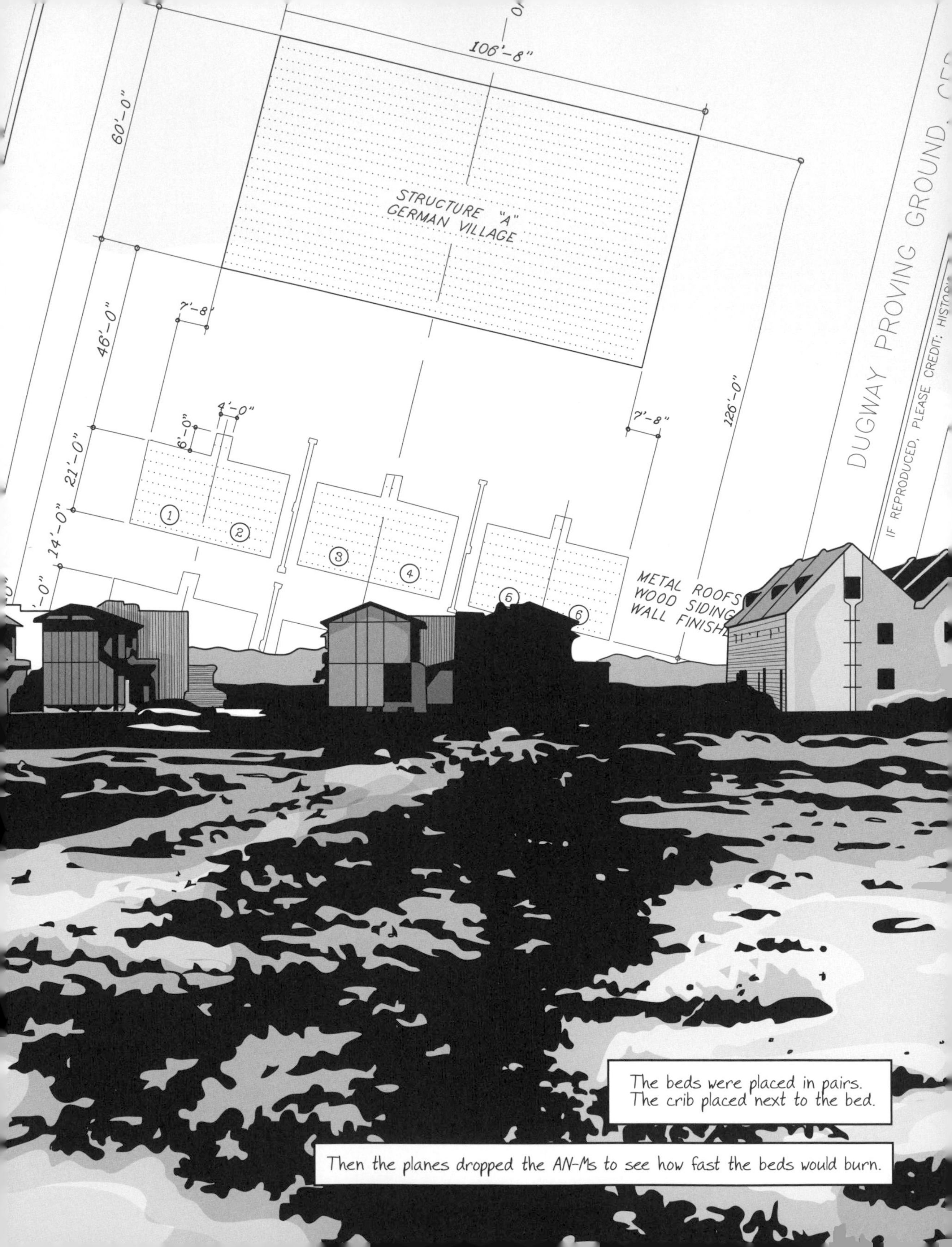
106'–8"
60'–0"
STRUCTURE "A"
GERMAN VILLAGE
7'–8"
46'–0"
4'–0"
6'–0"
21'–0"
14'–0"
7'–8"
126'–0"
METAL ROOFS
WOOD SIDING
WALL FINISH
DUGWAY PROVING GROUND,
IF REPRODUCED, PLEASE CREDIT:
The beds were placed in pairs.
The crib placed next to the bed.
Then the planes dropped the AN-Ms to see how fast the beds would burn.

The combination of wind, topography and ignition sources that created the [...] s of human [...]m.[25] **The**

Maybe an overzealous researcher had made a connection that simply wasn't there, had imagined a relationship of cause and effect when all they housed was similarity. Or maybe there is a classified government document somewhere that admits to what these sourceless books and websites have already reported.

[...] **ary during World War II to learn how to recreate firestorm conditions for bombing campaigns against cities in Germany and Japan.** The bombing of Dresden and the even more severe one of Tokyo by incendiary devices resulted in death tolls comparable to or exceeding those of the atomic bombings of

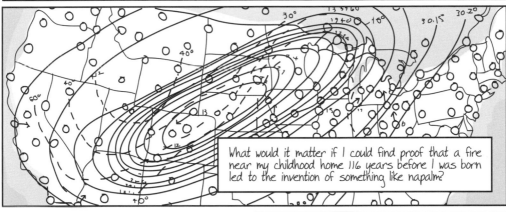

What would it matter if I could find proof that a fire near my childhood home 116 years before I was born led to the invention of something like napalm?

Perhaps nothing.

If it hadn't been napalm, it would have been something else.

There are so many ways to reach the same end.

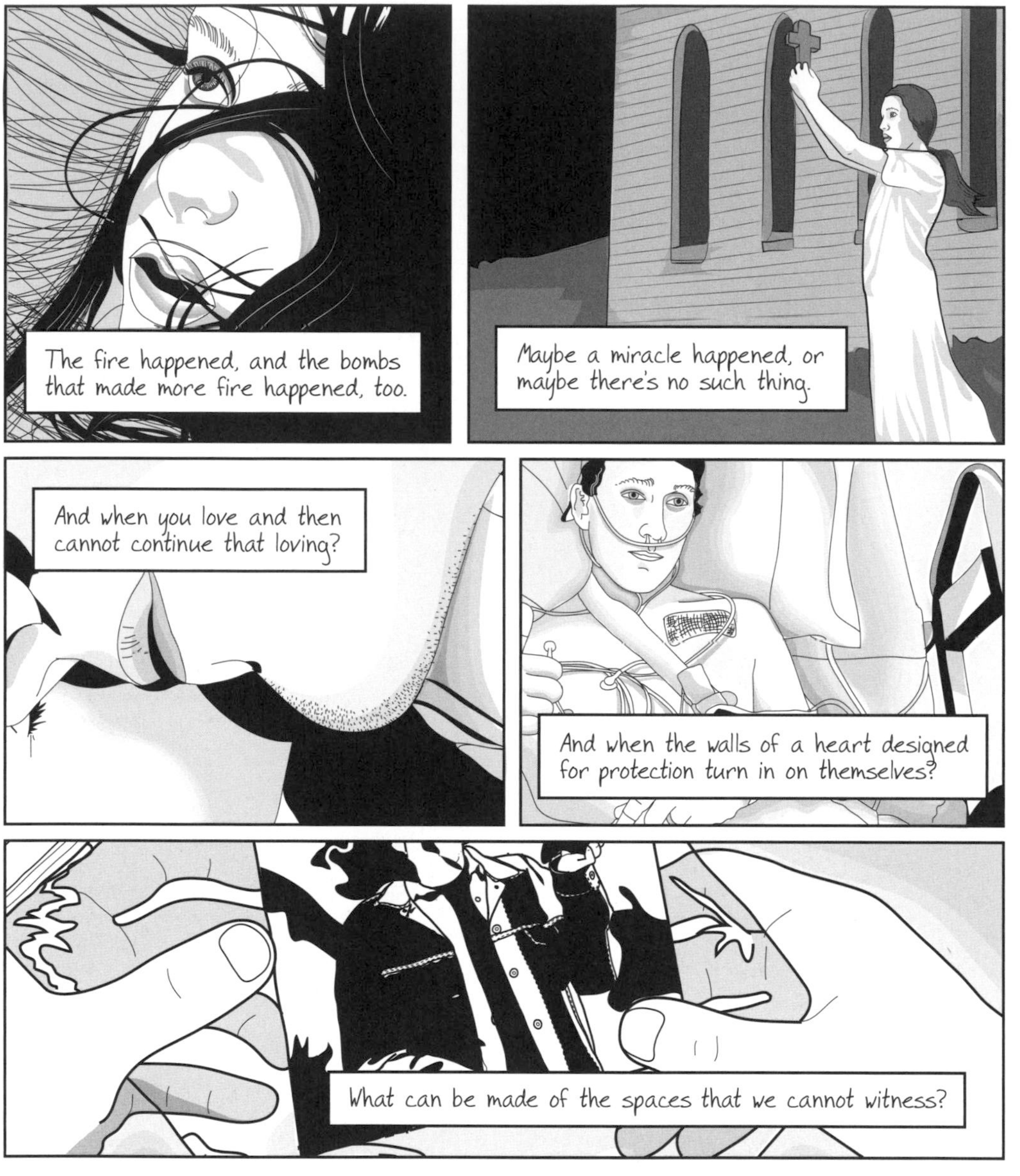
The fire happened, and the bombs that made more fire happened, too.
Maybe a miracle happened, or maybe there's no such thing.
And when you love and then cannot continue that loving?
And when the walls of a heart designed for protection turn in on themselves?
What can be made of the spaces that we cannot witness?

# Chapter 6

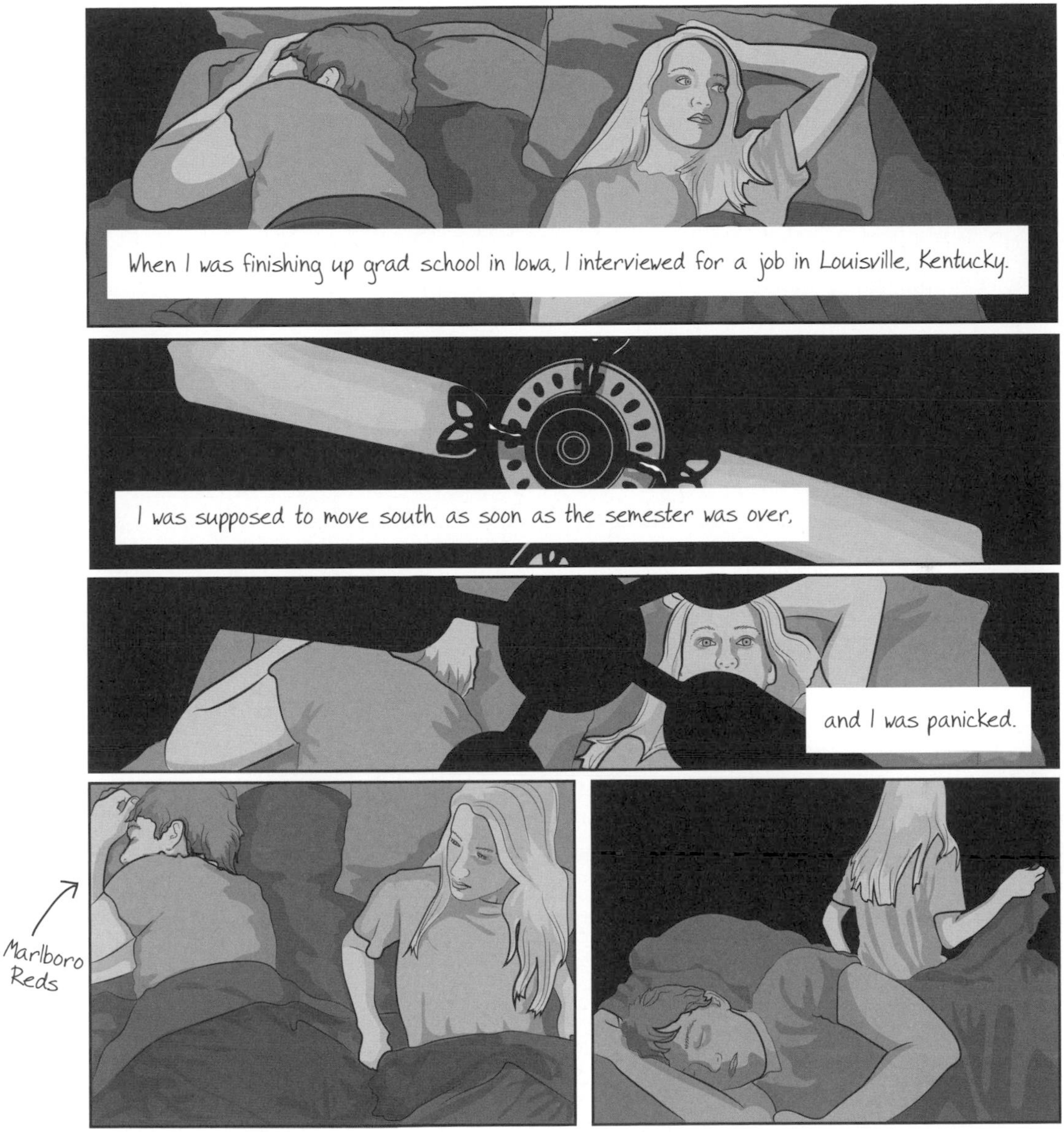
When I was finishing up grad school in Iowa, I interviewed for a job in Louisville, Kentucky.
I was supposed to move south as soon as the semester was over,
and I was panicked.
Marlboro Reds

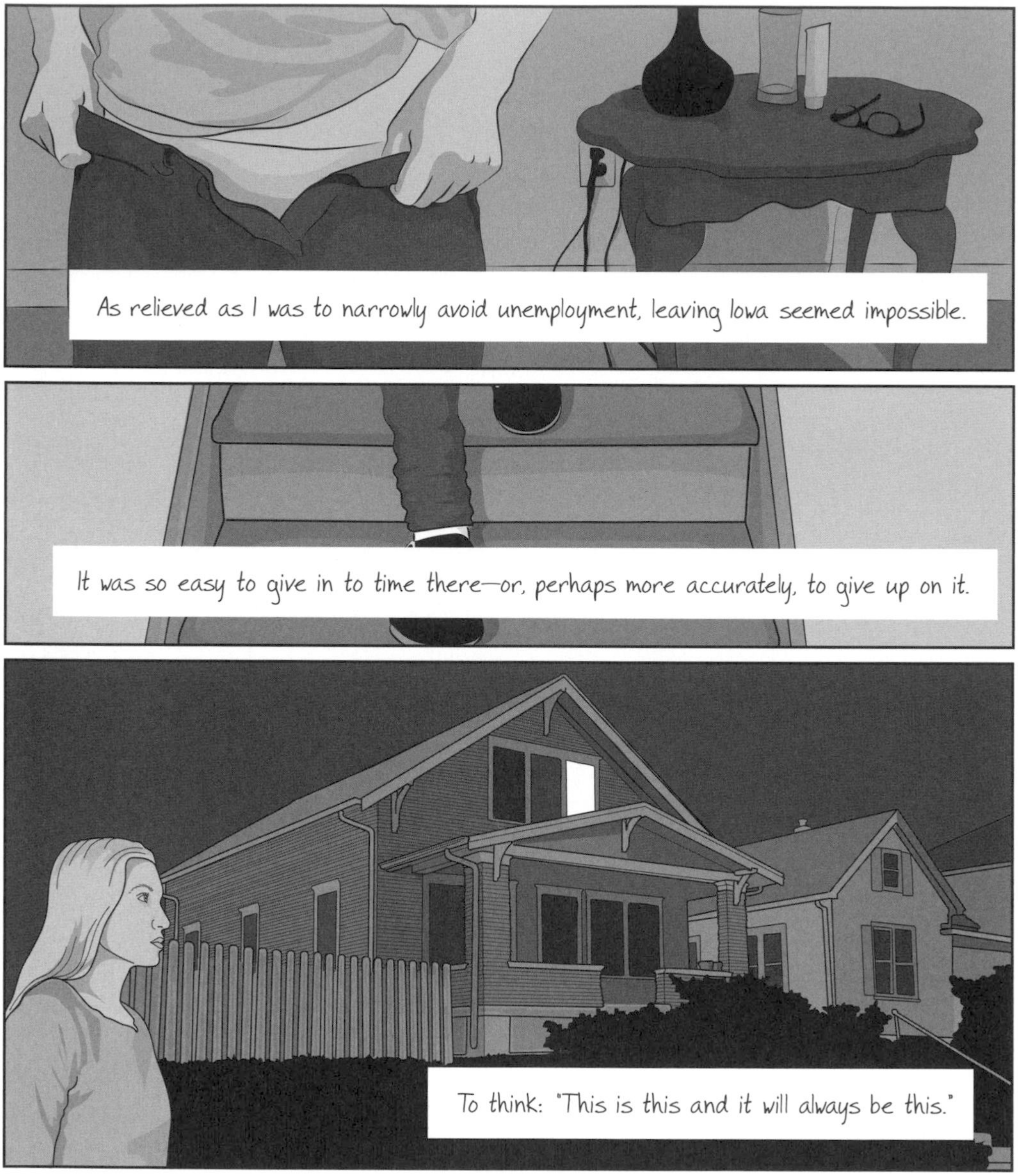
As relieved as I was to narrowly avoid unemployment, leaving Iowa seemed impossible.
It was so easy to give in to time there—or, perhaps more accurately, to give up on it.
To think: "This is this and it will always be this."

Hey.
Hey, girl. What're you doing up?
I could picture the room around her when I looked up through the window, and it felt important to me that I could.
ironic/unironic church candle
lots of Ani DiFranco
PHILIP ROT
leftover lighter from before she quit smoking

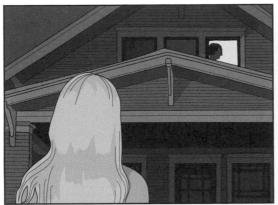

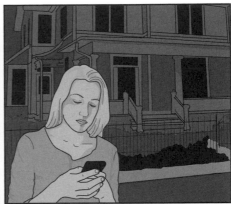

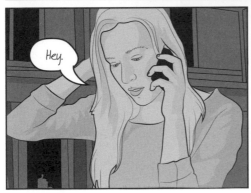

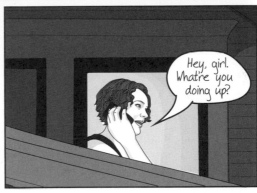

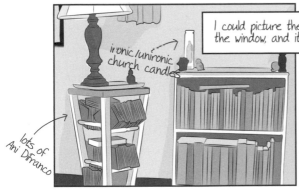

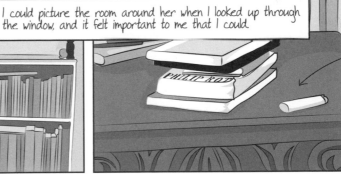

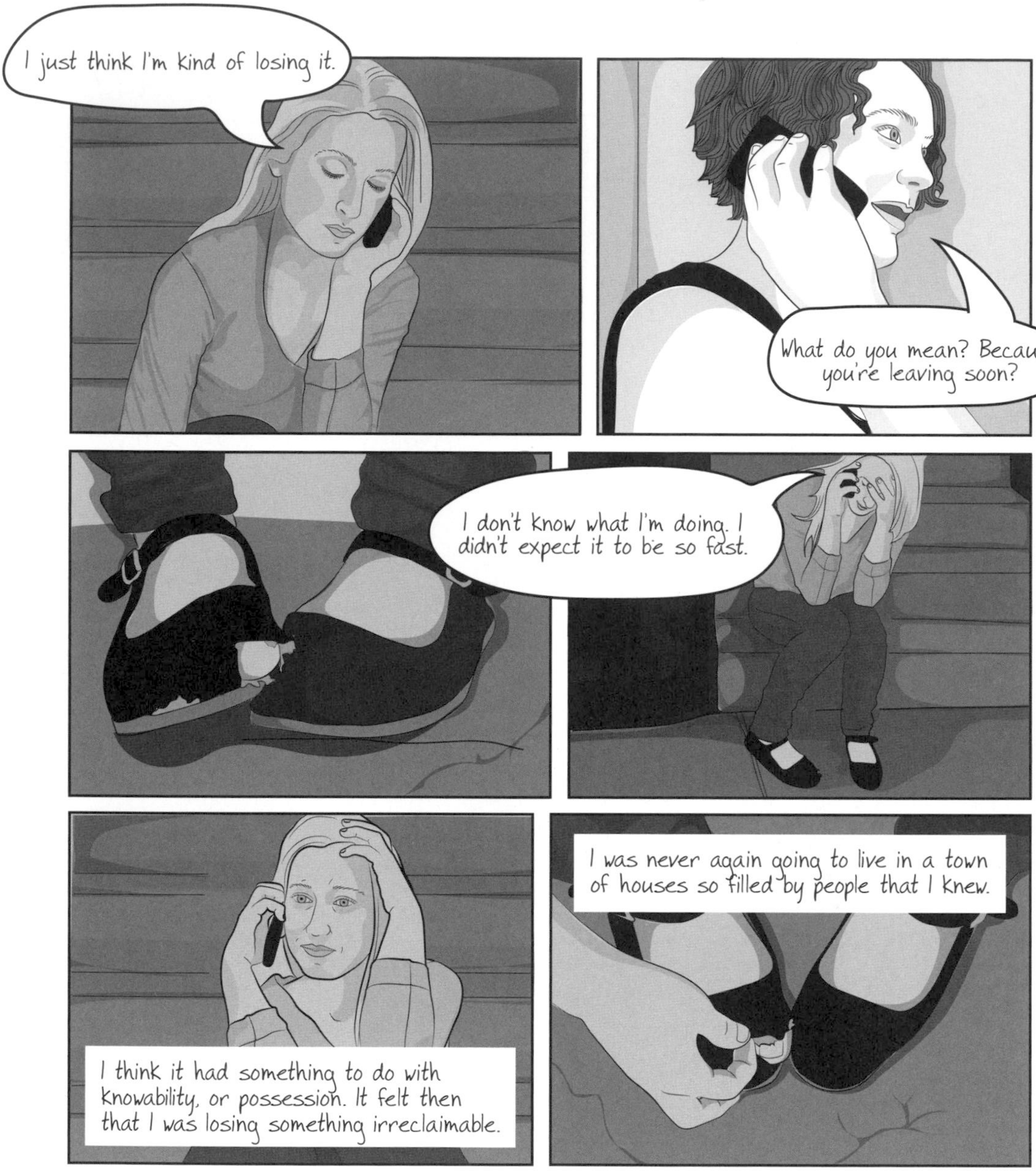
I just think I'm kind of losing it.
What do you mean? Because you're leaving soon?
I don't know what I'm doing. I didn't expect it to be so fast.
I think it had something to do with knowability, or possession. It felt then that I was losing something irreclaimable.
I was never again going to live in a town of houses so filled by people that I knew.

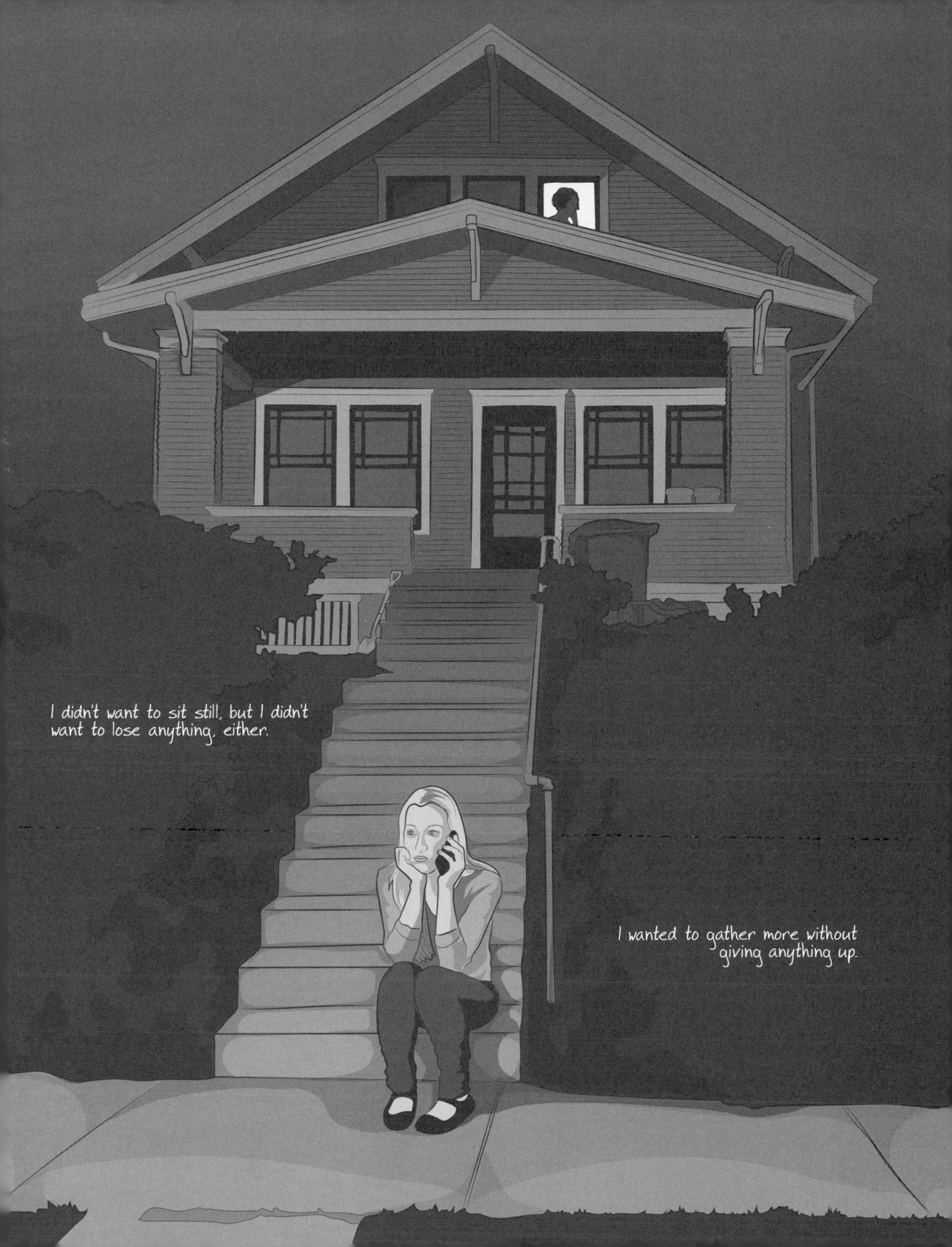
I didn't want to sit still, but I didn't want to lose anything, either.
I wanted to gather more without giving anything up.

Back at college in Chicago, Andrew and I often snuck into classrooms in the middle of the night to watch movies on the projectors.

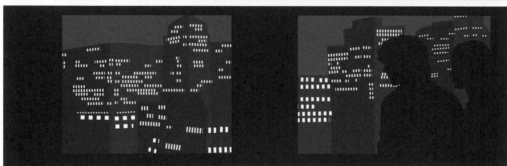

That was the first time I saw Chris Marker's <u>Sans Soleil</u>, a pseudo-travel documentary told in letters, which begins on the Icelandic island of Heimaey.

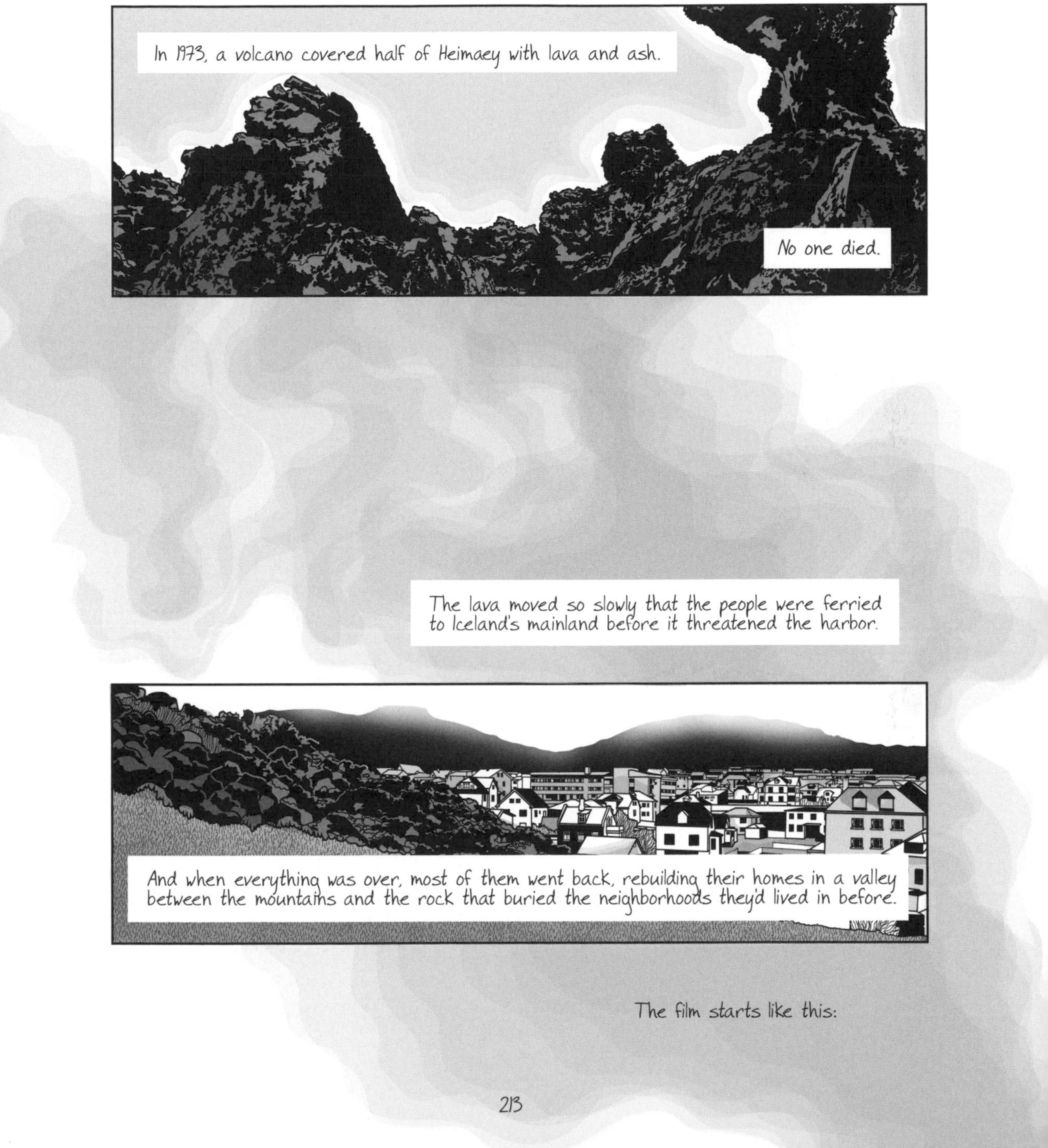
In 1973, a volcano covered half of Heimaey with lava and ash.
No one died.
The lava moved so slowly that the people were ferried to Iceland's mainland before it threatened the harbor.
And when everything was over, most of them went back, rebuilding their homes in a valley between the mountains and the rock that buried the neighborhoods they'd lived in before.
The film starts like this:

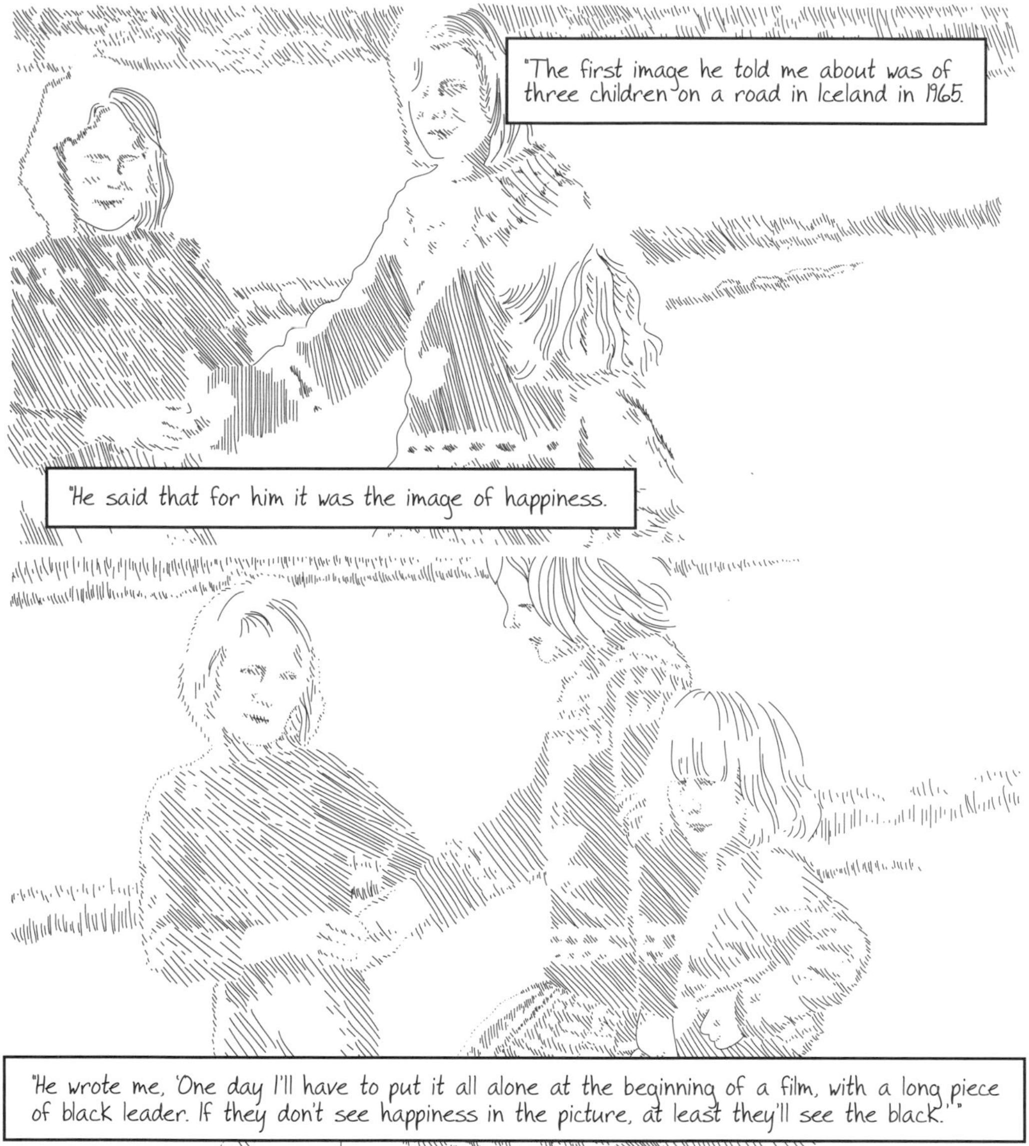
"The first image he told me about was of three children on a road in Iceland in 1965.
"He said that for him it was the image of happiness.
"He wrote me, 'One day I'll have to put it all alone at the beginning of a film, with a long piece of black leader. If they don't see happiness in the picture, at least they'll see the black.' "

215

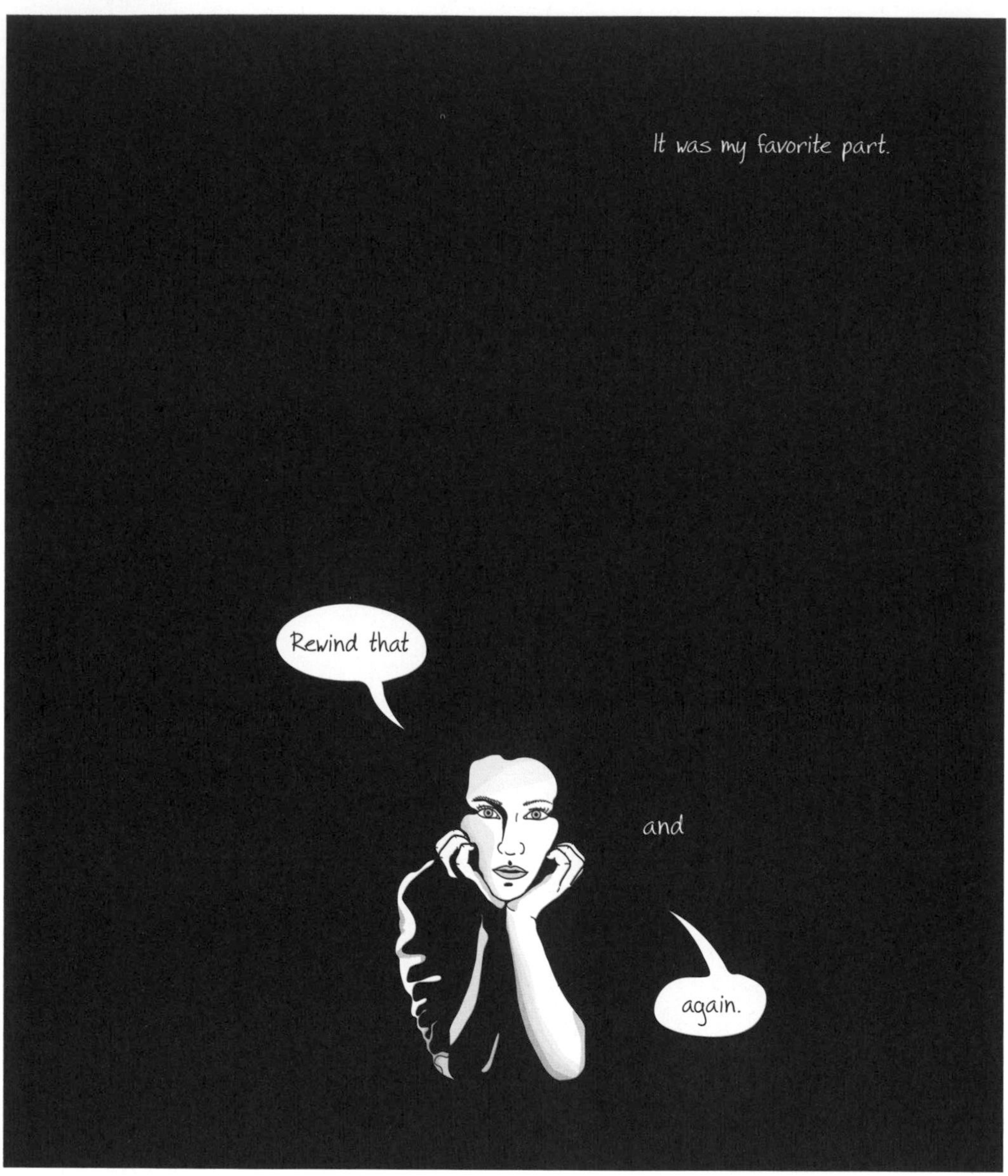
It was my favorite part.
Rewind that
and
again.

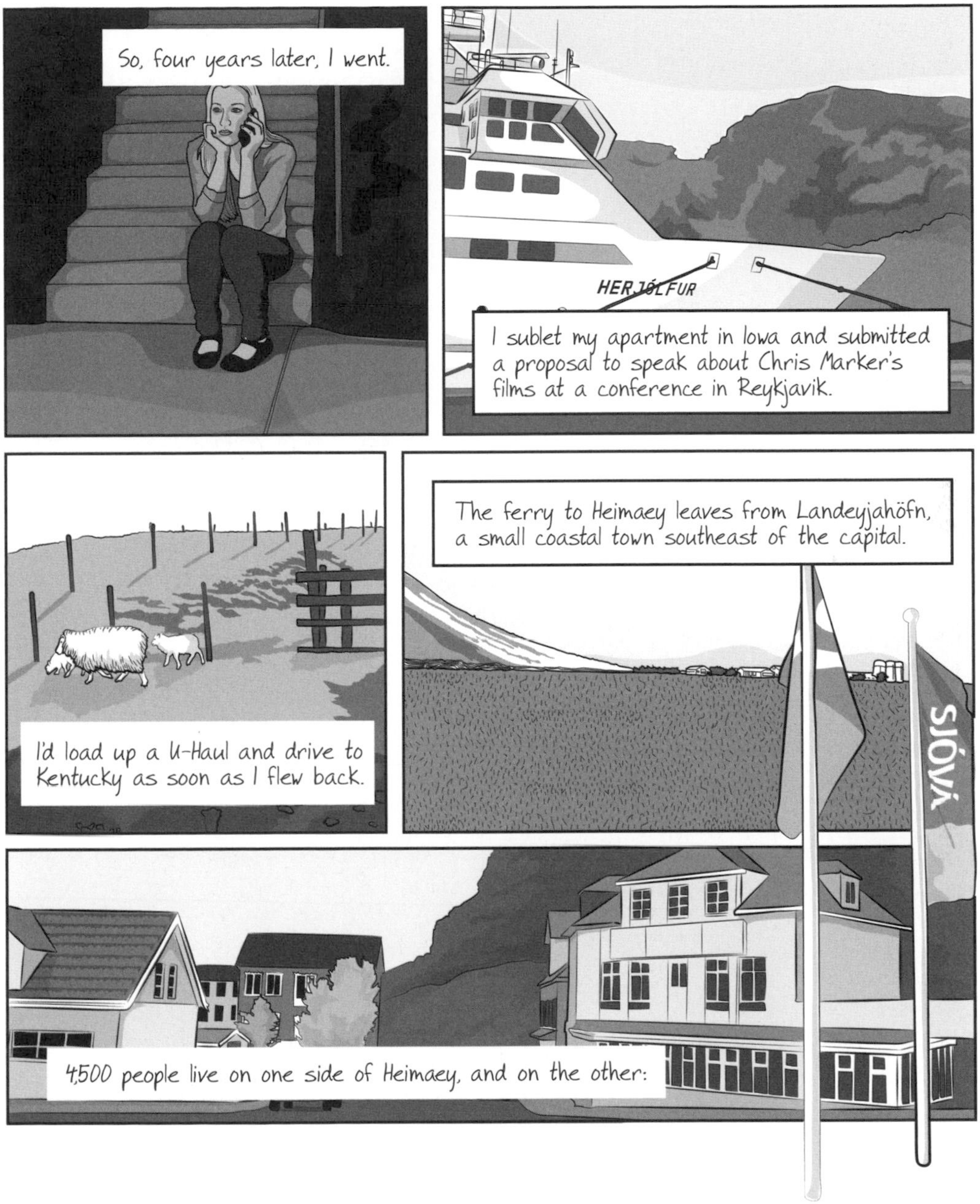
So, four years later, I went.
HERJÓLFUR
I sublet my apartment in Iowa and submitted a proposal to speak about Chris Marker's films at a conference in Reykjavik.
I'd load up a U-Haul and drive to Kentucky as soon as I flew back.
The ferry to Heimaey leaves from Landeyjahöfn, a small coastal town southeast of the capital.
SJÓVÁ
4,500 people live on one side of Heimaey, and on the other:

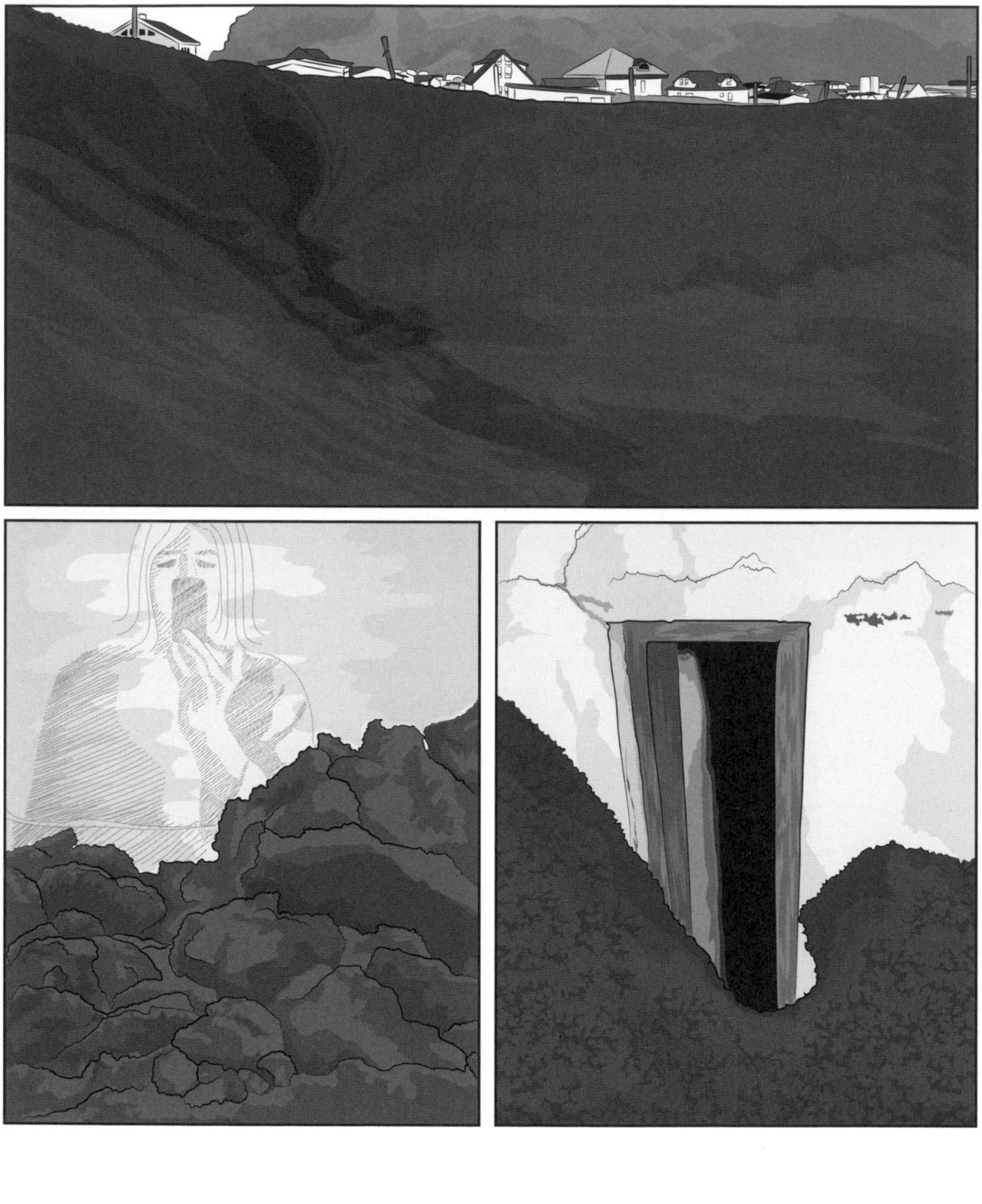

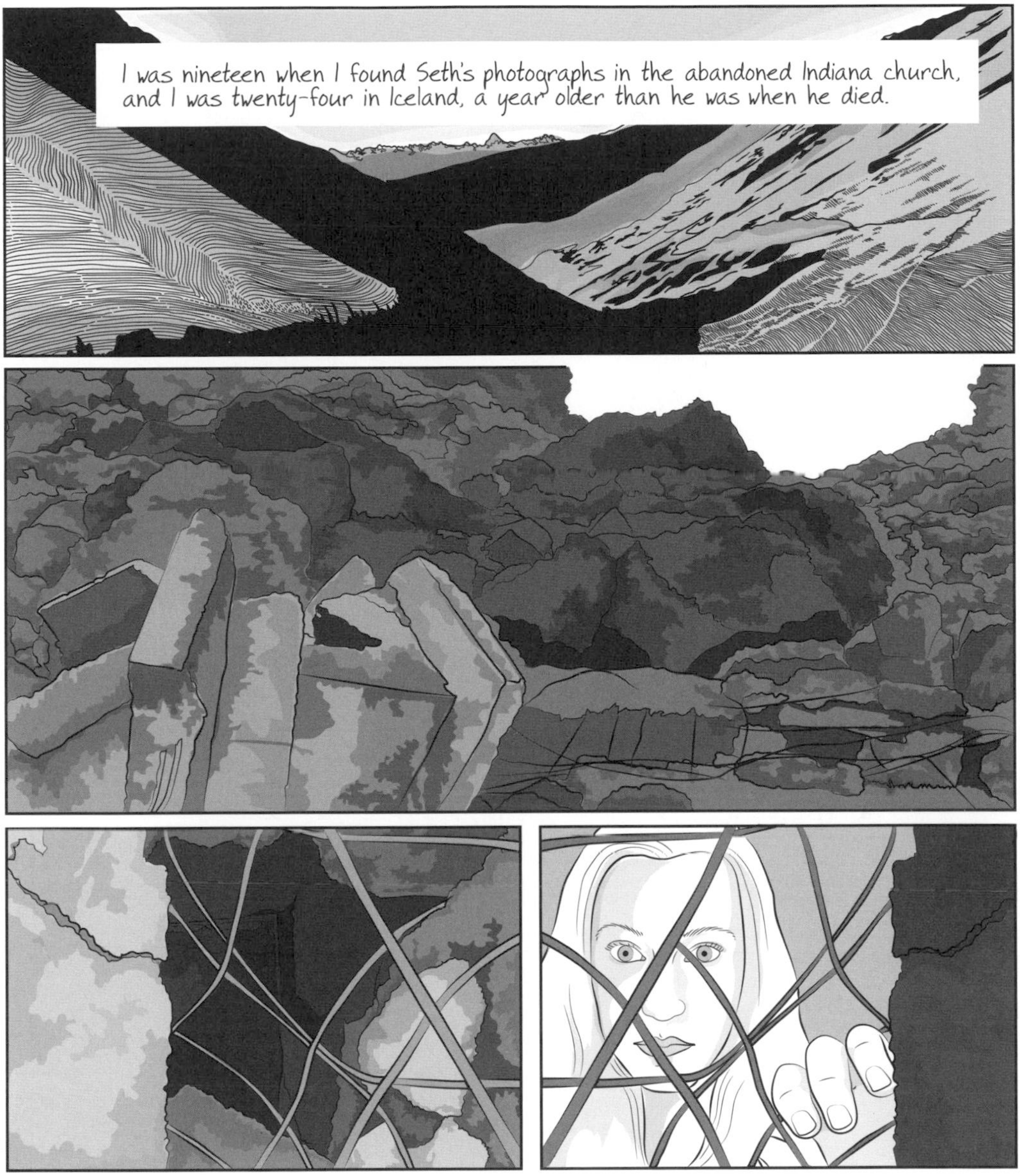
I was nineteen when I found Seth's photographs in the abandoned Indiana church, and I was twenty-four in Iceland, a year older than he was when he died.

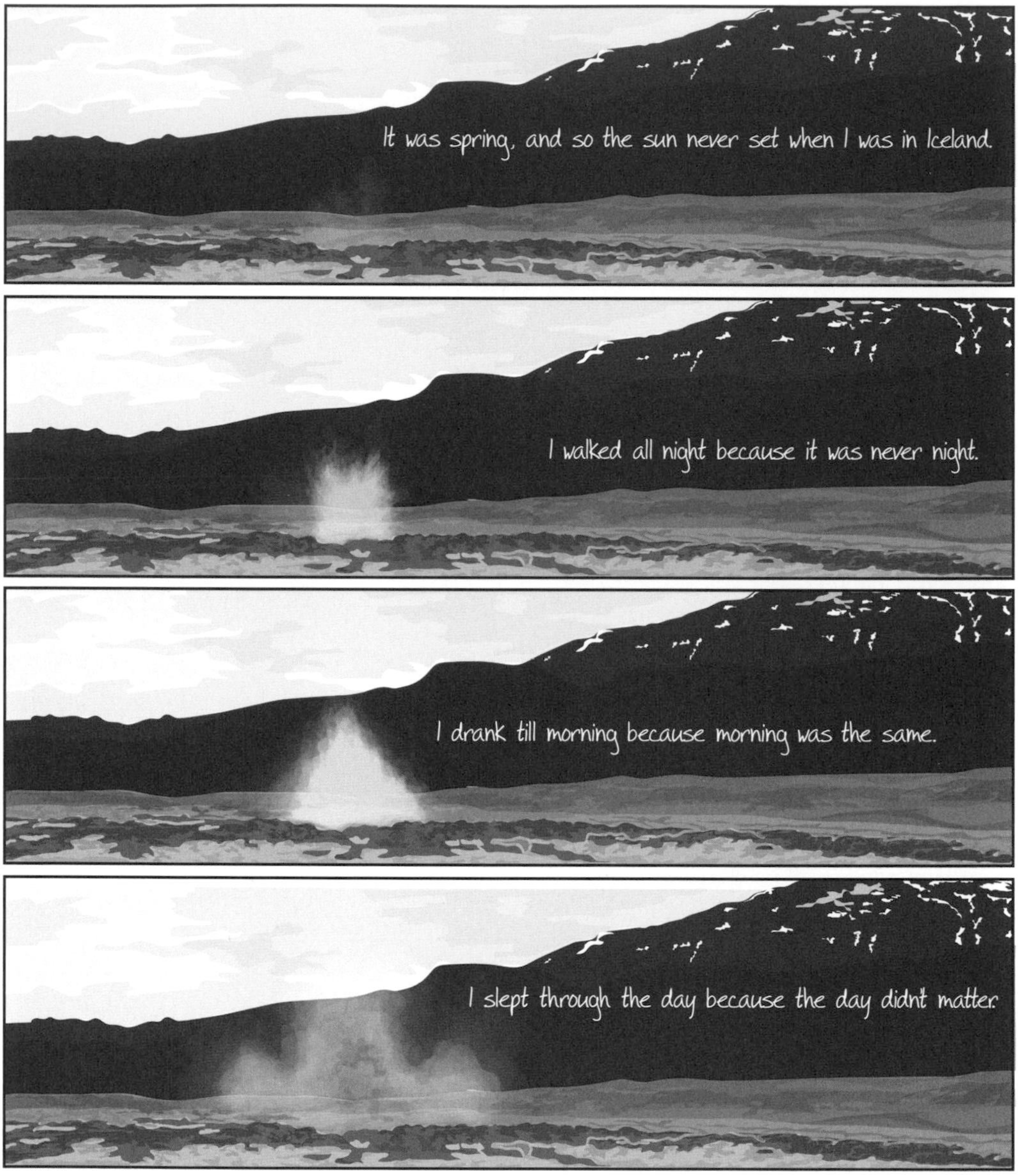

It was spring, and so the sun never set when I was in Iceland.
I walked all night because it was never night.
I drank till morning because morning was the same.
I slept through the day because the day didn't matter.

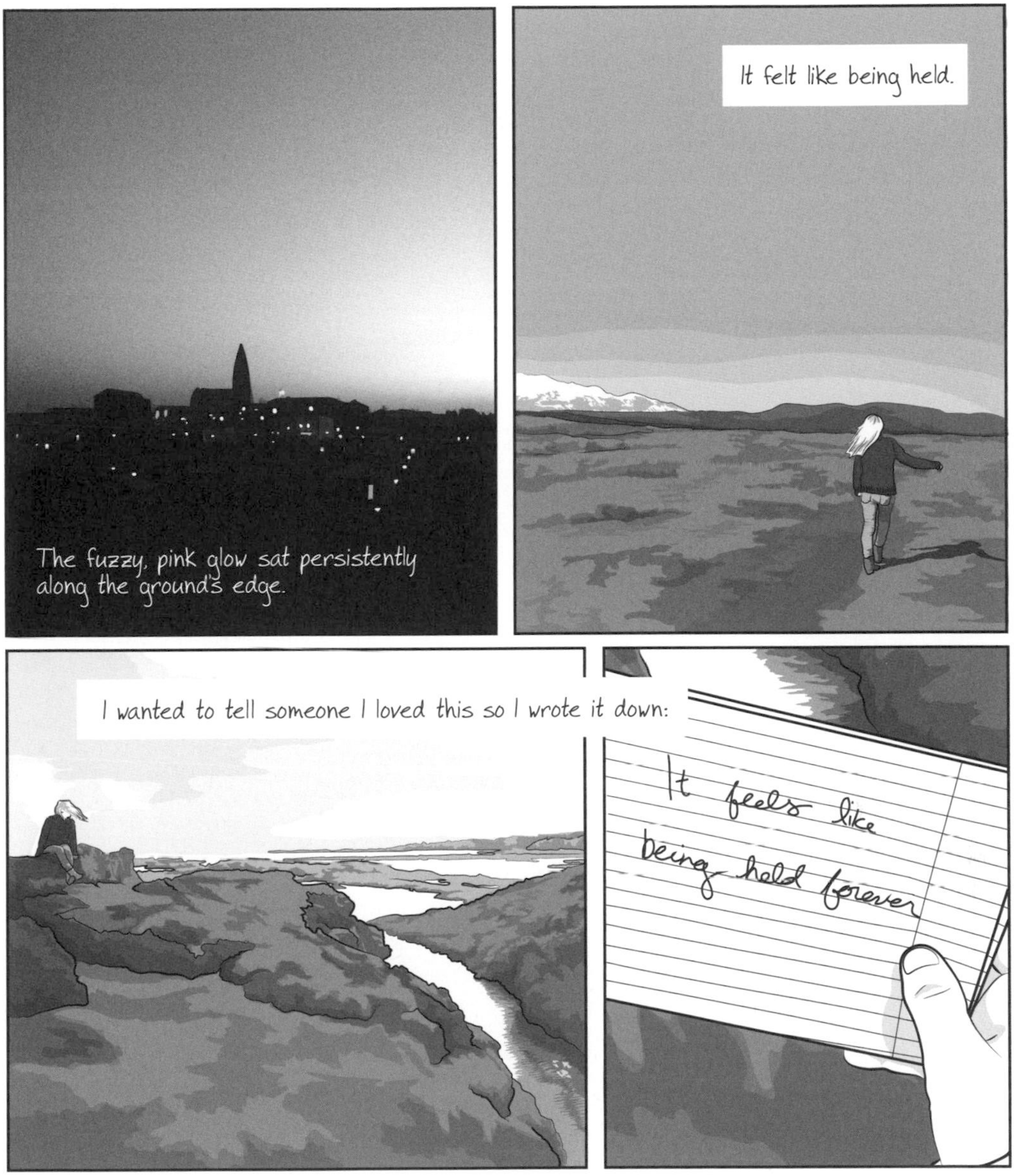
The fuzzy, pink glow sat persistently along the ground's edge.
It felt like being held.
I wanted to tell someone I loved this so I wrote it down:
It feels like being held forever

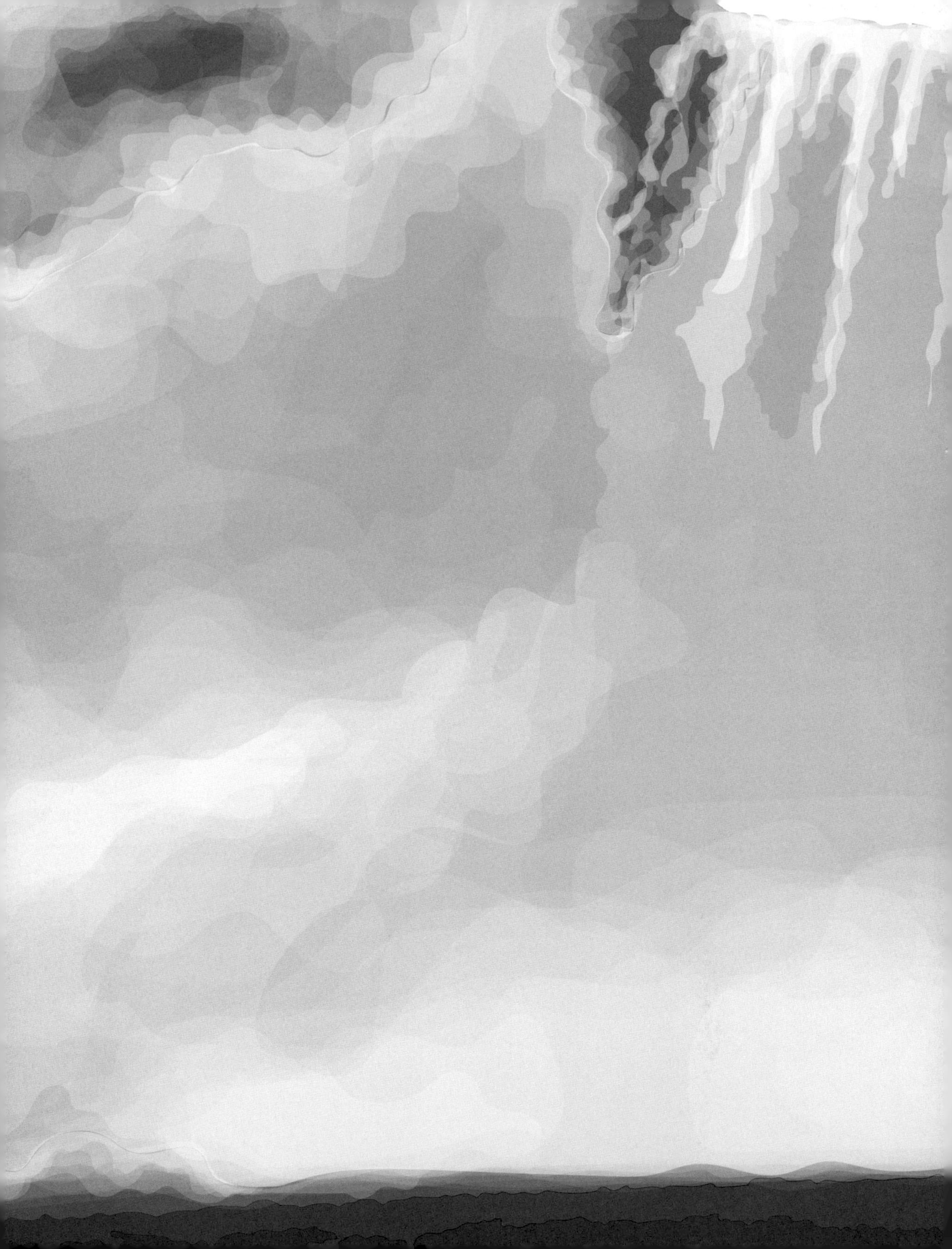

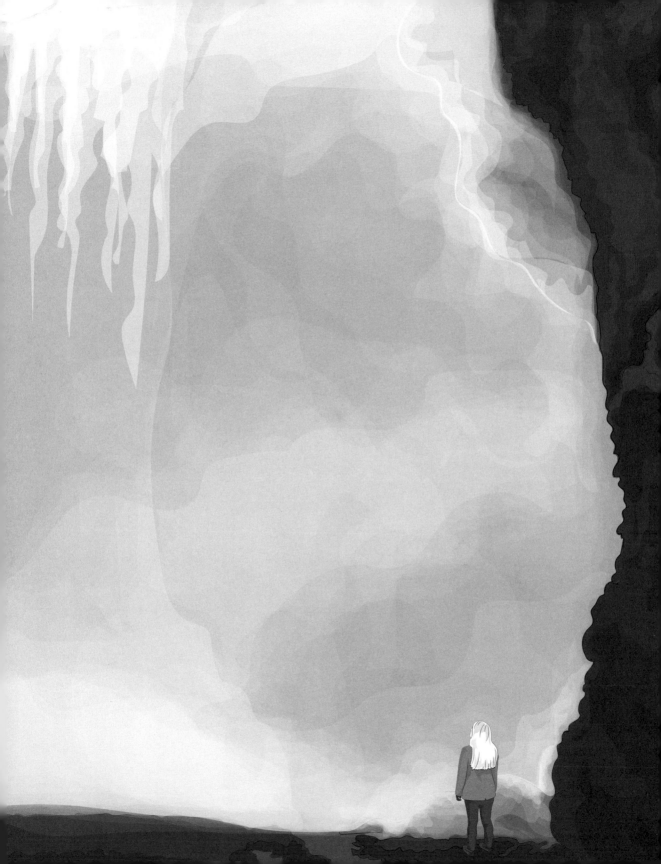

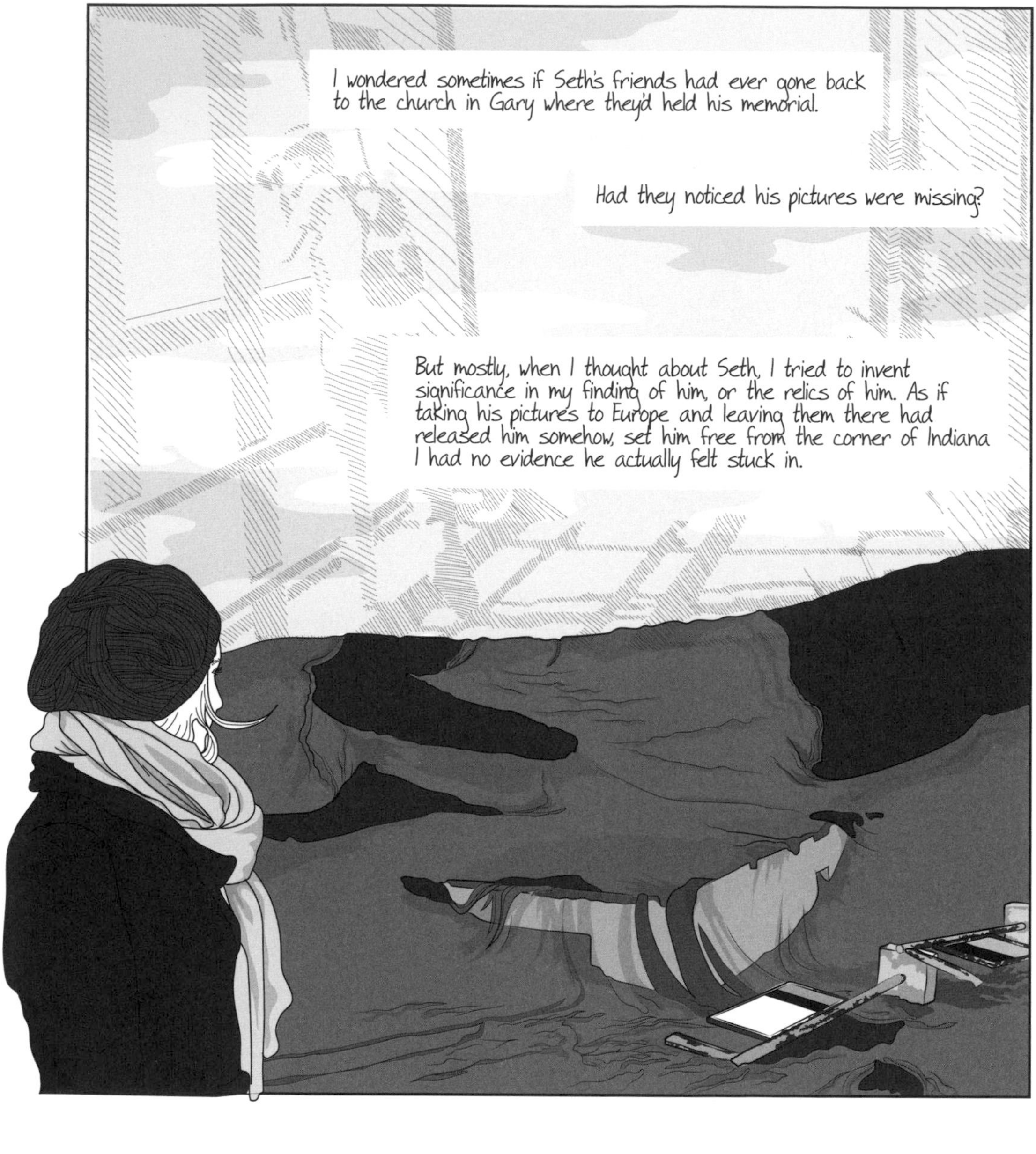
I wondered sometimes if Seth's friends had ever gone back to the church in Gary where they'd held his memorial.
Had they noticed his pictures were missing?
But mostly, when I thought about Seth, I tried to invent significance in my finding of him, or the relics of him. As if taking his pictures to Europe and leaving them there had released him somehow, set him free from the corner of Indiana I had no evidence he actually felt stuck in.

So, I'll begin by showing a clip from Chris Marker's Sans Soleil, which includes footage shot about 150 kilometers from here...

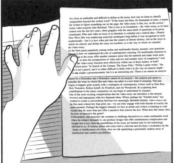

Near the end of the film, Marker revisits footage of Heimaey after the volcano's eruption.

"So, it sufficed to wait, and the planet itself staged the working of time.

"I saw what had been my window again. I saw emerge familiar roofs and balconies, the landmarks of the walks I took through town every day, down to the cliff where I had met the children."

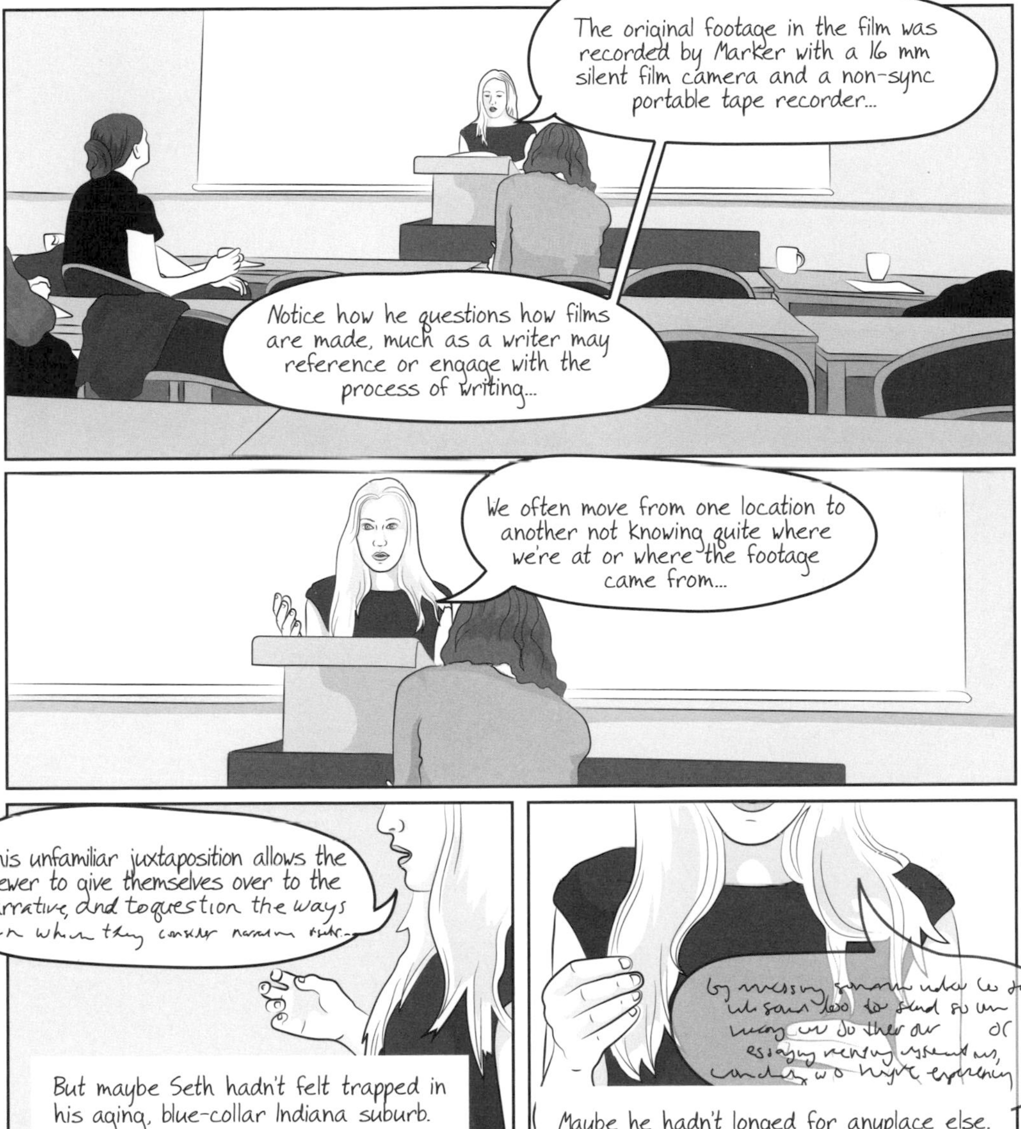
The original footage in the film was recorded by Marker with a 16 mm silent film camera and a non-sync portable tape recorder...
Notice how he questions how films are made, much as a writer may reference or engage with the process of writing...
We often move from one location to another not knowing quite where we're at or where the footage came from...
This unfamiliar juxtaposition allows the viewer to give themselves over to the narrative, and to question the ways
But maybe Seth hadn't felt trapped in his aging, blue-collar Indiana suburb.
Maybe he hadn't longed for anyplace else.

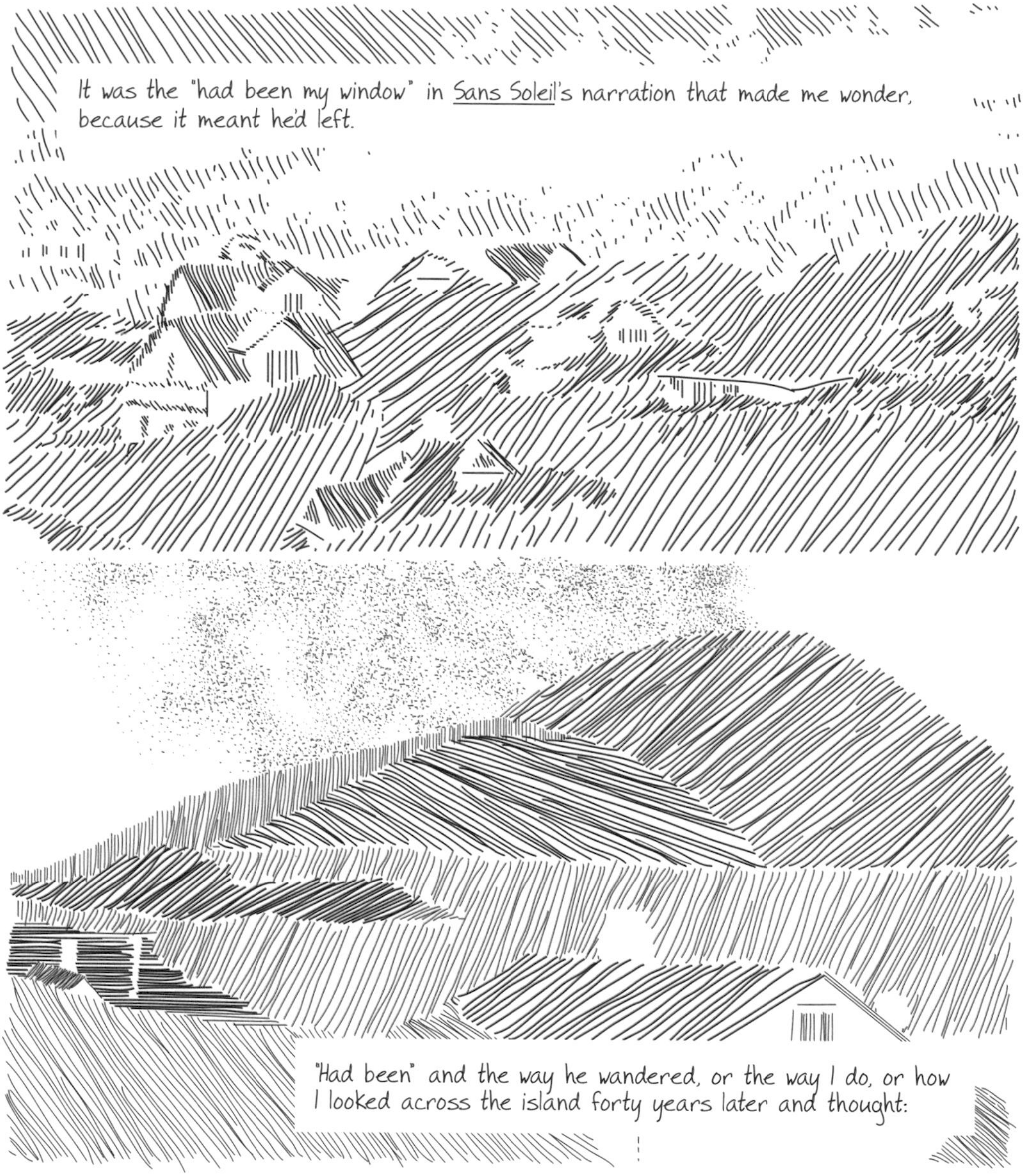
It was the "had been my window" in Sans Soleil's narration that made me wonder, because it meant he'd left.
"Had been" and the way he wandered, or the way I do, or how I looked across the island forty years later and thought:

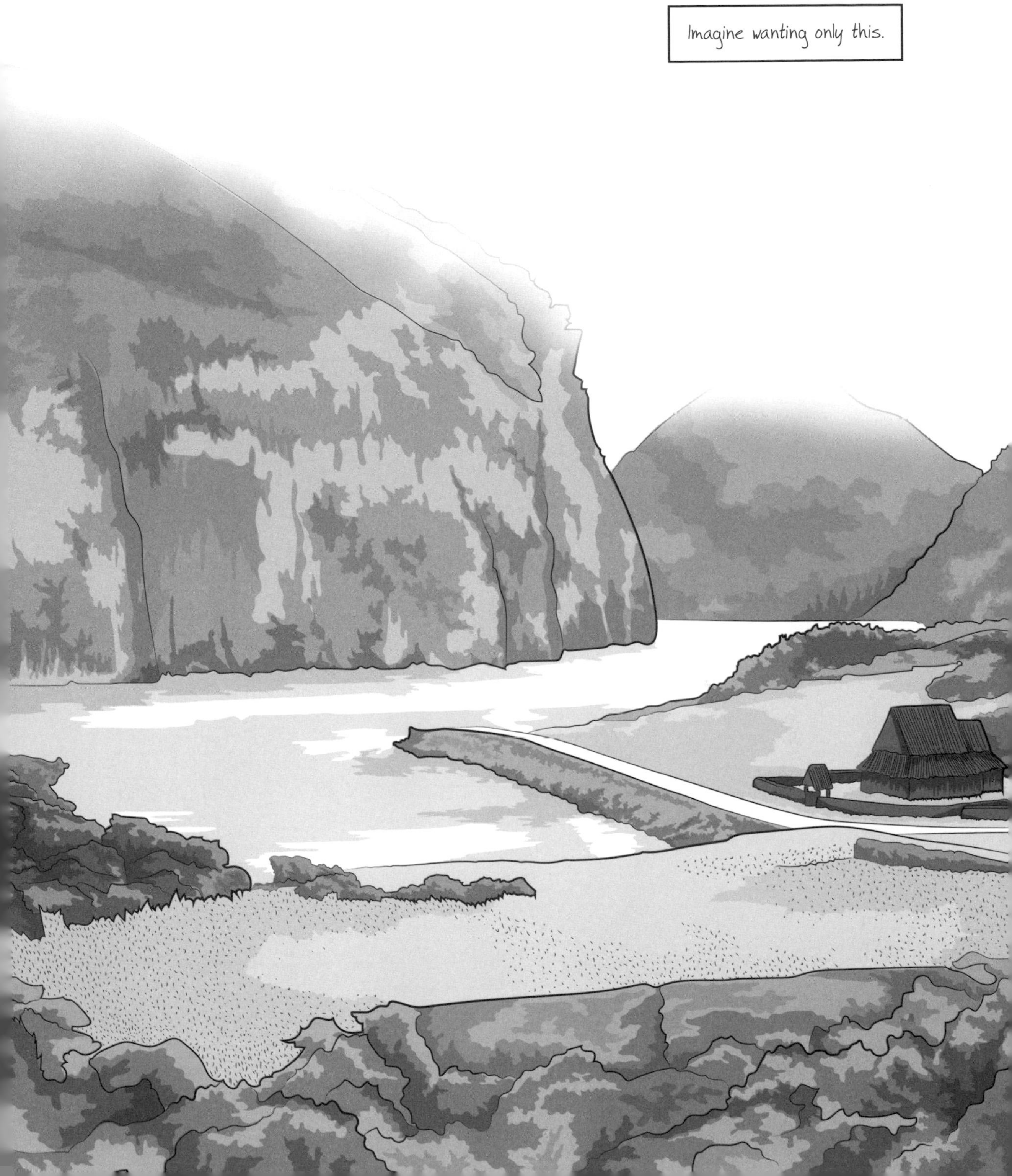
Imagine wanting only this.

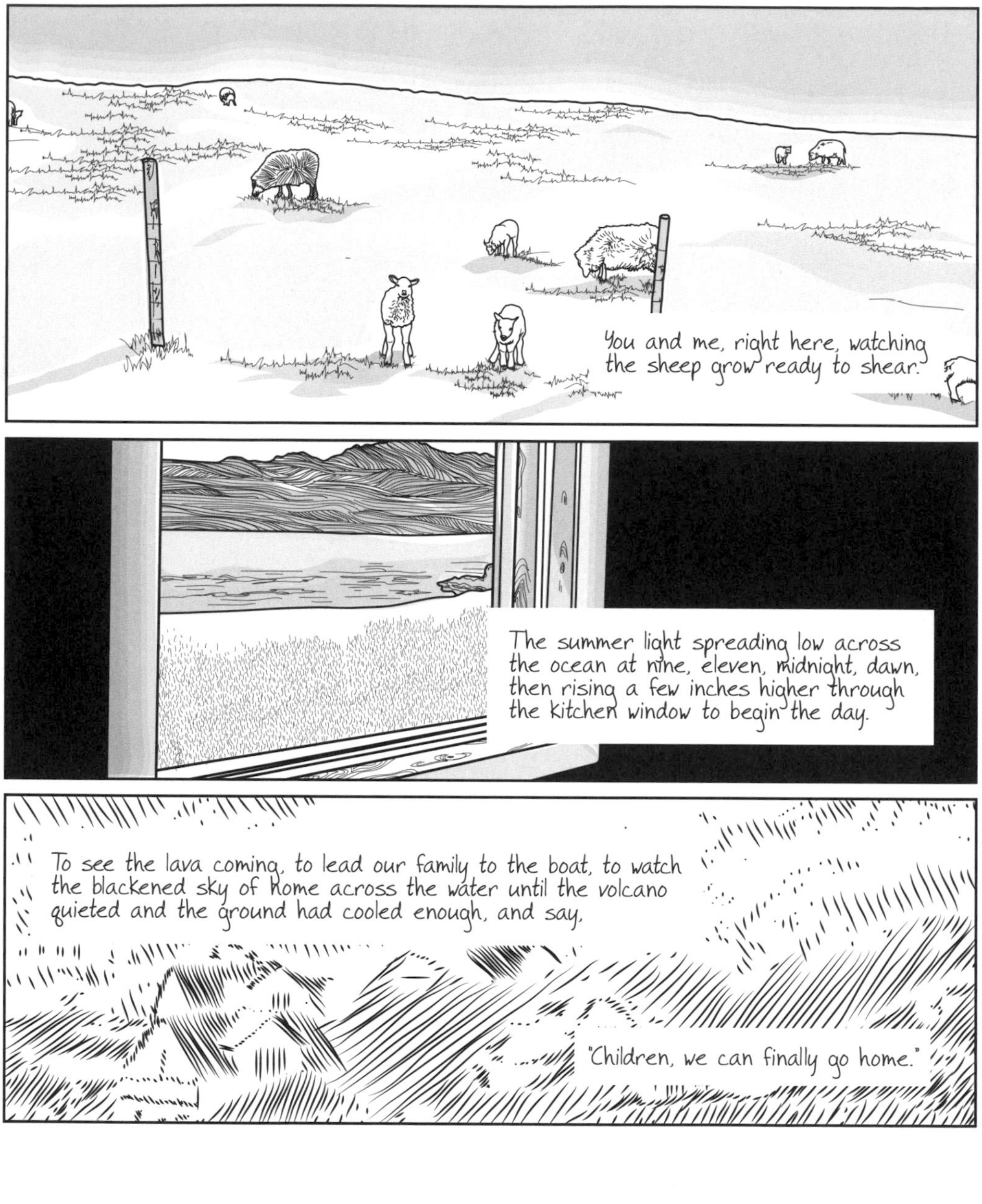
You and me, right here, watching the sheep grow ready to shear.
The summer light spreading low across the ocean at nine, eleven, midnight, dawn, then rising a few inches higher through the kitchen window to begin the day.
To see the lava coming, to lead our family to the boat, to watch the blackened sky of home across the water until the volcano quieted and the ground had cooled enough, and say,
"Children, we can finally go home."

# Chapter 7

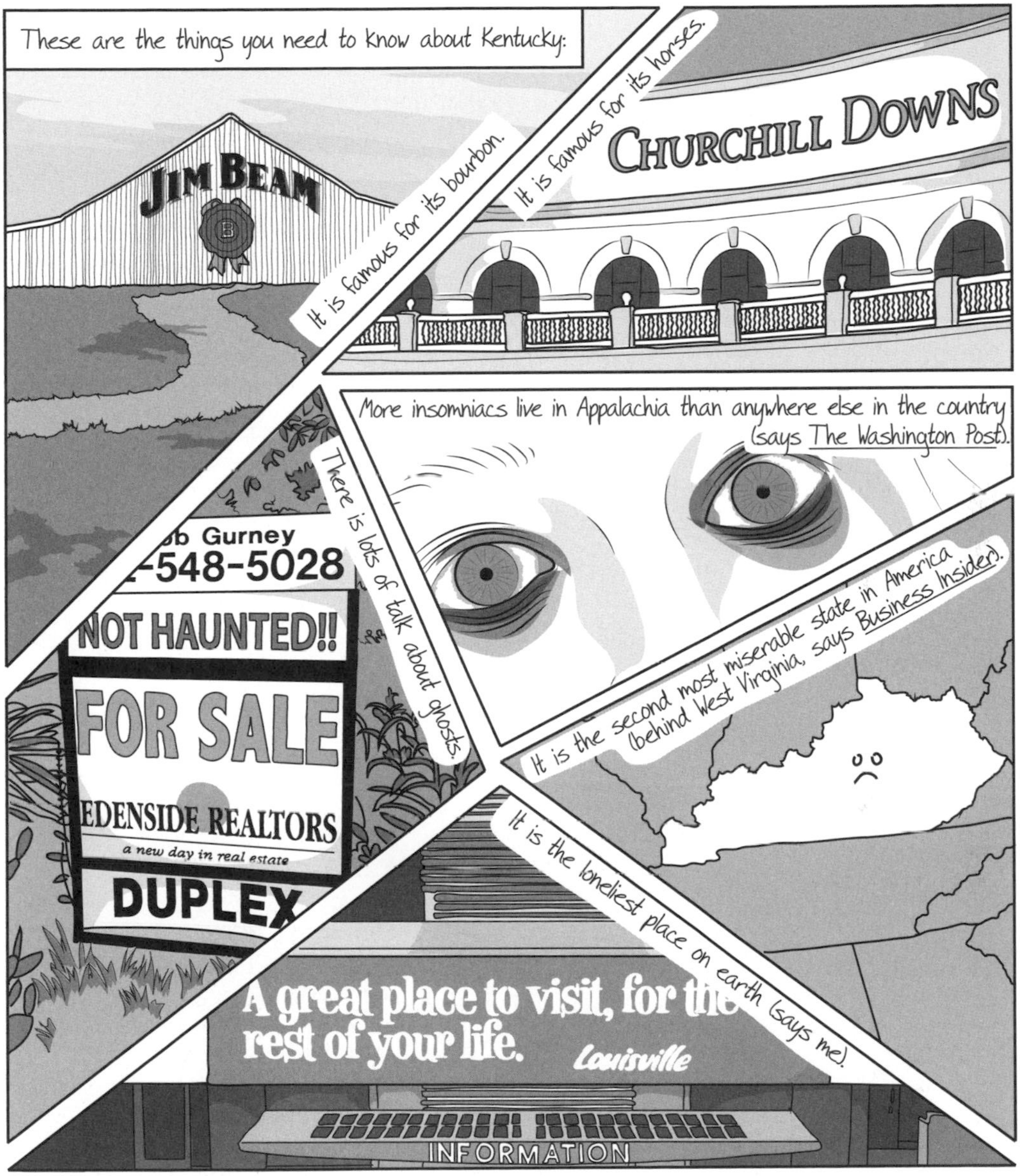

These are the things you need to know about Kentucky:
JIM BEAM
It is famous for its bourbon.
It is famous for its horses.
CHURCHILL DOWNS
More insomniacs live in Appalachia than anywhere else in the country
(says The Washington Post).
There is lots of talk about ghosts.
Gurney
548-5028
NOT HAUNTED!!
FOR SALE
EDENSIDE REALTORS
a new day in real estate
DUPLEX
It is the second most miserable state in America
(behind West Virginia, says Business Insider).
It is the loneliest place on earth (says me).
A great place to visit, for the rest of your life.
Louisville
INFORMATION

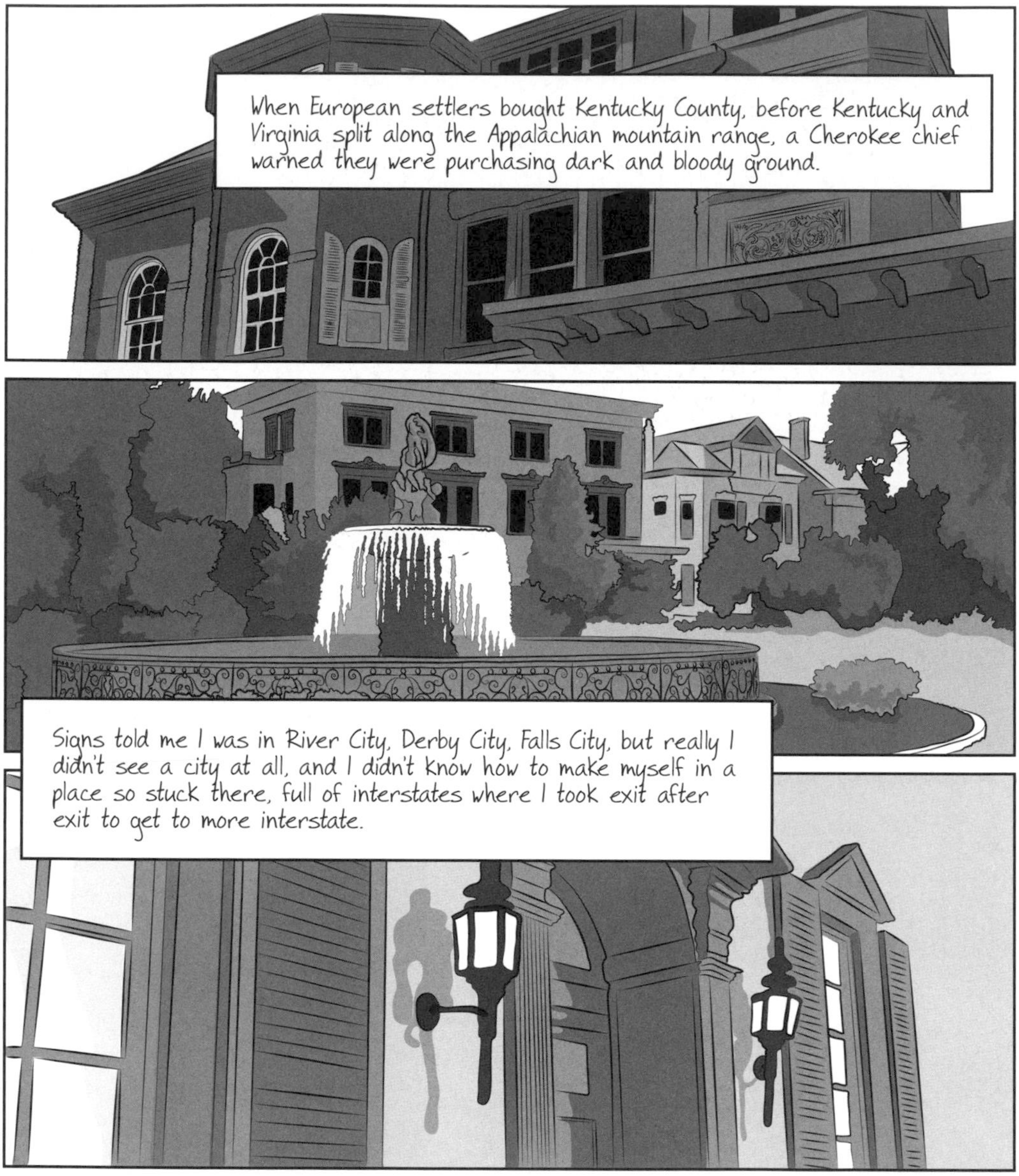
When European settlers bought Kentucky County, before Kentucky and Virginia split along the Appalachian mountain range, a Cherokee chief warned they were purchasing dark and bloody ground.
Signs told me I was in River City, Derby City, Falls City, but really I didn't see a city at all, and I didn't know how to make myself in a place so stuck there, full of interstates where I took exit after exit to get to more interstate.

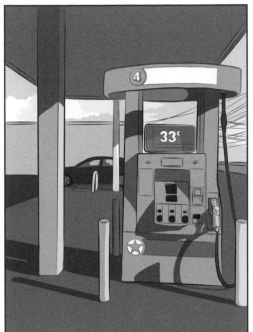

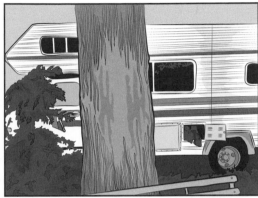

4
33¢
I never bumped into anyone on the sidewalk, never brushed a shoulder as I passed. I missed the grids of a city life I hadn't lived in years and wound myself lost on curved and cracking streets.
WELCOME
SUNDAY 10 AM
WED 630 PM

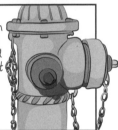

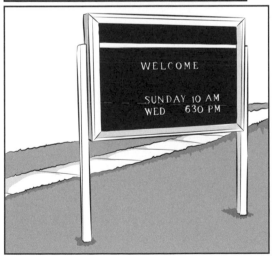

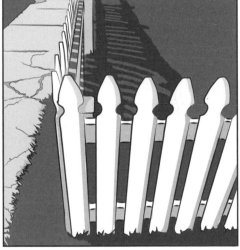

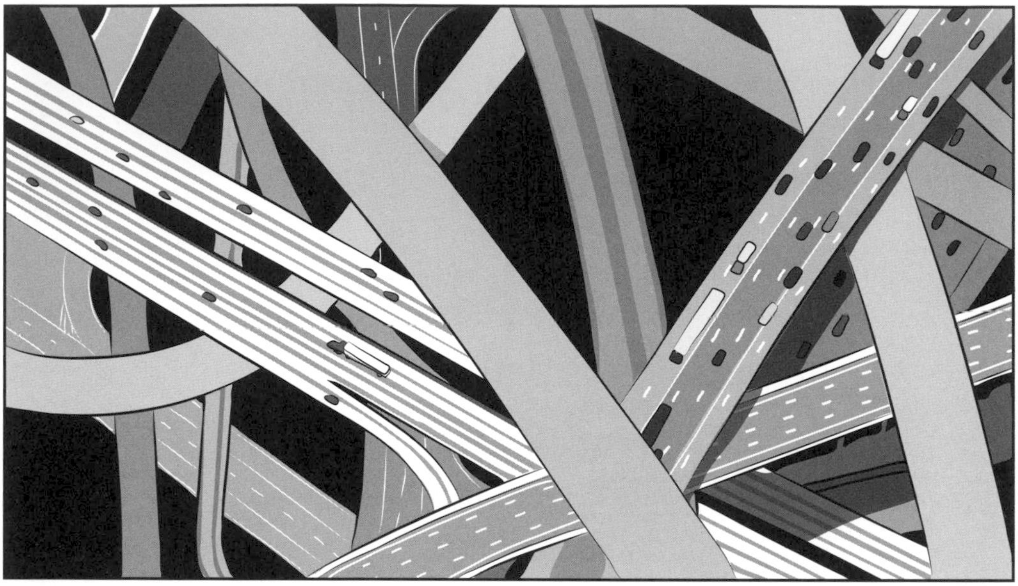

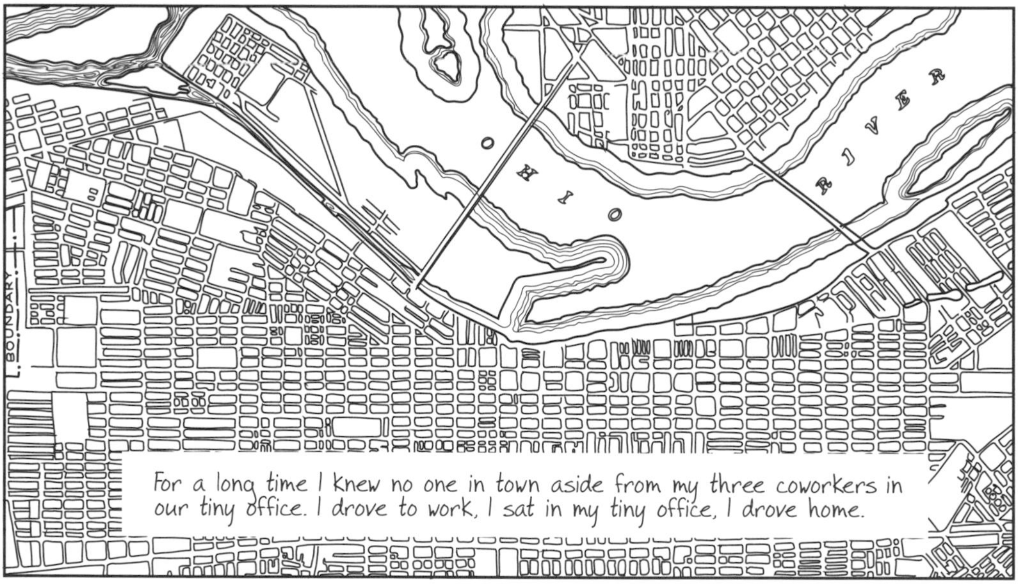
OHIO RIVER
BOUNDARY
For a long time I knew no one in town aside from my three coworkers in our tiny office. I drove to work, I sat in my tiny office, I drove home.

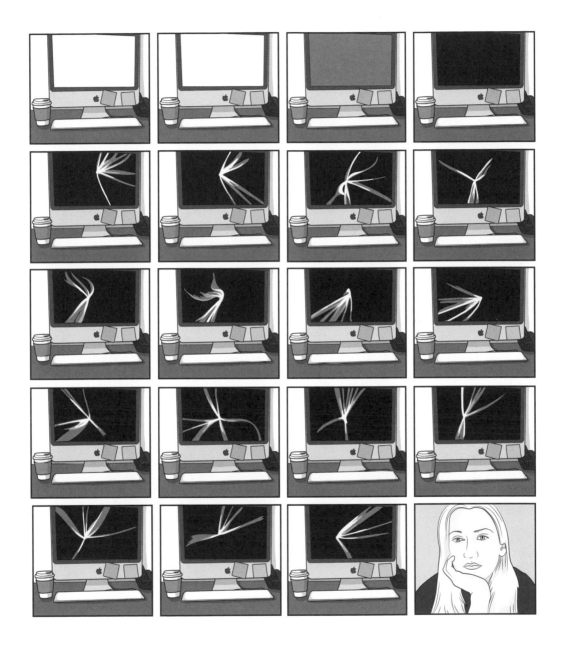

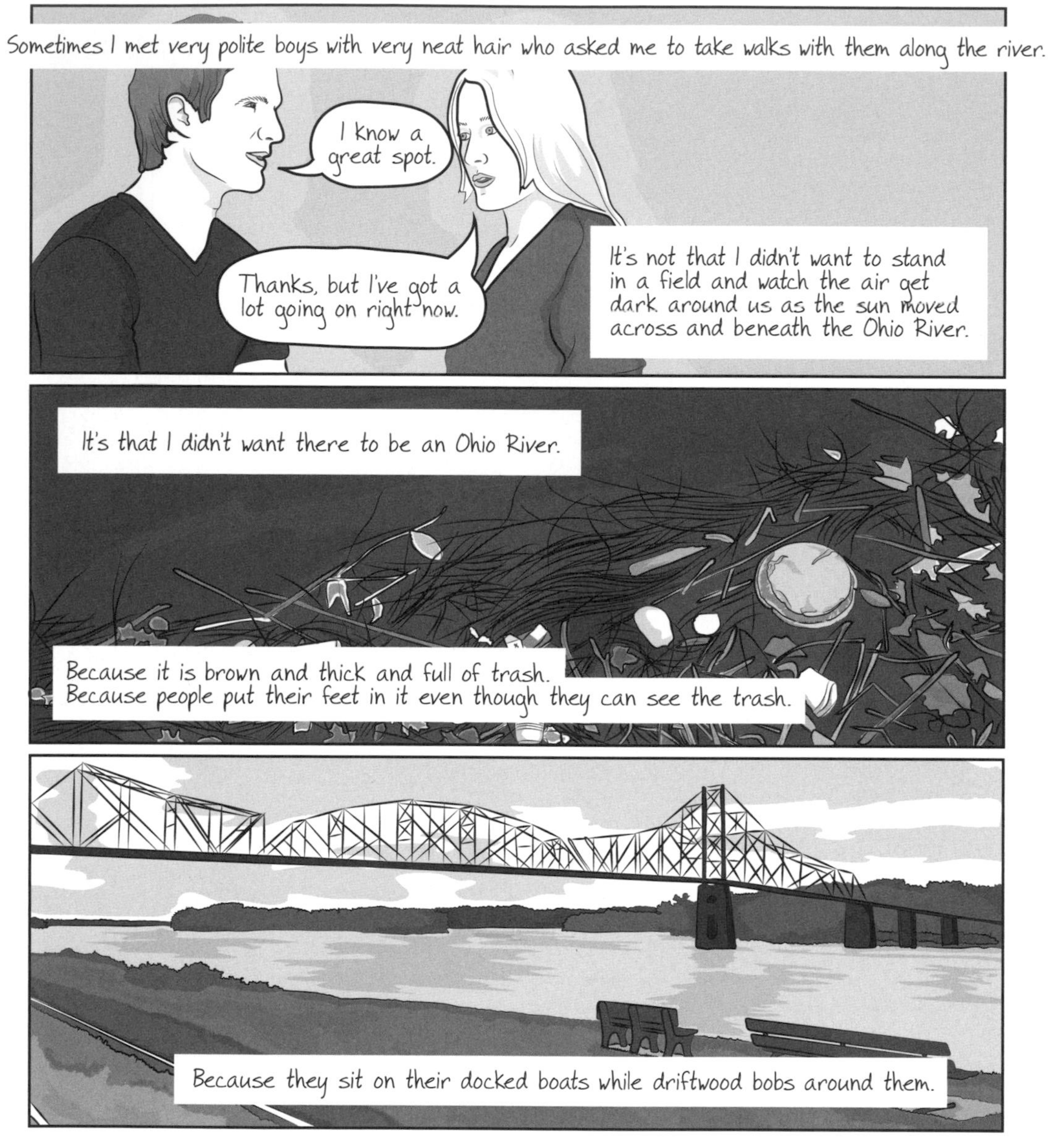
Sometimes I met very polite boys with very neat hair who asked me to take walks with them along the river.
I know a great spot.
Thanks, but I've got a lot going on right now.
It's not that I didn't want to stand in a field and watch the air get dark around us as the sun moved across and beneath the Ohio River.
It's that I didn't want there to be an Ohio River.
Because it is brown and thick and full of trash.
Because people put their feet in it even though they can see the trash.
Because they sit on their docked boats while driftwood bobs around them.

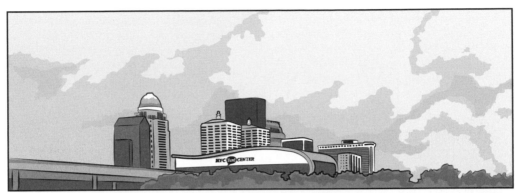

When the air is still the water looks like earth.

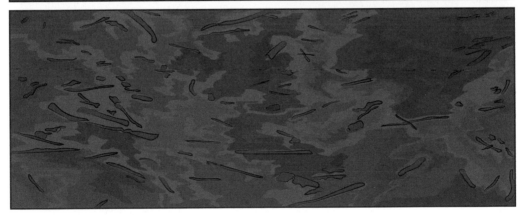

I never slept in Kentucky, because every night airplanes that I wasn't in flew over my apartment. The deeper I got into my unsleep the faster they started coming, every ten minutes at 3:30, every five at 4:00.

When I heard the planes every night I assumed they held passengers, but I was confused as to why so many in a town of not-quite-a-million where abandoned warehouses butt up against below-the-Mason-Dixon nineteenth-century mansions, until I drove past the UPS warehouse on the airport's lot, where Louisville headquarters the whole country's distribution.

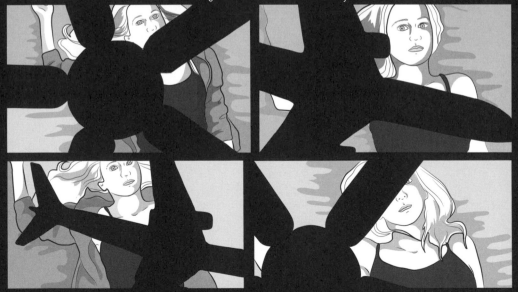

So then there was one less thing to wonder about as I stared at my ceiling and listened to them come in and over, carrying brown-wrapped iPads and Nike shoes and kitchenware but empty all the same.

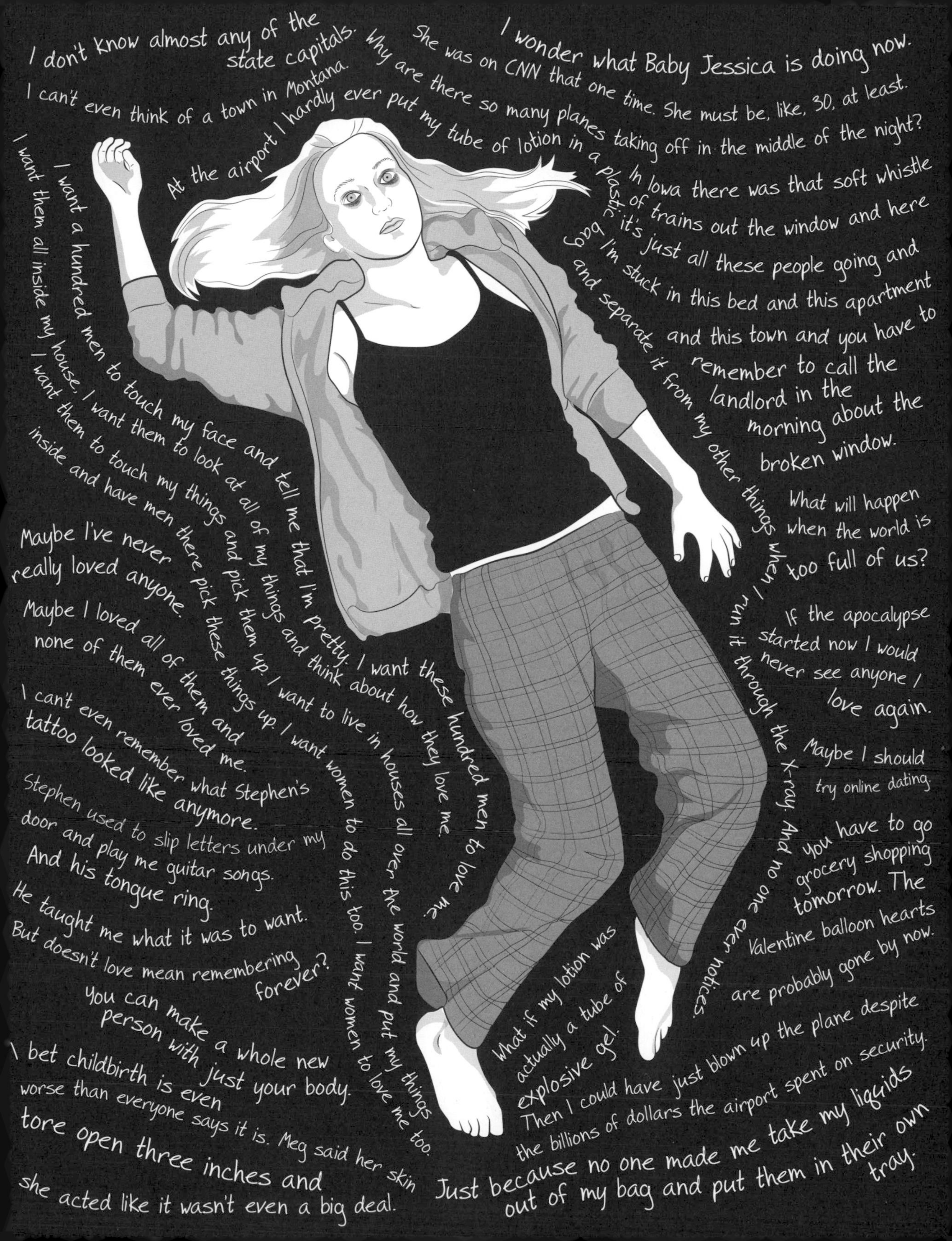
I don't know almost any of the state capitals.
I can't even think of a town in Montana.
I wonder what Baby Jessica is doing now.
She was on CNN that one time. She must be, like, 30, at least.
Why are there so many planes taking off in the middle of the night?
At the airport I hardly ever put my tube of lotion in a plastic bag and separate it from my other things when I run it through the X-ray. And no one ever notices.
In Iowa there was that soft whistle of trains out the window and here it's just all these people going and I'm stuck in this bed and this apartment and this town and you have to remember to call the landlord in the morning about the broken window.
What will happen when the world is too full of us?
If the apocalypse started now I would never see anyone I love again.
Maybe I should try online dating.
You have to go grocery shopping tomorrow. The Valentine balloon hearts are probably gone by now.
What if my lotion was actually a tube of explosive gel?
Then I could have just blown up the plane despite the billions of dollars the airport spent on security.
Just because no one made me take my liquids out of my bag and put them in their own tray.
I want a hundred men to touch my face and tell me that I'm pretty. I want these hundred men to love me.
I want them all inside my house, I want them to look at all of my things and think about how they love me.
I want them to touch my things and pick them up. I want to live in houses all over the world and put my things
inside and have men there pick these things up. I want women to do this too. I want women to love me too.
Maybe I've never really loved anyone.
Maybe I loved all of them and none of them ever loved me.
I can't even remember what Stephen's tattoo looked like anymore.
Stephen used to slip letters under my door and play me guitar songs.
And his tongue ring.
He taught me what it was to want.
But doesn't love mean remembering forever?
You can make a whole new person with just your body.
I bet childbirth is even worse than everyone says it is. Meg said her skin tore open three inches and she acted like it wasn't even a big deal.

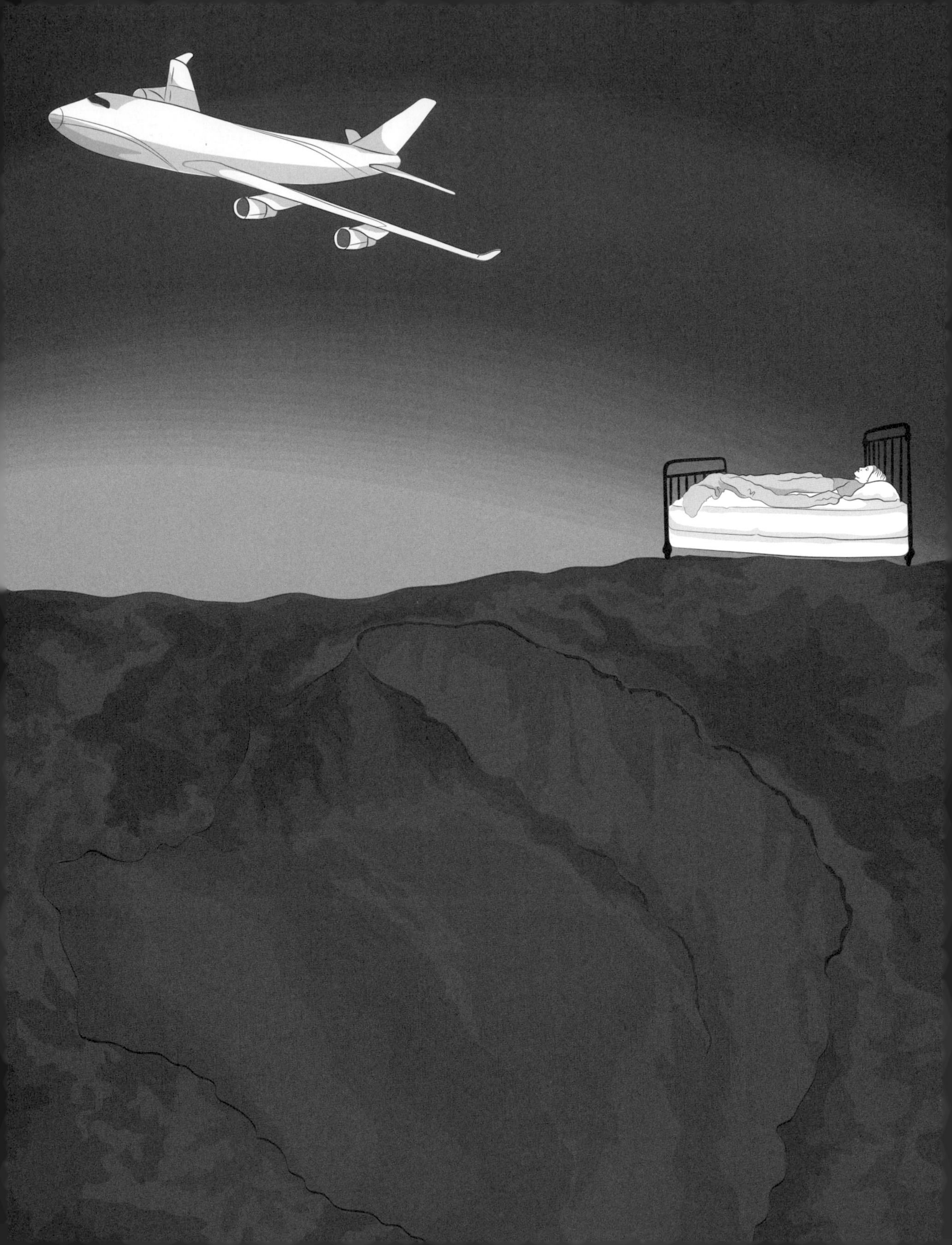

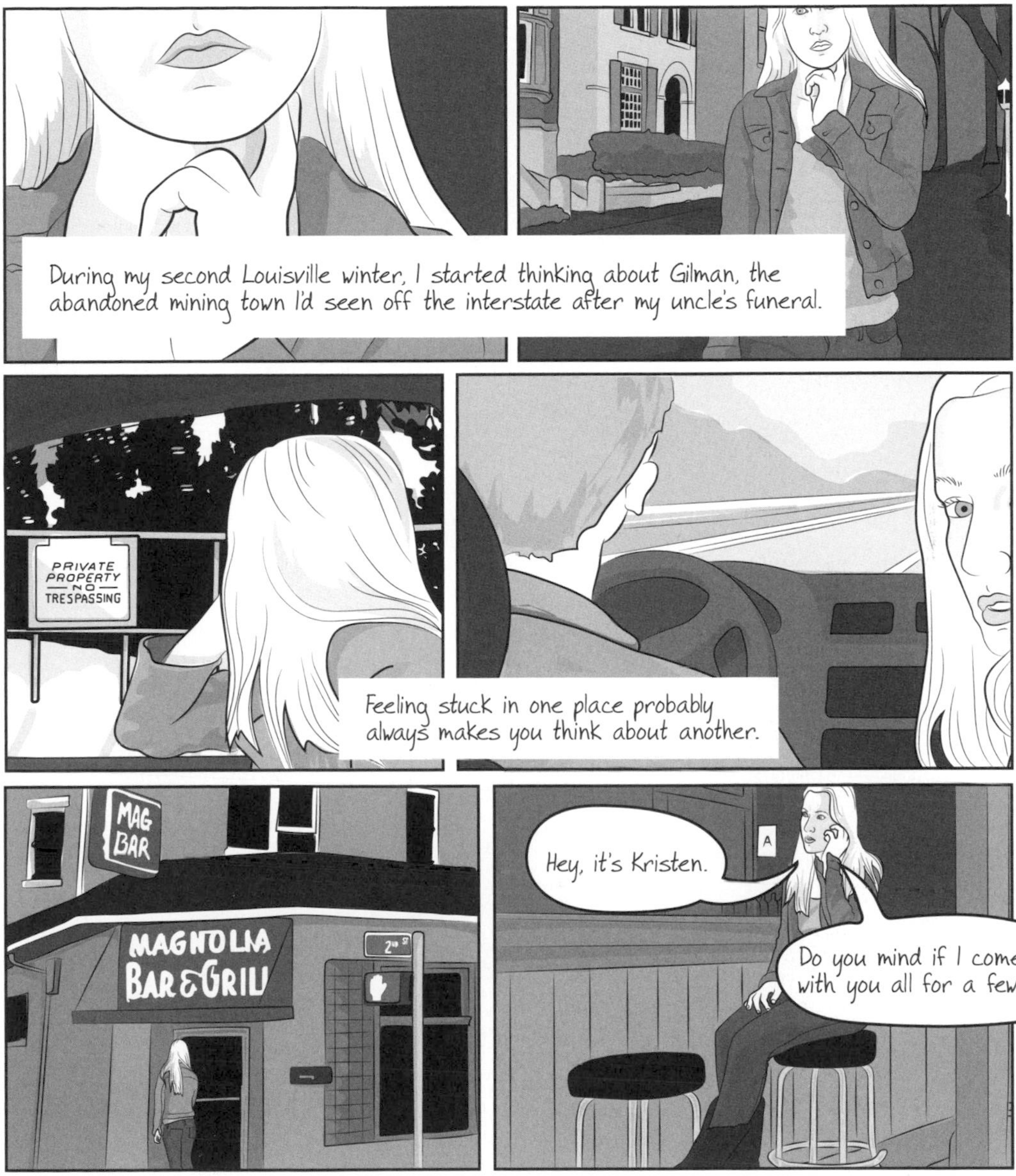
During my second Louisville winter, I started thinking about Gilman, the abandoned mining town I'd seen off the interstate after my uncle's funeral.
PRIVATE PROPERTY NO TRESPASSING
Feeling stuck in one place probably always makes you think about another.
MAG BAR
MAGNOLIA BAR & GRILL
2ND ST
A
Hey, it's Kristen.
Do you mind if I come stay with you all for a few days?

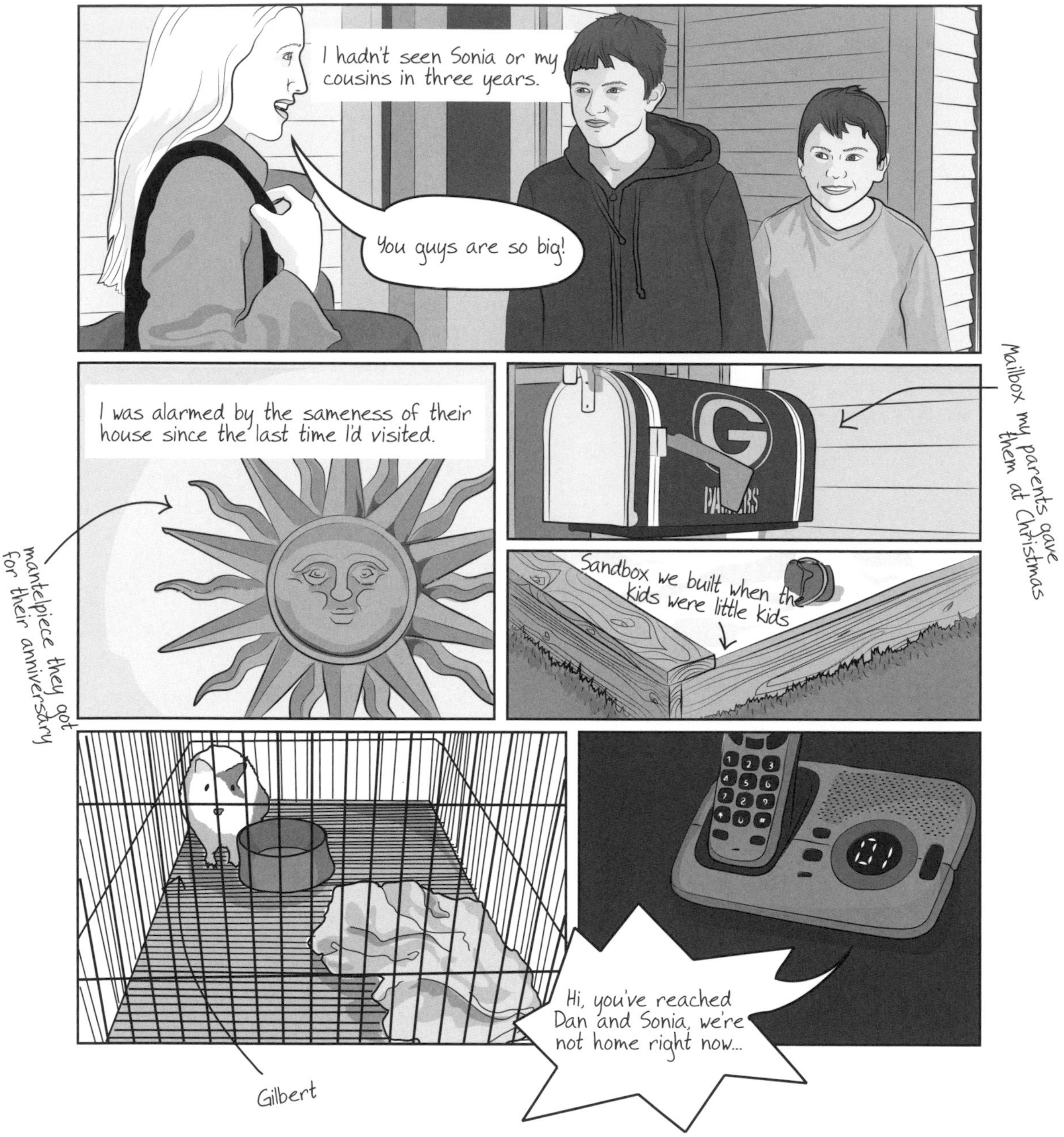

I hadn't seen Sonia or my cousins in three years.
You guys are so big!
I was alarmed by the sameness of their house since the last time I'd visited.
mantelpiece they got for their anniversary
Mailbox my parents gave them at Christmas
G
PACKERS
Sandbox we built when the kids were little kids
Gilbert
Hi, you've reached Dan and Sonia, we're not home right now...

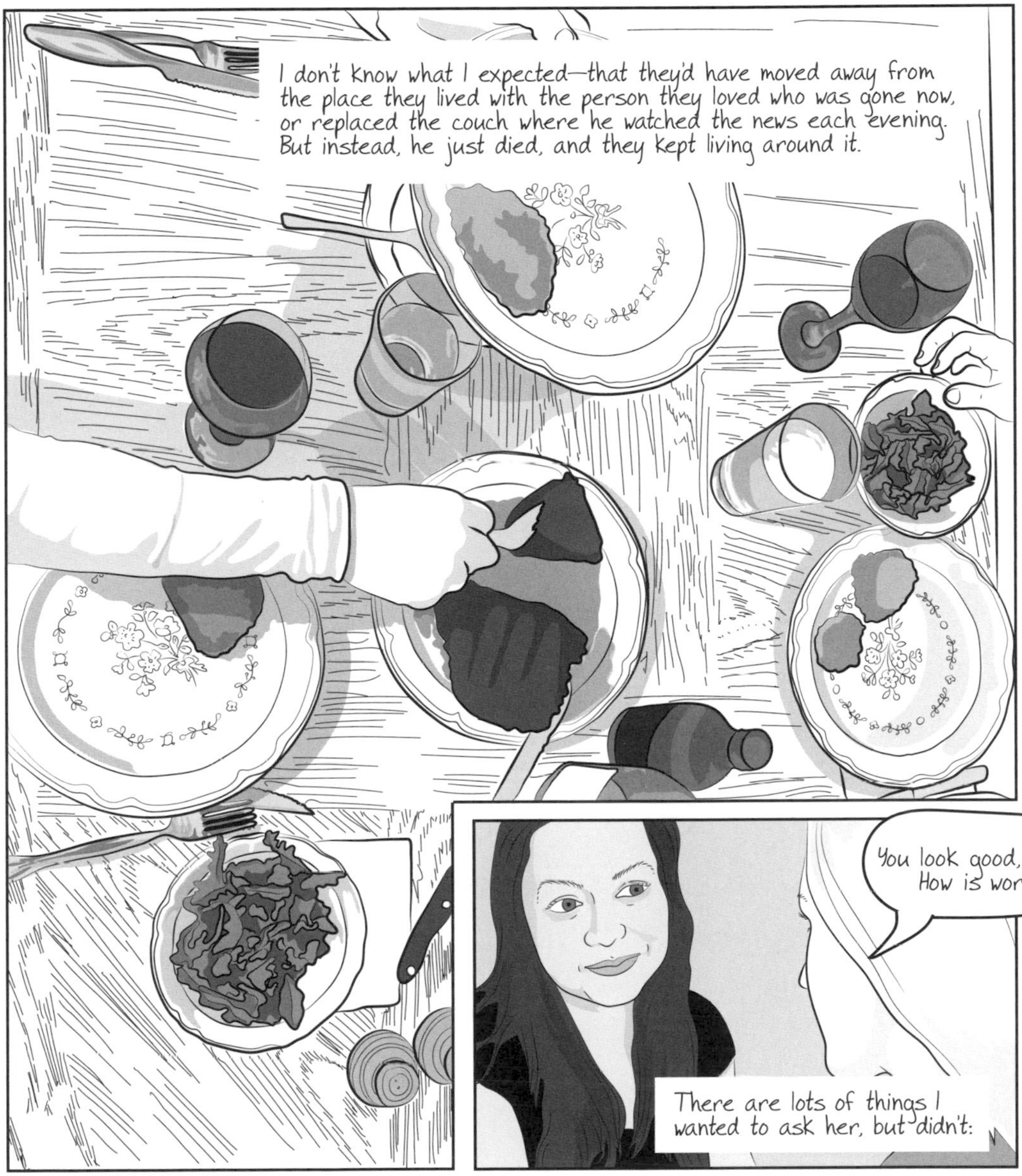
I don't know what I expected—that they'd have moved away from the place they lived with the person they loved who was gone now, or replaced the couch where he watched the news each evening. But instead, he just died, and they kept living around it.
You look good, Sonia! How is work?
There are lots of things I wanted to ask her, but didn't:

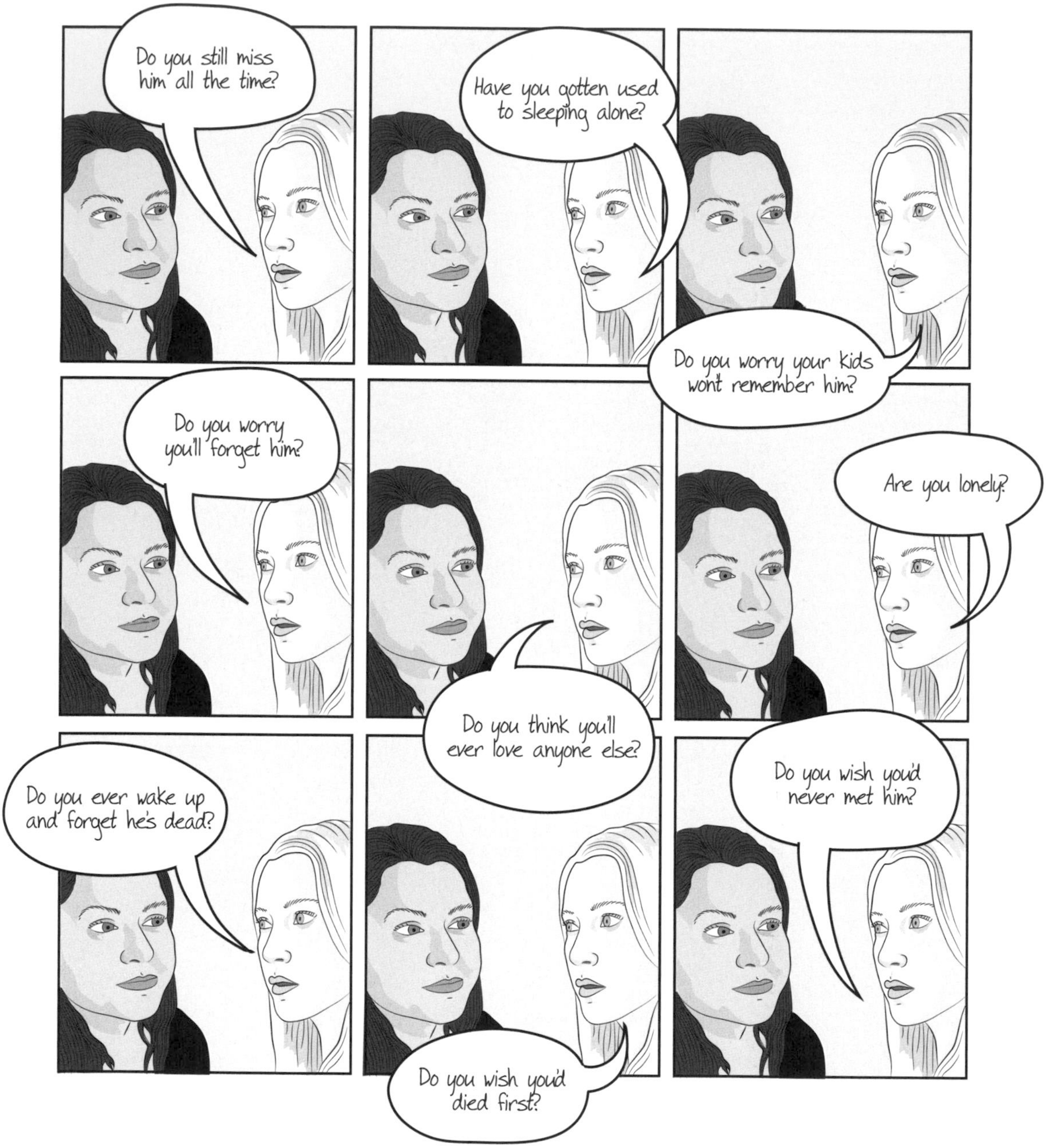
Do you still miss him all the time?
Have you gotten used to sleeping alone?
Do you worry your kids won't remember him?
Do you worry you'll forget him?
Do you think you'll ever love anyone else?
Are you lonely?
Do you ever wake up and forget he's dead?
Do you wish you'd died first?
Do you wish you'd never met him?

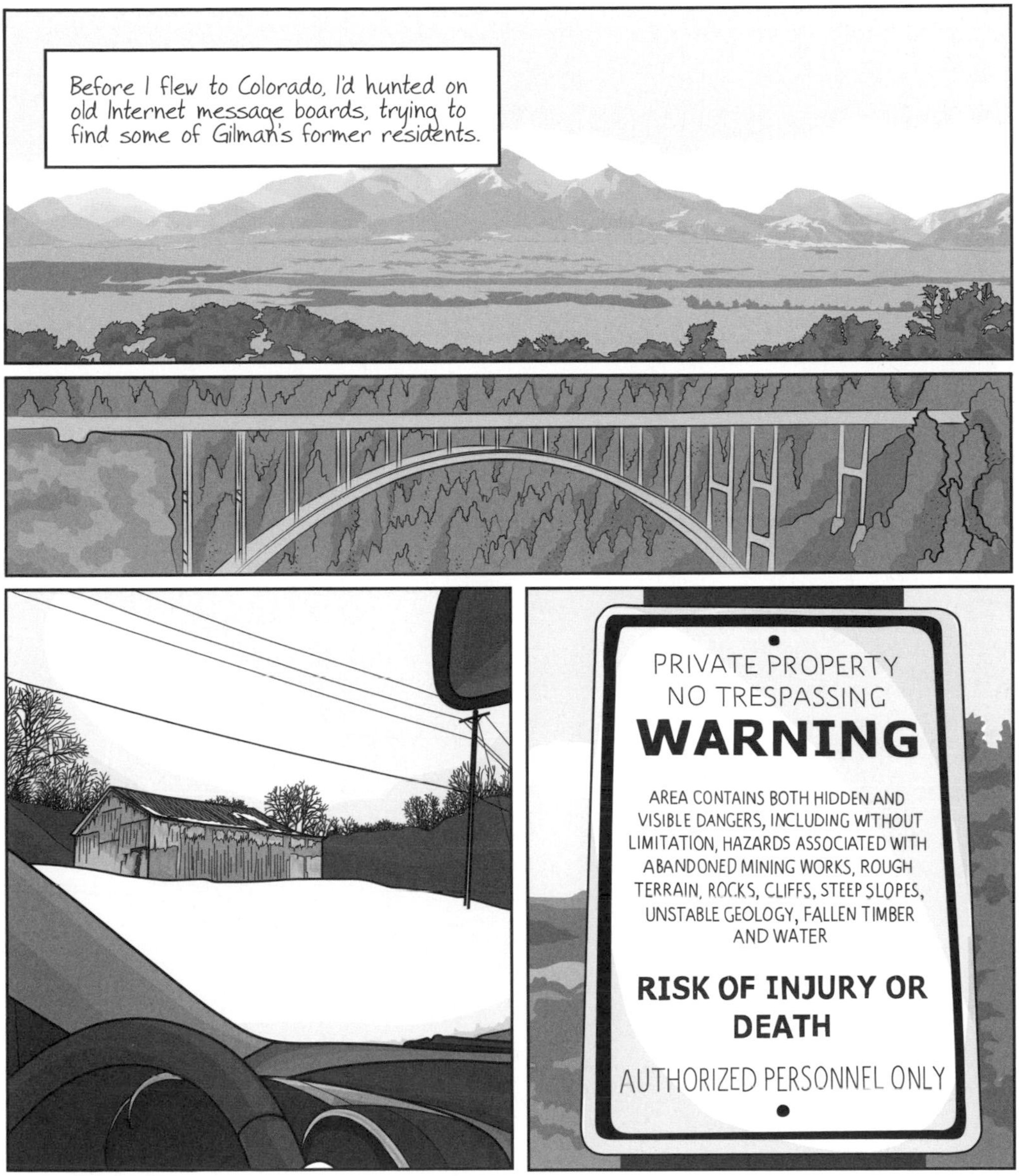

Before I flew to Colorado, I'd hunted on old Internet message boards, trying to find some of Gilman's former residents.
PRIVATE PROPERTY
NO TRESPASSING
WARNING
AREA CONTAINS BOTH HIDDEN AND VISIBLE DANGERS, INCLUDING WITHOUT LIMITATION, HAZARDS ASSOCIATED WITH ABANDONED MINING WORKS, ROUGH TERRAIN, ROCKS, CLIFFS, STEEP SLOPES, UNSTABLE GEOLOGY, FALLEN TIMBER AND WATER
RISK OF INJURY OR DEATH
AUTHORIZED PERSONNEL ONLY

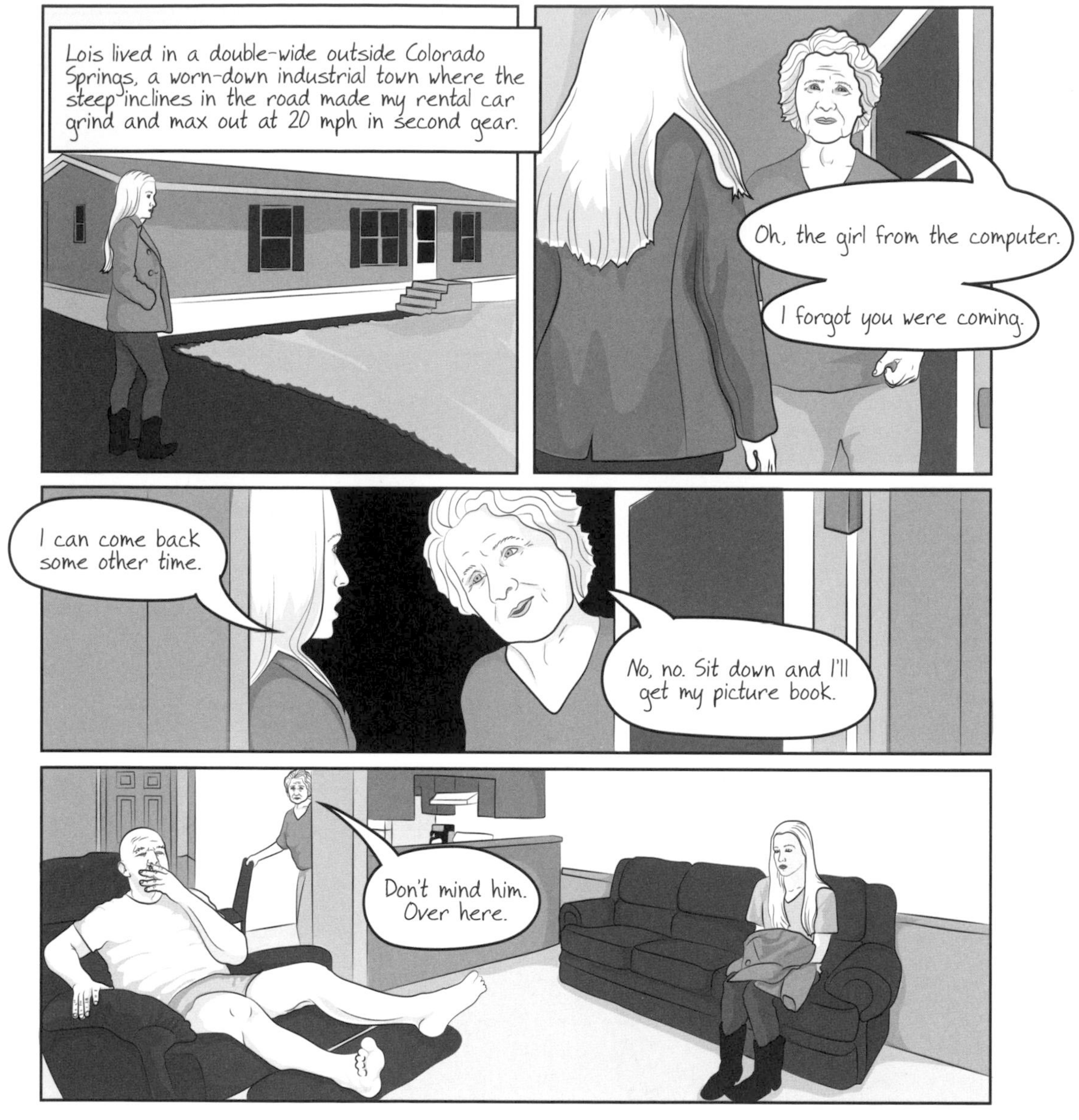
Lois lived in a double-wide outside Colorado Springs, a worn-down industrial town where the steep inclines in the road made my rental car grind and max out at 20 mph in second gear.
Oh, the girl from the computer.
I forgot you were coming.
I can come back some other time.
No, no. Sit down and I'll get my picture book.
Don't mind him. Over here.

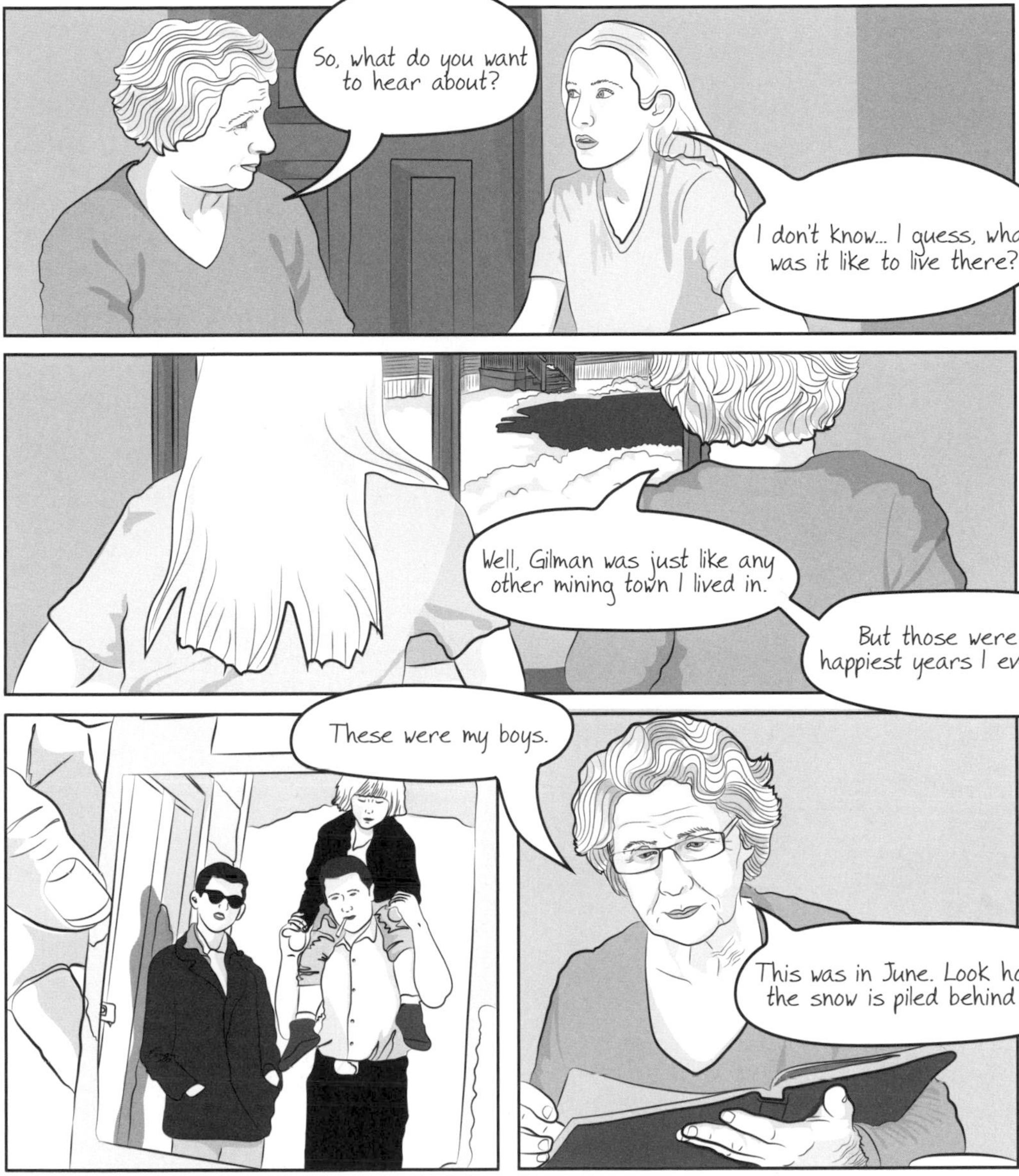
So, what do you want to hear about?
I don't know... I guess, what was it like to live there?
Well, Gilman was just like any other mining town I lived in.
But those were my happiest years I ever had.
These were my boys.
This was in June. Look how high the snow is piled behind them.

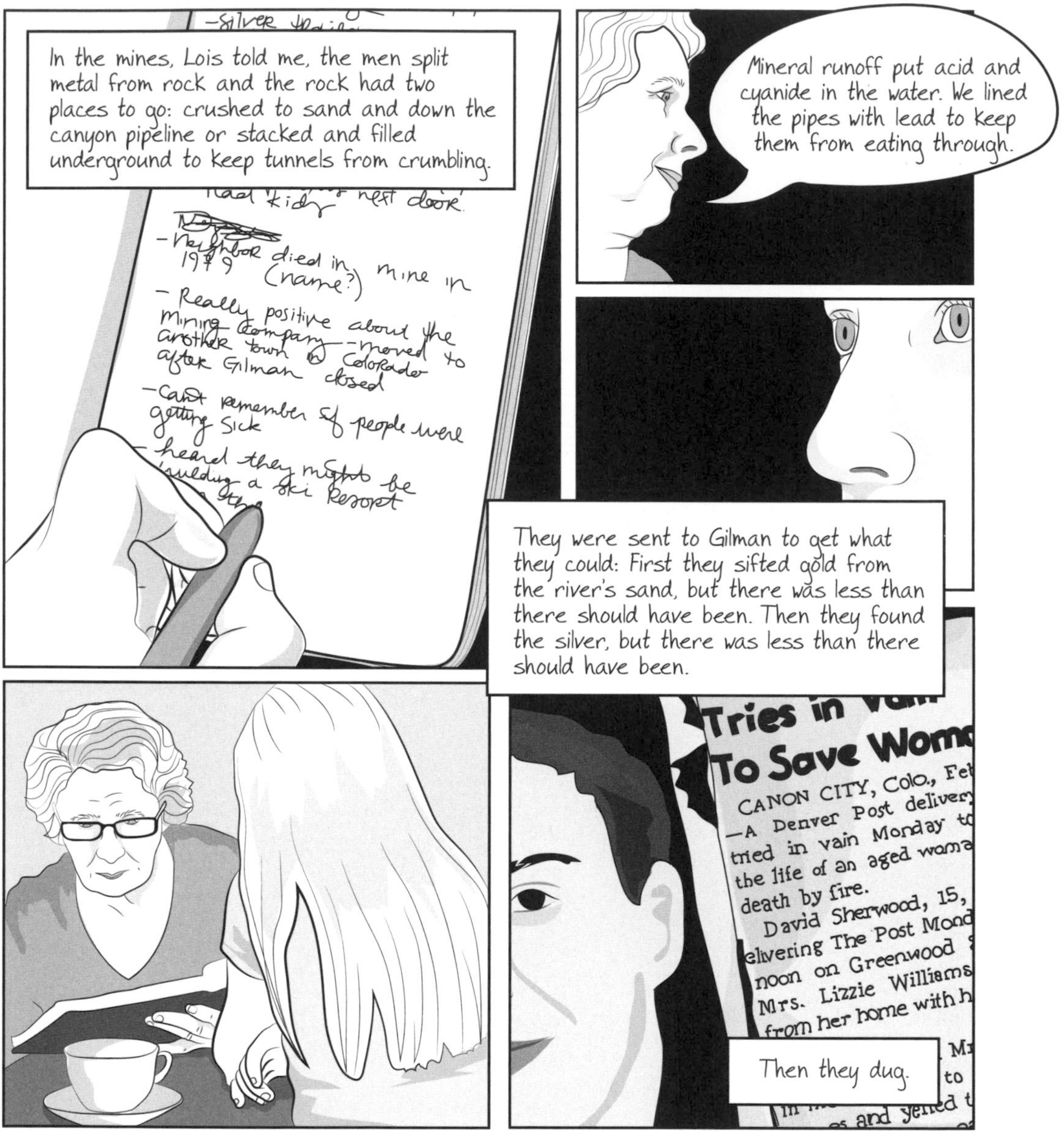

In the mines, Lois told me, the men split metal from rock and the rock had two places to go: crushed to sand and down the canyon pipeline or stacked and filled underground to keep tunnels from crumbling.
-Neighbor died in 1979 (name?) mine in
-Really positive about the mining company—moved to another town in Colorado after Gilman closed
-Can't remember if people were getting sick
-heard they might be building a ski Resort
Mineral runoff put acid and cyanide in the water. We lined the pipes with lead to keep them from eating through.
They were sent to Gilman to get what they could: First they sifted gold from the river's sand, but there was less than there should have been. Then they found the silver, but there was less than there should have been.
Tries in
To Save Wom
CANON CITY, Colo., Fe
—A Denver Post deliver
tried in vain Monday t
the life of an aged wom
death by fire.
David Sherwood, 15,
elivering The Post Mon
noon on Greenwood
Mrs. Lizzie William
from her home with
Then they dug.

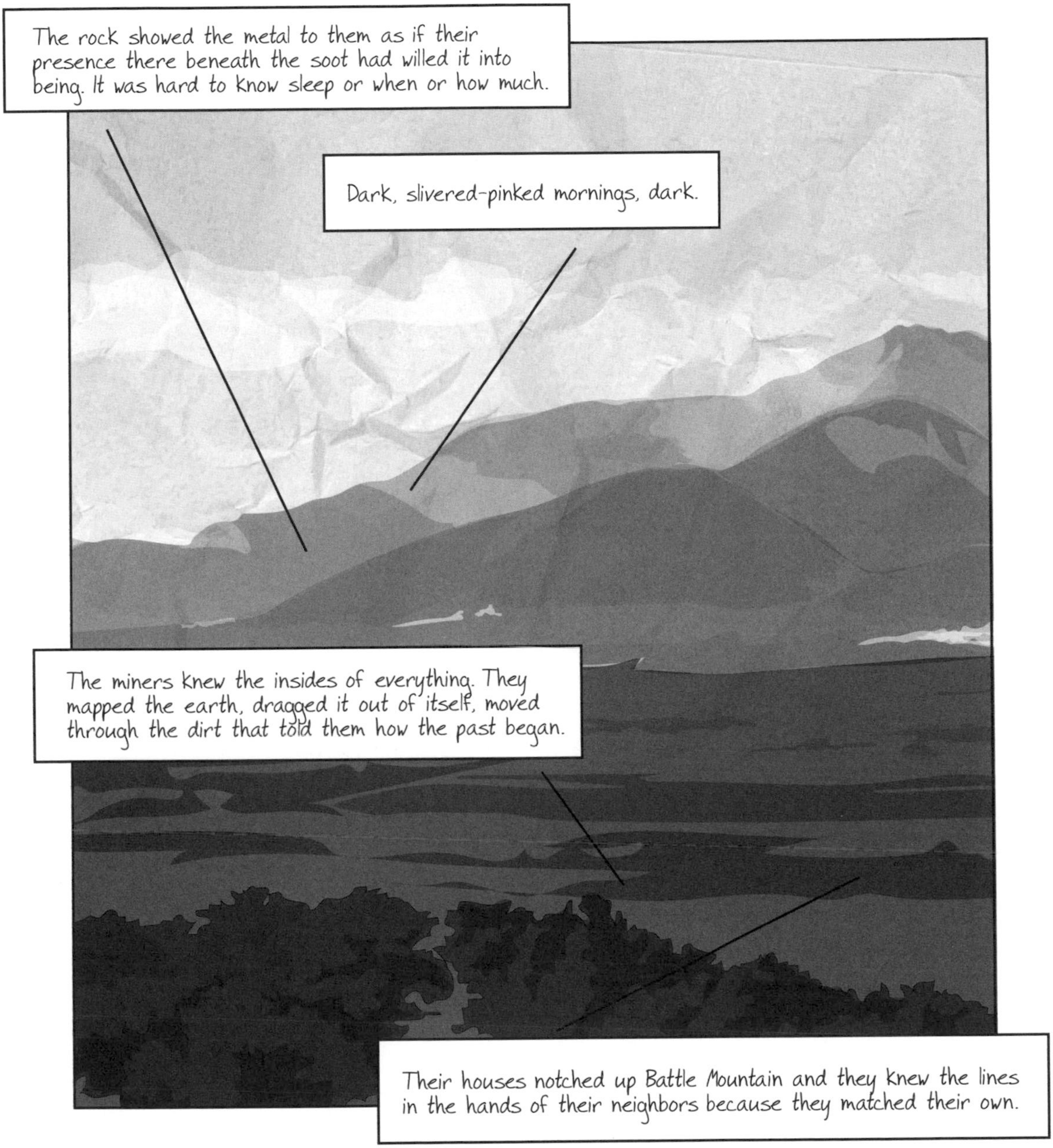
The rock showed the metal to them as if their presence there beneath the soot had willed it into being. It was hard to know sleep or when or how much.
Dark, slivered-pinked mornings, dark.
The miners knew the insides of everything. They mapped the earth, dragged it out of itself, moved through the dirt that told them how the past began.
Their houses notched up Battle Mountain and they knew the lines in the hands of their neighbors because they matched their own.

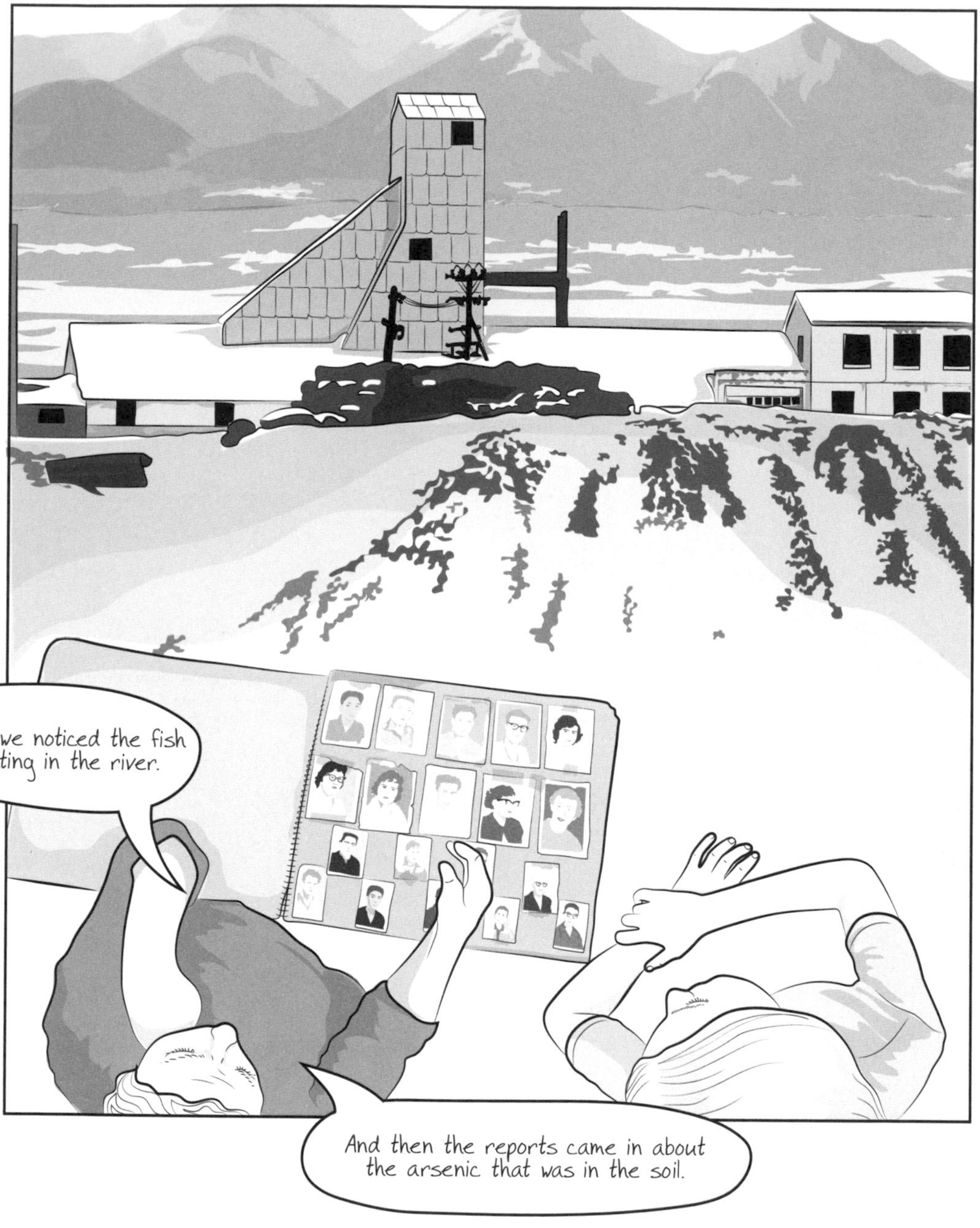
In '83 we noticed the fish floating in the river.
And then the reports came in about the arsenic that was in the soil.

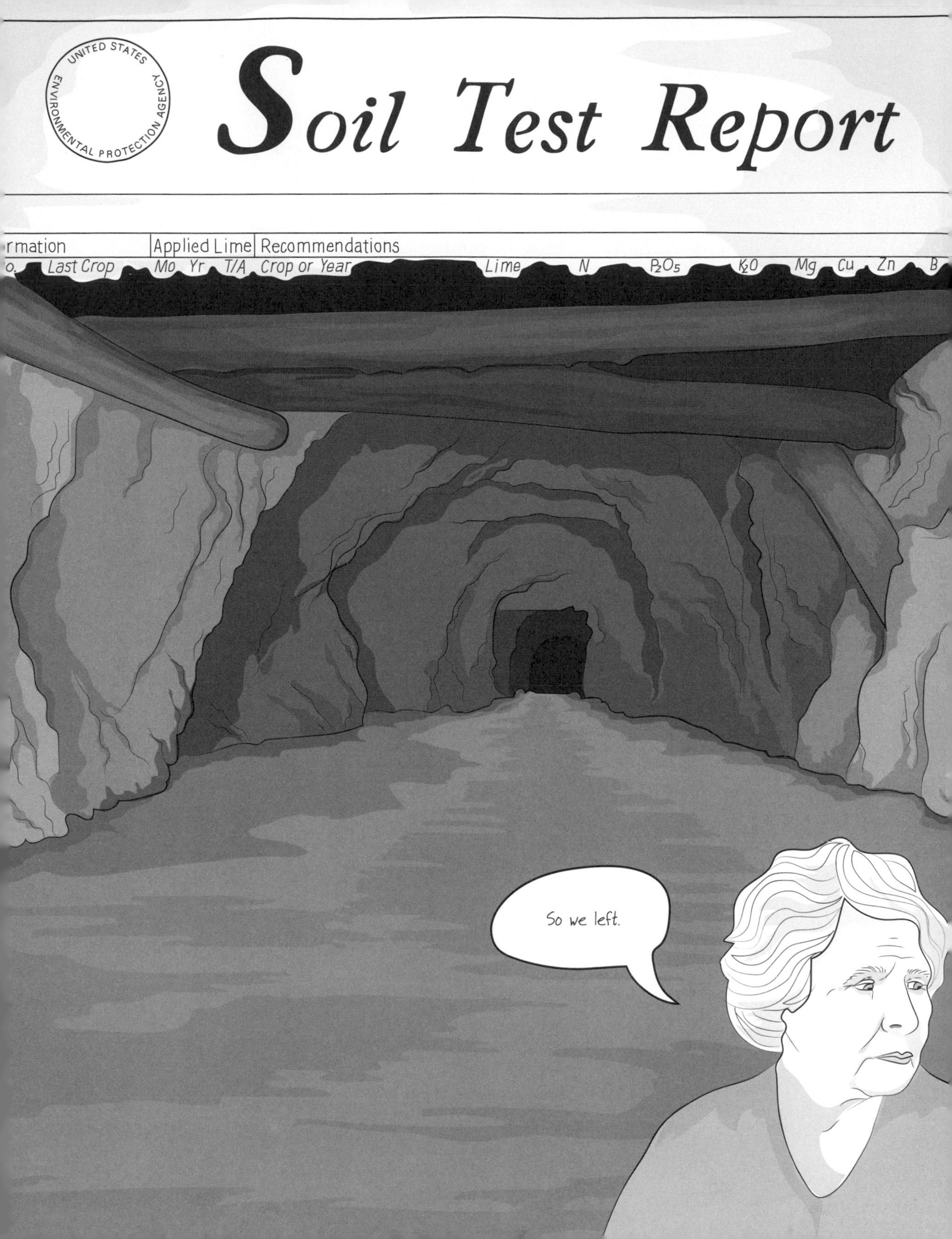
UNITED STATES ENVIRONMENTAL PROTECTION AGENCY
Soil Test Report
rmation | Applied Lime | Recommendations
o. Last Crop Mo Yr T/A Crop or Year Lime N P2O5 K2O Mg Cu Zn B
So we left.

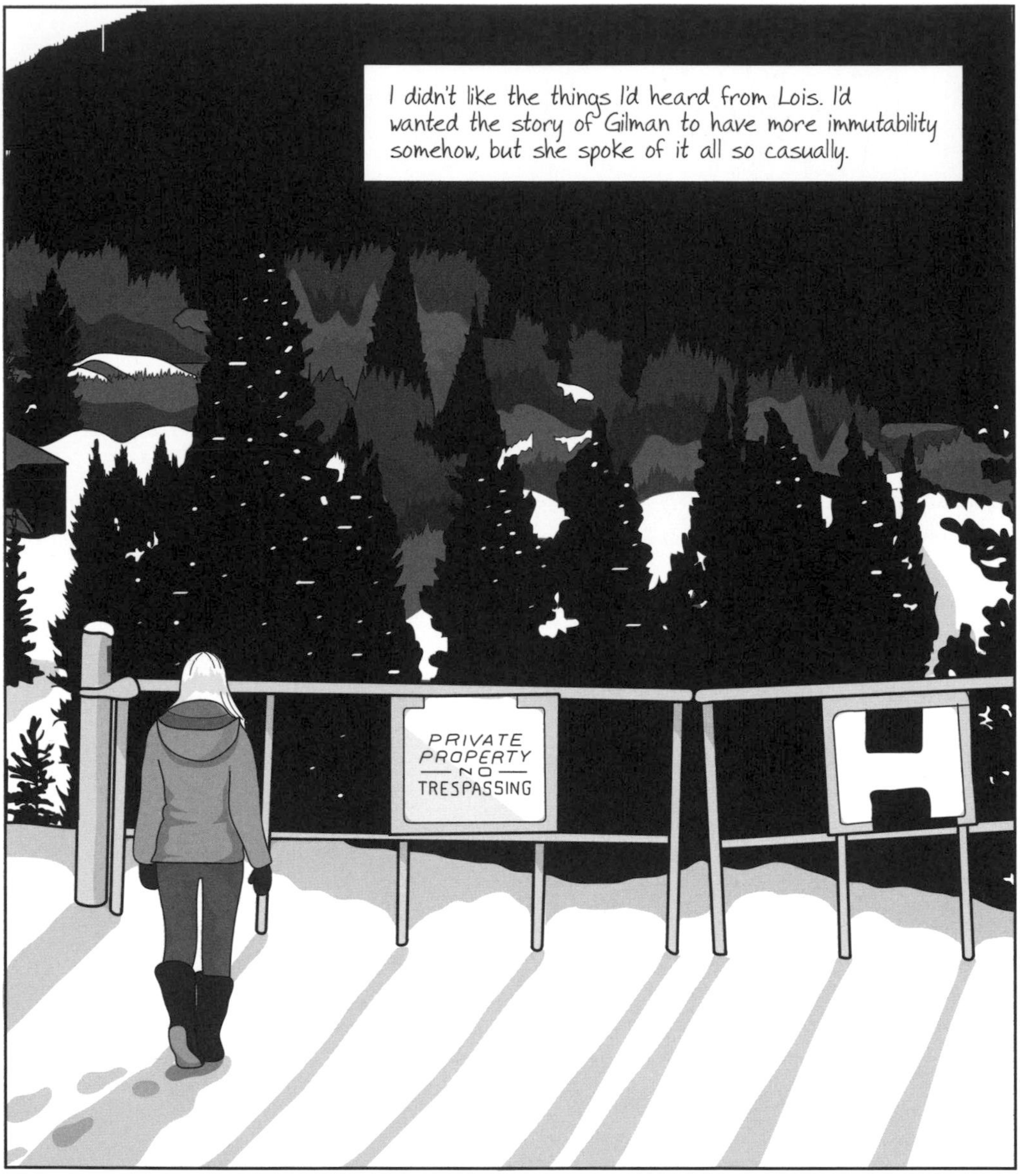
I didn't like the things I'd heard from Lois. I'd wanted the story of Gilman to have more immutability somehow, but she spoke of it all so casually.
PRIVATE PROPERTY —NO— TRESPASSING

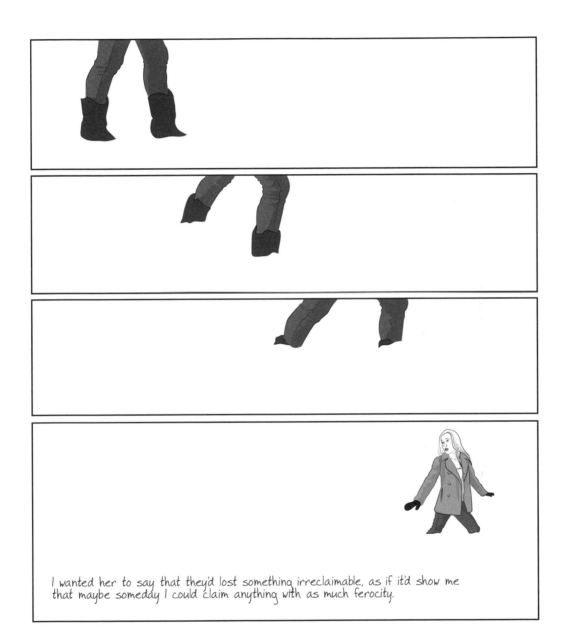

I wanted her to say that they'd lost something irreclaimable, as if it'd show me that maybe someday I could claim anything with as much ferocity.

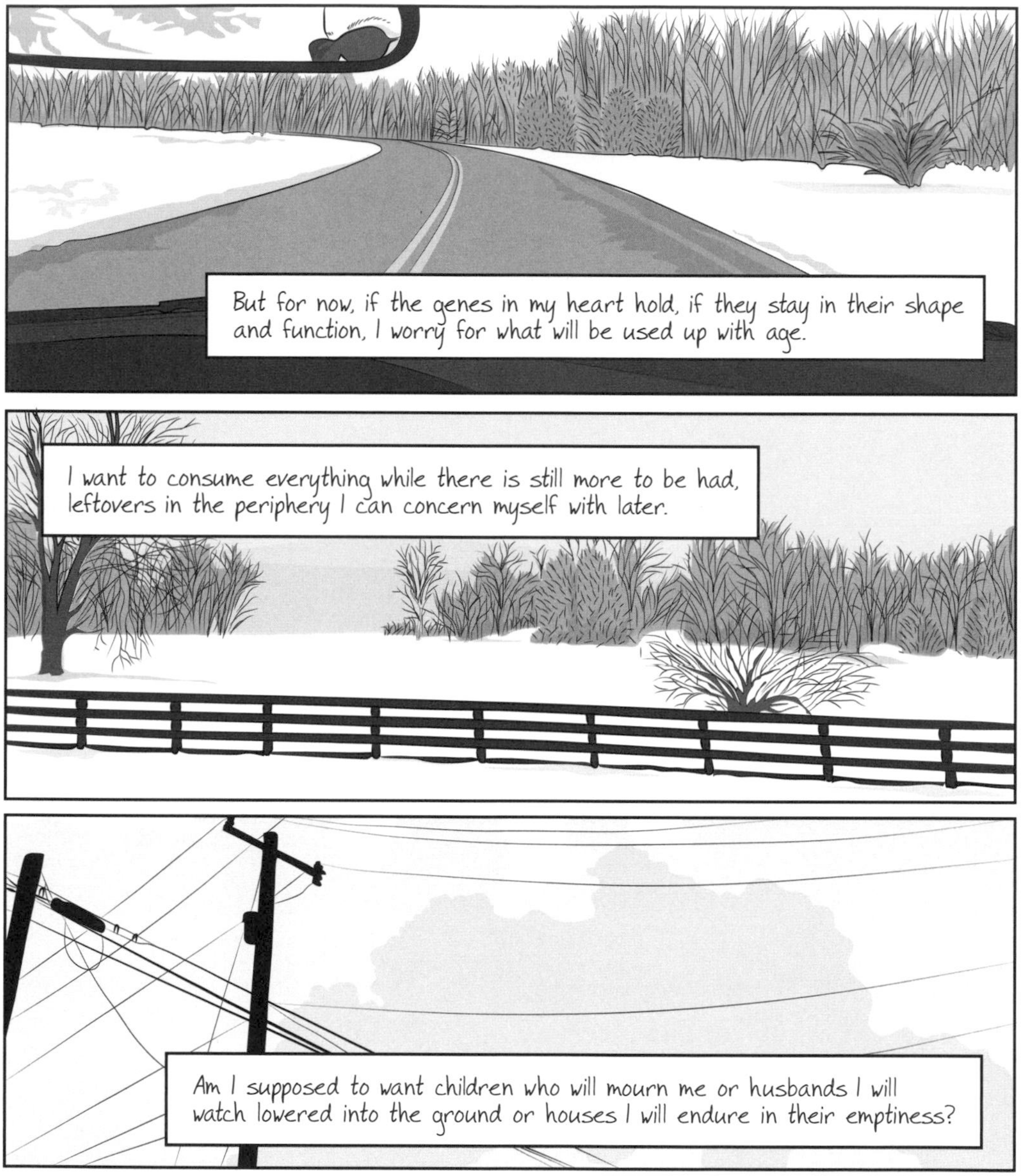
But for now, if the genes in my heart hold, if they stay in their shape and function, I worry for what will be used up with age.
I want to consume everything while there is still more to be had, leftovers in the periphery I can concern myself with later.
Am I supposed to want children who will mourn me or husbands I will watch lowered into the ground or houses I will endure in their emptiness?

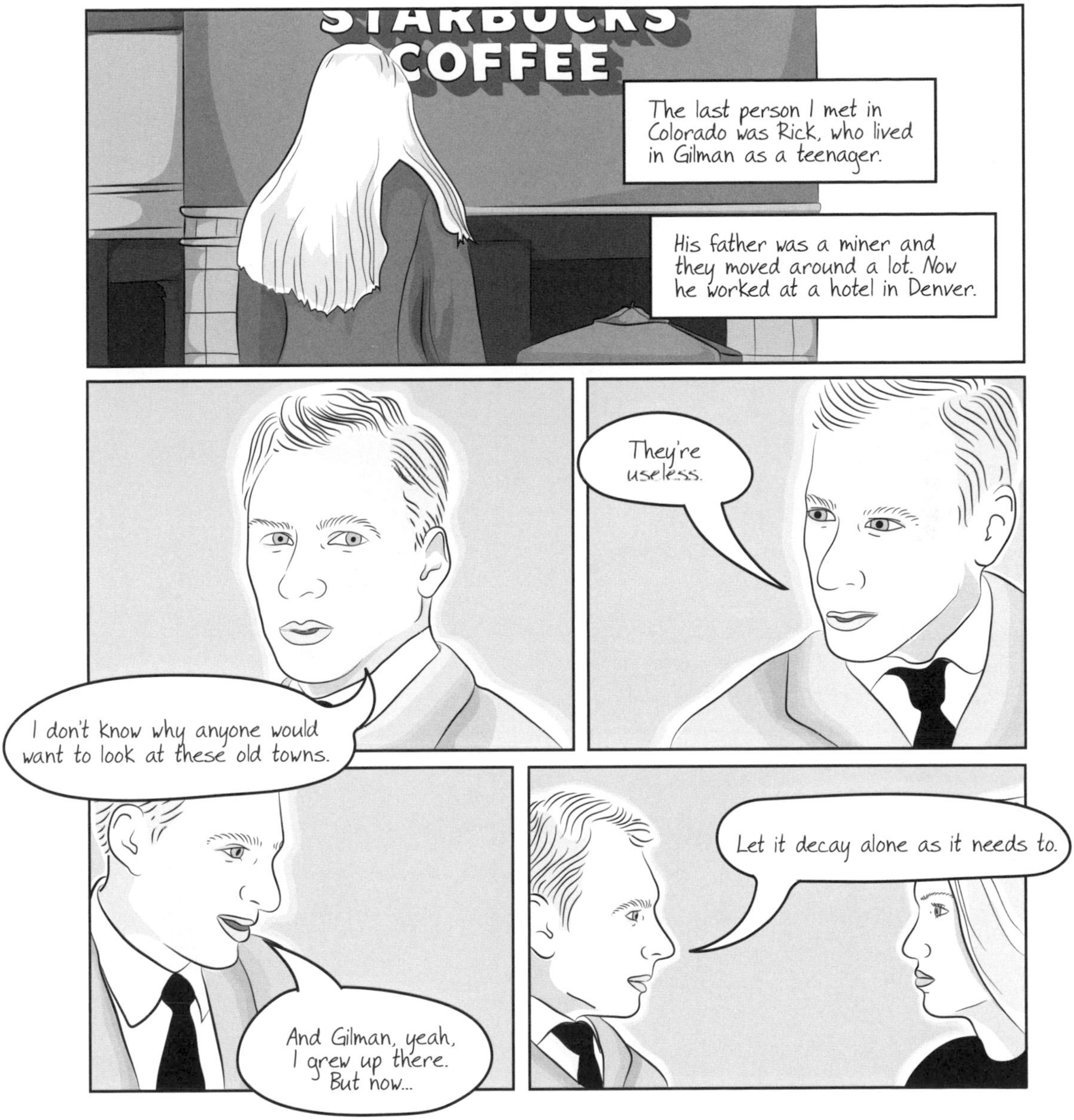
STARBUCKS COFFEE
The last person I met in Colorado was Rick, who lived in Gilman as a teenager.
His father was a miner and they moved around a lot. Now he worked at a hotel in Denver.
I don't know why anyone would want to look at these old towns.
They're useless.
And Gilman, yeah, I grew up there. But now...
Let it decay alone as it needs to.

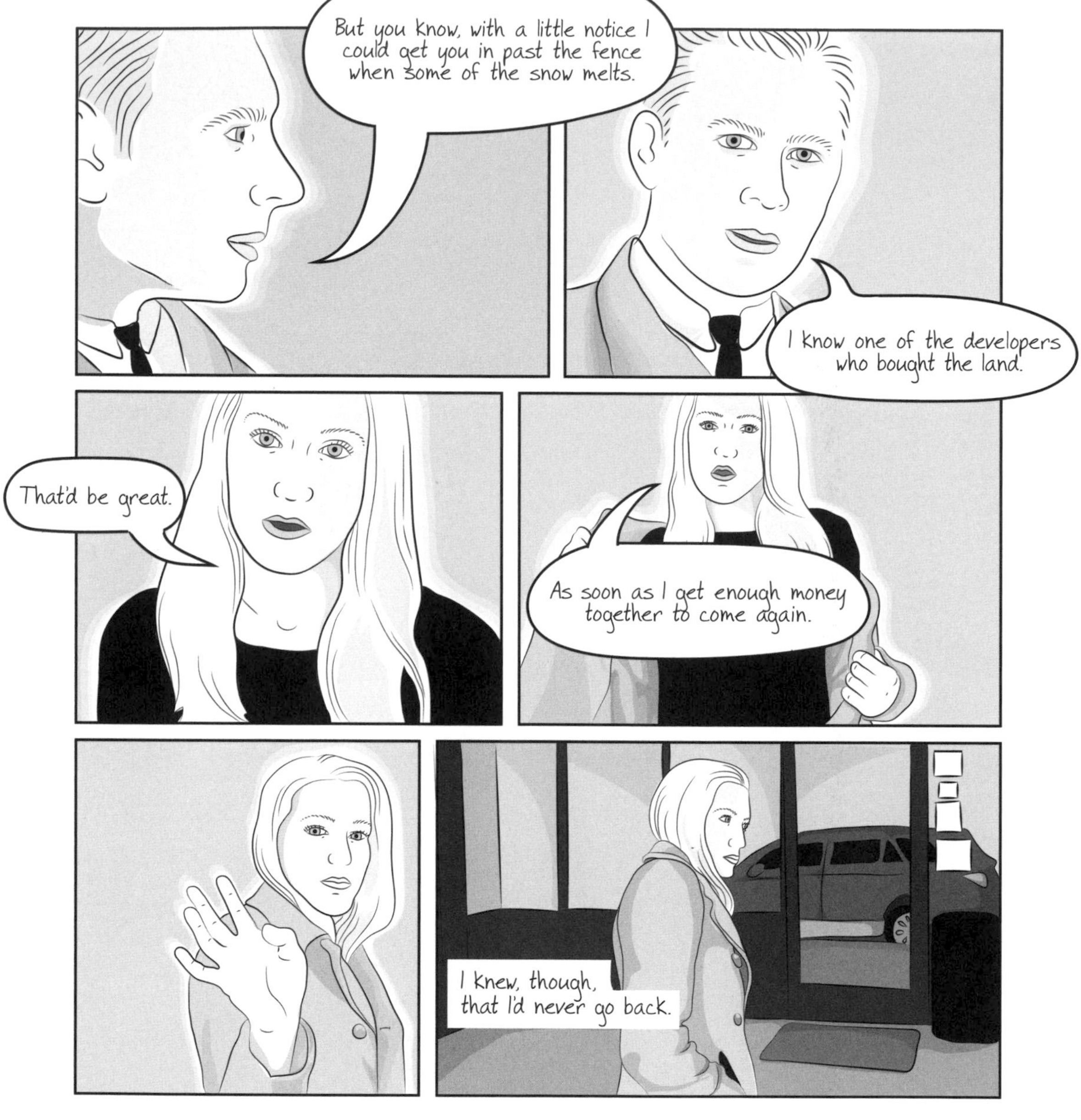
But you know, with a little notice I could get you in past the fence when some of the snow melts.
I know one of the developers who bought the land.
That'd be great.
As soon as I get enough money together to come again.
I knew, though, that I'd never go back.

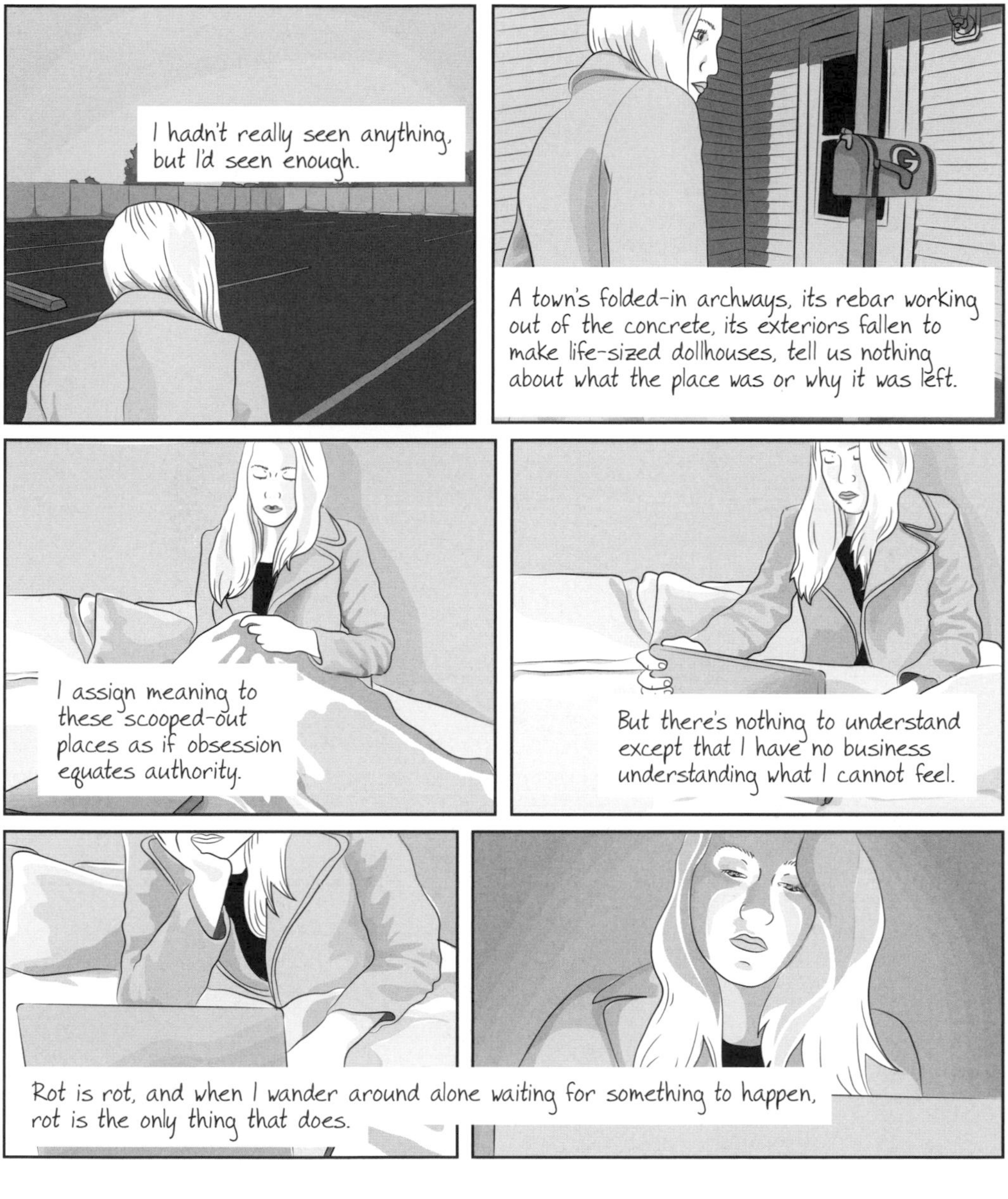
I hadn't really seen anything, but I'd seen enough.
A town's folded-in archways, its rebar working out of the concrete, its exteriors fallen to make life-sized dollhouses, tell us nothing about what the place was or why it was left.
I assign meaning to these scooped-out places as if obsession equates authority.
But there's nothing to understand except that I have no business understanding what I cannot feel.
Rot is rot, and when I wander around alone waiting for something to happen, rot is the only thing that does.

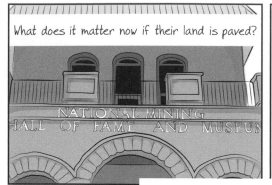

What does it matter now if their land is paved?
NATIONAL MINING
HALL OF FAME AND MUSEUM
Present-day mining takes place only after extensive consideration of environmental impacts and how they can be reduced. These exhibits illustrate
They worked and came to love it and left.
mental concerns.
Places are filled and made empty when the function of habitation wears out, contaminated and shelled like bodies left to waste.
The people of Gilman drilled and carved and hollowed and slid their roughness between cracks, and they have become things that resemble nothing of what they were.
The characteristics once belonging to them have slipped away, leaving gray, slouching bodies, unique to nothing but age.

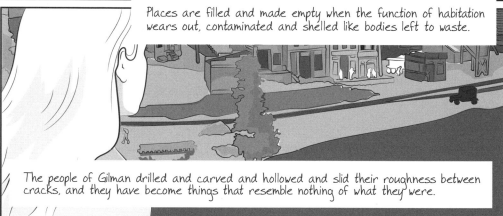

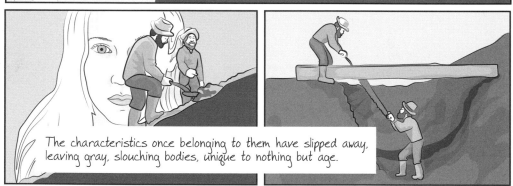

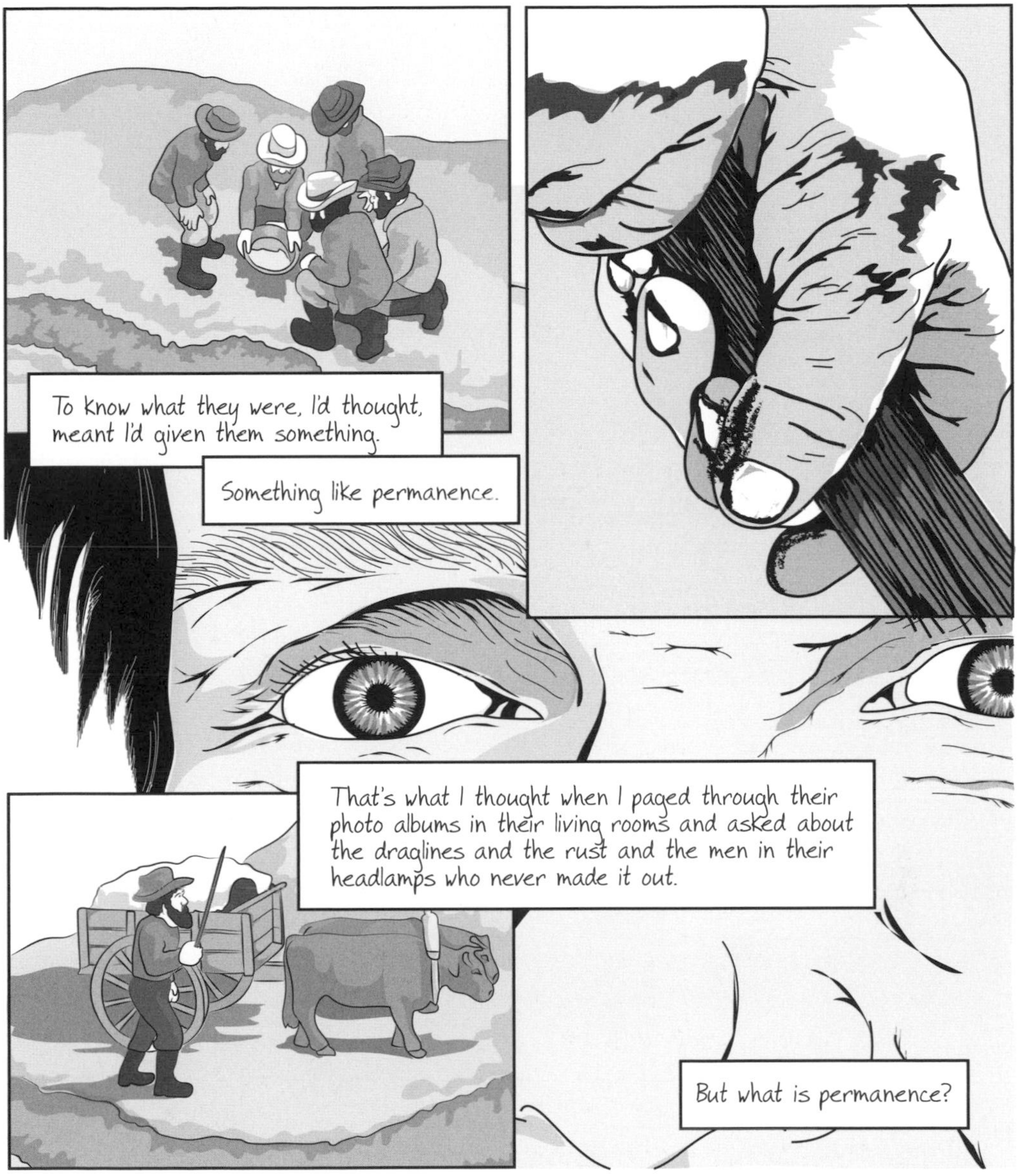
To know what they were, I'd thought, meant I'd given them something.
Something like permanence.
That's what I thought when I paged through their photo albums in their living rooms and asked about the draglines and the rust and the men in their headlamps who never made it out.
But what is permanence?

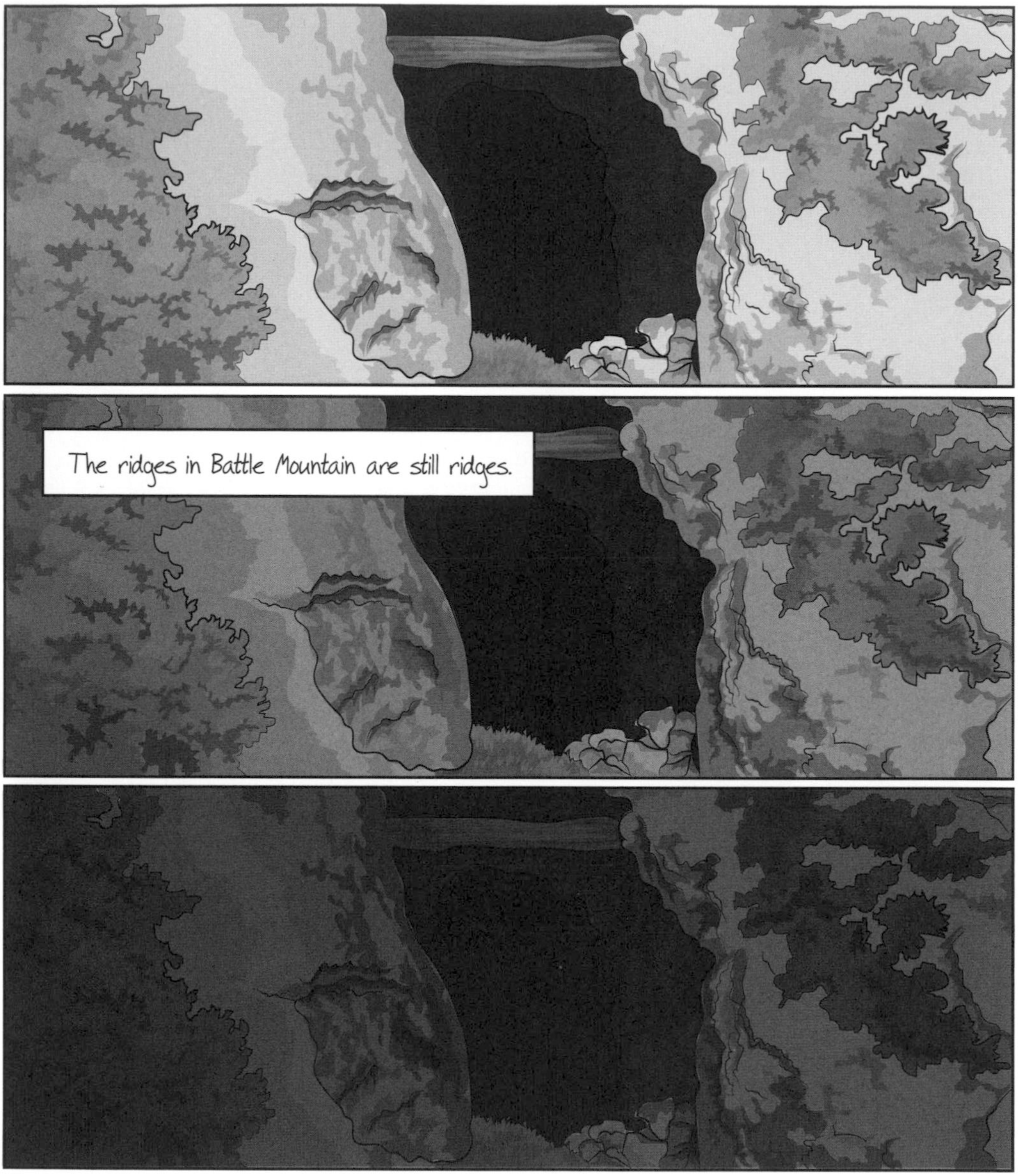
The ridges in Battle Mountain are still ridges.

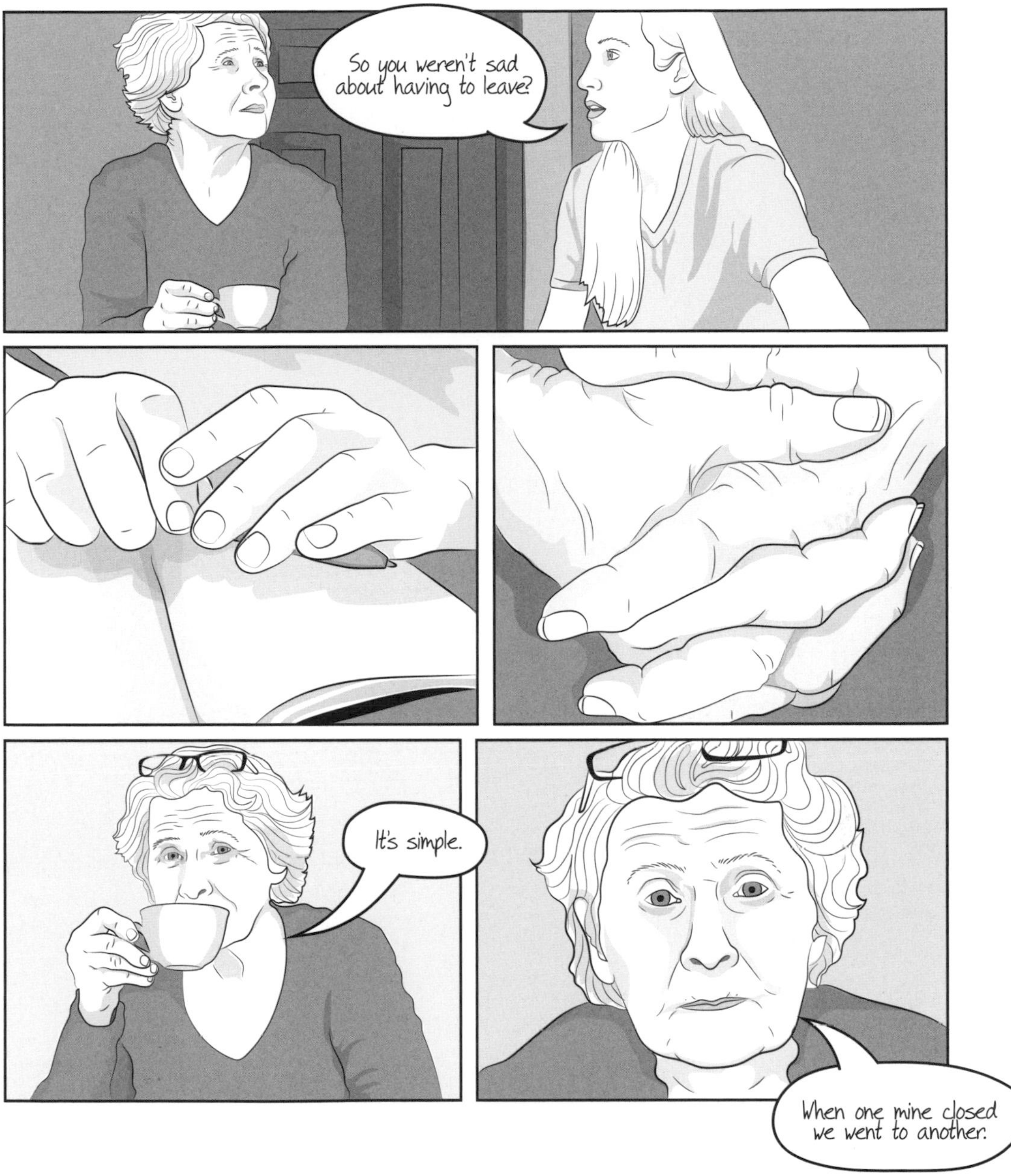
So you weren't sad about having to leave?
It's simple.
When one mine closed we went to another.

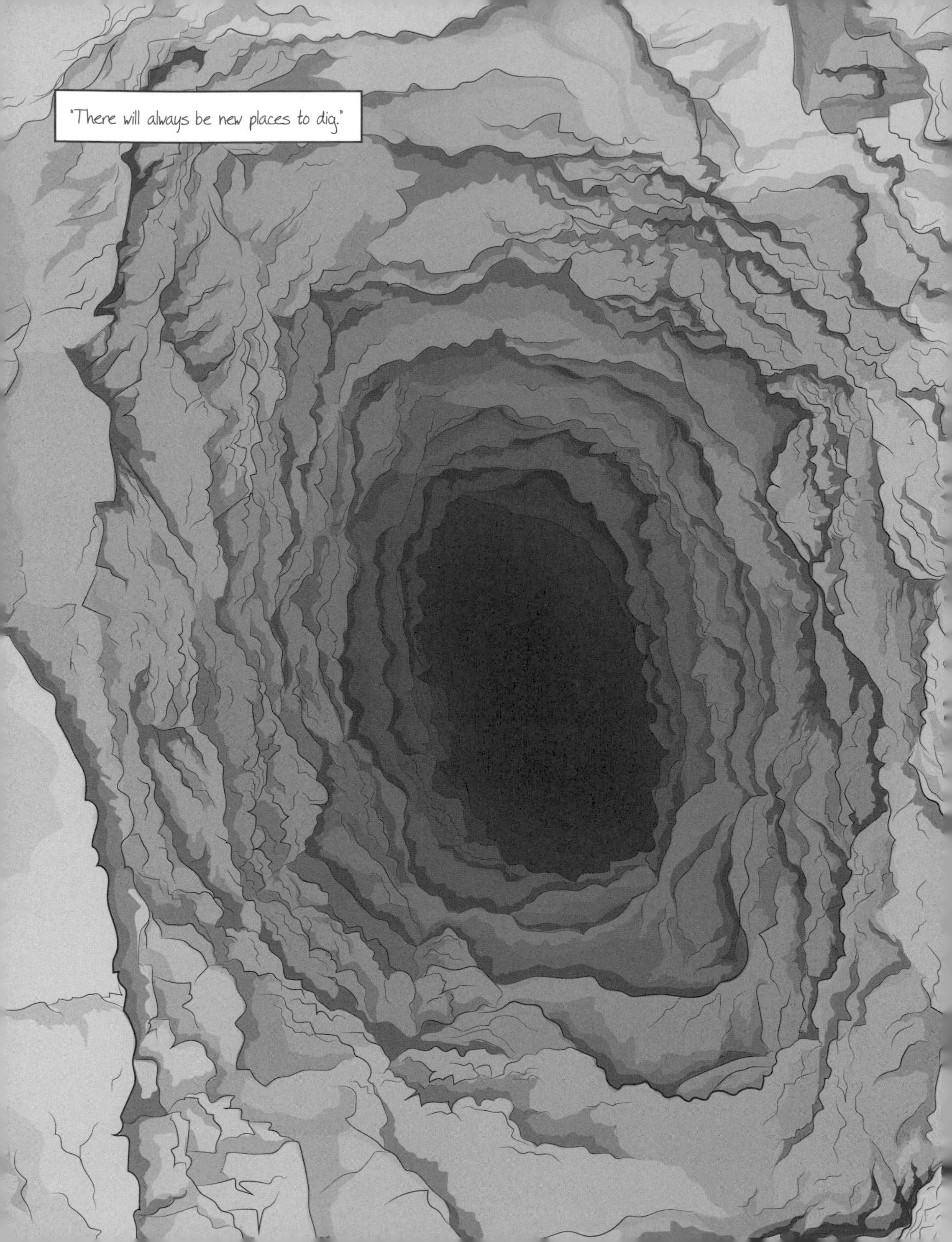
"There will always be new places to dig."

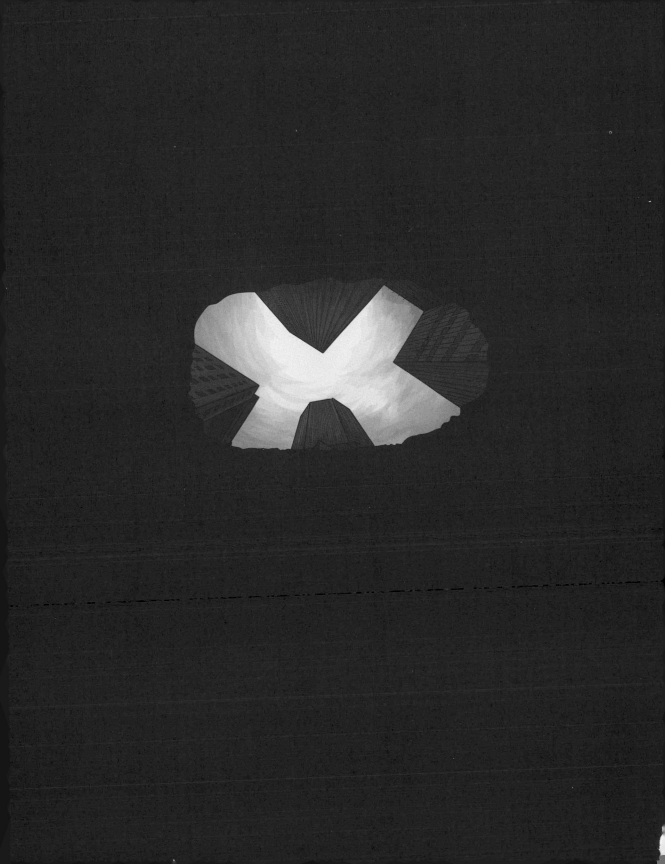

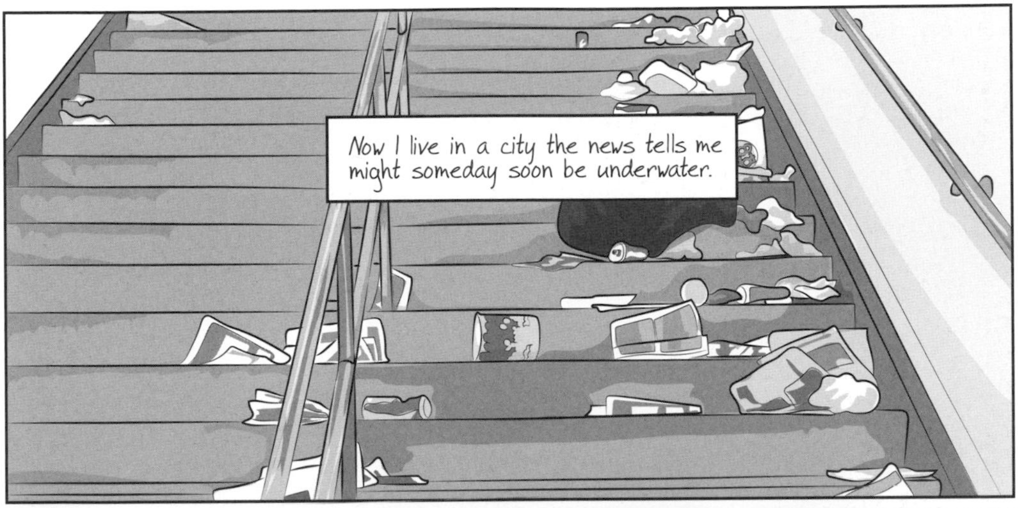
Now I live in a city the news tells me might someday soon be underwater.

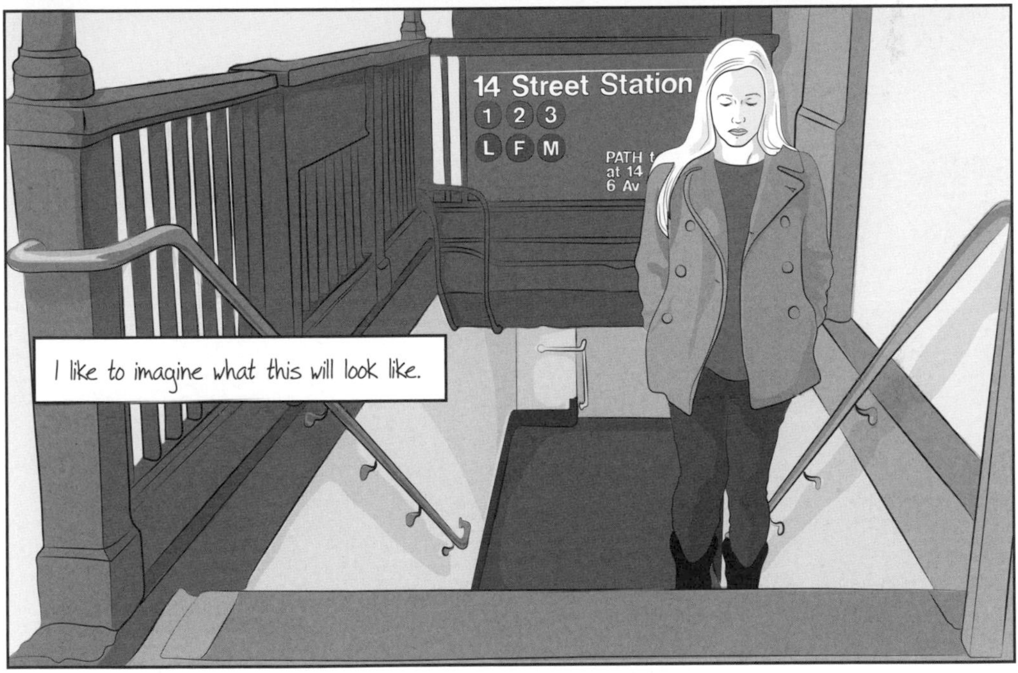
14 Street Station
1 2 3
L F M
I like to imagine what this will look like.

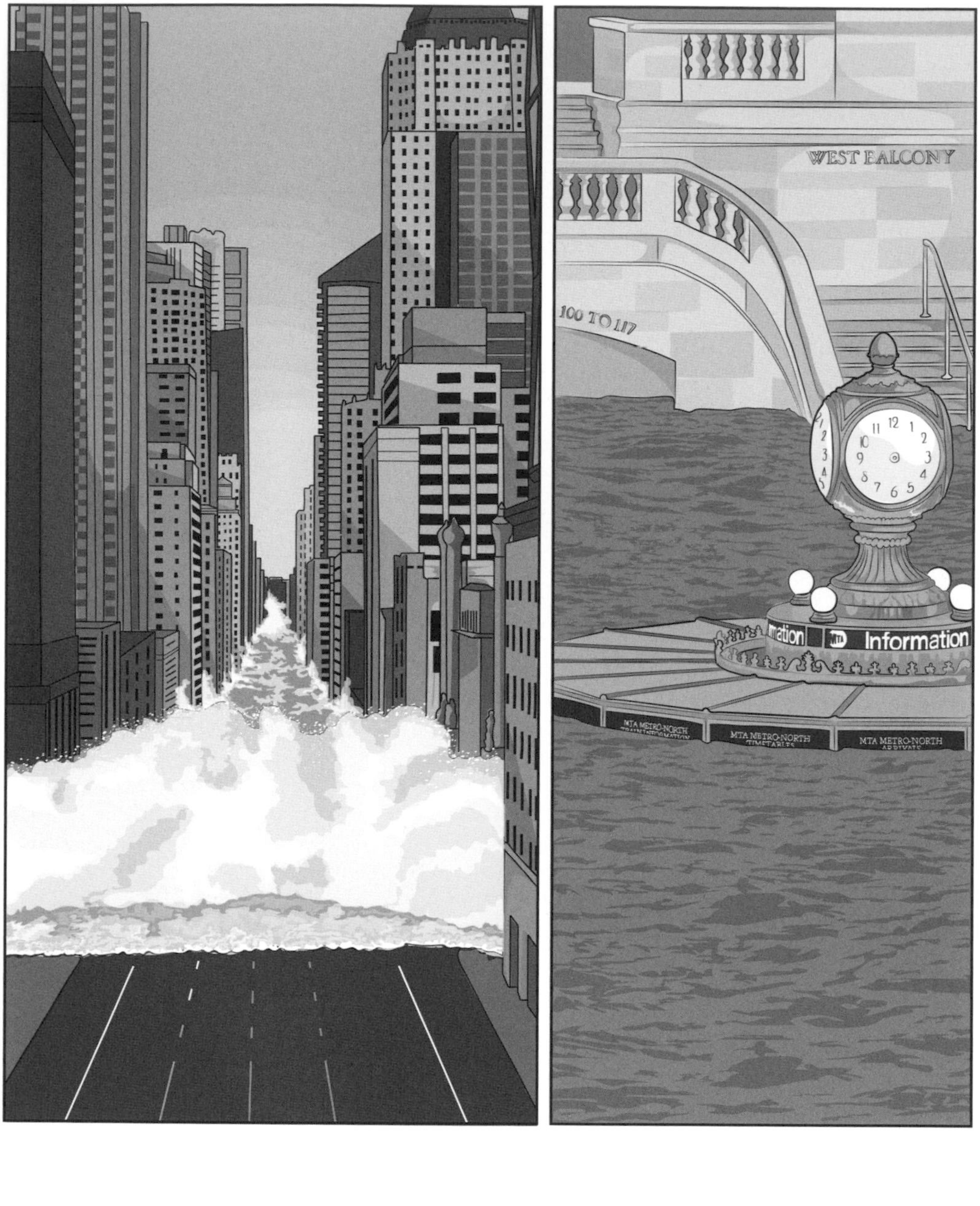
WEST BALCONY
100 TO 117
Information
MTA METRO-NORTH
MTA METRO-NORTH
MTA METRO-NORTH

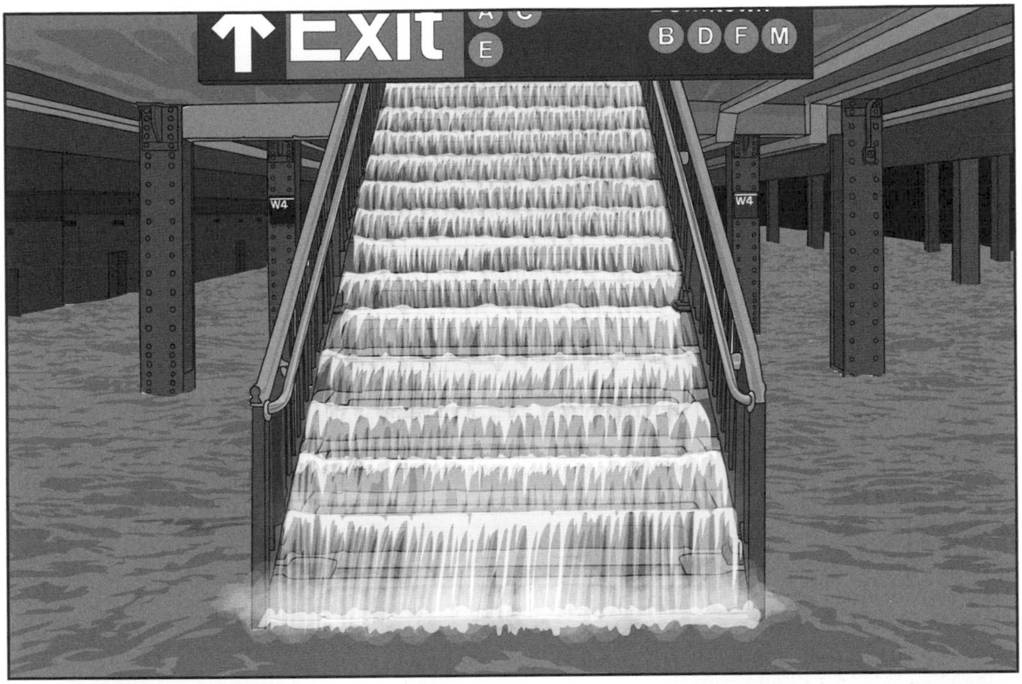
Exit
E
B D F M
W4
W4

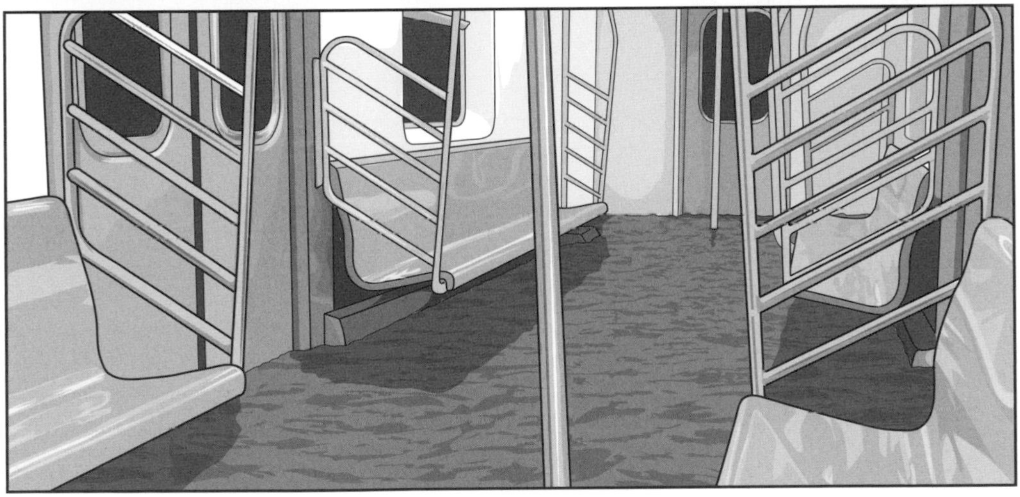

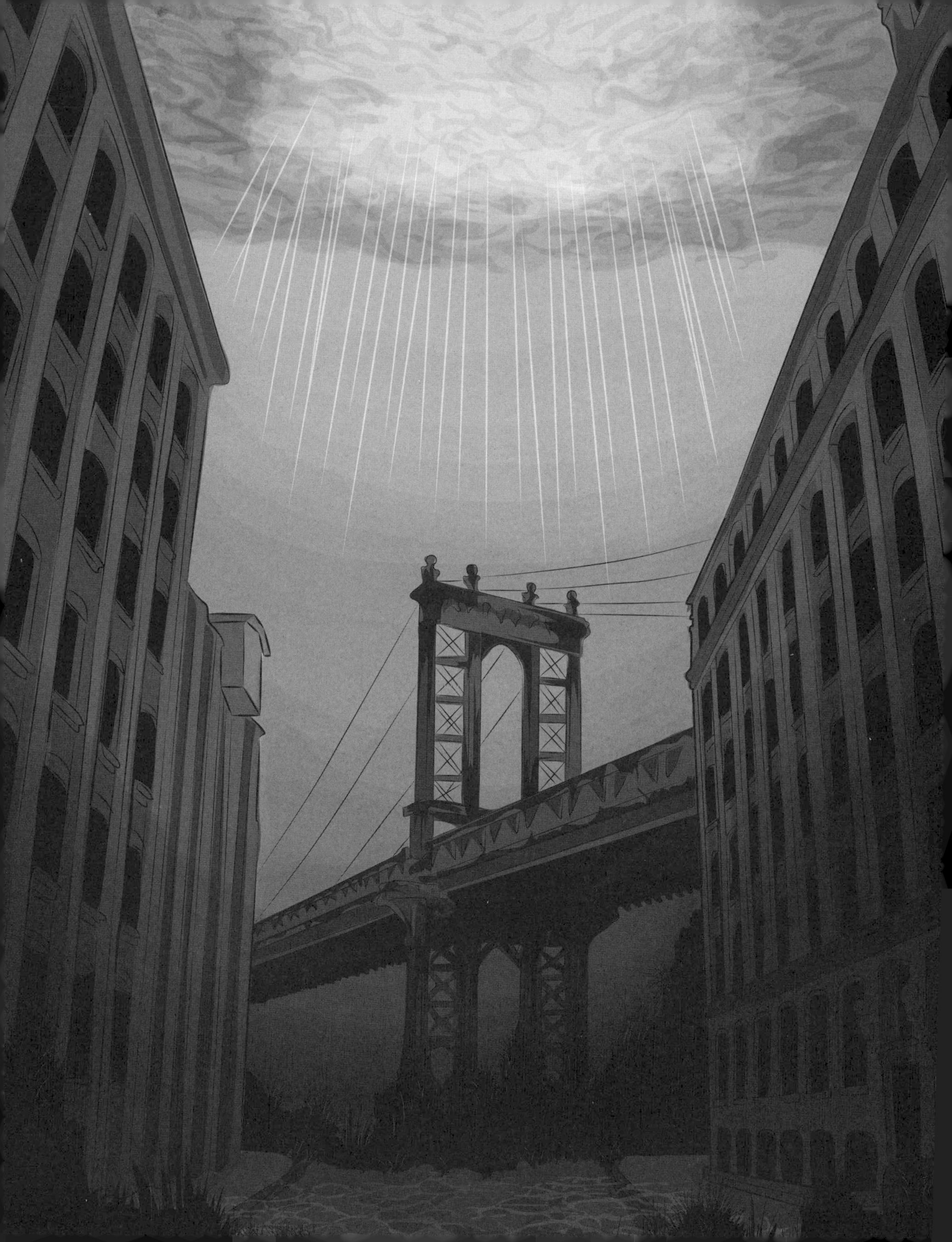

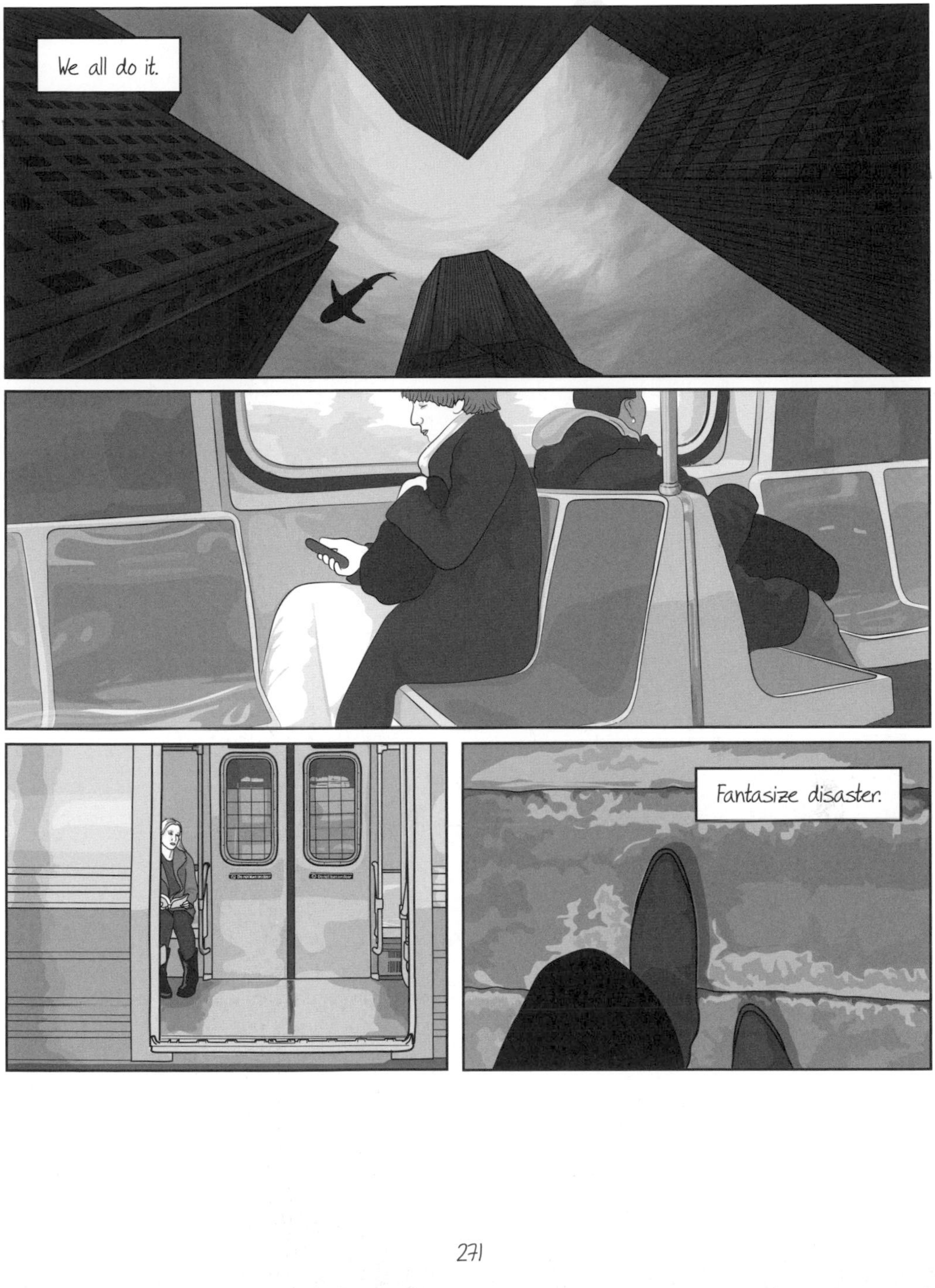
We all do it.
Fantasize disaster.

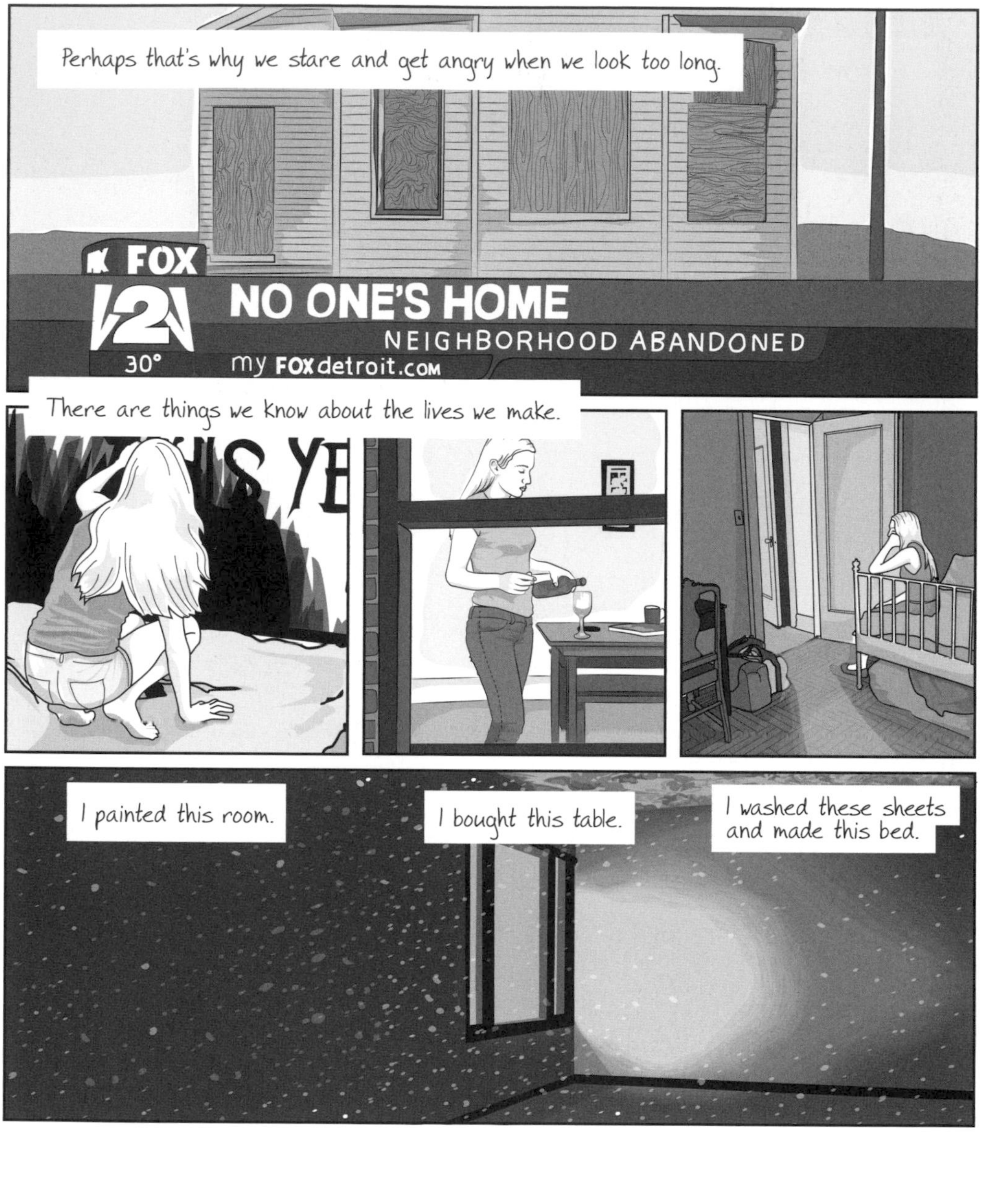
Perhaps that's why we stare and get angry when we look too long.
FOX
2
30°
NO ONE'S HOME
NEIGHBORHOOD ABANDONED
my FOXdetroit.com
There are things we know about the lives we make.
I painted this room.
I bought this table.
I washed these sheets and made this bed.

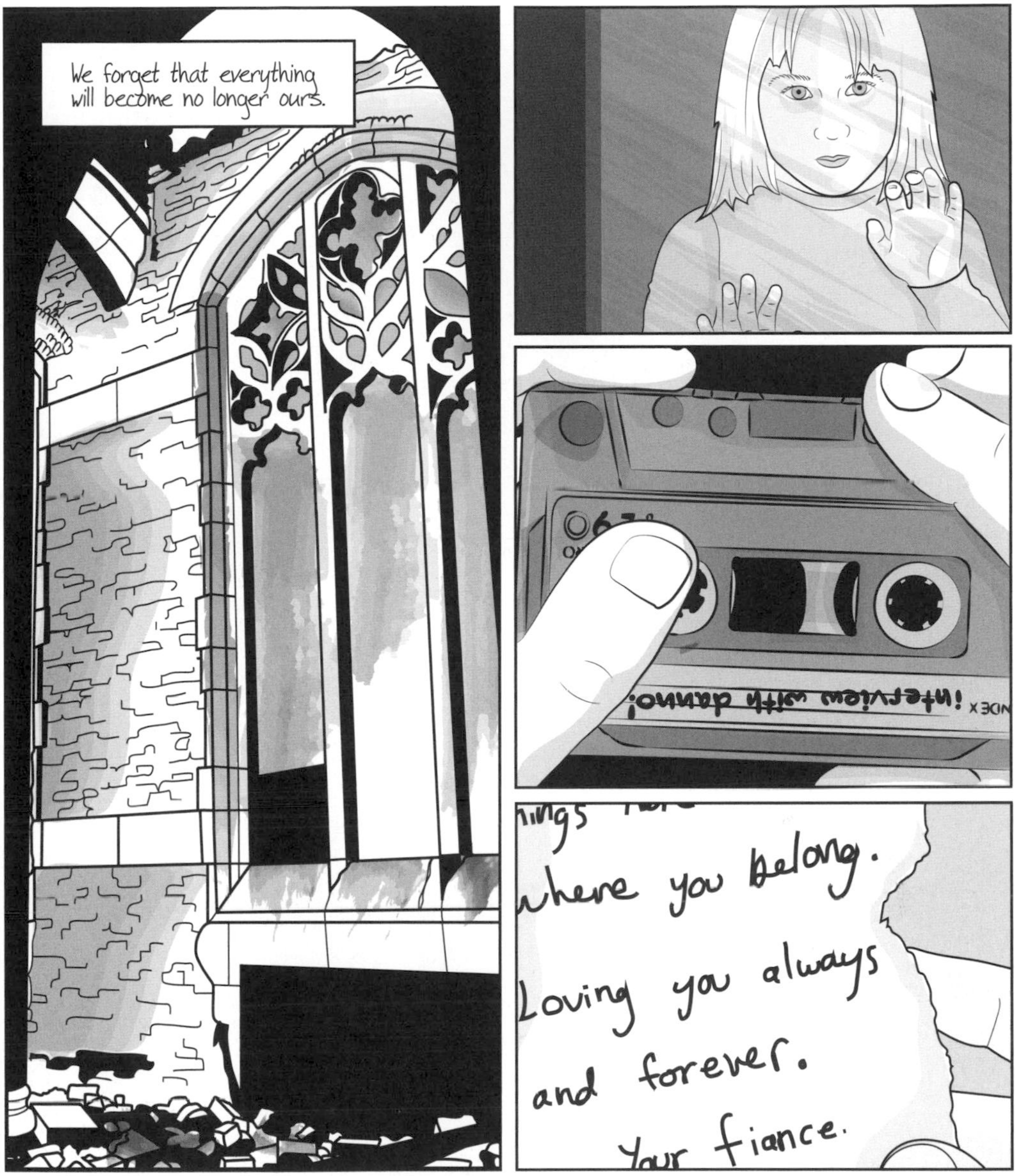
We forget that everything will become no longer ours.
interview with danno!
where you belong.
Loving you always
and forever.
Your fiance.

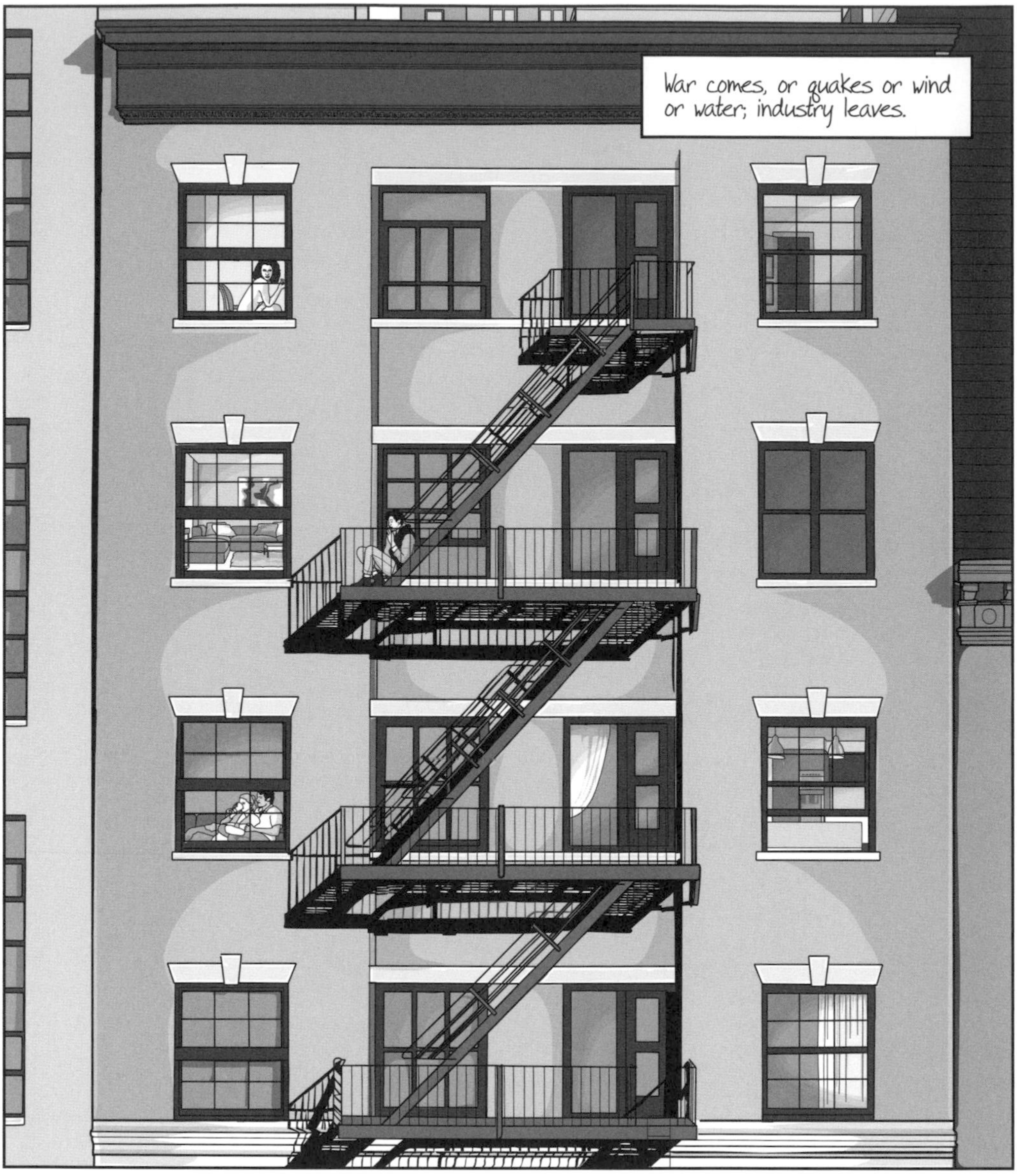
War comes, or quakes or wind or water; industry leaves.

It doesn't matter that your feet are touching the ground they're touching now.

The floors will rot, the carpet will be torn out, the cement will crack and shift and be pulled from the earth, the dirt will be tilled and changed and rained away, and someday there will be nothing left that you have touched.

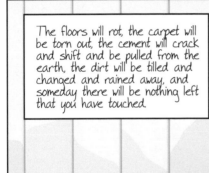

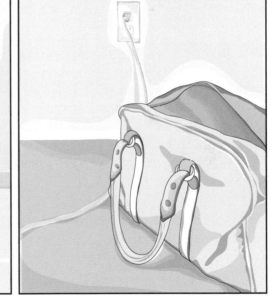

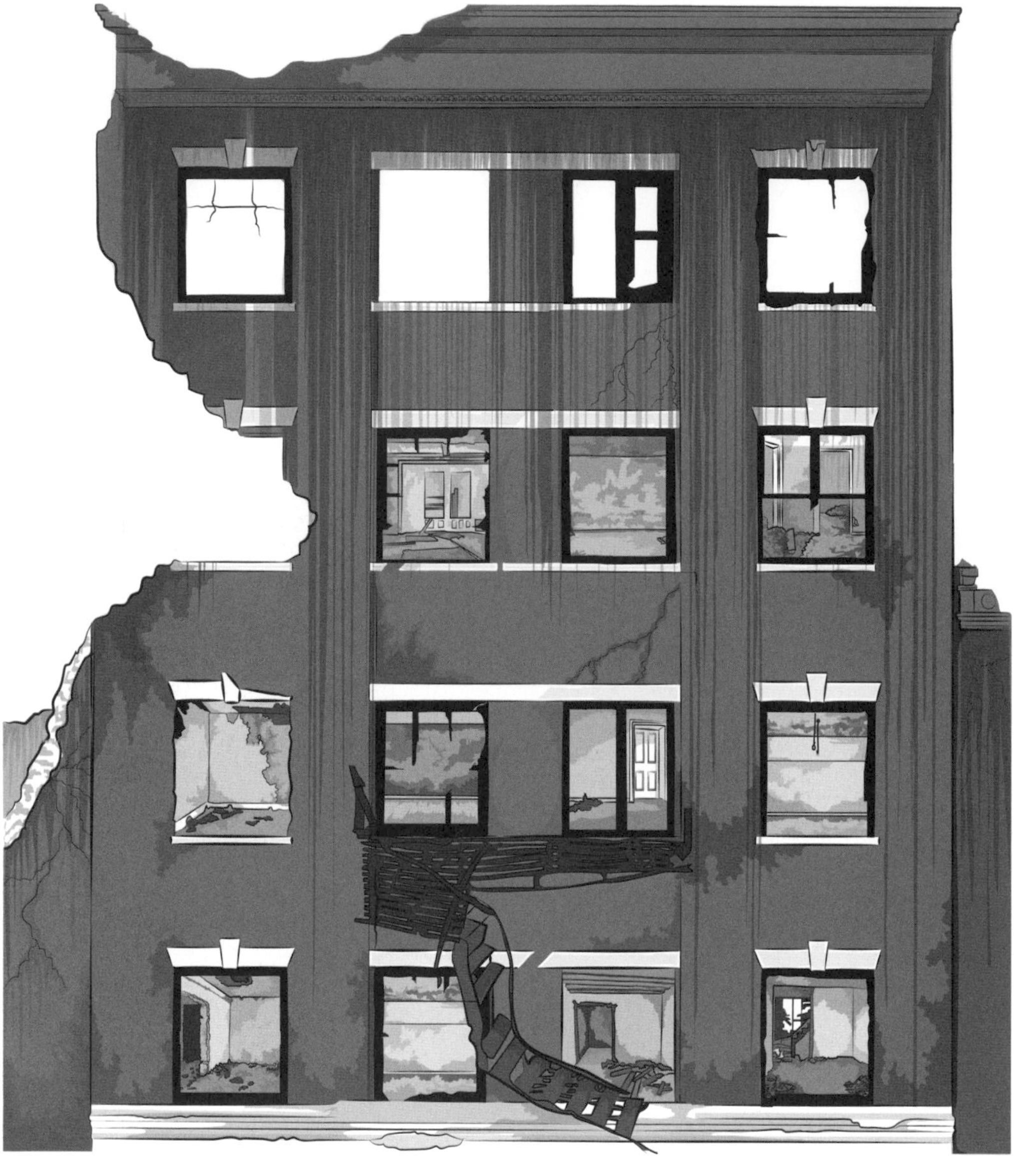

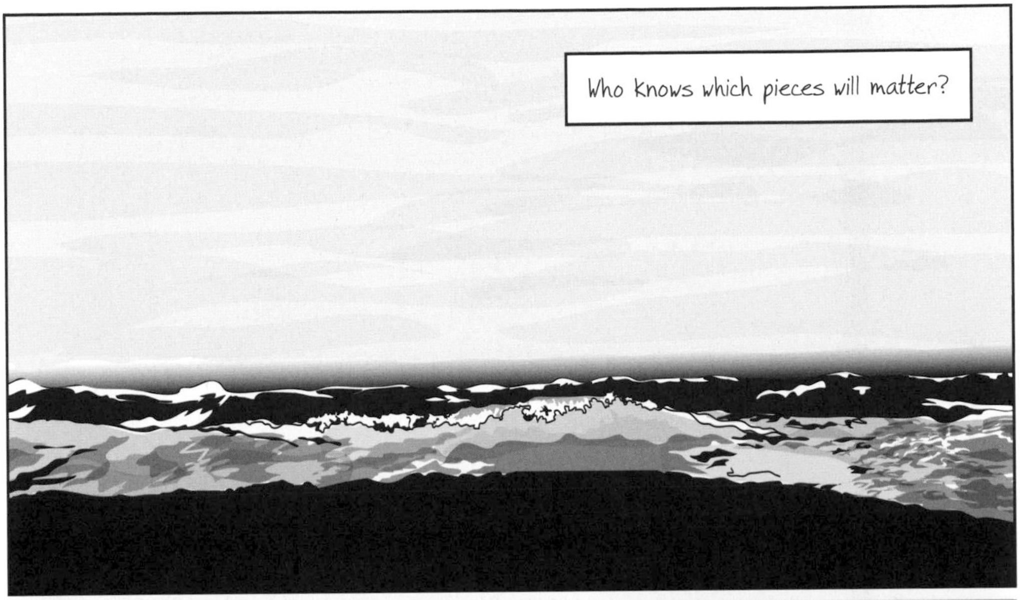
Who knows which pieces will matter?

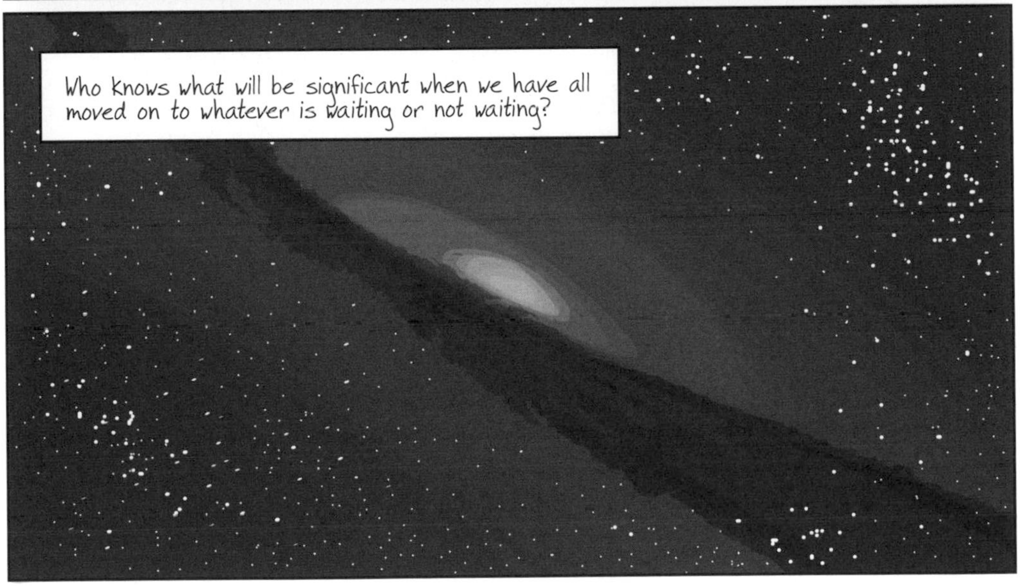
Who knows what will be significant when we have all moved on to whatever is waiting or not waiting?

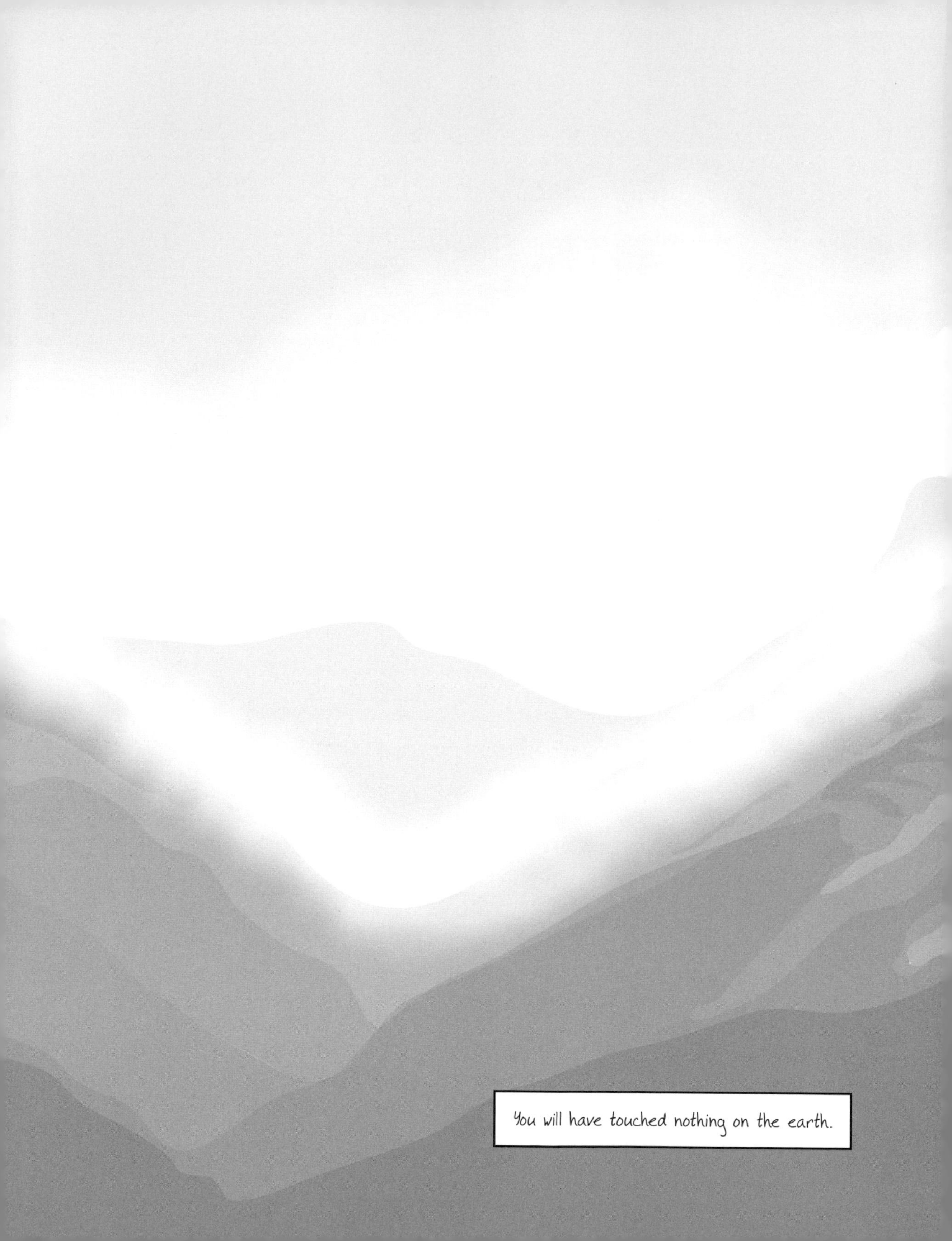
You will have touched nothing on the earth.

It takes so many people to make a book.

Jin Auh, Jessica Friedman, and everyone at the Wylie Agency: I could never ask for a better, more ferociously brilliant team.

Victoria Marini took a chance on this project when no one else would. I owe her forever.

This book would simply not exist without Tim O'Connell and Dan Frank. Every elegy for the publishing industry's former glory is alive and well in them. Thank you also to Josephine Kals, Altie Karper, Andy Hughes, Andrew Ridker, Tammy Tarng, and everyone at Pantheon.

Michael Taeckens: Thank you for keeping me calm, tethered, and well cared for.

To the former weekly residents of Canada House: Thank you, Lina Maria Ferreira Cabeza-Vanegas, Mary Helen Kennerly, Angela Pelster, and most of all in the years since, Ariel Lewiton and Lucas Mann. You all: for life.

Jeffery Gleaves, Kyle Minor, Kerry Howley, Miles Fuller, Mira Jacob, Jonathan Lee, John Bresland, Eula Biss, Leslie Jamison, Tom Hart, Jen Percy, Steven Yaccino, Caitlin Kranz Yaccino, Tony Tulathimutte, Blair Braverman, Dylan Nice, Joshua Wheeler, Landon Bates, Zachary Tyler Vickers, Kisha Schlegel, Amy Butcher, and Olivia Baker: I am so grateful for the intelligence you brought to my work and life.

Thank you to my teachers: John D'Agata (who thinks graphic novels are "too hip," but who is also relatively hip himself), Robin Hemley (who encouraged me to draw in the first place), Honor Moore, Jeff Porter, Stephen Kussisto, Bonnie Sunstein, Jenny Boully, and Aviya Kushner. And to David Lazar, without whom nothing.

I'm grateful to the University of Iowa's Nonfiction Writing Program, Columbia College Chicago, the Virginia Center for the Creative Arts, Sarabande Books, and the Stanley Grant for International Research, for the time and financial support they provided.

Parts of this book, often in dramatically different forms, appeared in: Oxford American, The Normal School, Witness, After Montaigne: Contemporary Essayists Cover the Essays, Essay Daily, and Gulf Coast. Thank you to Caitlin Love, Eliza Borne, Steven Church, Patrick Madden, Ander Monson, and all of the editors who have been kind enough to support my work.

Every woman who has ever put a comic into the world has made it a little more possible for me to do so.

Most of all, thank you to my parents and my family. This book is for and because of you.